CAMBRIDGE LIBRA
Books of enduring s

C000076042

Classics

From the Renaissance to the nineteenth century, Latin and Greek were
compulsory subjects in almost all European universities, and most early
modern scholars published their research and conducted international
correspondence in Latin. Latin had continued in use in Western Europe long
after the fall of the Roman empire as the lingua franca of the educated classes
and of law, diplomacy, religion and university teaching. The flight of Greek
scholars to the West after the fall of Constantinople in 1453 gave impetus
to the study of ancient Greek literature and the Greek New Testament.
Eventually, just as nineteenth-century reforms of university curricula were
beginning to erode this ascendancy, developments in textual criticism and
linguistic analysis, and new ways of studying ancient societies, especially
archaeology, led to renewed enthusiasm for the Classics. This collection
offers works of criticism, interpretation and synthesis by the outstanding
scholars of the nineteenth century.

The Golden Bough: The Third Edition

This work by Sir James Frazer (1854–1941) is widely considered to be one of
the most important early texts in the fields of psychology and anthropology.
At the same time, by applying modern methods of comparative ethnography
to the classical world, and revealing the superstition and irrationality beneath
the surface of the classical culture which had for so long been a model for
Western civilisation, it was extremely controversial. Frazer was greatly
influenced by E.B. Tylor's *Primitive Culture* (also reissued in this series), and
by the work of the biblical scholar William Robertson Smith, to whom the
first edition is dedicated. The twelve-volume third edition, reissued here,
was greatly revised and enlarged, and published between 1911 and 1915; the
two-volume first edition (1890) is also available in this series. Volumes 10
and 11 (1913) continue to examine taboo behaviour, and consider the role of
sunlight and firelight in ritual.

The Golden Bough
The Third Edition

Volume 11: Balder the Beautiful:
The Fire-Festivals of Europe and
the Doctrine of the External Soul 2

J.G. Frazer

CAMBRIDGE UNIVERSITY PRESS

Cambridge, New York, Melbourne, Madrid, Cape Town,
Singapore, São Paolo, Delhi, Mexico City

Published in the United States of America by Cambridge University Press, New York

www.cambridge.org
Information on this title: www.cambridge.org/9781108047418

© in this compilation Cambridge University Press 2012

This edition first published 1913
This digitally printed version 2012

ISBN 978-1-108-04741-8 Paperback

THE GOLDEN BOUGH

A STUDY IN MAGIC AND RELIGION

THIRD EDITION

PART VII

BALDER THE BEAUTIFUL

VOL. II

MACMILLAN AND CO., Limited
LONDON · BOMBAY · CALCUTTA
MELBOURNE

THE MACMILLAN COMPANY
NEW YORK · BOSTON · CHICAGO
DALLAS · SAN FRANCISCO

THE MACMILLAN CO. OF CANADA, Ltd.
TORONTO

BALDER
THE BEAUTIFUL

THE FIRE-FESTIVALS OF EUROPE
AND THE DOCTRINE OF THE EXTERNAL SOUL

BY

J. G. FRAZER, D.C.L., LL.D., LITT.D.

FELLOW OF TRINITY COLLEGE, CAMBRIDGE
PROFESSOR OF SOCIAL ANTHROPOLOGY IN THE UNIVERSITY OF LIVERPOOL

IN TWO VOLUMES
VOL. II

MACMILLAN AND CO., LIMITED
ST. MARTIN'S STREET, LONDON

1913

COPYRIGHT

CONTENTS

Chapter X.—The External Soul in Folk-Tales . . . . . Pp. 95-152

Chapter XI.—The External Soul in Folk-Custom . . . . . Pp. 153-278

CHAPTER XII.—THE GOLDEN BOUGH   . Pp. 279-303

CHAPTER XIII.—FAREWELL TO NEMI   Pp. 304-309

CHAPTER VI

FIRE-FESTIVALS IN OTHER LANDS

§ 1. *The Fire-walk*

AT first sight the interpretation of the European fire customs Bonfires at
the Pongol
festival in
Southern
India. as charms for making sunshine is confirmed by a parallel custom observed by the Hindoos of Southern India at the Pongol or Feast of Ingathering. The festival is celebrated in the early part of January, when, according to Hindoo astrologers, the sun enters the tropic of Capricorn, and the chief event of the festival coincides with the passage of the sun. For some days previously the boys gather heaps of sticks, straw, dead leaves, and everything that will burn. On the morning of the first day of the festival the heaps are fired. Every street and lane has its bonfire. The young folk leap over the flames or pile on fresh fuel. This fire is an offering to Sûrya, the sun-god, or to Agni, the deity of fire ; it " wakes him from his sleep, calling on him again to gladden the earth with his light and heat." [1] If this is indeed the explanation which the people themselves give of the festival, it seems decisive in favour of the solar explanation of the fires ; for to say that the fires waken the sun-god from his sleep is only a metaphorical or mythical way of saying that they actually help to rekindle the sun's light and heat. But the hesitation which the writer indicates between the two distinct deities of sun and fire seems to prove that he is merely giving his own interpretation of the rite, not reporting the views of the celebrants. If

---

[1] Ch. E. Gover, " The Pongol Festival in Southern India," *Journal* *of the Royal Asiatic Society*, N.S., v. (1870) pp. 96 *sq.*

that is so, the expression of his opinion has no claim to authority.

Bonfires at the Holi festival in Northern India.

A festival of Northern India which presents points of resemblance to the popular European celebrations which we have been considering is the Holi. This is a village festival held in early spring at the full moon of the month Phalgun. Large bonfires are lit and young people dance round them. The people believe that the fires prevent blight, and that the ashes cure disease.

The village priest expected to pass through the fire.

At Barsana the local village priest is expected to pass through the Holi bonfire, which, in the opinion of the faithful, cannot burn him. Indeed he holds his land rent-free simply on the score of his being fire-proof. On one occasion when the priest disappointed the expectant crowd by merely jumping over the outermost verge of the smouldering ashes and then bolting into his cell, they threatened to deprive him of his benefice if he did not discharge his spiritual functions better when the next Holi season came round. Another feature of the festival which has, or once had, its counterpart in the corresponding European ceremonies is the unchecked profligacy which prevails among the Hindoos at this time.[1] In Kumaon, a district of North-West India, at the foot of the Himalayas, each clan celebrates the Holi festival by cutting down a tree, which is thereupon stripped of its leaves, decked with shreds of cloth, and burnt at some convenient place in the quarter of the town inhabited by the clan. Some of the songs sung

Leaping over the ashes of the fire to get rid of disease.

on this occasion are of a ribald character. The people leap over the ashes of the fire, believing that they thus rid themselves of itch and other diseases of the skin. While the trees are burning, each clan tries to carry off strips of cloth from the tree of another clan, and success in the attempt is thought to ensure good luck. In Gwalior large heaps of cow-dung are burnt instead of trees. Among the Marwaris the festival is celebrated by the women with obscene songs

<hr/>

[1] W. Crooke, *Popular Religion and Folk-lore of Northern India* (Westminster, 1896), ii. 314 *sqq.*; Captain G. R. Hearn, "Passing through the Fire at Phalon," *Man*, v. (1905) pp. 154 *sq.* On the custom of walking through fire, or rather over a furnace, see Andrew Lang, *Modern Mythology* (London, 1897), pp. 148-175; *id.*, in *Athenaeum*, 26th August and 14th October, 1899; *id.*, in *Folk-lore*, xii. (1901) pp. 452-455; *id.*, in *Folk-lore*, xiv. (1903) pp. 87-89. Mr. Lang was the first to call attention to the wide prevalence of the rite in many parts of the world.

and gestures. A monstrous and disgusting image of a certain Nathuram, who is said to have been a notorious profligate, is set up in a bazaar and then smashed with blows of shoes and bludgeons while the bonfire of cow-dung is blazing. No household can be without an image of Nathuram, and on the night when the bride first visits her husband, the image of this disreputable personage is placed beside her couch. Barren women and mothers whose children have died look to Nathuram for deliverance from their troubles.[1] Various stories are told to account for the origin of the Holi festival. According to one legend it was instituted in order to get rid of a troublesome demon (*rákshasí*). The people were directed to kindle a bonfire and circumambulate it, singing and uttering fearlessly whatever might come into their minds. Appalled by these vociferations, by the oblations to fire, and by the laughter of the children, the demon was to be destroyed.[2]

In the Chinese province of Fo-Kien we also meet with a vernal festival of fire which may be compared to the fire-festivals of Europe. The ceremony, according to an eminent authority, is a solar festival in honour of the renewal of vegetation and of the vernal warmth. It falls in April, on the thirteenth day of the third month in the Chinese calendar, and is doubtless connected with the ancient custom of renewing the fire, which, as we saw, used to be observed in China at this season.[3] The chief performers in the ceremony are labourers, who refrain from women for seven days, and fast for three days before the festival. During these days they are taught in the temple how to discharge the difficult and dangerous duty which is to be laid upon them. On the eve of the festival an enormous brazier of charcoal, sometimes twenty feet wide, is prepared in front of the temple of the Great God, the protector of life. At sunrise next morning the brazier is lighted and kept

Vernal festival of fire in China.

[1] Pandit Janardan Joshi, in *North Indian Notes and Queries*, iii. pp. 92 *sq.*, § 199 (September, 1893); W. Crooke, *Popular Religion and Folk-lore of Northern India* (Westminster, 1896), ii. 318 *sq.*

[2] E. T. Atkinson, "Notes on the History of Religion in the Himalayas of the N.W. Provinces," *Journal of the Asiatic Society of Bengal*, liii. Part i. (Calcutta, 1884) p. 60. Compare W. Crooke, *Popular Religion and Folk-lore of Northern India* (Westminster, 1896), ii. 313 *sq.*

[3] See above, vol. i. pp. 136 *sq.*

Ceremony to ensure an abundant year.

Walking through the fire.

burning by fresh supplies of fuel. A Taoist priest throws a mixture of salt and rice on the fire to conjure the flames and ensure an abundant year.   Further, two exorcists, barefooted and followed by two peasants, traverse the fire again and again till it is somewhat beaten down.   Meantime the procession is forming in the temple.   The image of the god of the temple is placed in a sedan-chair, resplendent with red paint and gilding, and is carried forth by a score or more of barefooted peasants.   On the shafts of the sedan-chair, behind the image, stands a magician with a dagger stuck through the upper parts of his arms and grasping in each hand a great sword, with which he essays to deal himself violent blows on the back ; however, the strokes as they descend are mostly parried by peasants, who walk behind him and interpose bamboo rods between his back and the swords.   Wild music now strikes up, and under the excitement caused by its stirring strains the procession passes thrice across the furnace.   At their third passage the performers are followed by other peasants carrying the utensils of the temple ; and the rustic mob, electrified by the frenzied spectacle, falls in behind.   Strange as it may seem, burns are comparatively rare.   Inured from infancy to walking barefoot, the peasants can step with impunity over the glowing charcoal, provided they plant their feet squarely and do not stumble ; for usage has so hardened their soles that the skin is converted into a sort of leathery or horny substance which is almost callous to heat. But sometimes, when they slip and a hot coal touches the sides of their feet or ankles, they may be seen to pull a wry face and jump out of the furnace amid the laughter of the spectators.   When this part of the ceremony is over, the procession defiles round the village, and the priests distribute to every family a leaf of yellow paper inscribed with a magic character, which is thereupon glued over the door of the

Ashes of the fire mixed with the fodder of the cattle.

house.   The peasants carry off the charred embers from the furnace, pound them to ashes, and mix the ashes with the fodder of their cattle, believing that it fattens them.   However, the Chinese Government disapproves of these performances, and next morning a number of the performers may generally be seen in the hands of the police, laid face downwards on the ground and receiving a sound castigation on a part of their person which is probably more sensitive than the soles of their feet.[1]

In this last festival the essential feature of the ceremony appears to be the passage of the image of the deity across the fire ; it may be compared to the passage of the straw effigy of Kupalo across the midsummer bonfire in Russia.[2] As we shall see presently, such customs may perhaps be interpreted as magical rites designed to produce light and warmth by subjecting the deity himself to the heat and glow of the furnace ; and where, as at Barsana, priests or sorcerers have been accustomed in the discharge of their functions to walk through or over fire, they have sometimes done so as the living representatives or embodiments of deities, spirits, or other supernatural beings. Some confirmation of this view is furnished by the beliefs and practices of the Dosadhs, a low Indian caste in Behar and Chota Nagpur. On the fifth, tenth, and full-moon days of three months in the year, the priest walks over a narrow trench filled with smouldering wood ashes, and is supposed thus to be inspired by the tribal god Rahu, who becomes incarnate in him for a time. Full of the spirit and also, it is surmised, of drink, the man of god then mounts a bamboo platform, where he sings hymns and distributes to the crowd leaves of *tulsi*, which cure incurable diseases, and flowers which cause barren women to become happy mothers. The service winds up with a feast lasting far into the night, at which the line that divides religious fervour from drunken revelry cannot always be drawn with absolute precision.[3] Similarly the Bhuiyas, a Dravidian tribe of Mirzapur, worship

[marginal notes:] Passage of the image of the deity through the fire.

Passage of inspired men through the fire in India.

[1] G. Schlegel, *Uranographie Chinoise* (The Hague and Leyden, 1875), pp. 143 *sq.* ; *id.*, "La fête de fouler le feu célébrée en Chine et par les Chinois a Java," *Internationales Archiv für Ethnographie*, ix. (1896) pp. 193-195. Compare J. J. M. de Groot, *The Religious System of China*, vi. (Leyden, 1910) pp. 1292 *sq.* According to Professor Schlegel, the connexion between this festival and the old custom of solemnly extinguishing and relighting the fire in spring is unquestionable.

[2] *The Dying God*, p. 262.

[3] (Sir) H. H. Risley, *Tribes and Castes of Bengal, Ethnographic Glossary* (Calcutta, 1891–1892), i. 255 *sq.* Compare W. Crooke, *Popular Religion and Folk-lore of Northern India* (Westminster, 1896), i. 19 ; *id.*, *Tribes and Castes of the North-Western Provinces and Oudh* (Calcutta, 1896), ii. 355. According to Sir Herbert Risley, the trench filled with smouldering ashes is so narrow (only a span and a quarter wide) "that very little dexterity would enable a man to walk with his feet on either edge, so as not to touch the smouldering ashes at the bottom."

their tribal hero Bir by walking over a short trench filled with fire, and they say that the man who is possessed by the hero does not feel any pain in the soles of his feet.[1]   Ceremonies of this sort used to be observed in most districts of the Madras Presidency, sometimes in discharge of vows made in time of sickness or distress, sometimes periodically in honour of a deity.   Where the ceremony was observed periodically, it generally occurred in March or June, which are the months of the vernal equinox and the summer solstice respectively.   A narrow trench, sometimes twenty yards long and half a foot deep, was filled with small sticks and twigs, mostly of tamarind, which were kindled and kept burning till they sank into a mass of glowing embers.   Along this the devotees, often fifty or sixty in succession, walked, ran, or leaped barefoot.   In 1854 the Madras Government instituted an enquiry into the custom, but found that it was not attended by danger or instances of injury sufficient to call for governmental interference.[2]

Hindoo fire-festival in honour of Darma Rajah and Draupadi.

The French traveller Sonnerat has described how, in the eighteenth century, the Hindoos celebrated a fire-festival of this sort in honour of the god Darma Rajah and his wife

---

[1] W. Crooke, *Tribes and Castes of the North-Western Provinces and Oudh*, ii. 82.

[2] M. J. Walhouse, "Passing through the Fire," *Indian Antiquary*, vii. (1878) pp. 126 *sq.*   Compare J. A. Dubois, *Mœurs, Institutions et Cérémonies des Peuples de l'Inde* (Paris, 1825), ii. 373 ; E. Thurston, *Ethnographic Notes in Southern India* (Madras, 1906), pp. 471-486 ; G. F. D'Penha, in *Indian Antiquary*, xxxi. (1902) p. 392 ; "Fire-walking in Ganjam," *Madras Government Museum Bulletin*, vol. iv. No. 3 (Madras, 1903), pp. 214-216.   At Akka timanhully, one of the many villages which help to make up the town of Bangalore in Southern India, one woman at least from every house is expected to walk through the fire at the village festival. Captain J. S. F. Mackenzie witnessed the ceremony in 1873.   A trench, four feet long by two feet wide, was filled with live embers.   The priest walked through it thrice, and the women afterwards passed through it in batches. Capt. Mackenzie remarks : " From the description one reads of walking through fire, I expected something sensational. Nothing could be more tame than the ceremony we saw performed ; in which there never was nor ever could be the slightest danger to life.   Some young girl, whose soles were tender, might next morning find that she had a blister, but this would be the extent of harm she could receive." See Captain J. S. F. Mackenzie, " The Village Feast," *Indian Antiquary*, iii. (1874) pp. 6-9. But to fall on the hot embers might result in injuries which would prove fatal, and such an accident is known to have occurred at a village in Bengal.   See H. J. Stokes, "Walking through Fire," *Indian Antiquary*, ii. (1873) pp. 190 *sq.* At Afkanbour, five days' march from Delhi, the Arab traveller Ibn Batutah saw a troop of fakirs dancing and even rolling on the glowing embers of a wood fire.   See *Voyages d'Ibn Batoutah* (Paris, 1853–1858), ii. 6 *sq.*, iii. 439.

Drobedé (Draupadi). The festival lasted eighteen days, during which all who had vowed to take part in it were bound to fast, to practise continence, to sleep on the ground without a mat, and to walk on a furnace.   On the eighteenth day the images of Darma Rajah and his spouse were carried in procession to the furnace, and the performers followed dancing, their heads crowned with flowers and their bodies smeared with saffron.   The furnace consisted of a trench about forty feet long, filled with hot embers.   When the images had been carried thrice round it, the worshippers walked over the embers, faster or slower, according to the degree of their religious fervour, some carrying their children in their arms, others brandishing spears, swords, and standards.   This part of the ceremony being over, the bystanders hastened to rub their foreheads with ashes from the furnace, and to beg from the performers the flowers which they had worn in their hair ; and such as obtained them preserved the flowers carefully.   The rite was performed in honour of the goddess Drobedé (Draupadi), the heroine of the great Indian epic, the *Mahabharata*.   For she married five brothers all at once ; every year she left one of her husbands to betake herself to another, but before doing so she had to purify herself by fire.   There was no fixed date for the celebration of the rite, but it could only be held in one of the first three months of the year.[1]   In some villages the ceremony is performed annually ; in others, which cannot afford the expense every year, it is observed either at longer intervals, perhaps once in three, seven, ten, or twelve years, or only in special emergencies, such as the outbreak of smallpox, cholera, or plague.   Anybody but a pariah or other person of very low degree may take part in the ceremony in fulfilment of a vow. For example, if a man suffers from some chronic malady, he may vow to Draupadi that, should he be healed of his disease, he will walk over the fire at her festival.   As a preparation for the solemnity he sleeps in the temple and observes a fast. The celebration of the rite in any village is believed to protect the cattle and the crops and to guard the inhabitants from dangers of all kinds.   When it is over, many people carry

Worshippers walking through the fire.

---

[1] Sonnerat, *Voyage aux Indes orientales et à la Chine* (Paris, 1782), i. 247 *sq.*

home the holy ashes of the fire as a talisman which will drive
away devils and demons.[1]

Fire-festival of the Badagas in Southern India.

The Badagas, an agricultural tribe of the Neilgherry Hills
in Southern India, annually celebrate a festival of fire in various parts of their country.   For example, at Nidugala the
festival is held with much ceremony in the month of January.
Omens are taken by boiling two pots of milk side by side
on two hearths.   If the milk overflows uniformly on all sides,
the crops will be abundant for all the villages ; but if it flows
over on one side only, the harvest will be good for villages
on that side only.   The sacred fire is made by friction, a
vertical stick of *Rhodomyrtus tomentosus* being twirled by
means of a cord in a socket let into a thick bough of *Debregeasia velutina*.   With this holy flame a heap of wood of
two sorts, the *Eugenia Jambolana* and *Phyllanthus Emblica*, is
kindled, and the hot embers are spread over a fire-pit about
five yards long and three yards broad.   When all is ready,
the priest ties bells on his legs and approaches the fire-pit,
carrying milk freshly drawn from a cow which has calved
for the first time, and also bearing flowers of *Rhododendron
arboreum, Leucas aspera*, or jasmine.   After doing obeisance,
he throws the flowers on the embers and then pours some of
the milk over them.   If the omens are propitious, that is, if
the flowers remain for a few seconds unscorched and the milk
does not hiss when it falls on the embers, the priest walks
boldly over the embers and is followed by a crowd of celebrants, who before they submit to the ordeal count the hairs
on their feet.   If any of the hairs are found to be singed
after the passage through the fire-pit, it is an ill omen.
Sometimes the Badagas drive their cattle, which have recovered from sickness, over the hot embers in performance
of a vow.[2]   At Melur, another place of the Badagas in the

Sacred fire made by friction.

Walking through the fire.

Cattle driven over the hot embers.

[1] *Madras Government Museum,
Bulletin*, vol. iv. No. 1 (Madras,
1901), pp. 55-59; E. Thurston,
Ethnographic Notes in Southern India
(Madras, 1906), pp. 471-474.   One
of the places where the fire-festival
in honour of Draupadi takes place
annually is the Allandur Temple, at
St. Thomas's Mount, near Madras.
Compare " Fire-walking Ceremony at

the Dharmaraja Festival," *The Quar-
terly Journal of the Mythic Society*,
vol. ii. No. 1 (October, 1910), pp.
29-32.

[2] E. Thurston, *Castes and Tribes
of Southern India* (Madras, 1909), i.
98 *sq.* ; *id., Ethnographic Notes in
Southern India* (Madras, 1906), pp.
476 *sq.*

Neilgherry Hills, three, five, or seven men are chosen to walk through the fire at the festival ; and before they perform the ceremony they pour into an adjacent stream milk from cows which have calved for the first time during the year. A general feast follows the performance of the rite, and next day the land is ploughed and sown for the first time that season. At Jakkaneri, another place of the Badagas in the Neilgherry Hills, the passage through the fire at the festival " seems to have originally had some connection with agri-cultural prospects, as a young bull is made to go partly across the fire-pit before the other devotees, and the owners of young cows which have had their first calves during the year take precedence of others in the ceremony, and bring offerings of milk, which are sprinkled over the burning embers." [1]   According to another account the ceremony among the Badagas was performed every second year at a harvest festival, and the performers were a set of degenerate Brahmans called Haruvarus, who " used to walk on burning coals with bare feet, pretending that the god they worshipped could allay the heat and make fire like cold water to them. As they only remained a few seconds, however, on the coals, it was impossible that they could receive much injury." [2]

In Japan the fire-walk is performed as a religious rite twice a year at a temple in the Kanda quarter of Tokio. One of the performances takes place in September.   It was witnessed in the year 1903 by the wife of an American naval officer, who has described it.   In a court of the temple a bed of charcoal about six yards long, two yards wide, and two feet deep was laid down and covered with a deep layer of straw.   Being ignited, the straw blazed up, and when the flames had died down the bed of hot charcoal was fanned by attendants into a red glow.   Priests dressed in robes of white cotton then walked round the fire, striking sparks from flint and steel and carrying trays full of salt.   When mats had been laid down at the two ends of the fire and salt poured on them, the priests rubbed their bare feet twice in the salt and then walked calmly down the middle of the fire.

[1] E. Thurston, *Castes and Tribes of Southern India* (Madras, 1909), i. 100 *sq.*

[2] F. Metz, *The Tribes inhabiting the Neilgherry Hills*, Second Edition (Mangalore, 1864), p. 55.

They were followed by a number of people, including some boys and a woman with a baby in her arms. "The Shinto-ists claim that, having been perfectly purified by their prayers and ceremonies, no evil has any power over them. Fire they regard as the very spirit of evil; so twice a year, I believe, they go through this fire-walking as a kind of 'outward and visible sign of inward spiritual grace.'"[1]

The fire-walk in Fiji.

In the island of Mbengga, one of the Fijian archipelago, once every year a dracaena, which grows in profusion on the grassy hillsides, becomes fit to yield the sugar of which its fibrous root is full. To render the roots edible it is necessary to bake them among hot stones for four days. A great pit is dug and filled with great stones and blazing logs, and when the flames have died down and the stones are at white heat, the oven is ready to receive the roots. At this moment the members of a certain clan called Na Ivilankata, favoured of the gods, leap into the oven and walk unharmed upon the hot stones, which would scorch the feet of any other persons. On one occasion when the ceremony was witnessed by Europeans fifteen men of the clan, dressed in garlands and fringes, walked unscathed through the furnace, where tongues of fire played among the hot stones. The pit was about nineteen feet wide and the men marched round it, planting their feet squarely and firmly on each stone. When they emerged from the pit,

---

[1] "A Japanese Fire-walk," *American Anthropologist*, New Series, v. (1903) pp. 377-380. The ceremony has been described to me by two eye-witnesses, Mr. Ernest Foxwell of St. John's College, Cambridge, and Miss E. P. Hughes, formerly Principal of the Teachers' Training College, Cambridge. Mr. Foxwell examined the feet of the performers both before and after their passage through the fire and found no hurt. The heat was so great that the sweat ran down him as he stood near the bed of glowing charcoal. He cannot explain the immunity of the performers. He informs me that the American writer Percival Lowell walked in the fire and was burned so severely that he was laid up in bed for three weeks; while on the other hand a Scotch engineer named Hillhouse passed over the hot charcoal unscathed. Several of Miss Hughes's Japanese pupils also went through the ordeal with impunity, but one of them burned a toe. Both before and after walking through the fire the people dipped their feet in a white stuff which Miss Hughes was told was salt. Compare W. G. Aston, *Shinto* (London, 1905), p. 348: "At the present day plunging the hand into boiling water, walking barefoot over a bed of live coals, and climbing a ladder formed of sword-blades set edge upwards are practised, not by way of ordeal, but to excite the awe and stimulate the piety of the ignorant spectators."

the feet of several were examined and shewed no trace of scorching; even the anklets of dried tree-fern leaves which they wore on their legs were unburnt. The immunity thus enjoyed by members of the clan in the fiery furnace is explained by a legend that in former days a chief of the clan, named Tui Nkualita, received for himself and his descendants this remarkable privilege from a certain god, whom the chief had accidentally dragged out of a deep pool of water by the hair of his head.[1] A similar cere-mony of walking through fire, or rather over a furnace of hot charcoal or hot stones, has also been observed in Tahiti,[2] the Marquesas Islands,[3] and by Hindoo coolies in the West Indian island of Trinidad;[4] but the eye-witnesses who have described the rite, as it is observed in these islands, have said little or nothing as to its meaning and purpose, their whole attention having been apparently concentrated on the heat of the furnace and the state of the performers' legs before and after passing through it.

The fire-walk in Tahiti, the Mar-quesas Islands, and Trinidad.

"Another grand custom of the Hottentots, which they likewise term *andersmaken*, is the driving their sheep at certain times through the fire. Early in the day appointed by a kraal for the observance of this custom, the women

Hottentot custom of driving their sheep through fire and smoke.

---

[1] Basil Thomson, *South Sea Yarns* (Edinburgh and London, 1894), pp. 195-207. Compare F. Arthur Jackson, "A Fijian Legend of the Origin of the *Vilavilairevo* or Fire Ceremony," *Journal of the Polynesian Society*, vol. iii. No. 2 (June, 1894), pp. 72-75; R. Fulton, "An Account of the Fiji Fire-walking Ceremony, or *Vilavilairevo*, with a probable explanation of the mystery," *Transactions and Proceedings of the New Zealand Institute*, xxxv. (1902) pp. 187-201; Lieutenant Vernon H. Haggard, in *Folk-lore*, xiv. (1903) pp. 88 *sq.*

[2] S. P. Langley, "The Fire-walk Ceremony in Tahiti," *Report of the Smithsonian Institution for 1901* (Washington, 1902), pp. 539-544; *id.*, in *Folk-lore*, xiv. (1901) pp. 446-452; "More about Fire-walking," *Journal of the Polynesian Society*, vol. x. No. 1 (March, 1901), pp. 53 *sq.*

In his *Modern Mythology* (pp. 162-165) Andrew Lang quotes from *The Polynesian Society's Journal*, vol. ii. No. 2, pp. 105-108, an account of the fire-walk by Miss Tenira Henry, which seems to refer to Raiatea, one of the Tahitian group of islands.

[3] *Annales de l'Association de la Propagation de la Foi*, lxix. (1897) pp. 130-133. But in the ceremony here described the chief performer was a native of Huahine, one of the Tahitian group of islands. The wood burned in the furnace was hibiscus and native chestnut (*Inocarpus edulis*). Before stepping on the hot stones the principal performer beat the edge of the furnace twice or thrice with *ti* leaves (dracaena).

[4] *Les Missions Catholiques*, x. (1878) pp. 141 *sq.*; A. Lang, *Modern Mythology*, p. 167, quoting Mr. Henry R. St. Clair.

milk all their cows, and set the whole produce before their husbands. 'Tis a strict rule at those times that the women neither taste, nor suffer their children to touch, a drop of it. The whole quantity is sacred to the men, who drink it all up before they address themselves to the business of the fire. Having consumed the milk, some go and bring the sheep together to the place where the fire is to be lighted, while others repair to the place to light it. The fire is made of chips and dry twigs and thinly spread into a long square. Upon the coming up of the sheep, the fire, scattered into this figure, is covered with green twigs to raise a great smoak ; and a number of men range themselves closely on both sides of it, making a lane for the sheep to pass through, and extending themselves to a good distance beyond the fire on the side where the sheep are to enter. Things being in this posture, the sheep are driven into the lane close up to the fire, which now smoaks in the thickest clouds. The foremost boggle, and being forced forward by the press behind, seek their escape by attempting breaches in the ranks. The men stand close and firm, and whoop and goad them forward ; when a few hands, planted at the front of the fire, catch three or four of the foremost sheep by the head, and drag them through, and bring them round into the sight of the rest ; which sometimes upon this, the whooping and goading continuing, follow with a tantivy, jumping and pouring themselves through the fire and smoak with a mighty clattering and fury. At other times they are not so tractable, but put the Hottentots to the trouble of dragging numbers of them through ; and sometimes, in a great press and fright, sturdily attacking the ranks, they make a breach and escape. This is a very mortifying event at all times, the Hottentots, upon whatever account, looking upon it as a heavy disgrace and a very ill omen into the bargain. But when their labours here are attended with such success, that the sheep pass readily through or over the fire, 'tis hardly in the power of language to describe them in all the sallies of their joy." The writer who thus describes the custom had great difficulty in extracting an explanation of it from the Hottentots. At last one of them informed him that their country was much infested by wild dogs, which made terrible havoc among the cattle, worrying the animals to death even when they did not devour them. " Now we have it," he said, " from our ancestors, that if sheep are driven through the fire, as we say, that is, through a thick smoak, the wild dogs will not be fond of attacking them while the scent of the smoak remains upon their fleeces. We therefore from time to time, for the security of our flocks, perform this *andersmaken*." [1]

When disease breaks out in a herd of the Nandi, a pastoral tribe of British East Africa, a large bonfire is made with the wood of a certain tree (*Olea chrysophilla*), and brushwood of two sorts of shrubs is thrown on the top. Then the sick herd is driven to the fire, and while the animals are standing near it, a sheep big with young is brought to them and anointed with milk by an elder, after which it is strangled by two men belonging to clans that may intermarry. The intestines are then inspected, and if the omens prove favourable, the meat is roasted and eaten ; moreover rings are made out of the skin and worn by the cattle-owners. After the meat has been eaten, the herd is driven round the fire, and milk is poured on each beast.[2] When their cattle are sick, the Zulus of Natal will collect their herds in a kraal, where a medicine-man kindles a fire, burns medicine in it, and so fumigates the cattle with the medicated smoke. Afterwards he sprinkles the herd with a decoction, and, taking some melted fat of the dead oxen in his mouth, squirts it on a fire-brand and holds the brand to each animal in succession.[3] Such a custom is probably equivalent to the Hottentot and European practice of driving cattle through a fire.

Fire applied to sick cattle by the Nandi and Zulus.

Among the Indians of Yucatan the year which was marked in their calendar by the sign of *Cauac* was reputed to be very unlucky ; they thought that in the course of it the death-rate would be high, the maize crops would be withered up by the extreme heat of the sun, and what remained of the harvest would be devoured by swarms of ants and birds. To avert these calamities they used to erect a great pyre of

Indians of Yucatan walk over hot embers in order to avert calamities.

[1] Peter Kolben, *The Present State of the Cape of Good Hope*, Second Edition (London, 1738), i. 129-133.
[2] A. C. Hollis, *The Nandi* (Oxford, 1909), pp. 45 *sq.*
[3] Rev. Joseph Shooter, *The Kafirs of Natal* (London, 1857), p. 35.

wood, to which most persons contributed a faggot.   Having danced about it during the day, they set fire to it at night-fall, and when the flames had died down, they spread out the red embers and walked or ran barefoot over them, some of them escaping unsmirched by the flames, but others burning themselves more or less severely.   In this way they hoped to conjure away the evils that threatened them, and to undo the sinister omens of the year.[1]

The fire-walk in antiquity, at Castabala in Cappadocia and at Mount Soracte near Rome.

Similar rites were performed at more than one place in classical antiquity.   At Castabala, in Cappadocia, the priestesses of an Asiatic goddess, whom the Greeks called Artemis Perasia, used to walk barefoot through a furnace of hot charcoal and take no harm.[2]   Again, at the foot of Mount Soracte, in Italy, there was a sanctuary of a goddess Feronia, where once a year the men of certain families walked barefoot, but unscathed, over the glowing embers and ashes of a great fire of pinewood in presence of a vast multitude, who had assembled from all the country round about to pay their devotions to the deity or to ply their business at the fair.   The families from whom the performers of the rite were drawn went by the name of Hirpi Sorani, or "Soranian Wolves"; and in consideration of the services which they rendered the state by walking through the fire, they were exempted, by a special decree of the senate, from military service and all public burdens.   In the discharge of their sacred function, if we can trust the testimony of Strabo, they were believed to be inspired by the goddess Feronia. The ceremony certainly took place in her sanctuary, which was held in the highest reverence alike by Latins and Sabines; but according to Virgil and Pliny the rite was performed in honour of the god of the mountain, whom they call by the Greek name of Apollo, but whose real name appears to have been Soranus.[3]   If Soranus was a sun-god, as his

[1] Diego de Landa, *Relation des choses de Yucatan* (Paris, 1864), pp. 231, 233.

[2] Strabo, xii. 2. 7, p. 537.   Compare *Adonis, Attis, Osiris*, Second Edition, pp. 89, 134 *sqq.*

[3] Pliny, *Nat. Hist.* vii. 19; Virgil, *Aen.* xi. 784 *sqq.* with the comment of Servius; Strabo, v. 2. 9, p. 226;

Dionysius Halicarnasensis, *Antiquit. Rom.* iii. 32.   From a reference to the custom in Silius Italicus (v. 175 *sqq.*) it seems that the men passed thrice through the furnace holding the entrails of the sacrificial victims in their hands.   The learned but sceptical Varro attributed their immunity in the fire to a drug with which they took

name has by some been thought to indicate,[1] we might perhaps conclude that the passage of his priests through the fire was a magical ceremony designed to procure a due supply of light and warmth for the earth by mimicking the sun's passage across the firmament. For so priceless a service, rendered at some personal risk, it would be natural that the magicians should be handsomely rewarded by a grateful country, and that they should be released from the common obligations of earth in order the better to devote themselves to their celestial mission. The neighbouring towns paid the first-fruits of their harvest as tribute to the shrine, and loaded it besides with offerings of gold and silver, of which, however, it was swept clean by Hannibal when he hung with his dusky army, like a storm-cloud about to break, within sight of the sentinels on the walls of Rome.[2]

§ 2. *The Meaning of the Fire-walk*

The foregoing customs, observed in many different parts of the world, present at least a superficial resemblance to the modern European practices of leaping over fires and driving cattle through them ; and we naturally ask whether it is not possible to discover a general explanation which will include them all. We have seen that two general theories have been proposed to account for the European practices ; according to one theory the customs in question are sun-charms,

Little evidence to shew that the fire-walk is a sun-charm.

care to anoint the soles of their feet before they planted them in the furnace. See Varro, cited by Servius, on Virgil, *Aen.* xi. 787. The whole subject has been treated by W. Mannhardt (*Antike Wald- und Feldkulte*, Berlin, 1877, pp. 327 *sqq.*), who compares the rites of these "Soranian Wolves" with the ceremonies performed by the brotherhood of the Green Wolf at Jumièges in Normandy. See above, vol. i. pp. 185 *sq.*

[1] L. Preller (*Römische Mythologie*,[3] i. 268), following G. Curtius, would connect the first syllable of Soranus and Soracte with the Latin *sol*, "sun." However, this etymology appears to be at the best very doubtful. My friend Prof. J. H. Moulton doubts

whether *Soranus* can be connected with *sol*; he tells me that the interchange of *l* and *r* is rare. He would rather connect *Soracte* with the Greek ὕραξ, "a shrew-mouse." In that case Apollo Soranus might be the equivalent of the Greek Apollo Smintheus, "the Mouse Apollo." Professor R. S. Conway also writes to me (11th November 1902) that *Soranus* and *Soracte* "have nothing to do with *sol*; *r* and *l* are not confused in Italic."

[2] Livy, xxvi. 11. About this time the Carthaginian army encamped only three miles from Rome, and Hannibal in person, at the head of two thousand cavalry, rode close up to the walls and leisurely reconnoitered them. See Livy, xxvi. 10; Polybius, ix. 5-7.

according to the other they are purifications.   Let us see how the two rival theories fit the other facts which we have just passed in review.   To take the solar theory first, it is supported, first, by a statement that the fires at the Pongol festival in Southern India are intended to wake the sun-god or the fire-god from his sleep;[1] and, second, by the etymology which connects Soranus, the god of Soracte, with the sun.[2]   But for reasons which have already been given, neither of these arguments carries much weight ; and apart from them there appears to be nothing in the foregoing customs to suggest that they are sun-charms.   Nay, some of the customs appear hardly reconcilable with such a view. For it is to be observed that the fire-walk is frequently practised in India and other tropical countries, where as a rule people would more naturally wish to abate than to increase the fierce heat of the sun.   In Yucatan certainly the intention of kindling the bonfires cannot possibly have been to fan the solar flames, since one of the principal evils which the bonfires were designed to remedy was precisely the excessive heat of the sun, which had withered up the maize crops.[3]   Thus the solar theory is not strongly supported by any of the facts which we are considering, and it is actually inconsistent with some of them.

On the other hand there is much to be said for the view that the fire-walk is a form of purification, the flames being thought either to burn up or repel the powers of evil.

Not so with the purificatory theory.   It is obviously applicable to some of the facts, and apparently consistent with them all.   Thus we have seen that sick men make a vow to walk over the fire, and that sick cattle are driven over it.   In such cases clearly the intention is to cleanse the suffering man or beast from the infection of disease, and thereby to restore him or it to health ; and the fire is supposed to effect this salutary end, either by burning up the powers of evil or by interposing an insurmountable barrier between them and the sufferer.   For it is to be remembered that evils which civilized men regard as impersonal are often conceived by uncivilized man in the personal shape of witches and wizards, of ghosts and hobgoblins ; so tnat measures which we should consider as simple disinfectants the savage looks upon as obstacles opportunely presented to

---

[1] Above, p. 1.   [2] Above, p. 15.

[3] Above, pp. 13 *sq.*

the attacks of demons or other uncanny beings. Now of all such obstacles fire seems generally to be thought the most effective; hence in passing through or leaping over it our primitive philosopher often imagines that he is not so much annihilating his spiritual foe as merely giving him the slip; the ghostly pursuer shrinks back appalled at the flames through which his intended victim, driven to desperation by his fears, has safely passed before him. This interpretation of the ceremony is confirmed, first, by the observation that in India the ashes of the bonfire are used as a talisman against devils and demons;[1] and, second, by the employment of the ceremony for the avowed purpose of escaping from the pursuit of a troublesome ghost. For example, in China "they believe that a beheaded man wanders about a headless spectre in the World of Shades. Such spectres are frequently to be seen in walled towns, especially in the neighbourhood of places of execution. Here they often visit the people with disease and disaster, causing a considerable depreciation in the value of the houses around such scenes. Whenever an execution takes place, the people fire crackers to frighten the headless ghost away from the spot; and the mandarin who has superintended the bloody work, on entering the gate of his mansion, has himself carried in his sedan chair over a fire lighted on the pavement, lest the headless apparition should enter there along with him; for disembodied spirits are afraid of fire."[2] For a like reason Chinese mourners after a funeral, and persons who have paid a visit of condolence to a house of death, often purify themselves by stepping over a fire of straw;[3] the purification, we cannot doubt, consists simply in shaking off the ghost who is supposed to dog their steps. Similarly at a coroner's inquest in China the mandarin and his subordinates hold pocket handkerchiefs or towels to their mouths and noses while they are inspecting the corpse, no doubt to hinder the ghost from insinuating himself into their bodies by these apertures; and when they have discharged their dangerous

Custom of stepping over fire for the purpose of getting rid of a ghost.

---

[1] Above, p. 8, compare p. 3.

[2] J. J. M. de Groot, *The Religious System of China*, i. (Leyden, 1892), p. 355; *id.* vi. (Leyden, 1910) p. 942.

[3] Rev. J. H. Gray, *China* (London, 1878), i. 287, 305; J. J. M. de Groot, *op. cit.* i. 32, vi. 942.

duty, they purify themselves by passing through a small fire of straw kindled on the pavement before they enter their sedan-chairs to return home, while at the same time the crowd of idlers, who have gathered about the door, assist in keeping the ghost at bay by a liberal discharge of crackers. The same double process of purification, or rather of repelling the ghost, by means of fire and crackers is repeated at the gate of the mandarin's residence when the procession defiles into it.[1] Among some of the Tartars it used to be customary for all persons returning from a burial to leap over a fire made for the purpose, " in order that the dead man might not follow them ; for apparently in their opinion he would be afraid of the fire." [2] " The Yakuts bury their dead as a rule on the day of the death, and in order not to take the demon of death home with them, they kindle fires on the way back from the burial and jump over them in the belief that the demon of death, who dreads fire, will not follow them, and that in this way they will be freed from the persecutions of the hated demon of death." [3] In Sikkhim, when members of the Khambu caste have buried a corpse, all persons present at the burial " adjourn to a stream for a bath of purification, and, on re-entering the house, have to tread on a bit of burning cloth, to prevent the evil spirits who attend at funerals from following them in." [4] Among the Fans of West Africa, " when the mourning is over, the wives of the deceased must pass over a small lighted brazier in the middle of the village, then they sit down while some leaves are still burning under their feet ; their heads are shaved, and from that moment they are purified from the mourning—perhaps we should translate : ' delivered from the ghost of their husband '—and may be divided among the heirs." [5] At Agweh, on the Slave Coast of West Africa, a widow used to remain shut up for six

[1] J. J. M. de Groot, op. cit. i. 137, vi. 942.

[2] J. G. Gmelin, Reise durch Sibirien (Göttingen, 1751–1752), i. 333.

[3] W. L. Priklonski, "Ueber das Schamenthum bei den Jakuten," in A. Bastian's Allerlei aus Volks- und Menschenkunde (Berlin, 1888), i. 219. Compare Vasilij Priklonski, "Todten-gebräuche der Jakuten," Globus, lix. (1891) p. 85.

[4] J. A. H. Louis, The Gates of Thibet (Calcutta, 1894), p. 116.

[5] E. Allegret, "Les Idées religieuses des Fañ (Afrique Occidentale)," Revue de l'Histoire des Religions, l. (1904) p. 220.

months in the room where her husband was buried ; at the Widows fumigated to free them from their husbands' ghosts.
end of the time a fire was lighted on the floor, and red
peppers strewn in it, until in the pungent fumes the widow
was nearly stifled.[1]   No doubt the intention was to rid her
of her husband's ghost in order that she might mingle again
in the world with safety to herself and others.

On the analogy of these customs, in which the purpose Hence it seems probable that the chief use of the fire in the fire-festivals of Europe was to destroy or repel the witches, to whose maleficent arts the people ascribed most of their troubles.
of the passage through the fire appears to be unmistakable,
we may suppose that the motive of the rite is similar at the
popular festivals of Europe and the like observances in
other lands.   In every case the ritual appears to be explained
in a simple and natural way by the supposition that the
performers believe themselves to be freed from certain evils,
actual or threatened, through the beneficent agency of fire,
which either burns up and destroys the noxious things or
at all events repels and keeps them at bay.   Indeed this
belief, or at least this hope, is definitely expressed by
some of the people who leap across the bonfires : they
imagine that all ills are burnt up and consumed in the
flames, or that they leave their sins, or at all events their
fleas, behind them on the far side of the fire.[2]   But we may
conjecture that originally all the evils from which the people
thus thought to deliver themselves were conceived by them
to be caused by personal beings, such as ghosts and demons
or witches and warlocks, and that the fires were kindled
for the sole purpose of burning or banning these noxious
creatures.   Of these evil powers witches and warlocks
appear to have been the most dreaded by our European
peasantry ; and it is therefore significant that the fires kindled
on these occasions are often expressly alleged to burn the
witches,[3] that effigies of witches are not uncommonly consumed in them,[4] and that two of the great periodic fire-
festivals of the year, namely May Day and Midsummer Eve,
coincide with the seasons when witches are believed to be
most active and mischievous, and when accordingly many
other precautions are taken against them.[5]   Thus if witch-

[1] A. B. Ellis, *The Ewe-speaking Peoples of the Slave Coast of West Africa* (London, 1890), p. 160.
[2] Above, pp. 162, 163, 211, 212, 214, 215, 217.

[3] See the references above, vol. i. p. 342 note [2].
[4] See the references above, vol. i. p. 342 note [3].
[5] See *The Magic Art and the Evolu-*

craft, as a great part of mankind has believed, is the fertile source of almost all the calamities that afflict our species, and if the surest means of frustrating witchcraft is fire, then it follows as clearly as day follows night that to jump over a fire must be a sovereign panacea for practically all the ills that flesh is heir to. We can now, perhaps, fully understand why festivals of fire played so prominent a part in the religion or superstition of our heathen forefathers ; the observance of such festivals flowed directly from their overmastering fear of witchcraft and from their theory as to the best way of combating that dreadful evil.

---

tion of Kings, ii. 52 *sqq.*, 127 ; *The Scapegoat*, pp. 157 *sqq.* Compare R. Kühnau, *Schlesische Sagen* (Berlin, 1910–1913), iii. p. 69, No. 1428 : "In the county of Glatz the people believe that on Walpurgis Night (the Eve of May Day) the witches under cover of the darkness seek to harm men in all sorts of ways. To guard themselves against them the people set small birch trees in front of the house-door on the previous day, and are of opinion that the witches must count all the leaves on these little trees before they can get into the house. While they are still at this laborious task, the day dawns and the dreaded guests must retire to their own realm " ; *id.*, iii. p. 39, No. 1394 : "On St. John's Night (between the 23rd and 24th of June) the witches again busily bestir themselves to force their way into the houses of men and the stalls of cattle. People stick small twigs of oak in the windows and doors of the houses and cattle-stalls to keep out the witches. This is done in the neighbourhood of Patschkau and generally in the districts of Frankenstein, Münsterberg, Grottkau, and Neisse. In the same regions they hang garlands, composed of oak leaves intertwined with flowers, at the windows. The garland must be woven in the house itself and may not be carried over any threshold ; it must be hung out of the window on a nail, which is inserted there." Similar evidence might be multiplied almost indefinitely.

CHAPTER VII

THE BURNING OF HUMAN BEINGS IN THE FIRES

§ 1. *The Burning of Effigies in the Fires*

WE have still to ask, What is the meaning of burning effigies in the fire at these festivals? After the preceding investigation the answer to the question seems obvious. As the fires are often alleged to be kindled for the purpose of burning the witches, and as the effigy burnt in them is sometimes called "the Witch," we might naturally be disposed to conclude that all the effigies consumed in the flames on these occasions represent witches or warlocks, and that the custom of burning them is merely a substitute for burning the wicked men and women themselves, since on the principle of homoeopathic or imitative magic you practically destroy the witch herself in destroying her effigy. On the whole this explanation of the burning of straw figures in human shape at the festivals appears to be the most probable.

Yet it may be that this explanation does not apply to all the cases, and that certain of them may admit and even require another interpretation, in favour of which I formerly argued as follows:—[1]

"It remains to ask, What is the meaning of burning an effigy in these bonfires? The effigies so burned, as I have already remarked, can hardly be separated from the effigies of Death which are burned or otherwise destroyed in spring; and grounds have been already given for regarding the so-called effigies of Death as really representatives of the tree-

---

[1] *The Golden Bough*, Second Edition (London, 1900), ii. 314-316.

spirit or spirit of vegetation.[1]   Are the other effigies, which
are burned in the spring and midsummer bonfires, susceptible
of the same explanation?   It would seem so.   For just as
the fragments of the so-called Death are stuck in the fields
to make the crops grow, so the charred embers of the figure
burned in the spring bonfires are sometimes laid on the
fields in the belief that they will keep vermin from the crop.[2]
Again, the rule that the last married bride must leap over
the fire in which the straw-man is burned on Shrove Tuesday,
is probably intended to make her fruitful.[3]   But, as we have
seen, the power of blessing women with offspring is a special
attribute of tree-spirits ;[4] it is therefore a fair presumption
that the burning effigy over which the bride must leap is a
representative of the fertilizing tree-spirit or spirit of vegetation.   This character of the effigy, as representative of the
spirit of vegetation, is almost unmistakable when the figure is
composed of an unthreshed sheaf of corn or is covered from
head to foot with flowers.[5]   Again, it is to be noted that,
instead of a puppet, trees, either living or felled, are sometimes burned both in the spring and midsummer bonfires.[6]
Now, considering the frequency with which the tree-spirit is
represented in human shape, it is hardly rash to suppose that
when sometimes a tree and sometimes an effigy is burned in
these fires, the effigy and the tree are regarded as equivalent
to each other, each being a representative of the tree-spirit.
This, again, is confirmed by observing, first, that sometimes the
effigy which is to be burned is carried about simultaneously
with a May-tree, the former being carried by the boys, the
latter by the girls ;[7] and, second, that the effigy is sometimes
tied to a living tree and burned with it.[8]   In these cases, we
can scarcely doubt, the tree-spirit is represented, as we have
found it represented before, in duplicate, both by the tree and
by the effigy.   That the true character of the effigy as a
representative of the beneficent spirit of vegetation should
sometimes be forgotten, is natural.   The custom of burning

[1] *The Dying God*, pp. 249 *sqq.*

[2] Above, vol. i. p. 117, compare
pp. 143, 144.

[3] See above, vol. i. p. 120.

[4] *The Magic Art and the Evolution
of Kings*, ii. 56 *sqq.*

[5] Above, vol. i. pp. 120, 167.

[6] Above, vol. i. pp. 115 *sq.*, 116,
142, 173 *sq.*, 185, 191, 192, 193, 209.

[7] Above, vol. i. p. 120.

[8] Above, vol. i. p. 116.   But the
effigy is called the Witch.

a beneficent god is too foreign to later modes of thought to escape misinterpretation.   Naturally enough the people who continued to burn his image came in time to identify it as the effigy of persons, whom, on various grounds, they regarded with aversion, such as Judas Iscariot, Luther, and a witch.

"The general reasons for killing a god or his repre- sentative have been examined in the preceding chapter.[1] But when the god happens to be a deity of vegetation, there are special reasons why he should die by fire.   For light and heat are necessary to vegetable growth ; and, on the principle of sympathetic magic, by subjecting the personal representative of vegetation to their influence, you secure a supply of these necessaries for trees and crops. In other words, by burning the spirit of vegetation in a fire which represents the sun, you make sure that, for a time at least, vegetation shall have plenty of sun.   It may be objected that, if the intention is simply to secure enough sunshine for vegetation, this end would be better attained, on the principles of sympathetic magic, by merely passing the representative of vegetation through the fire instead of burning him.   In point of fact this is sometimes done.   In Russia, as we have seen, the straw figure of Kupalo is not burned in the midsummer fire, but merely carried backwards and forwards across it.[2]   But, for the reasons already given, it is necessary that the god should die ; so next day Kupalo is stripped of her ornaments and thrown into a stream.   In this Russian custom, therefore, the passage of the image through the fire is a sun-charm pure and simple ; the killing of the god is a separate act, and the mode of killing him— by drowning—is probably a rain-charm.   But usually people have not thought it necessary to draw this fine distinction ; for the various reasons already assigned, it is advantageous, they think, to expose the god of vegetation to a considerable degree of heat, and it is also advantageous to kill him, and they combine these advantages in a rough-and-ready way by burning him."

On the foregoing argument, which I do not now find very cogent, I would remark that we must distinguish the cases in

Reasons for burning effigies of the spirit of vegetation or for passing them through the fire.

---

[1] The chapter has since been ex- panded into the four volumes of *The Dying God, Spirits of the Corn and of* *the Wild,* and *The Scapegoat.*

[2] *The Dying God,* p. 262.

The custom of passing images of gods or their living representatives through the fires may be simply a form of purification.

which an effigy or an image is burnt in the fire from the cases in which it is simply carried through or over it. We have seen that in the Chinese festival of fire the image of the god is carried thrice by bearers over the glowing furnace. Here the motive for subjecting a god to the heat of the furnace must surely be the same as the motive for subjecting his worshippers to the same ordeal; and if the motive in the case of the worshippers is purificatory, it is probably the same in the case of the deity. In other words we may suppose that the image of a god is periodically carried over a furnace in order to purify him from the taint of corruption, the spells of magicians, or any other evil influences that might impair or impede his divine energies. The same theory would explain the custom of obliging the priest ceremonially to pass through the fire; the custom need not be a mitigation of an older practice of burning him in the flames, it may only be a purification designed to enable him the better to discharge his sacred duties as representative of the deity in the coming year. Similarly, when the rite is obligatory, not on the people as a whole, but only on certain persons chosen for the purpose,[1] we may suppose that these persons act as representatives of the entire community, which thus passes through the fire by deputy and consequently participates in all the benefits which are believed to accrue from the purificatory character of the rite.[2]   In both cases, therefore, if my interpretation of them is correct, the passage over or through a fire is not a substitute for human sacrifice; it is nothing but a stringent form of purification.

§ 2. *The Burning of Men and Animals in the Fires*

Yet in the popular customs connected with the fire-festivals of Europe there are certain features which appear to

---

[1] Above, pp. 9, 10, 14.

[2] Among the Klings of Southern India the ceremony of walking over a bed of red-hot ashes is performed by a few chosen individuals, who are prepared for the rite by a devil-doctor or medicine-man. The eye-witness who describes the ceremony adds : "As I understood it, they took on themselves and expiated the sins of the Kling community for the past year." See the letter of Stephen Ponder, quoted by Andrew Lang, *Modern Mythology* (London, 1897), p. 160.

point to a former practice of human sacrifice. We have seen reasons for believing that in Europe living persons have often acted as representatives of the tree-spirit and corn-spirit and have suffered death as such.[1] There is no reason, therefore, why they should not have been burned, if any special advantages were likely to be attained by putting them to death in that way. The consideration of human suffering is not one which enters into the calculations of primitive man. Now, in the fire-festivals which we are discussing, the pretence of burning people is sometimes carried so far that it seems reasonable to regard it as a mitigated survival of an older custom of actually burning them. Thus in Aachen, as we saw, the man clad in peas-straw acts so cleverly that the children really believe he is being burned.[2] At Jumièges in Normandy the man clad all in green, who bore the title of the Green Wolf, was pursued by his comrades, and when they caught him they feigned to fling him upon the mid-summer bonfire.[3] Similarly at the Beltane fires in Scotland the pretended victim was seized, and a show made of throwing him into the flames, and for some time afterwards people affected to speak of him as dead.[4] Again, in the Hallowe'en bonfires of north-eastern Scotland we may perhaps detect a similar pretence in the custom observed by a lad of lying down as close to the fire as possible and allowing the other lads to leap over him.[5] The titular king at Aix, who reigned for a year and danced the first dance round the midsummer bonfire,[6] may perhaps in days of old have discharged the less agreeable duty of serving as fuel for that fire which in later times he only kindled. In the following customs Mannhardt is probably right in recognizing traces of an old custom of burning a leaf-clad representative of the spirit of vegetation. At Wolfeck, in Austria, on Midsummer Day, a boy completely clad in green fir branches goes from house to house, accompanied by a noisy crew, collecting wood for the bonfire. As he gets the wood he sings—

Yet at some of the fire-festivals the pretence of burning live persons in the fires points to a former custom of human sacrifice.

---

[1] *The Dying God*, pp. 205 *sqq.*; *Spirits of the Corn and of the Wild*, i. 216 *sqq.*

[2] Above, vol. i. p. 120.

[3] Above, vol. i. p. 186.

[4] Above, vol. i. p. 148.

[5] Above, vol. i. p. 233.

[6] Above, vol. i. p. 194.

> "*Forest trees I want,*
> *No sour milk for me,*
> *But beer and wine,*
> *So can the wood-man be jolly and gay.*"[1]

In some parts of Bavaria, also, the boys who go from house to house collecting fuel for the midsummer bonfire envelop one of their number from head to foot in green branches of firs, and lead him by a rope through the whole village.[2]   At Moosheim, in Wurtemberg, the festival of St. John's Fire usually lasted for fourteen days, ending on the second Sunday after Midsummer Day.   On this last day the bonfire was left in charge of the children, while the older people retired to a wood.   Here they encased a young fellow in leaves and twigs, who, thus disguised, went to the fire, scattered it, and trod it out.   All the people present fled at the sight of him.[3]

In pagan Europe the water as well as the fire seems to have claimed its human victim on Midsummer Day.

In this connexion it is worth while to note that in pagan Europe the water as well as the fire seems to have claimed its human victim on Midsummer Day.   Some German rivers, such as the Saale and the Spree, are believed still to require their victim on that day; hence people are careful not to bathe at this perilous season.   Where the beautiful Neckar flows, between vine-clad and wooded hills, under the majestic ruins of Heidelberg castle, the spirit of the river seeks to drown three persons, one on Midsummer Eve, one on Midsummer Day, and one on the day after.   On these nights, if you hear a shriek as of a drowning man or woman from the water, beware of running to the rescue; for it is only the water-fairy shrieking to lure you to your doom.   Many a fisherman of the Elbe knows better than to launch his boat and trust himself to the treacherous river on Midsummer Day.   And Samland fishermen will not go to sea at this season, because they are aware that the sea is then hollow and demands a victim.   In the neighbourhood of the Lake of Constance

---

[1] W. Mannhardt, *Baumkultus*, p. 524.

[2] *Bavaria, Landes- und Volkskunde des Königreichs Bayern* (Munich, 1860–1867), iii. 956; W. Mannhardt, *Baumkultus*, p. 524.   In the neighbourhood of Breitenbrunn the lad who collects fuel at this season has his face blackened and is called "the Charcoal Man" (*Bavaria*, etc., ii. 261).

[3] A. Birlinger, *Volksthümliches aus Schwaben* (Freiburg im Breisgau, 1861–1862), ii. 121 *sq.*, § 146; W. Mannhardt, *Baumkultus*, pp. 524 *sq.*

the Swabian peasants say that on St. John's Day the Angel or St. John must have a swimmer and a climber; hence no one will climb a tree or bathe even in a brook on that day.[1] According to others, St. John will have three dead men on his day; one of them must die by water, one by a fall, and one by lightning; therefore old-fashioned people warn their children not to climb or bathe, and are very careful themselves not to run into any kind of danger on Midsummer Day.[2] So in some parts of Switzerland people are warned against bathing on St. John's Night, because the saint's day demands its victims. Thus in the Emmenthal they say, "This day will have three persons; one must perish in the air, one in the fire, and the third in the water." At Schaffhausen the saying runs, "St. John the Baptist must have a runner, must have a swimmer, must have a climber." That is the reason why you should not climb cherry-trees on the saint's day, lest you should fall down and break your valuable neck.[3] In Cologne the saint is more exacting; on his day he requires no less than fourteen dead men; seven of them must be swimmers and seven climbers.[4] Accordingly when we find that, in one of the districts where a belief of this sort prevails, it used to be customary to throw a person into the water on Midsummer Day, we can hardly help concluding that this was only a modification of an older custom of actually drowning a human being in the river at that time. In Voigtland it was formerly the practice to set up a fine May tree, adorned with all kinds of things, on St. John's Day. The people danced round it, and when the lads had fetched down the things with which it was tricked out, the tree was thrown into the water. But before this was

Custom of throwing a man and a tree into the water on St. John's Day.

[1] E. Meier, *Deutsche Sagen, Sitten und Gebräuche aus Schwaben* (Stuttgart, 1852), pp. 428 *sq.*, §§ 120, 122; O. Freiherr von Reinsberg-Düringsfeld, *Das festliche Jahr* (Leipsic, 1863), p. 194; J. A. E. Köhler, *Volksbrauch, Aberglauben, Sagen und andre alte Ueberlieferungen im Voigtlande* (Leipsic, 1867), p. 176; J. V. Grohmann, *Aberglauben und Gebräuche aus Böhmen und Mähren* (Prague and Leipsic, 1864), p. 49, § 311; W. J. A. Tettau und J. D. H. Temme, *Die Volkssagen Ost-preussens, Litthauens und West-*

preussens (Berlin, 1837), pp. 277 *sq.*; K. Haupt, *Sagenbuch der Lausitz* (Leipsic, 1862–1863), i. 48; R. Eisel, *Sagenbuch des Voigtlandes* (Gera, 1871), p. 31, Nr. 62.

[2] Montanus, *Die deutschen Volksfeste, Volksbräuche und deutscher Volksglaube* (Iserlohn, N.D.), p. 34.

[3] E. Hoffmann-Krayer, *Feste und Bräuche des Schweizervolkes* (Zurich, 1913), p. 163.

[4] E. H. Meyer, *Badisches Volksleben* (Strasburg, 1900), p. 507.

done, they sought out somebody whom they treated in the same manner, and the victim of this horseplay was called "the John." The brawls and disorders, which such a custom naturally provoked, led to the suppression of the whole ceremony.[1]

Loaves and flowers thrown into the water on St. John's Day, perhaps as substitutes for human beings.

At Rotenburg on the Neckar they throw a loaf of bread into the water on St. John's Day ; were this offering not made, the river would grow angry and take away a man.[2] Clearly, therefore, the loaf is regarded as a substitute which the spirit of the river consents to accept instead of a human victim. Elsewhere the water-sprite is content with flowers. Thus in Bohemia people sometimes cast garlands into water on Midsummer Eve ; and if the water-sprite pulls one of them down, it is a sign that the person who threw the garland in will die.[3] In the villages of Hesse the girl who first comes to the well early on the morning of Midsummer Day, places on the mouth of the well a gay garland composed of many sorts of flowers which she has culled from the fields and meadows. Sometimes a number of such garlands are twined together to form a crown, with which the well is decked. At Fulda, in addition to the flowery decoration of the wells, the neighbours choose a Lord of the Wells and announce his election by sending him a great nosegay of flowers ; his house, too, is decorated with green boughs, and children walk in procession to it. He goes from house to house collecting materials for a feast, of which the neighbours partake on the following Sunday.[4] What the other duties of the Lord of the Wells may be, we are not told. We may conjecture that in old days he had to see to it that the spirits of the water received their dues from men and maidens on that important day.

[1] J. A. E. Köhler, *loc. cit.* Tacitus tells us that the image of the goddess Nerthus, her vestments, and chariot were washed in a certain lake, and that immediately afterwards the slaves who ministered to the goddess were swallowed by the lake (*Germania*, 40). The statement may perhaps be understood to mean that the slaves were drowned as a sacrifice to the deity. Certainly we know from Tacitus (*Germania*, 9 and 39) that the ancient Germans offered human sacrifices.

[2] E. Meier, *Deutsche Sagen, Sitten und Gebräuche aus Schwaben* (Stuttgart, 1852), p. 429, § 121.

[3] O. Frh. von Reinsberg-Düringsfeld, *Fest-Kalender aus Böhmen* (Prague, N.D.), p. 311.

[4] Karl Lynker, *Deutsche Sagen und Sitten in hessischen Gauen*[2] (Cassel and Göttingen, 1860), pp. 253, 254, §§ 335, 336.

The belief that the spirits of the water exact a human life on Midsummer Day may partly explain why that day is regarded by some people as unlucky. At Neuburg, in Baden, people who meet on Midsummer. Day bid each other beware.[1] Sicilian mothers on that ominous day warn their little sons not to go out of the house, or, if they do go out, not to stray far, not to walk on solitary unfrequented paths, to avoid horses and carriages and persons with firearms, and not to dare to swim ; in short they bid them be on their guard at every turn. The Sicilian writer who tells us this adds : " This I know and sadly remember ever since the year 1848, when, not yet seven years old, I beheld in the dusk of the evening on St. John's Day some women of my acquaintance bringing back in their arms my little brother, who had gone to play in a garden near our house, and there had found his death, my poor Francesco ! In their simplicity the women who strove to console my inconsolable mother, driven distracted by the dreadful blow, kept repeating that St. John must have his due, that on that day he must be appeased. ' Who knows,' said they, ' how many other mothers are weeping now for other little sons forlorn ! ' "[2]

Yet curiously enough, though the water-spirits call for human victims on Midsummer Eve or Midsummer Day, water in general is supposed at that season to acquire certain wonderful medicinal virtues, so that he who bathes in it then or drinks of it is not only healed of all his infirmities but will be well and hearty throughout the year. Hence in many parts of Europe, from Sweden in the north to Sicily in the south, and from Ireland and Spain in the west to Esthonia in the east it used to be customary for men, women, and children to bathe in crowds in rivers, the sea, or springs on Midsummer Eve or Midsummer Day, hoping thus to fortify themselves for the next twelve months. The usual time for taking the bath was the night which intervenes between Midsummer Eve and Midsummer Day ;[3]

Marginal notes: Midsummer Day deemed unlucky and dangerous.

In Europe people used to bathe on Midsummer Eve or Midsummer Day, because water was thought to acquire wonderful medicinal virtues at that time.

[1] E. H. Meyer, *Badisches Volksleben* (Strasburg, 1900), p. 506.

[2] Giuseppe Pitrè, *Spettacoli e Feste Popolari Siciliane* (Palermo, 1881), p. 313.

[3] J. Grimm, *Deutsche Mythologie*,[4] i. 489 *sq.*, iii. 487 ; A. Wuttke, *Der deutsche Volksaberglaube*[2] (Berlin, 1869), p. 77 § 92 ; O. Freiherr von Reinsberg - Düringsfeld, *Das festliche*

but in Belgium the hour was noon on Midsummer Day. It was a curious sight, we are told, to see the banks of a river lined with naked children waiting for the first stroke of noon to plunge into the healing water. The dip was supposed to have a remarkable effect in strengthening the legs. People who were ashamed to bathe in public used to have cans of water brought to their houses from the river at midday, and then performed their ablutions in the privacy of their chambers. Nor did they throw away the precious fluid ; on the contrary they bottled it up and kept it as a sort of elixir for use throughout the year. It was thought never to grow foul and to be as blessed as holy water fetched from a church, which we may well believe. Hence it served to guard the house against a thunder-storm ; when the clouds were heavy and threatening, all you had to do was to take the palm branches (that is, the twigs of box-wood) which were blessed on Palm Sunday, dip them in the midsummer water, and burn them. That averted the tempest.[1] In the Swiss canton of Lucerne a bath on Mid-summer Eve is thought to be especially wholesome, though in other parts of Switzerland, as we saw, bathing at that season is accounted dangerous.[2]

Similar customs and beliefs as to water at Midsummer in Morocco.   Nor are such customs and beliefs confined to the Christian peoples of Europe ; they are shared also by the Mohammedan peoples of Morocco. There, too, on Mid-summer Day all water is thought to be endowed with such marvellous virtue that it not only heals but prevents sickness for the rest of the year ; hence men, women, and children bathe in the sea, in rivers, or in their houses at

---

Jahr (Leipsic, 1863), p. 193 ; F. J. Vonbun, *Beiträge zur deutschen Mythologie* (Chur, 1862), p. 133 ; P. Drechsler, *Sitte, Brauch und Volksglaube in Schlesien* (Leipsic, 1903–1906), i. 143 § 161 ; Karl Haupt, *Sagenbuch der Lausitz* (Leipsic, 1862–1863), i. 248, No. 303 ; F. J. Wiedemann, *Aus dem inneren und äusseren Leben der Ehsten* (St. Petersburg, 1876), p. 415 ; L. Lloyd, *Peasant Life in Sweden* (London, 1870), pp. 261 *sq.* ; Paul Sébillot, *Le Folk-lore de France* (Paris, 1904–1907), ii. 160 *sq.* ; T. F. Thiselton Dyer,

British Popular Customs (London, 1876), pp. 322 *sq.*, 329 *sq.* For more evidence, see above, vol. i. pp. 193, 194, 205 *sq.*, 208, 210, 216 ; *Adonis, Attis, Osiris*, Second Edition, pp. 204 *sqq.*

[1] Le Baron de Reinsberg-Düringsfeld, *Calendrier Belge* (Brussels, 1861–1862), i. 420 *sq.* ; E. Monseur, *Le Folklore Wallon* (Brussels, N.D.), p. 130 ; P. Sébillot, *Le Folk-lore de France*, ii. 374 *sq.*

[2] E. Hoffmann-Krayer, *Feste und Bräuche des Schweizervolkes* (Zurich, 1913), p. 163. See above, p. 27.

that time for the sake of their health.   In Fez and other places
on this day people pour or squirt water over each other in the
streets or from the house-tops, so that the streets become
almost as muddy as after a fall of rain.   More than that, in
the Andjra they bathe their animals also ; horses, mules,
donkeys, cattle, sheep, and goats, all must participate in the
miraculous benefits of midsummer water.[1]   The rite forms
part of that old heathen celebration of Midsummer which
appears to have been common to the peoples on both sides
of the Mediterranean ;[2] and as the aim of bathing in the
midsummer water is undoubtedly purification, it is reasonable
to assign the same motive for the custom of leaping over
the midsummer bonfire.   On the other hand some people in
Morocco, like some people in Europe, think that water on
Midsummer Day is unclean or dangerous.   A Berber told
Dr. Westermarck that water is haunted on Midsummer
Day, and that people therefore avoid bathing in it and keep
animals from drinking of it.   And among the Beni Ahsen
persons who swim in the river on that day are careful, before
plunging into the water, to throw burning straw into it as an
offering, in order that the spirits may not harm them.[3]   The
parallelism between the rites of water and fire at this season
is certainly in favour of interpreting both in the same way ;[4]
and the traces of human sacrifice which we have detected in
the rite of water may therefore be allowed to strengthen the
inference of a similar sacrifice in the rite of fire.

But it seems possible to go farther than this.   Of human
sacrifices offered on these occasions the most unequivocal
traces, as we have seen, are those which, about a hundred
years ago, still lingered at the Beltane fires in the Highlands of Scotland, that is, among a Celtic people who,
situated in a remote corner of Europe and almost com-

Human sacrifices by fire among the ancient Gauls.

[1] E. Westermarck, " Midsummer
Customs in Morocco," *Folk-lore*, xvi.
(1905) pp. 31 *sq.* ; *id.*, *Ceremonies and
Beliefs connected with Agriculture,
certain Dates of the Solar Year, and
the Weather in Morocco* (Helsingfors,
1913), pp. 84-86 ; E. Douttè, *Magie
et Religion dans l'Afrique du Nord*
(Algiers, 1908), pp. 567 *sq.* See also
above, vol. i. p. 216.

[2] See above, vol. i. pp. 213-219.
[3] E. Westermarck, *Ceremonies and
Beliefs connected with Agriculture,
certain Dates of the Solar Year, and
the Weather in Morocco* (Helsingfors,
1913), pp. 94 *sq.*
[4] This has been rightly pointed out
by Dr. Edward Westermarck (" Midsummer Customs in Morocco," *Folk-
lore*, xvi. (1905) p. 46).

pletely isolated from foreign influence, had till then conserved their old heathenism better perhaps than any other people in the West of Europe. It is significant, therefore, that human sacrifices by fire are known, on unquestionable evidence, to have been systematically practised by the Celts. The earliest description of these sacrifices has been bequeathed to us by Julius Caesar. As conqueror of the hitherto independent Celts of Gaul, Caesar had ample opportunity of observing the national Celtic religion and manners, while these were still fresh and crisp from the native mint and had not yet been fused in the melting-pot of Roman civilization. With his own notes Caesar appears to have incorporated the observations of a Greek explorer, by name Posidonius, who travelled in Gaul about fifty years before Caesar carried the Roman arms to the English Channel. The Greek geographer Strabo and the historian Diodorus seem also to have derived their descriptions of the Celtic sacrifices from the work of Posidonius, but independently of each other, and of Caesar, for each of the three derivative accounts contain some details which are not to be found in either of the others. By combining them, therefore, we can restore the original account of Posidonius with some probability, and thus obtain a picture of the sacrifices offered by the Celts of Gaul at the close of the second century before our era.[1] The following seem to have been the main outlines of the custom. Condemned criminals were reserved by the Celts in order to be sacrificed to the gods at a great festival which took place once in every five years. The more there were of such victims, the greater was believed to be the fertility of the land.[2] If there were not enough criminals to furnish victims, captives taken in war were immolated to supply the deficiency. When the time came the victims were sacrificed by the Druids or priests. Some they shot down with arrows, some they impaled, and some they burned alive in the following manner. Colossal images of

Men and animals enclosed in great

[1] Caesar, *Bell. Gall.* vi. 15 ; Strabo, iv. 4. 5, p. 198 ; Diodorus Siculus, v. 32. See W. Mannhardt, *Baumkultus,* pp. 525 *sqq.*

[2] Strabo, iv. 4. 4, p. 197 : τὰς δὲ φονικὰς δίκας μάλιστα τούτοις [*i.e.* the Druids] ἐπετέτραπτο δικάζειν, ὅταν τε φορὰ τούτων ᾖ, φορὰν καὶ τῆς χώρας νομίζουσιν ὑπάρχειν. On this passage see W. Mannhardt, *Baumkultus,* pp. 529 *sqq.*; and below, pp. 42 *sq.*

wicker-work or of wood and grass were constructed ; these were filled with live men, cattle, and animals of other kinds ; fire was then applied to the images, and they were burned with their living contents.

wicker-work images and burnt alive.

Such were the great festivals held once every five years. But besides these quinquennial festivals, celebrated on so grand a scale, and with, apparently, so large an expenditure of human life, it seems reasonable to suppose that festivals of the same sort, only on a lesser scale, were held annually, and that from these annual festivals are lineally descended some at least of the fire-festivals which, with their traces of human sacrifices, are still celebrated year by year in many parts of Europe. The gigantic images constructed of osiers or covered with grass in which the Druids enclosed their victims remind us of the leafy framework in which the human representative of the tree-spirit is still so often encased.[1] Hence, seeing that the fertility of the land was apparently supposed to depend upon the due performance of these sacrifices, Mannhardt interpreted the Celtic victims, cased in osiers and grass, as representatives of the tree-spirit or spirit of vegetation.

As the fertility of the land was supposed to depend on these sacrifices, Mannhardt interpreted the victims as representatives of tree-spirits or spirits of vegetation.

These wicker giants of the Druids seem to have had till lately their representatives at the spring and mid-summer festivals of modern Europe. At Douay, down to the early part of the nineteenth century, a procession took place annually on the Sunday nearest to the seventh of July. The great feature of the procession was a colossal figure, some twenty or thirty feet high, made of osiers, and called " the giant," which was moved through the streets by means of rollers and ropes worked by men who were enclosed within the effigy. The wooden head of the giant is said to have been carved and painted by Rubens. The figure was armed as a knight with lance and sword, helmet and shield. Behind him marched his wife and his three children, all constructed of osiers on the same principle, but on a smaller scale.[2] At

Wicker-work giants at popular festivals in modern Europe. The giant at Douay on July the seventh.

---

[1] *The Magic Art and the Evolution of Kings*, ii. 80 *sqq.*

[2] Madame Clément, *Histoire des fêtes civiles et religieuses du départe-* ment du Nord[2] (Cambrai, 1836), pp. 193-200; A. de Nore, *Coutumes, Mythes et Traditions des Provinces de France*, (Paris and Lyons, 1846), pp. 323 *sq.* ;

Dunkirk the procession of the giants took place on Midsummer Day, the twenty-fourth of June. The festival,
which was known as the Follies of Dunkirk, attracted such
multitudes of spectators, that the inns and private houses
could not lodge them all, and many had to sleep in cellars
or in the streets. In 1755 an eye-witness estimated that
the number of onlookers was not less than forty thousand,
without counting the inhabitants of the town. The streets
through which the procession took its way were lined with
double ranks of soldiers, and the houses crammed with
spectators from top to bottom. High mass was celebrated in
the principal church and then the procession got under weigh.
First came the guilds or brotherhoods, the members walking
two and two with great waxen tapers, lighted, in their hands.
They were followed by the friars and the secular priests, and
then came the Abbot, magnificently attired, with the Host
borne before him by a venerable old man. When these
were past, the real " Follies of Dunkirk " began. They consisted of pageants of various sorts wheeled through the streets
in cars. These appear to have varied somewhat from year
to year ; but if we may judge from the processions of 1755
and 1757, both of which have been described by eye-witnesses,
a standing show was a car decked with foliage and branches
to imitate a wood, and carrying a number of men dressed in
leaves or in green scaly skins, who squirted water on the
people from pewter syringes. An English spectator has
compared these maskers to the Green Men of our own country
on May Day. Last of all came the giant and giantess.
The giant was a huge figure of wicker-work, occasionally as
much as forty-five feet high, dressed in a long blue robe with
gold stripes, which reached to his feet, concealing the dozen
or more men who made it dance and bob its head to the
spectators. This colossal effigy went by the name of Papa

F. W. Fairholt, *Gog and Magog, the
Giants in Guildhall, their real and
legendary History* (London, 1859), pp.
78-87 ; W. Mannhardt, *Baumkultus*,
p. 523, note. It is said that the giantess
made her first appearance in 1665, and
that the children were not added to the
show till the end of the seventeenth
century. In the eighteenth century the
procession took place on the third
Sunday in June, which must always
have been within about a week of
Midsummer Day (H. Gaidoz, " Le dieu
gaulois du soleil et le symbolisme de
la roue," *Revue Archéologique*, iii.
série iv. 32 *sq.*).

Reuss, and carried in its pocket a bouncing infant of Brob-
dingnagian proportions, who kept bawling " Papa ! papa ! "
in a voice of thunder, only pausing from time to time to
devour the victuals which were handed out to him from the
windows. The rear was brought up by the daughter of the
giant, constructed, like her sire, of wicker-work, and little, if
at all, inferior to him in size. She wore a rose-coloured robe,
with a gold watch as large as a warming pan at her side :
her breast glittered with jewels : her complexion was high,
and her eyes and head turned with as easy a grace as the
men inside could contrive to impart to their motions. The
procession came to an end with the revolution of 1789, and
has never been revived. The giant himself indeed, who had
won the affections of the townspeople, survived his ancient
glory for a little while and made shift to appear in public a
few times more at the Carnival and other festal occasions ;
but his days were numbered, and within fifty years even his
memory had seemingly perished.[1]

Most towns and even villages of Brabant and Flanders
have, or used to have, similar wicker giants which were
annually led about to the delight of the populace, who
loved these grotesque figures, spoke of them with patriotic
enthusiasm, and never wearied of gazing at them. The
name by which the giants went was Reuzes, and a special
song called the Reuze song was sung in the Flemish dialect
while they were making their triumphal progress through
the streets. The most celebrated of these monstrous effigies
were those of Antwerp and Wetteren. At Ypres a whole
family of giants contributed to the public hilarity at the
Carnival. At Cassel and Hazebrouch, in the French department of Nord, the giants made their annual appearance
on Shrove Tuesday.[2] At Antwerp the giant was so big

Wicker-work giants in Brabant and Flanders

[1] *The Gentleman's Magazine*, xxix.
(1759), pp. 263-265 ; Madame Clément,
*Histoire des fêtes civiles et religieuses
du département du Nord*,[2] pp. 169-175 ;
A. de Nore, *Coutumes, Mythes et Traditions des Provinces de France*, pp. 328-
332. Compare John Milner, *The
History, Civil and Ecclesiastical, and
Survey of the Antiquities of Winchester* (Winchester, N.D.), i. 8 *sq.*

note [6] ; John Brand, *Popular Antiquities of Great Britain* (London, 1882–
1883), i. 325 *sq.* ; James Logan, *The
Scottish Gael or Celtic Manners*, edited
by Rev. Alex. Stewart (Inverness, N.D.),
ii. 358. According to the writer in *The
Gentleman's Magazine* the name of the
procession was the Cor-mass.
[2] Madame Clément, *Histoire des
fêtes civiles et religieuses*, etc., de la Bel-

that no gate in the city was large enough to let him go through; hence he could not visit his brother giants in neighbouring towns, as the other Belgian giants used to do on solemn occasions. He was designed in 1534 by Peter van Aelst, painter to the Emperor Charles the Fifth, and is still preserved with other colossal figures in a large hall at Antwerp.[1] At Ath, in the Belgian province of Hainaut, the popular procession of the giants took place annually in August down to the year 1869 at least. For three days the colossal effigies of Goliath and his wife, of Samson and an Archer (*Tirant*), together with a two-headed eagle, were led about the streets on the shoulders of twenty bearers concealed under the flowing drapery of the giants, to the great delight of the towns-people and a crowd of strangers who assembled to witness the pageant. The custom can be traced back by documentary evidence to the middle of the fifteenth century; but it appears that the practice of giving Goliath a wife dates only from the year 1715. Their nuptials were solemnized every year on the eve of the festival in the church of St. Julien, whither the two huge figures were escorted by the magistrates in procession.[2]

Mid-summer giants in England.

In England artificial giants seem to have been a standing feature of the midsummer festival. A writer of the sixteenth century speaks of "Midsommer pageants in London, where to make the people wonder, are set forth great and uglie gyants marching as if they were alive, and armed at all points, but within they are stuffed full of browne paper and tow, which the shrewd boyes, underpeering,

---

gique méridionale, etc. (Avesnes, 1846), p. 252; Le Baron de Reinsberg-Düringsfeld, *Calendrier Belge* (Brussels, 1861–1862), i. 123-126. We may conjecture that the Flemish *Reuze*, like the *Reuss* of Dunkirk, is only another form of the German *Riese*, "giant."

[1] F. W. Fairholt, *Gog and Magog, the Giants in Guildhall, their real and legendary History* (London, 1859), pp. 64-78. For the loan of this work and of the one cited in the next note I have to thank Mrs. Wherry, of St. Peter's Terrace, Cambridge.

[2] E. Fourdin, "La foire d'Ath," *Annales du Cercle Archéologique de Mons*, ix. (Mons, 1869) pp. 7, 8, 12, 36 *sq.* The history of the festival has been carefully investigated, with the help of documents by M. Fourdin. According to him, the procession was religious in its origin and took its rise from a pestilence which desolated Hainaut in 1215 (*op. cit.* pp. 1 *sqq.*). He thinks that the effigies of giants were not introduced into the procession till between 1450 and 1460 (*op. cit.* p. 8).

do guilefully discover, and turne to a greate derision."[1]
At Chester the annual pageant on Midsummer Eve included
the effigies of four giants, with animals, hobby-horses, and
other figures. An officious mayor of the town suppressed
the giants in 1599, but they were restored by another mayor
in 1601. Under the Commonwealth the pageant was discontinued, and the giants and beasts were destroyed ; but
after the restoration of Charles II. the old ceremony was
revived on the old date, new effigies being constructed to
replace those which had fallen victims to Roundhead bigotry.
The accounts preserve a record not only of the hoops, buck-
ram, tinfoil, gold and silver leaf, paint, glue, and paste which
went to make up these gorgeous figures ; they also mention
the arsenic which was mixed with the paste in order to preserve the poor giants from being eaten alive by the rats.[2]
At Coventry the accounts of the Cappers' and Drapers'
Companies in the sixteenth century shed light on the giants
which there also were carried about the town at Midsummer ;
from some of the entries it appears that the giant's wife
figured beside the giant.[3]   At Burford, in Oxfordshire, Midsummer Eve used to be celebrated with great jollity by the
carrying of a giant and a dragon up and down the town.
The last survivor of these perambulating English giants
dragged out a miserable existence at Salisbury, where an
antiquary found him mouldering to decay in the neglected
hall of the Tailors' Company about the year 1844. His
bodily framework was of lath and hoop like the one which
used to be worn by Jack-in-the-Green on May Day. The
drapery, which concealed the bearer, was of coloured chintz,
bordered with red and purple, and trimmed with yellow
fringe. His head was modelled in paste-board and adorned
with a gold-laced cocked hat : his flowing locks were of
tow ; and in his big right hand he brandished a branch of

[1] George Puttenham, *The Arte of
English Poesie* (London, 1811, reprint
of the original edition of London,
1589), book iii. chapter vi. p. 128.
On the history of the English giants
and their relation to those of the
continent, see F. W. Fairholt, *Gog
and Magog, the Giants in Guildhall,
their real and legendary History*

(London, 1859).
[2] Joseph Strutt, *The Sports and
Pastimes of the People of England*,
New Edition, by W. Hone (London,
1834), pp. xliii.-xlv. ; F. W. Fairholt,
*Gog and Magog, the Giants in Guild-
hall* (London, 1859), pp. 52-59.
[3] F. W. Fairholt, *op. cit.* pp. 59-
61.

artificial laurel.   In the days of his glory he promenaded about the streets, dancing clumsily and attended by two men grotesquely attired, who kept a watchful eye on his movements and checked by the wooden sword and club which they carried any incipient tendency to lose his balance and topple over in an undignified manner, which would have exposed to the derision of the populace the mystery of his inner man.   The learned called him St. Christopher, the vulgar simply the giant.[1]

Wicker-work giants burnt at or near Midsummer.

In these cases the giants only figure in the processions.   But sometimes they were burned in the summer bonfires.   Thus the people of the Rue aux Ours in Paris used annually to make a great wicker-work figure, dressed as a soldier, which they promenaded up and down the streets for several days, and solemnly burned on the third of July, the crowd of spectators singing *Salve Regina*. A personage who bore the title of king presided over the ceremony with a lighted torch in his hand.   The burning fragments of the image were scattered among the people, who eagerly scrambled for them.   The custom was abolished in 1743.[2]   In Brie, Isle de France, a wicker-work giant, eighteen feet high, was annually burned on Midsummer Eve.[3]

Animals burnt in the Midsummer bonfires.

Again, the Druidical custom of burning live animals, enclosed in wicker-work, has its counterpart at the spring and midsummer festivals.   At Luchon in the Pyrenees on Midsummer Eve " a hollow column, composed of strong wicker-work, is raised to the height of about sixty feet in the centre of the principal suburb, and interlaced with green foliage up to the very top ; while the most beautiful flowers and shrubs procurable are artistically arranged in groups below, so as to form a sort of background to the scene.   The column is then filled with combustible materials, ready for ignition. At an appointed hour—about 8 P.M.—a grand procession, composed of the clergy, followed by young men and maidens in holiday attire, pour forth from the town chanting hymns,

[1] F. W. Fairholt, *op. cit.* pp. 61-63.

[2] Felix Liebrecht, *Des Gervasius von Tilbury Otia Imperialia* (Hanover, 1856), pp. 212 *sq.*; A. de Nore, *Coutumes,*

Mythes, et Traditions des Provinces de France, pp. 354 *sq.* ; W. Mannhardt, *Baumkultus,* p. 514.

[3] W. Mannhardt, *Baumkultus,* pp. 514, 523.

and take up their position around the column. Meanwhile, bonfires are lit, with beautiful effect, in the surrounding hills. As many living serpents as could be collected are now thrown into the column, which is set on fire at the base by means of torches, armed with which about fifty boys and men dance around with frantic gestures. The serpents, to avoid the flames, wriggle their way to the top, whence they are seen lashing out laterally until finally obliged to drop, their struggles for life giving rise to enthusiastic delight among the surrounding spectators. This is a favourite annual ceremony for the inhabitants of Luchon and its neighbourhood, and local tradition assigns it to a heathen origin."[1] In the midsummer fires formerly kindled on the Place de Grève at Paris it was the custom to burn a basket, barrel, or sack full of live cats, which was hung from a tall mast in the midst of the bonfire; sometimes a fox was burned. The people collected the embers and ashes of the fire and took them home, believing that they brought good luck. The French kings often witnessed these spectacles and even lit the bonfire with their own hands. In 1648 Louis the Fourteenth, crowned with a wreath of roses and carrying a bunch of roses in his hand, kindled the fire, danced at it and partook of the banquet afterwards in the town hall. But this was the last occasion when a monarch presided at the midsummer bonfire in Paris.[2] At Metz midsummer fires were lighted with great pomp on the esplanade, and a dozen cats, enclosed in wicker-cages, were burned alive in them, to the amusement of the people.[3] Similarly at Gap, in the depart-

Marginal notes: Serpents formerly burnt in the Midsummer fire at Luchon. Cats formerly burnt in the Midsummer, Easter, and Lenten bonfires.

---

[1] *Athenaeum*, 24th July 1869, p. 115; W. Mannhardt, *Baumkultus*, pp. 515 *sq.* From a later account we learn that about the year 1890 the custom of lighting a bonfire and dancing round it was still observed at Bagnères de Luchon on Midsummer Eve, but the practice of burning live serpents in it had been discontinued. The fire was kindled by a priest. See *Folk-lore*, xii. (1901) pp. 315-317.

[2] A. Breuil, "Du culte de St.-Jean Baptiste," *Mémoires de la Société des Antiquaires de Picardie*, viii. (1845) pp. 187 *sq.*; Collin de Plancy, *Dictionnaire Infernal* (Paris, 1825-1826), iii.

40; A. de Nore, *Coutumes, Mythes et Traditions des Provinces de France*, pp. 355 *sq.*; J. W. Wolf, *Beiträge zur deutschen Mythologie* (Göttingen and Leipsic, 1852-1857), ii. 388; E. Cortet, *Essai sur les Fêtes Religieuses* (Paris, 1867), pp. 213 *sq.*; Laisnel de la Salle, *Croyances et Légendes du Centre de la France* (Paris, 1875), i. 82; W. Mannhardt, *Baumkultus*, p. 515.

[3] Tessier, in *Mémoires et Dissertations publiés par la Société Royale des Antiquaires de France*, v. (1823) p. 388; W. Mannhardt, *Baumkultus*, p. 515.

ment of the High Alps, cats used to be roasted over the midsummer bonfire.[1]   In Russia a white cock was sometimes burned in the midsummer bonfire;[2] in Meissen or Thuringia a horse's head used to be thrown into it.[3]   Sometimes animals are burned in the spring bonfires.   In the Vosges cats were burned on Shrove Tuesday; in Alsace they were thrown into the Easter bonfire.[4]   In the department of the Ardennes cats were flung into the bonfires kindled on the first Sunday in Lent; sometimes, by a refinement of cruelty, they were hung over the fire from the end of a pole and roasted alive.   " The cat, which represented the devil, could never suffer enough."   While the creatures were perishing in the flames, the shepherds guarded their flocks and forced them to leap over the fire, esteeming this an infallible means of preserving them from disease and witchcraft.[5]   We have seen that squirrels were sometimes burned in the Easter fire.[6]

Thus the sacrificial rites of the ancient Gauls have their counterparts in the popular festivals of modern Europe.

Thus it appears that the sacrificial rites of the Celts of ancient Gaul can be traced in the popular festivals of modern Europe.   Naturally it is in France, or rather in the wider area comprised within the limits of ancient Gaul, that these rites have left the clearest traces in the customs of burning giants of wicker-work and animals enclosed in wicker-work or baskets.   These customs, it will have been remarked, are generally observed at or about midsummer.   From this we may infer that the original rites of which these are the degenerate successors were solemnized at midsummer.   This inference harmonizes with the conclusion suggested by a general survey of European folk-custom, that the midsummer festival must on the whole have been the most widely diffused and the most solemn of all the yearly festivals celebrated by the primitive Aryans in Europe.   At the same time we must bear in mind that among the British Celts the chief fire-festivals of the year appear certainly to have been those

[1] Alexandre Bertrand, *La Religion des Gaulois* (Paris, 1897), p. 407.

[2] J. Grimm, *Deutsche Mythologie*,[4] i. 519; W. Mannhardt, *Baumkultus*, p. 515.

[3] W. Mannhardt, *Baumkultus*, p. 515; Montanus, *Die deutschen Volksfesten, Volksbräuche und deutscher Volks-* *glaube* (Iserlohn, N.D.), p. 34.

[4] W. Mannhardt, *Baumkultus*, p. 515.

[5] A. Meyrac, *Traditions, Coutumes, Légendes, et Contes des Ardennes* (Charleville, 1890), p. 68.

[6] Above, vol. i. p. 142.

of Beltane (May Day) and Hallowe'en (the last day of October); and this suggests a doubt whether the Celts of Gaul also may not have celebrated their principal rites of fire, including their burnt sacrifices of men and animals, at the beginning of May or the beginning of November rather than at Midsummer.

We have still to ask, What is the meaning of such sacrifices? Why were men and animals burnt to death at these festivals? If we are right in interpreting the modern European fire-festivals as attempts to break the power of witchcraft by burning or banning the witches and warlocks, it seems to follow that we must explain the human sacrifices of the Celts in the same manner; that is, we must suppose that the men whom the Druids burnt in wicker-work images were condemned to death on the ground that they were witches or wizards, and that the mode of execution by fire was chosen because, as we have seen, burning alive is deemed the surest mode of getting rid of these noxious and dangerous beings. The same explanation would apply to the cattle and wild animals of many kinds which the Celts burned along with the men.[1] They, too, we may conjecture, were supposed to be either under the spell of witchcraft or actually to be the witches and wizards, who had transformed themselves into animals for the purpose of prosecuting their infernal plots against the welfare of their fellow creatures. This conjecture is confirmed by the observation that the victims most commonly burned in modern bonfires have been cats, and that cats are precisely the animals into which, with the possible exception of hares, witches were most usually supposed to transform themselves. Again, we have seen that serpents and foxes used sometimes to be burnt in the midsummer fires;[2] and Welsh and German witches are reported to have assumed the form both of foxes and serpents.[3] In short,

The men women, and animals burnt at these festivals were perhaps thought to be witches or wizards in disguise.

---

[1] Strabo, iv. 4. 5, p. 198, καὶ ἄλλα δὲ ἀνθρωποθυσιῶν εἴδη λέγεται· καὶ γὰρ κατετόξευόν τινας καὶ ἀνεσταύρουν ἐν τοῖς ἱεροῖς καὶ κατασκευάσαντες κολοσσὸν χόρτου καὶ ξύλων, ἐμβαλόντες εἰς τοῦτον βοσκήματα καὶ θηρία παντοῖα καὶ ἀνθρώπους ὡλοκαύτουν.

[2] Above, p. 39.

[3] Marie Trevelyan, Folk - lore and Folk-stories of Wales (London, 1909), pp. 214, 301 sq.; Ulrich Jahn, Hexenwesen und Zauberei in Pommern (Breslau, 1886), p. 7; id., Volkssagen aus Pommern und Rügen (Stettin, 1886), p. 353, No. 446.

when we remember the great variety of animals whose forms witches can assume at pleasure,[1] it seems easy on this hypothesis to account for the variety of living creatures that have been burnt at festivals both in ancient Gaul and modern Europe ; all these victims, we may surmise, were doomed to the flames, not because they were animals, but because they were believed to be witches who had taken the shape of animals for their nefarious purposes. One advantage of explaining the ancient Celtic sacrifices in this way is that it introduces, as it were, a harmony and consistency into the treatment which Europe has meted out to witches from the earliest times down to about two centuries ago, when the growing influence of rationalism discredited the belief in witchcraft and put a stop to the custom of burning witches. On this view the Christian Church in its dealings with the black art merely carried out the traditional policy of Druidism, and it might be a nice question to decide which of the two, in pursuance of that policy, exterminated the larger number of innocent men and women.[2] Be that as it may, we can now perhaps understand why the Druids believed that the more persons they sentenced to death, the greater would be the fertility of the land.[3] To a modern reader the connexion at first sight may not be obvious between the activity of the hangman and the productivity of the earth. But a little reflection may satisfy him that when the criminals who perish at the stake or on the

---

[1] See above, vol. i. p. 315 *n*[1].

[2] The treatment of magic and witchcraft by the Christian Church is described by W. E. H. Lecky, *History of the Rise and Influence of the Spirit of Rationalism in Europe*, New Edition (London, 1882), i. 1 *sqq.* Four hundred witches were burned at one time in the great square of Toulouse (W. E. H. Lecky, *op. cit.* ii. 38). Writing at the beginning of the eighteenth century Addison observes : "Before I leave Switzerland I cannot but observe, that the notion of witchcraft reigns very much in this country. I have often been tired with accounts of this nature from very sensible men, who are most of them furnished with matters of fact which have happened, as they pretend, within the compass of their own knowledge. It is certain there have been many executions on this account, as in the canton of Berne there were some put to death during my stay at Geneva. The people are so universally infatuated with the notion, that if a cow falls sick, it is ten to one but an old woman is clapt up in prison for it, and if the poor creature chance to think herself a witch, the whole country is for hanging her up without mercy." See *The Works of Joseph Addison*, with notes by R. Hurd, D.D. (London, 1811), vol. ii., "Remarks on several Parts of Italy," p. 196.

[3] Strabo, iv. 4. 4, p. 197. See the passage quoted above, p. 32, note [2].

gallows are witches, whose delight it is to blight the crops of the farmer or to lay them low under storms of hail, the execution of these wretches is really calculated to ensure an abundant harvest by removing one of the principal causes which paralyze the efforts and blast the hopes of the husbandman.

The Druidical sacrifices which we are considering were explained in a different way by W. Mannhardt. He supposed that the men whom the Druids burned in wickerwork images represented the spirits of vegetation, and accordingly that the custom of burning them was a magical ceremony intended to secure the necessary sunshine for the crops. Similarly, he seems to have inclined to the view that the animals which used to be burnt in the bonfires represented the corn-spirit,[1] which, as we saw in an earlier part of this work, is often supposed to assume the shape of an animal.[2] This theory is no doubt tenable, and the great authority of W. Mannhardt entitles it to careful consideration. I adopted it in former editions of this book ; but on reconsideration it seems to me on the whole to be less probable than the theory that the men and animals burnt in the fires perished in the character of witches. This latter view is strongly supported by the testimony of the people who celebrate the fire-festivals, since a popular name for the custom of kindling the fires is "burning the witches," effigies of witches are sometimes consumed in the flames, and the fires, their embers, or their ashes are supposed to furnish protection against witchcraft. On the other hand there is little to shew that the effigies or the animals burnt in the fires are regarded by the people as representatives of the vegetation-spirit, and that the bonfires are sun-charms. With regard to serpents in particular, which used to be burnt in the midsummer fire at Luchon, I am not aware of any certain evidence that in Europe snakes have been regarded as embodiments of the tree-spirit or corn-spirit,[3] though in other parts of the world

Mannhardt thought that the men and animals whom the Druids burned in wickerwork images represented spirits of vegetation, and that the burning of them was a charm to secure a supply of sunshine for the crops.

---

[1] W. Mannhardt, *Baumkultus*, pp. 532-534.

[2] *Spirits of the Corn and of the Wild*, i. 270-305.

[3] Some of the serpents worshipped by the old Prussians lived in hollow oaks, and as oaks were sacred among the Prussians, the serpents may possibly have been regarded as genii of the trees. See Simon Grunau, *Preussischer Chronik*, herausgegeben von Dr. M. Perlbach, i. (Leipsic, 1876) p. 89 ;

the conception appears to be not unknown.[1]   Whereas the popular faith in the transformation of witches into animals is so general and deeply rooted, and the fear of these uncanny beings is so strong, that it seems safer to suppose that the cats and other animals which were burnt in the fire suffered death as embodiments of witches than that they perished as representatives of vegetation-spirits.

Christophor Hartknoch, *Alt und Neues Preussen* (Frankfort and Leipsic, 1684), pp. 143, 163.   Serpents played an important part in the worship of Demeter, but we can hardly assume that they were regarded as embodiments of the goddess.   See *Spirits of the Corn and of the Wild*, ii. 17 *sq.*

[1] For example, in China the spirits of plants are thought to assume the form of snakes oftener than that of any other animal. Chinese literature abounds with stories illustrative of such transformations. See J. J. M. de Groot, *The Religious System of China*, iv. (Leyden, 1901) pp. 283-286. In Siam the spirit of the *takhien* tree is said to appear

sometimes in the shape of a serpent and sometimes in that of a woman. See Adolph Bastian, *Die Voelker des Oestlichen Asien*, iii. (Jena, 1867) p. 251.   The vipers that haunted the balsam trees in Arabia were regarded by the Arabs as sacred to the trees (Pausanias, ix. 28. 4);   and once in Arabia, when a wood hitherto untouched by man was burned down to make room for the plough, certain white snakes flew out of it with loud lamentations.   No doubt they were supposed to be the dispossessed spirits of the trees.   See J. Wellhausen, *Reste Arabischen Heidentums*[2] (Berlin, 1897), pp. 108 *sq.*

CHAPTER VIII

THE MAGIC FLOWERS OF MIDSUMMER EVE

A FEATURE of the great midsummer festival remains to be considered, which may perhaps help to clear up the doubt as to the meaning of the fire-ceremonies and their relation to Druidism. For in France and England, the countries where the sway of the Druids is known to have been most firmly established, Midsummer Eve is still the time for culling certain magic plants, whose evanescent virtue can be secured at this mystic season alone. Indeed all over Europe antique fancies of the same sort have lingered about Midsummer Eve, imparting to it a fragrance of the past, like withered rose leaves that, found by chance in the pages of an old volume, still smell of departed summers. Thus in Saintonge and Aunis, two of the ancient provinces of Western France, we read that "of all the festivals for which the merry bells ring out there is not one which has given rise to a greater number of superstitious practices than the festival of St. John the Baptist. The Eve of St. John was the day of all days for gathering the wonderful herbs by means of which you could combat fever, cure a host of diseases, and guard yourself against sorcerers and their spells. But in order to attain these results two conditions had to be observed ; first, you must be fasting when you gathered the herbs, and second, you must cull them before the sun rose. If these conditions were not fulfilled, the plants had no special virtue."[1]

It is a common belief in Europe that plants acquire certain magical, but transient, virtues on Midsummer Eve.

Magical plants culled on Midsummer Eve (St. John's Eve) or Midsummer Day (St. John's Day) in France.

[1] J. L. M. Noguès, *Les mœurs d'autrefois en Saintonge et en Aunis* (Saintes, 1891), p. 71. Amongst the superstitious practices denounced by the French writer J. B. Thiers in the seventeenth century was "the gathering of certain herbs between the Eve of St. John and the Eve of St. Peter and keeping them in a bottle to heal certain maladies." See J. B. Thiers, *Traité des Superstitions* (Paris, 1679), p. 321.

In the neighbouring province of Perigord the person who gathered the magic herbs before sunrise at this season had to walk backwards, to mutter some mystic words, and to perform certain ceremonies. The plants thus collected were carefully kept as an infallible cure for fever; placed above beds and the doors of houses and of cattle-sheds they protected man and beast from disease, witchcraft, and accident.[1] In Normandy a belief in the marvellous properties of herbs and plants, of flowers and seeds and leaves gathered, with certain traditional rites, on the Eve or the Day of St. John has remained part of the peasant's creed to this day. Thus he fancies that seeds of vegetables and plants, which have been collected on St. John's Eve, will keep better than others, and that flowers plucked that day will never fade.[2] Indeed so widespread in France used to be the faith in the magic virtue of herbs culled on that day that there is a French proverb "to employ all the herbs of St. John in an affair," meaning "to leave no stone unturned."[3] In the early years of the nineteenth century a traveller reported that at Marseilles, "on the Eve of St. John, the Place de Noailles and the course are cleaned. From three o'clock in the morning the country-people flock thither, and by six o'clock the whole place is covered with a considerable quantity of flowers and herbs, aromatic or otherwise. The folk attribute superstitious virtues to these plants; they are persuaded that if they have been gathered the same day before sunrise they are fitted to heal many ailments. People buy them emulously to give away in presents and to fill the house with."[4] On the Eve of St. John (Midsummer Eve), before sunset, the peasants of Perche still gather the herb called St. John's herb. It is a creeping plant, very aromatic, with small flowers of a violet blue. Other scented flowers

St. John's herb.

---

[1] A. de Nore, *Coutumes, Mythes et Traditions des Provinces de France* (Paris and Lyons, 1846), pp. 150 *sq.*

[2] Jules Lecœur, *Esquisses du Bocage Normand* (Condé-sur-Noireau, 1883–1887), ii. 8, 244; Amélie Bosquet, *La Normandie romanesque et merveilleuse* (Paris and Rouen, 1845), p. 294.

[3] De la Loubere, *Du Royaume de Siam* (Amsterdam, 1691), i. 202. The writer here mentions an Italian mode of divination practised on Midsummer Eve. People washed their feet in wine and threw the wine out of the window. After that, the first words they heard spoken by passersby were deemed oracular.

[4] Aubin-Louis Millin, *Voyage dans les Départemens du Midi de la France* (Paris, 1807–1811), iii. 344 *sq.*

are added, and out of the posies they make floral crosses
and crowns, which they hang up over the doors of houses
and stables.   Such floral decorations are sold like the box-
wood on Palm Sunday, and the withered wreaths are kept
from year to year.   If an animal dies, it may be a cow, they
carefully clean the byre or the stable, make a pile of these
faded garlands, and set them on fire, having previously closed
up all the openings and interstices, so that the whole place
is thoroughly fumigated.   This is thought to eradicate the
germs of disease from the byre or stable.[1]   At Nellingen,
near Saaralben, in Lorraine the hedge doctors collect their
store of simples between eleven o'clock and noon on Midsummer Day ; and on that day nut-water is brewed from
nuts that have been picked on the stroke of noon.   Such
water is a panacea for all ailments.[2]   In the Vosges
Mountains they say that wizards have but one day in the
year, and but one hour in that day, to find and cull the
baleful herbs which they use in their black art.   That day
is the Eve of St. John, and that hour is the time when the
church bells are ringing the noonday Angelus.   Hence in
many villages they say that the bells ought not to ring at
noon on that day.[3]

In the Tyrol also they think that the witching hour
is when the *Ave Maria* bell is ringing on Midsummer
Eve, for then the witches go forth to gather the noxious
plants whereby they raise thunderstorms.   Therefore in
many districts the bells ring for a shorter time than usual
that evening ;[4] at Folgareit the sexton used to steal quietly
into the church, and when the clock struck three he contented
himself with giving a few pulls to the smallest of the bells.[5]

Magical plants culled on Midsummer Eve or Midsummer Day in the Tyrol and Germany.

---

[1] Alexandre Bertrand, *La Religion des Gaulois* (Paris, 1897), p. 124.   In French the name of St. John's herb (*herbe de la Saint-Jean*) is usually given to *millepertius*, that is, St. John's wort, which is quite a different flower.   See below, pp. 54 *sqq.*   But "St. John's herb" may well be a general term which in different places is applied to different plants.

[2] Bruno Stehle, " Aberglauben, Sitten und Gebräuche in Lothringen," *Globus*, lix. (1891) p. 379.

[3] L. F. Sauvé, *Le Folk-lore des Hautes-Vosges* (Paris, 1889), pp. 168 *sq.*

[4] I. V. Zingerle, "Wald, Bäume, Kräuter," *Zeitschrift für deutsche Mythologie und Sittenkunde*, i. (1853) pp. 332 *sq.* ; *id.*, *Sitten, Bräuche und Meinungen des Tiroler Volkes*[2] (Innsbruck, 1871), p. 158, §§ 1345, 1348.

[5] Christian Schneller, *Märchen und Sagen aus Wälschtirol* (Innsbruck, 1867), p. 237, § 24.

At Rengen, in the Eifel Mountains, the sexton rings the church bell for an hour on the afternoon of Midsummer Day. As soon as the bell begins to ring, the children run out into the meadows, gather flowers, and weave them into garlands which they throw on the roofs of the houses and buildings. There the garlands remain till the wind blows them away. It is believed that they protect the houses against fire and thunderstorms.[1] At Niederehe, in the Eifel Mountains, on Midsummer Day little children used to make wreaths and posies out of " St. John's flowers and Maiden-flax " and throw them on the roofs. Some time afterwards, when the wild gooseberries were ripe, all the children would gather round an old woman on a Sunday afternoon, and taking the now withered wreaths and posies with them march out of the village, praying while they walked. Wreaths and posies were then thrown in a heap and kindled, whereupon the children snatched them up, still burning, and ran and fumigated the wild gooseberry bushes with the smoke. Then they returned with the old woman to the village, knelt down before her, and received her blessing. From that time the children were free to pick and eat the wild gooseberries.[2] In the Mark of Brandenburg the peasants gather all sorts of simples on Midsummer Day, because they are of opinion that the drugs produce their medicinal effect only if they have been culled at that time. Many of these plants, especially roots, must be dug up at midnight and in silence.[3] In Mecklenburg not merely is a special healing virtue ascribed to simples collected on Midsummer Day ; the very smoke of such plants, if they are burned in the fire, is believed to protect a house against thunder and lightning, and to still the raging of the storm.[4] The Wends of the Spreewald twine wreaths of herbs and flowers at midsummer, and hang them up in their rooms ; and when any one gets a fright he will lay some of the leaves and blossoms on hot coals and fumigate himself with the smoke.[5] In Eastern Prussia, some

[1] J. H. Schmitz, *Sitten und Bräuche, Lieder, Sprüchwörter und Räthsel des Eifler Volkes* (Treves, 1856–1858), i. 40.

[2] J. H. Schmitz, *op. cit.* i. 42.

[3] A. Kuhn, *Märkische Sagen und Märchen* (Berlin, 1843), p. 330.

[4] K. Bartsch, *Sagen, Märchen und Gebräuche aus Mecklenburg* (Vienna, 1879–1880), ii. p. 287, § 1436.

[5] W. von Schulenburg, *Wendische Volkssagen und Gebräuche aus dem Spreewald* (Leipsic, 1880), p. 254.

two hundred years ago, it used to be customary on Midsummer Day to make up a bunch of herbs of various sorts
and fasten it to a pole, which was then put up over the gate
or door through which the corn would be brought in at
harvest. Such a pole was called Kaupole, and it remained
in its place till the crops had been reaped and garnered.
Then the bunch of herbs was taken down ; part of it was
put with the corn in the barn to keep rats and mice from
the grain, and part was kept as a remedy for diseases of all
sorts.[1]

The Germans of West Bohemia collect simples on St. Magical
John's Night, because they believe the healing virtue of the plants
culled on
plants to be especially powerful at that time.[2]   The theory Mid-
summer
and practice of the Huzuls in the Carpathian Mountains are Eve (St.
similar ; they imagine that the plants gathered on that night John's Eve)
are not only medicinal but possess the power of restraining or Mid-
summer
the witches ; some say that the herbs should be plucked in Day in
twelve gardens or meadows.[3]   Among the simples which the Austria and
Russia.
Czechs and Moravians of Silesia cull at this season are
dandelions, ribwort, and the bloom of the lime-tree.[4]   The
Esthonians of the island of Oesel gather St. John's herbs
(*Jani rohhud*) on St. John's Day, tie them up in bunches, and
hang them up about the houses to prevent evil spirits from
entering. A subsidiary use of the plants is to cure diseases ;
gathered at that time they have a greater medical value than
if they were collected at any other season. Everybody does
not choose exactly the same sorts of plants ; some gather
more and some less, but in the collection St. John's wort
(*Jani rohhi, Hypericum perforatum*) should never be wanting.[5]
A writer of the early part of the seventeenth century informs
us that the Livonians, among whom he lived, were impressed
with a belief in the great and marvellous properties possessed

[1] M. Prätorius, *Deliciae Prussicae*
(Berlin, 1871), pp. 24 *sq.*   Kaupole is
probably identical in name with Kupole
or Kupalo, as to whom see *The Dying
God*, pp. 261 *sq.*

[2] Alois John, *Sitte, Brauch und
Volksglaube im deutschen Westböhmen*
(Prague, 1905), p. 86.

[3] R. F. Kaindl, *Die Huzulen*
(Vienna, 1894), pp. 78, 90, 93, 105 ;

id., "Zauberglaube bei den Huzulen,"
Globus, lxxvi. (1899) p. 256.

[4] Dr. F. Tetzner, "Die Tschechen
und Mährer in Schlesien," *Globus*,
lxxviii. (1900) p. 340.

[5] J. B. Holzmayer, "Osiliana,"
*Verhandlungen der gelehrten Est-
nischen Gesellschaft*, vii. Heft 2 (Dor-
pat, 1872), p. 62.

by simples which had been culled on Midsummer Day. Such simples, they thought, were sure remedies for fever and for sickness and pestilence in man and beast; but if gathered one day too late they lost all their virtue.[1] Among the Letts of the Baltic provinces of Russia girls and women go about on Midsummer Day crowned with wreaths of aromatic plants, which are afterwards hung up for good luck in the houses. The plants are also dried and given to cows to eat, because they are supposed to help the animals to calve.[2]

Magical plants culled on St. John's Eve or St. John's Day among the South Slavs, in Macedonia, and Bolivia.

In Bulgaria St. John's Day is the special season for culling simples. On this day, too, Bulgarian girls gather nosegays of a certain white flower, throw them into a vessel of water, and place the vessel under a rose-tree in bloom. Here it remains all night. Next morning they set it in the courtyard and dance singing round it. An old woman then takes the flowers out of the vessel, and the girls wash themselves with the water, praying that God would grant them health throughout the year. After that the old woman restores her nosegay to each girl and promises her a rich husband.[3] Among the South Slavs generally on St. John's Eve it is the custom for girls to gather white flowers in the meadows and to place them in a sieve or behind the rafters. A flower is assigned to each member of the household: next morning the flowers are inspected; and he or she whose flower is fresh will be well the whole year, but he or she whose flower is faded will be sickly or die. Garlands are then woven out of the flowers and laid on roofs, folds, and beehives.[4] In some parts of Macedonia on St. John's Eve the peasants are wont to festoon their cottages and gird their own waists with wreaths of what they call St. John's flower; it is the blossom of a creeping plant which resembles honeysuckle.[5] Similar notions as to the magical virtue which plants acquire at midsummer have been transported by Europeans to the New World. At La Paz in Bolivia people

[1] P. Einhorn, "Wiederlegunge der Abgötterey: der ander (sic) Theil," printed at Riga in 1627, and reprinted in *Scriptores rerum Livonicarum*, ii. (Riga and Leipsic, 1848) pp. 651 *sq.*

[2] J. G. Kohl, *Die deutsch-russischen Ostseeprovinzen* (Dresden and Leipsic, 1841), ii. 26.

[3] A. Strausz, *Die Bulgaren* (Leipsic, 1898), pp. 348, 386.

[4] F. S. Krauss, *Volksglaube und religiöser Brauch der Südslaven* (Münster i. W., 1890), p. 34.

[5] G. F. Abbott, *Macedonian Folklore* (Cambridge, 1903), pp. 54, 58.

believe that flowers of mint (*Yerba buena*) gathered before sunrise on St. John's Day foretell an endless felicity to such as are so lucky as to find them.[1]

Nor is the superstition confined to Europe and to people of European descent.   In Morocco also the Mohammedans are of opinion that certain plants, such as penny-royal, marjoram, and the oleander, acquire a special magic virtue (*baraka*) when they are gathered shortly before midsummer. Hence the people collect these plants at this season and preserve them for magical or medical purposes.   For example, branches of oleander are brought into the houses before midsummer and kept under the roof as a charm against the evil eye; but while the branches are being brought in they may not touch the ground, else they would lose their marvellous properties.   Cases of sickness caused by the evil eye are cured by fumigating the patients with the smoke of these boughs.   The greatest efficacy is ascribed to "the sultan of the oleander," which is a stalk with four pairs of leaves clustered round it.   Such a stalk is always endowed with magical virtue, but that virtue is greatest when the stalk has been cut just before midsummer.   Arab women in the Hiaina district of Morocco gather *Daphne gnidium* on Midsummer Day, dry it in the sun, and make it into a powder which, mixed with water, they daub on the heads of their little children to protect them from sunstroke and vermin and to make their hair grow well.   Indeed such marvellous powers do these Arabs attribute to plants at this mystic season that a barren woman will walk naked about a vegetable garden on Midsummer Night in the hope of conceiving a child through the fertilizing influence of the vegetables.[2]

Magical plants culled at Midsummer among the Mohammedans of Morocco.

Sometimes in order to produce the desired effect it is deemed necessary that seven or nine different sorts of plants should be gathered at this mystic season.   Norman peasants, who wish to fortify themselves for the toil of harvest, will

Seven different sorts of magical plants gathered at Midsummer.

[1] H. A. Weddell, *Voyage dans le Nord de la Bolivie et dans les parties voisines du Pérou* (Paris and London, 1853), p. 181.

[2] W. Westermarck, "Midsummer Customs in Morocco," *Folk-lore*, xvi. (1905) p. 35; *id.*, *Ceremonies and Beliefs connected with Agriculture, certain Dates of the Solar Year, and the Weather in Morocco* (Helsingfors, 1913), pp. 88 *sq.*

sometimes go out at dawn on St. John's Day and pull seven kinds of plants, which they afterwards eat in their soup as a means of imparting strength and suppleness to their limbs in the harvest field.[1] In Mecklenburg maidens are wont to gather seven sorts of flowers at noon on Midsummer Eve. These they weave into garlands, and sleep with them under their pillows. Then they are sure to dream of the men who will marry them.[2] But the flowers on which youthful lovers dream at Midsummer Eve are oftener nine in number. Thus in Voigtland nine different kinds of flowers are twined into a garland at the hour of noon, but they may not enter the dwelling by the door in the usual way ; they must be passed through the window, or, if they come in at the door, they must be thrown, not carried, into the house. Sleeping on them that night you will dream of your future wife or future husband.[3] The Bohemian maid, who gathers nine kinds of flowers on which to dream of love at Midsummer Eve, takes care to wrap her hand in a white cloth, and afterwards to wash it in dew ; and when she brings her garland home she must speak no word to any soul she meets by the way, for then all the magic virtue of the flowers would be gone.[4] Other Bohemian girls look into the book of fate at this season after a different fashion. They twine their hair with wreaths made of nine sorts of leaves, and go, when the stars of the summer night are twinkling in the sky, to a brook that flows beside a tree. There, gazing on the stream, the girl beholds, beside the broken reflections of the tree and the stars, the watery image of her future lord.[5] So in Masuren maidens gather nosegays of wild flowers in silence on Midsummer Eve. At the midnight hour each girl takes the nosegay and a glass of water, and when she has spoken certain words she sees her lover mirrored in the water.[6]

Sometimes Bohemian damsels make a different use of their midsummer garlands twined of nine sorts of flowers.

Nine different sorts of plants gathered at Midsummer.

Dreams of love on flowers at Midsummer Eve.

Love's watery mirror at Midsummer Eve.

[1] J. Lecœur, *Esquisses du Bocage Normand* (Condé-sur-Noireau, 1883–1887), ii. 9.

[2] K. Bartsch, *Sagen, Märchen und Gebräuche aus Mecklenburg* (Vienna, 1879–1890), ii. 285.

[3] J. A. E. Köhler, *Volksbrauch, Aberglauben, Sagen und andre alte*

Ueberlieferungen im Voigtlande (Leipsic, 1867), p. 376.

[4] O. Freiherr von Reinsberg-Düringsfeld, *Fest-Kalender aus Böhmen* (Prague, N.D.), p. 312.

[5] Reinsberg-Düringsfeld, *loc. cit.*

[6] M. Töppen, *Aberglaube aus Masuren*[2] (Danzig, 1867), p. 72.

They lie down with the garland laid as a pillow under their
right ear, and a hollow voice, swooning from underground,
proclaims their destiny.[1]   Yet another mode of consulting the
oracle by means of these same garlands is to throw them
backwards and in silence upon a tree at the hour of noon,
just when the flowers have been gathered.   For every time
that the wreath is thrown without sticking to the branches
of the tree the girl will have a year to wait before she weds.
This mode of divination is practised in Voigtland,[2] East
Prussia,[3] Silesia,[4] Belgium,[5] and Wales,[6] and the same thing
is done in Masuren, although we are not told that there the
wreaths must be composed of nine sorts of flowers.[7]   However,
in Masuren chaplets of nine kinds of herbs are gathered on
St. John's Eve and put to a more prosaic use than that of
presaging the course of true love.   They are carefully preserved, and the people brew a sort of tea from them, which
they administer as a remedy for many ailments ; or they keep
the chaplets under their pillows till they are dry, and thereupon dose their sick cattle with them.[8]   In Esthonia the
virtues popularly ascribed to wreaths of this sort are many
and various.   These wreaths, composed of nine kinds of
herbs culled on the Eve or the Day of St. John, are sometimes inserted in the roof or hung up on the walls of the
house, and each of them receives the name of one of the
inmates.   If the plants which have been thus dedicated to
a girl happen to take root and grow in the chinks and
crannies, she will soon wed ; if they have been dedicated to
an older person and wither away, that person will die.   The
people also give them as medicine to cattle at the time when
the animals are driven forth to pasture ; or they fumigate
the beasts with the smoke of the herbs, which are burnt
along with shavings from the wooden threshold.   Bunches
of the plants are also hung about the house to keep off evil

Garlands
of flowers
of nine
sorts
gathered
at Mid-
summer
and used
in divina-
tion and
medicine.

[1] Reinsberg-Düringsfeld, *loc. cit.*

[2] J. A. E. Köhler, *Volksbrauch*, etc.,
im Voigtlande, p. 376.

[3] C. Lemke, *Volksthümliches in
Ostpreussen* (Mohrungen, 1884–1887),
i. 20.

[4] P. Drechsler, *Sitte, Brauch und
Volksglaube in Schlesien* (Leipsic,
1903–1906), i. 144 *sq.*

[5] Le Baron de Reinsberg-Düringsfeld, *Calendrier Belge* (Brussels, 1861–
1862), i. 423.

[6] Marie Trevelyan, *Folk-lore and
Folk-stories of Wales* (London, 1909),
p. 252.

[7] M. Töppen, *Aberglauben aus Masuren*,[2] p. 72.

[8] M. Töppen, *op. cit.* p. 71.

spirits, and maidens lay them under their pillows to dream on.[1]   In Sweden the " Midsummer Brooms," made up of nine sorts of flowers gathered on Midsummer Eve, are put to nearly the same uses.   Fathers of families hang up such " brooms " to the rafters, one for each inmate of the house ; and he or she whose broom (*quast*) is the first to wither will be the first to die.   Girls also dream of their future husbands with these bunches of flowers under their pillows.   A decoction made from the flowers is, moreover, a panacea for all disorders, and if a bunch of them be hung up in the cattle shed, the Troll cannot enter to bewitch the beasts.[2]   The Germans of Moravia think that nine kinds of herbs gathered on St. John's Night (Midsummer Eve) are a remedy for fever ;[3] and some of the Wends attribute a curative virtue in general to such plants.[4]

St John's wort (*Hypericum perforatum*) gathered for magical purposes at Midsummer.
Of the flowers which it has been customary to gather for purposes of magic or divination at midsummer none perhaps is so widely popular as St. John's wort (*Hypericum perforatum*).   The reason for associating this particular plant with the great summer festival is perhaps not far to seek, for the flower blooms about Midsummer Day, and with its bright yellow petals and masses of golden stamens it might well pass for a tiny copy on earth of the great sun which reaches its culminating point in heaven at this season.   Gathered on Midsummer Eve, or on Midsummer Day before sunrise, the blossoms are hung on doorways and windows to preserve the house against thunder, witches, and evil spirits ; and various healing properties are attributed to the different species of the plant.   In the Tyrol they say that if you put St. John's wort in your shoe before sunrise on Midsummer Day you may walk as far as you please without growing weary.   In Scotland people carried it about their persons as an amulet against witchcraft.   On the lower Rhine children twine chaplets of St. John's wort on the morning of Midsummer Day, and throw them on the roofs of the houses.   Here, too, the people who danced round the midsummer bonfires used

[1] A. Wiedemann, *Aus dem inneren und äussern Leben der Ehsten* (St. Petersburg, 1876), pp. 362 *sq.*

[2] L. Lloyd, *Peasant Life in Sweden* (London, 1870), pp. 267 *sq.*

[3] Willibald Müller, *Beiträge zur Volkskunde der Deutschen in Mähren* (Vienna and Olmütz, 1893), p. 264.

[4] W. von Schulenburg, *Wendisches Volksthum* (Berlin, 1882), p. 145.

to wear wreaths of these yellow flowers in their hair, and to deck the images of the saints at wayside shrines with the blossoms.   Sometimes they flung the flowers into the bonfires.   In Sicily they dip St. John's wort in oil, and so apply it as a balm for every wound.   During the Middle Ages the power which the plant notoriously possesses of banning devils won for it the name of *fuga daemonum* ; and before witches and wizards were stretched on the rack or otherwise tortured, the flower used to be administered to them as a means of wringing the truth from their lips.[1]   In North Wales people used to fix sprigs of St. John's wort over their doors, and sometimes over their windows, " in order to purify their houses, and by that means drive away all fiends and evil spirits." [2]   In Saintonge and Aunis the flowers served to detect the presence of sorcerers, for if one of these pestilent fellows entered a house, the bunches of St. John's wort, which had been gathered on Midsummer Eve and hung on the walls, immediately dropped their yellow heads as if they had suddenly faded.[3]   However, the Germans

[1] Montanus, *Die deutschen Volksfeste, Volksbräuche und deutscher Volksglaube* (Iserlohn, N.D.), p. 145; A. Wuttke, *Der deutsche Volksaberglaube* [2] (Berlin, 1869), p. 100, § 134; I. V. Zingerle, "Wald, Bäume, Kräuter," *Zeitschrift für deutsche Mythologie und Sittenkunde*, i. (1853) p. 329; A. Schlossar, "Volksmeinung und Volksaberglaube aus der deutschen Steiermark," *Germania*, N.R., xxiv. (1891) p. 387; E. Meier, *Deutsche Sagen, Sitten und Gebräuche aus Schwaben* (Stuttgart, 1852), p. 428; J. Brand, *Popular Antiquities of Great Britain* (London, 1882–1883), i. 307, 312; T. F. Thiselton Dyer, *Folk-lore of Plants* (London, 1889), pp. 62, 286; Rev. Hilderic Friend, *Flowers and Flower Lore*, Third Edition (London, 1886), pp. 147, 149, 150, 540; G. Finamore, *Credenze, Usi e Costumi Abruzzesi* (Palermo, 1890), pp. 161 *sq.* ; G. Pitrè, *Spettacoli e Feste Popolari Siciliane* (Palermo, 1881), p. 309. One authority lays down the rule that you should gather the plant fasting and in silence (J. Brand, *op. cit.* p. 312). According to Sowerby, the *Hypericum*

perforatum flowers in England about July and August (*English Botany*, vol. v. London, 1796, p. 295).   We should remember, however, that in the old calendar Midsummer Day fell twelve days later than at present.   The reform of the calendar probably put many old floral superstitions out of joint.

[2] Bingley, *Tour round North Wales* (1800), ii. 237, quoted by T. F. Thiselton Dyer, *British Popular Customs* (London, 1876), p. 320.   Compare Marie Trevelyan, *Folk-lore and Folk-stories of Wales* (London, 1909), p. 251 : "St. John's, or Midsummer Day, was an important festival.   St. John's wort, gathered at noon on that day, was considered good for several complaints.   The old saying went that if anybody dug the devil's bit at midnight on the eve of St. John, the roots were then good for driving the devil and witches away." Apparently by "the devil's bit" we are to understand St. John's wort.

[3] J. L. M. Noguès, *Les mœurs d'autrefois en Saintonge et en Aunis* (Saintes, 1891), pp. 71 *sq.*

of Western Bohemia think that witches, far from dreading
St. John's wort, actually seek the plant on St. John's Eve.[1]

St. John's blood on St. John's Day.

Further, the edges of the calyx and petals of St. John's wort,
as well as their external surface, are marked with dark purple
spots and lines, which, if squeezed, yield a red essential oil
soluble in spirits.[2]   German peasants believe that this red
oil is the blood of St. John,[3] and this may be why the plant
is supposed to heal all sorts of wounds.[4]   In Mecklenburg
they say that if you pull up St. John's wort at noon on
Midsummer Day you will find at the root a bead of red
juice called St. John's blood ; smear this blood on your shirt
just over your heart, and no mad dog will bite you.[5]   In the
Mark of Brandenburg the same blood, procured in the same
manner and rubbed on the barrel of a gun, will make every
shot from that gun to hit the mark.[6]   According to others,
St. John's blood is found at noon on St. John's Day, and
only then, adhering in the form of beads to the root of a
weed called knawel, which grows in sandy soil.   But some
people say that these beads of red juice are not really the
blood of the martyred saint, but only insects resembling the
cochineal or kermes-berry.[7]   " About Hanover I have often
observed devout Roman Catholics going on the morning of
St. John's day to neighbouring sandhills, gathering on the
roots of herbs a certain insect (*Coccus Polonica*) looking
like drops of blood, and thought by them to be created
on purpose to keep alive the remembrance of the foul
murder of St. John the Baptist, and only to be met with
on the morning of the day set apart for him by the
Church.   I believe the life of this insect is very ephemeral,

---

[1] Alois John, *Sitte, Brauch und
Volksglaube im deutschen Westböhmen*
(Prague, 1905), p. 84.   They call the
plant " witch's herb" (*Hexenkraut*).

[2] James Sowerby, *English Botany*,
vol. v. (London, 1796), p. 295.

[3] Montanus, *Die deutschen Volksfeste, Volksbräuche und deutscher Volksglaube* (Iserlohn, N.D.), p. 35.

[4] T. F. Thiselton Dyer, *Folk-lore of
Plants* (London, 1889), p. 286 ; K.
Bartsch, *Sagen, Märchen und Gebräuche
aus Mecklenburg*, ii. p. 291, § 1450a.
The Germans of Bohemia ascribe
wonderful virtues to the red juice ex-

tracted from the yellow flowers of St.
John's wort (W. Müller, *Beitrage zur
Volkskunde der Deutschen in Mähren*,
Vienna and Olmütz, 1893, p. 264).

[5] K. Bartsch, *op. cit.* ii. p. 286, §
1433.   The blood is also a preservative against many diseases (*op. cit.* ii.
p. 290, § 1444).

[6] A. Kuhn, *Märkische Sagen und
Märchen* (Berlin, 1843), p. 387, § 105.

[7] *Die gestriegelte Rockenphilosophie*[5]
(Chemnitz, 1759), pp. 246 *sq.* ; Montanus, *Die deutschen Volksfesten, Volksbräuche und deutscher Volksglaube*, p.
147.

but by no means restricted to the twenty-fourth of June." [1]

Yet another plant whose root has been thought to yield the blood of St. John is the mouse-ear hawkweed (*Hieracium pilosella*), which grows very commonly in dry exposed places, such as gravelly banks, sunny lawns, and the tops of park walls. " It blossoms from May to the end of July, presenting its elegant sulphur-coloured flowers to the noontide sun, while the surrounding herbage, and even its own foliage, is withered and burnt up " ; [2] and these round yellow flowers may be likened not inaptly to the disc of the great luminary whose light they love. At Hildesheim, in Germany, people used to dig up hawkweed, especially on the Gallows' Hill, when the clocks were striking noon on Midsummer Day ; and the blood of St. John, which they found at the roots, was carefully preserved in quills for good luck. A little of it smeared secretly on the clothes was sure to make the wearer fortunate in the market that day.[3] According to some the plant ought to be dug up with a gold coin.[4] Near Gablonz, in Bohemia, it used to be customary to make a bed of St. John's flowers, as they were called, on St. John's Eve, and in the night the saint himself came and laid his head on the bed ; next morning you could see the print of his head on the flowers, which derived a healing virtue from his blessed touch, and were mixed with the fodder of sick cattle to make them whole.[5] But whether these St. John's flowers were the mouse-ear hawkweed or not is doubtful.[6]

More commonly in Germany the name of St. John's flowers (*Johannisblumen*) appears to be given to the mountain arnica. In Voigtland the mountain arnica if plucked on St. John's Eve and stuck in the fields, laid under

Mouse-ear hawkweed (Hieracium pilosella) gathered for magical purposes at Midsummer.

Mountain arnica gathered for magical purposes at Midsummer.

[1] Berthold Seeman, *Viti, An Account of a Government Mission to the Vitian or Fijian Islands in the years 1860–61* (Cambridge, 1862), p. 63.

[2] James Sowerby, *English Botany*, vol. xvi. (London, 1803) p. 1093.

[3] K. Seifart, *Sagen, Märchen, Schwänke und Gebräuche aus Stadt und Stift Hildesheim* [2] (Hildesheim, 1889), p. 177, § 12.

[4] C. L. Rochholz, *Deutscher Glaube und Brauch* (Berlin, 1867), i. 9.

[5] J. V. Grohmann, *Aberglauben und Gebräuche aus Böhmen und Mähren* (Prague and Leipsic, 1864), p. 98, § 681.

[6] A. Wuttke, *Der deutsche Volksaberglaube* [2] (Berlin, 1869), p. 100, § 134.

the roof, or hung on the wall, is believed to protect house and fields from lightning and hail.[1]   So in some parts of Bavaria they think that no thunderstorm can harm a house which has a blossom of mountain arnica in the window or the roof, and in the Tyrol the same flower fastened to the door will render the dwelling fire-proof.   But it is needless to remark that the flower, which takes its popular name from St. John, will be no protection against either fire or thunder unless it has been culled on the saint's own day.[2]

Mugwort (*Artemisia vulgaris*) gathered for magical purposes at Midsummer.

Another plant which possesses wondrous virtues, if only it be gathered on the Eve or the Day of St. John, is mugwort (*Artemisia vulgaris*).   Hence in France it goes by the name of the herb of St. John.[3]   Near Péronne, in the French department of Somme, people used to go out fasting before sunrise on St. John's Day to cull the plant; put among the wheat in the barn it protected the corn against

---

[1] J. A. E. Köhler, *Volksbrauch, Aberglauben, Sagen und andre alte Ueberlieferungen im Voigtlande* (Leipsic, 1867), p. 376.   The belief and practice are similar at Grün, near Asch, in Western Bohemia.   See Alois John, *Sitte, Brauch und Volksglaube im deutschen Westböhmen* (Prague, 1905), p. 84.

[2] F. Panzer, *Beitrag zur deutschen Mythologie* (Munich, 1848–1855), ii. 299; *Bavaria, Landes- und Volkskunde des Königreichs Bayern*, iii. (Munich, 1865), p. 342; I. V. Zingerle, *Sitten, Bräuche und Meinungen des Tiroler Volkes* [2] (Innsbruck, 1871), p. 160, § 1363.

[3] J. Grimm, *Deutsche Mythologie*, [4] ii. 1013; A. de Gubernatis, *Mythologie des Plantes* (Paris, 1878–1882), i. 189 *sq.*; Rev. Hilderic Friend, *Flowers and Flower Lore*, Third Edition (London, 1886), p. 75.   In England mugwort is very common in waste ground, hedges, and the borders of fields.   It flowers throughout August and later.   The root is woody and perennial.   The smooth stems, three or four feet high, are erect, branched, and leafy, and marked by many longitudinal purplish ribs.   The pinnatified leaves alternate on the stalk; they are smooth and dark green

above, cottony and very white below. The flowers are in simple leafy spikes or clusters; the florets are purplish, furnished with five stamens and five awl-shaped female flowers, which constitute the radius.   The whole plant has a weak aromatic scent and a slightly bitter flavour.   Its medical virtues are of no importance.   See James Sowerby, *English Botany*, xiv. (London, 1802) p. 978.   Altogether it is not easy to see why such an inconspicuous and insignificant flower should play so large a part in popular superstition.   Mugwort (*Artemisia vulgaris*) is not to be confounded with wormwood (*Artemisia absinthium*), which is quite a different flower in appearance, though it belongs to the same genus.   Wormwood is common in England, flowering about August.   The flowers are in clusters, each of them broad, hemispherical, and drooping, with a buff-coloured disc. The whole plant is of a pale whitish green and clothed with a short silky down.   It is remarkable for its intense bitterness united to a peculiar strong aromatic odour.   It is often used to keep insects from clothes and furniture, and as a medicine is one of the most active bitters.   See James Sowerby, *English Botany*, vol. xviii. (London, 1804) p. 1230.

mice.   In Artois people carried bunches of mugwort, or wore
it round their body ;[1] in Poitou they still wear girdles of
mugwort or hemp when they warm their backs at the midsummer fire as a preservative against backache at harvest ;[2]
and the custom of wearing girdles of mugwort on the Eve
or Day of St. John has caused the plant to be popularly
known in Germany and Bohemia as St. John's girdle.   In
Bohemia such girdles are believed to protect the wearer for
the whole year against ghosts, magic, misfortune, and sickness.   People also weave garlands of the plant and look
through them at the midsummer bonfire or put them on their
heads ; and by doing so they ensure that their heads will
not ache nor their eyes smart all that year.   Another
Bohemian practice is to make a decoction of mugwort which
has been gathered on St. John's Day ; then, when your cow
is bewitched and will yield no milk, you have only to wash
the animal thrice with the decoction and the spell will be
broken.[3]   In Germany, people used to crown their heads or
gird their bodies with mugwort, which they afterwards threw
into the midsummer bonfire, pronouncing certain rhymes
and believing that they thus rid themselves of all their ill-
luck.[4]   Sometimes wreaths or girdles of mugwort were kept
in houses, cattle-sheds, and sheep-folds throughout the year.[5]
In Normandy such wreaths are a protection against thunder
and thieves ;[6] and stalks of mugwort hinder witches from
laying their spells on the butter.[7]   In the Isle of Man on
Midsummer Eve people gathered *barran fealoin* or mugwort
" as a preventive against the influence of witchcraft " ;[8] in

---

[1] Breuil, "Du culte de St.-Jean-
Baptiste," *Mémoires de la Société des
Antiquaires de Picardie*, viii. (1845)
p. 224, note [1], quoting the curé of
Manancourt, near Péronne.

[2] L. Pineau, *Le folk-lore du Poitou*
(Paris, 1892), p. 499.

[3] J. V. Grohmann, *Aberglauben und
Gebräuche aus Böhmen und Mähren*
(Prague and Leipsic, 1864), pp. 90 *sq.*,
§§ 635-637.

[4] F. Panzer, *Beitrag zur deutschen
Mythologie*, i. p. 249, § 283 ; J.
Grimm, *Deutsche Mythologie*,[4] ii. 1013 ;
I. V. Zingerle, in *Zeitschrift für
deutsche Mythologie und Sittenkunde*,
i. (1853) p. 331, and *ib.* iv. (1859)

p. 42 (quoting a work of the seventeenth century); F. J. Vonbun, *Beiträge
zur deutschen Mythologie* (Chur, 1862),
p. 133, note **. See also above, vol. i.
pp. 162, 163, 165, 174, 177.

[5] A. de Gubernatis, *Mythologie der
Plantes* (Paris, 1878–1882), i. 190,
quoting Du Cange.

[6] A. de Nore, *Coutumes, Mythes et
Traditions des Provinces de France*
(Paris and Lyons, 1846), p. 262.

[7] Jules Lecœur, *Esquisses du Bocage
Normand* (Condé-sur-Noireau, 1883–
1886), ii. 8.

[8] Joseph Train, *Historical and Statis-
tical Account of the Isle of Man* (Douglas,
Isle of Man, 1845), ii. 120.

Mugwort in China and Japan.

Belgium bunches of mugwort gathered on St. John's Day or Eve and hung on the doors of stables and houses are believed to bring good luck and to furnish a protection against sorcery.[1] It is curious to find that in China a similar use is, or was formerly, made of mugwort at the same season of the year. In an old Chinese calendar we read that " on the fifth day of the fifth month the four classes of the people gambol in the herbage, and have competitive games with plants of all kinds. They pluck mugwort and make dolls of it, which they suspend over their gates and doors, in order to expel poisonous airs or influences." [2] On this custom Professor J. J. M. de Groot observes : " Notice that the plant owed its efficacy to the time when it was plucked : a day denoting the midsummer festival, when light and fire of the universe are in their apogee." [3] On account of this valuable property mugwort is used by Chinese surgeons in cautery.[4] The Ainos of Japan employ bunches of mugwort in exorcisms, " because it is thought that demons of disease dislike the smell and flavour of this herb." [5] It is an old German belief that he who carries mugwort in his shoes will not grow weary.[6] In Mecklenburg, they say that if you will dig up a plant of mugwort at noon on Midsummer Day, you will find under the root a burning coal, which vanishes away as soon as the church bells have ceased to ring. If you find the coal and carry it off in silence, it will prove a remedy for all sorts of maladies.[7] According to another German superstition, such a coal will turn to gold.[8] English writers record the popular belief that a rare coal is to be found under the root of mugwort at a single hour of a single day in the year, namely, at noon or midnight on Midsummer Eve, and that this coal will

[1] Le Baron de Reinsberg-Düringsfeld, *Calendrier Belge* (Brussels, 1861–1862), i. 422.

[2] J. J. M. de Groot, *The Religious System of China*, vi. (Leyden, 1910) p. 1079, compare p. 947.

[3] J. J. M. de Groot, *op. cit.* vi. 947.

[4] J. J. M. de Groot, *op. cit.* vi. 946 *sq.*

[5] Rev. John Batchelor, *The Ainu and their Folk-lore* (London, 1901), p. 318, compare pp. 315 *sq.*, 329, 370, 372.

[6] *Zeitschrift für deutsche Mythologie und Sittenkunde*, iv. (1859) p. 42 ; Montanus, *Die deutschen Volksfeste*, p. 141. The German name of mugwort (*Beifuss*) is said to be derived from this superstition.

[7] K. Bartsch, *Sagen, Märchen, und Gebräuche aus Mecklenburg* (Vienna, 1879–1880), ii. 290, § 1445.

[8] Montanus, *Die deutschen Volksfeste*, p. 141.

protect him who carries it on his person from plague, car-
buncle, lightning, fever, and ague.[1]   In Eastern Prussia, on
St. John's Eve, people can foretell a marriage by means of
mugwort ; they bend two stalks of the growing plant outward, and then observe whether the stalks, after straighten-
ing themselves again, incline towards each other or not.[2]

A similar mode of divination has been practised both in
England and in Germany with the orpine (*Sedum telephium*),
a plant which grows on a gravelly or chalky soil about
hedges, the borders of fields, and on bushy hills.   It flowers
in August, and the blossoms consist of dense clustered tufts
of crimson or purple petals ; sometimes, but rarely, the
flowers are white.[3]   In England the plant is popularly
known as Midsummer Men, because people used to plant
slips of them in pairs on Midsummer Eve, one slip standing
for a young man and the other for a young woman.   If the
plants, as they grew up, bent towards each other, the couple
would marry ; if either of them withered, he or she whom it
represented would die.[4]   In Masuren, Westphalia, and Switzerland the method of forecasting the future by means of the
orpine is precisely the same.[5]

*Orpine
(Sedum
telephium)
used in
divination
at Mid-
summer.*

[1] J. Brand, *Popular Antiquities of
Great Britain* (London, 1882–1883),
i. 334 *sq.*, quoting Lupton, Thomas
Hill, and Paul Barbette.   A precisely
similar belief is recorded with regard
to wormwood (*armoise*) by the French
writer J. B. Thiers, who adds that
only small children and virgins could
find the wonderful coal.   See J. B.
Thiers, *Traité des Superstitions* [5] (Paris,
1741), i. 300.   In Annam people think
that wormwood puts demons to flight ;
hence they hang up bunches of its
leaves in their houses at the New Year.
See Paul Giran, *Magie et Religion
Annamites* (Paris, 1912), p. 118,
compare pp. 185, 256.

[2] C. Lemke, *Volksthümliches in Ostpreussen* (Mohrungen, 1884–1887), i.
21.   As to mugwort (German *Beifuss*,
French *armoise*), see further A. de
Gubernatis, *Mythologie des Plantes*, ii.
16 *sqq.* ; J. Grimm, *Deutsche Mythologie*,[4] iii. 356 *sq.*

[3] James Sowerby, *English Botany*,
vol. xix. (London, 1804) p. 1319.

[4] John Aubrey, *Remains of Gentil-
isme and Judaisme* (London, 1881), pp.
25 *sq.* ; J. Brand, *Popular Antiquities
of Great Britain* (London, 1882–1883),
i. 329 *sqq.* ; Rev. Hilderic Friend,
Flowers and Flower Lore, Third Edition (London, 1886), p. 136 ; D. H.
Moutray Read, "Hampshire Folk-
lore," *Folk-lore*, xxii. (1911) p. 325.
Compare J. Sowerby, *English Botany*,
vol. xix. (London, 1804), p. 1319 :
"Like all succulent plants this is very
tenacious of life, and will keep growing long after it has been torn from its
native spot.   The country people in
Norfolk sometimes hang it up in their
cottages, judging by its vigour of the
health of some absent friend."   It
seems that in England the course of
love has sometimes been divined by
means of sprigs of red sage placed in a
basin of rose-water on Midsummer Eve
(J. Brand, *op. cit.* i. 333).

[5] M. Töppen, *Aberglauben aus
Masuren* [2] (Danzig, 1867), pp. 71 *sq.* ;
A. Kuhn, *Sagen, Gebräuche und*

Vervain
gathered
for magical
purposes
at Mid-
summer.

Another plant which popular superstition has often associated with the summer solstice is vervain.[1]   In some parts of Spain people gather vervain after sunset on Mid-summer Eve, and wash their faces next morning in the water in which the plants have been allowed to steep over-night.[2]   In Belgium vervain is gathered on St. John's Day and worn as a safeguard against rupture.[3]   In Normandy the peasants cull vervain on the Day or the Eve of St. John, believing that, besides its medical properties, it possesses at this season the power of protecting the house from thunder and lightning, from sorcerers, demons, and thieves.[4]   Bohemian poachers wash their guns with a decoction of vervain and southernwood, which they have gathered naked before sun-rise on Midsummer Day ; guns which have been thus treated never miss the mark.[5]   In our own country vervain used to

Magical
virtue of
four-
leaved
clover
on Mid-
summer
Eve.

be sought for its magical virtues on Midsummer Eve.[6]   In the Tyrol they think that he who finds a four-leaved clover while the vesper-bell is ringing on Midsummer Eve can work

---

Märchen aus Westfalen (Leipsic, 1859), ii. 176, § 487 ; E. Hoffmann-Krayer, *Feste und Bräuche des Schweizervolkes* (Zurich, 1913), p. 163.   In Switzerland the species employed for this purpose on Midsummer day is *Sedum reflexum.* The custom is reported from the Emmenthal.   In Germany a root of orpine, dug up on St. John's morn-ing and hung between the shoulders, is sometimes thought to be a cure for hemorrhoids (Montanus, *Die deutschen Volksfeste*, p. 145).   Perhaps the "ob-long, tapering, fleshy, white lumps" of the roots (J. Sowerby, *English Botany*, vol. xix. London, 1804, p. 1319) are thought to bear some likeness to the hemorrhoids, and to heal them on the principle that the remedy should resemble the disease.

[1] See above, vol. i. pp. 162, 163, 165.   In England vervain (*Verbena officinalis*) grows not uncommonly by road sides, in dry sunny pastures, and in waste places about villages.   It flowers in July.   The flowers are small and sessile, the corolla of a very pale lilac hue, its tube enclosing the four short curved stamens.   The root of

the plant, worn by a string round the neck, is an old superstitious medicine for scrofulous disorders.   See James Sowerby, *English Botany*, vol. xi. (London, 1800) p. 767.

[2] Dr. Otero Acevado, in *Le Temps*, September 1898.   See above, vol. i. p. 208, note [1].

[3] Le Baron de Reinsberg-Dürings-feld, *Calendrier Belge* (Brussels, 1861–1862), i. 422.

[4] A. de Nore, *Coutumes, Mythes et Traditions des Provinces de France*, p. 262 ; Amélie Bosquet, *La Normandie romanesque et merveilleuse*, p. 294 ; J. Lecœur, *Esquisses du Bocage Nor-mand*, i. 287, ii. 8.   In Saintonge and Aunis the plant was gathered on Mid-summer Eve for the purpose of evoking or exorcising spirits (J. L. M. Noguès, *Les mœurs d'autrefois en Saintonge et en Aunis*, p. 72).

[5] J. V. Grohmann, *Aberglauben und Gebräuche aus Böhmen und Mähren*, p. 207, § 1437.

[6] A. Kuhn, *Sagen, Gebräuche und Märchen aus Westfalen* (Leipsic, 1859), ii. 177, citing Chambers, *Edinburgh Journal*, 2nd July 1842.

magic from that time forth.[1]   People in Berry say that the four-leaved clover is endowed with all its marvellous virtues only when it has been plucked by a virgin on the night of Midsummer Eve.[2]   In Saintonge and Aunis the four-leaved clover, if it be found on the Eve of St. John, brings good luck at play ;[3] in Belgium it brings a girl a husband.[4]

At Kirchvers, in Hesse, people run out to the fields at noon on Midsummer Day to gather camomile ; for the flowers, plucked at the moment when the sun is at the highest point of his course, are supposed to possess the medicinal qualities of the plant in the highest degree.   In heathen times the camomile flower, with its healing qualities, its yellow calix and white stamens, is said to have been sacred to the kindly and shining Balder and to have borne his name, being called *Balders-brå*, that is, Balder's eyelashes.[5]   In Westphalia, also, the belief prevails that camomile is most potent as a drug when it has been gathered on Midsummer Day ;[6] in Masuren the plant must always be one of the nine different kinds of plants that are culled on Midsummer Eve to form wreaths, and tea brewed from the flower is a remedy for many sorts of maladies.[7]

Camomile gathered for magical purposes at Midsummer.

Thuringian peasants hold that if the root of the yellow mullein (*Verbascum*) has been dug up in silence with a ducat at midnight on Midsummer Eve, and is worn in a piece of linen next to the skin, it will preserve the wearer from epilepsy.[8] In Prussia girls go out into the fields on Midsummer Day, gather mullein, and hang it up over their beds.   The girl

Mullein (Verbascum) gathered for magical purposes at Midsummer.

[1] I. V. Zingerle, *Sitten, Bräuche und Meinungen des Tiroler Volkes*[2] (Innsbruck, 1871), p. 107, § 919.

[2] Laisnel de la Salle, *Croyances et Légendes du Centre de la France* (Paris, 1875), i. 288.

[3] J. L. M. Noguès, *Les mœurs d'autrefois en Saintonge et en Aunis*, pp. 71 *sq.*

[4] Le Baron de Reinsberg-Düringsfeld, *Calendrier Belge*, i. 423.

[5] W. Kolbe, *Hessische Volks-Sitten und Gebräuche*[2] (Marburg, 1888), p. 72 ; Sophus Bugge, *Studien über die Entstehung der nordischen Götter- und Heldensagen* (Munich, 1889), pp. 35, 295 *sq.*; Fr. Kauffmann, *Balder* (Strasburg, 1902), pp. 45, 61.   The flowers

of common camomile (*Anthemis nobilis*) are white with a yellow disk, which in time becomes conical.   The whole plant is intensely bitter, with a peculiar but agreeable smell.   As a medicine it is useful for stomachic troubles.   In England it does not generally grow wild.   See James Sowerby, *English Botany*, vol. xiv. (London, 1802) p. 980.

[6] A. Kuhn, *Sagen, Gebräuche und Märchen aus Westfalen* (Leipsic, 1859), ii. 177, § 488.

[7] M. Töppen, *Aberglauben aus Masuren*[2] (Danzig, 1867), p. 71.

[8] A. Witzschel, *Sagen, Sitten und Gebräuche aus Thüringen* (Vienna, 1878), p. 289, § 139.

whose flower is the first to wither will be the first to die.[1] Perhaps the bright yellow flowers of mullein, clustering round the stem like lighted candles, may partly account for the association of the plant with the summer solstice. In Germany great mullein (*Verbascum thapsus*) is called the King's Candle ; in England it is popularly known as High Taper. The yellow, hoary mullein (*Verbascum pulverulentum*) " forms a golden pyramid a yard high, of many hundreds of flowers, and is one of the most magnificent of British herbaceous plants." [2] We may trace a relation between mullein and the sun in the Prussian custom of bending the flower, after sunset, towards the point where the sun will rise, and praying at the same time that a sick person or a sick beast may be restored to health.[3]

Seeds of fir-cones, wild thyme, elder-flowers, and purple loosestrife gathered for magical purposes at Midsummer.

In Bohemia poachers fancy that they can render themselves invulnerable by swallowing the seed from a fir-cone which they have found growing upwards before sunrise on the morning of St. John's Day.[4] Again, wild thyme gathered on Midsummer Day is used in Bohemia to fumigate the trees on Christmas Eve in order that they may grow well ; [5] in Voigtland a tea brewed from wild thyme which has been pulled at noon on Midsummer Day is given to women in childbed.[6] The Germans of Western Bohemia brew a tea or wine from elder-flowers, but they say that the brew has no medicinal virtue unless the flowers have been gathered on Midsummer Eve. They do say, too, that whenever you see an elder-tree, you should take off your hat.[7] In the Tyrol dwarf-elder serves to detect witchcraft in cattle, provided of course that the shrub has been pulled up or the branches broken on Midsummer Day.[8]

---

[1] W. J. A. von Tettau und J. D. H. Temme, *Volkssagen Ostpreussens, Litthauens und Westpreussens* (Berlin, 1837), p. 283.

[2] James Sowerby, *English Botany*, vol. vii. (London, 1798), p. 487. As to great mullein or high taper, see *id.*, vol. viii. (London, 1799) p. 549.

[3] Tettau und Temme, *loc. cit.* As to mullein at Midsummer, see also above, vol. i. pp. 190, 191.

[4] J. V. Grohmann, *Aberglauben und Gebräuche aus Böhmen und Mähren*,

p. 205, § 1426.

[5] J. V. Grohmann, *op. cit.* p. 93, § 648.

[6] J. A. E. Köhler, *Volksbrauch, Aberglauben, Sagen und andre alte Ueberlieferungen im Voigtlande* (Leipsic, 1867), p. 377.

[7] Alois John, *Sitte, Brauch und Volksglaube im deutschen Westböhmen* (Prague, 1905), p. 84.

[8] J. N. Ritter von Alpenburg, *Mythen und Sagen Tirols* (Zurich, 1857), p. 397.

Russian peasants regard the plant known as purple loosestrife (*Lythrum salicaria*) with respect and even fear. Wizards make much use of it. They dig the root up on St. John's morning, at break of day, without the use of iron tools ; and they believe that by means of the root, as well as of the blossom, they can subdue evil spirits and make them serviceable, and also drive away witches and the demons that guard treasures.[1]

More famous, however, than these are the marvellous properties which popular superstition in many parts of Europe has attributed to the fern at this season. At midnight on Midsummer Eve the plant is supposed to bloom and soon afterwards to seed ; and whoever catches the bloom or the seed is thereby endowed with supernatural knowledge and miraculous powers ; above all, he knows where treasures lie hidden in the ground, and he can render himself invisible at will by putting the seed in his shoe. But great precautions must be observed in procuring the wondrous bloom or seed, which else quickly vanishes like dew on sand or mist in the air. The seeker must neither touch it with his hand nor let it touch the ground ; he spreads a white cloth under the plant, and the blossom or the seed falls into it. Beliefs of this sort concerning fernseed have prevailed, with trifling variations of detail, in England, France, Germany, Austria, Italy, and Russia.[2] In

Magical properties attributed to fern seed at Midsummer.

[1] C. Russwurm, "Aberglaube aus Russland," *Zeitschrift für deutsche Mythologie und Sittenkunde*, iv. (1859) pp. 153 *sq.* The purple loosestrife is one of our most showy English wild plants. In July and August it may be seen flowering on the banks of rivers, ponds, and ditches. The separate flowers are in axillary whorls, which together form a loose spike of a reddish variable purple. See James Sowerby, *English Botany*, vol. xv. (London, 1802) p. 1061.

[2] J. Brand, *Popular Antiquities*, i. 314 *sqq.*; Hilderic Friend, *Flowers and Flower Lore*, Third Edition (London, 1886), pp. 60, 78, 150, 279-283 ; Miss C. S. Burne and Miss G. F. Jackson, *Shropshire Folk-lore* (London, 1883), p. 242 ; Marie Trevelyan, *Folk-lore and Folk-stories of Wales* (London, 1909), pp. 89 *sq.* ; J. B.

Thiers, *Traité des Superstitions* (Paris, 1679), p. 314 ; J. Lecœur, *Esquisses du Bocage Normand*, i. 290 ; P. Sébillot, *Coutumes populaires de la Haute-Bretagne* (Paris, 1886), p. 217 ; id., *Traditions et Superstitions de la Haute-Bretagne* (Paris. 1882), ii. 336 ; A. Wuttke, *Der deutsche Volksaberglaube*[2] (Berlin, 1869), pp. 94 *sq.*, § 123 ; F. J. Vonbun, *Beiträge zur deutschen Mythologie* (Chur, 1862), pp. 133 *sqq.*; Montanus, *Die deutschen Volksfesten*, p. 144 ; K. Bartsch, *Sagen, Märchen und Gebräuche aus Mecklenburg*, ii. 288, § 1437 ; M. Töppen, *Aberglauben aus Masuren*,[2] p. 72 ; A. Schlossar, "Volksmeinung und Volksaberglaube aus der deutschen Steiermark," *Germania*, N.R., xxiv. (1891) p. 387 ; Theodor Vernaleken, *Mythen und Bräuche des Volkes in Oesterreich*

Bohemia the magic bloom is said to be golden, and to glow or sparkle like fire.[1]   In Russia, they say that at dead of night on Midsummer Eve the plant puts forth buds like glowing coals, which on the stroke of twelve burst open with a clap like thunder and light up everything near and far.[2]   In the Azores they say that the fern only blooms at midnight on St. John's Eve, and that no one ever sees the flower because the fairies instantly carry it off.   But if any one, watching till it opens, throws a cloth over it, and then, when the magic hour has passed, burns the blossoms carefully, the ashes will serve as a mirror in which you can read the fate of absent friends; if your friends are well and happy, the ashes will resume the shape of a lovely flower; but if they are unhappy or dead, the ashes will remain cold and lifeless.[3]   In Thuringia people think that he who has on his person or in his house the male fern (*Aspidium filix mas*) cannot be bewitched.   They call it St. John's root (*Johanniswurzel*), and say that it blooms thrice in the year, on Christmas Eve, Easter Eve, and the day of St. John the Baptist; it should be dug up when the sun enters the sign

(Vienna, 1859), p. 309; J. N. Ritter von Alpenburg, *Mythen und Sagen Tirols* (Zurich, 1857), pp. 407 *sq.*; I. V. Zingerle, *Sitten, Bräuche und Meinungen des Tiroler Volkes* [2] (Innsbruck, 1871), p. 103, § 882, p. 158, § 1350; Christian Schneller, *Märchen und Sagen aus Wälschtirol* (Innsbruck, 1867), p. 237; J. V. Grohmann, *Aberglauben und Gebräuche aus Böhmen und Mähren*, p. 97, §§ 673-677; Reinsberg-Düringsfeld, *Fest-Kalendar aus Böhmen* (Prague, N.D.), pp. 311 *sq.*; W. Müller, *Beiträge zur Volkskunde der Deutschen in Mähren* (Vienna and Olmutz, 1893), p. 265; R. F. Kaindl, *Die Huzulen* (Vienna, 1894), p. 106; *id.*, "Zauberglaube bei den Huzulen," *Globus*, lxxvi. (1899) p. 275; P. Drechsler, *Sitte, Brauch und Volksglaube in Schlesien* (Leipsic, 1903–1906), i. 142, § 159; G. Finamore, *Credenze, Usi e Costumi Abruzzesi* (Palermo, 1890), p. 161; C. Russwurm, "Aberglaube in Russland," *Zeitschrift für deutsche Mythologie und Sittenkunde*, iv. (1859) pp.

152 *sq.*; A. de Gubernatis, *Mythologie des Plantes* (Paris, 1878–1882), ii. 144 *sqq.*   The practice of gathering ferns or fern seed on the Eve of St. John was forbidden by the synod of Ferrara in 1612.   See J. B. Thiers, *Traité des Superstitions* [5] (Paris, 1741), i. 299 *sq.*   In a South Slavonian story we read how a cowherd understood the language of animals, because fern-seed accidentally fell into his shoe on Midsummer Day (F. S. Krauss, *Sagen und Märchen der Südslaven*, Leipsic, 1883–1884, ii. 424 *sqq.*, No. 159).   On this subject I may refer to my article, "The Language of Animals," *The Archaeological Review*, i. (1888) pp. 164 *sqq.*

[1] J. V. Grohmann, *op. cit.* p. 97, §§ 673, 675.

[2] *Zeitschrift für deutsche Mythologie und Sittenkunde*, iv. (1859) pp. 152 *sq.*; A. de Gubernatis, *Mythologie des Plantes*, ii. 146.

[3] M. Longworth Dames and E. Seemann, "Folk-lore of the Azores," *Folk-lore*, xiv. (1903) pp. 142 *sq.*

of the lion.   Armed with this powerful implement you can detect a sorcerer at any gathering, it may be a wedding feast or what not.   All you have to do is to put the root under the tablecloth unseen by the rest of the company, and, if there should be a sorcerer among them, he will turn as pale as death and get up and go away.   Fear and horror come over him when the fern-root is under the tablecloth. And when oxen, horses, or other domestic cattle are bewitched by wicked people, you need only take the root at full moon, soak it in water, and sprinkle the cattle with the water, or rub them down with a cloth that has been steeped in it, and witchcraft will have no more power over the animals.[1]

Once more, people have fancied that if they cut a branch of hazel on Midsummer Eve it would serve them as a diving-rod to discover treasures and water.   This belief has existed in Moravia, Mecklenburg, and apparently in Scotland.[2]   In the Mark of Brandenburg, they say that if you would procure the mystic wand you must go to the hazel by night on Midsummer Eve, walking backwards, and when you have come to the bush you must silently put your hands between your legs and cut a fork-shaped stick ; that stick will be the divining-rod, and, as such, will detect treasures buried in the ground.   If you have any doubt as to the quality of the wand, you have only to hold it in water ; for in that case your true divining-rod will squeak like a pig, but your spurious one will not.[3]   In Bavaria they say that the divining-rod should be cut from a hazel bush between eleven and twelve on St. John's Night, and that by means of it you can discover not only veins of metal and

---

[1] August Witzschel, *Sagen, Sitten und Gebräuche aus Thüringen* (Vienna, 1878), p. 275, § 82.

[2] W. Müller, *Beiträge zur Volkskunde der Deutschen in Mähren* (Vienna and Olmutz, 1893), p. 265 ; K. Bartsch, *Sagen, Märchen und Gebräuche aus Mecklenburg*, ii. p. 285, § 1431, p. 288, § 1439 ; J. Napier, *Folk-lore, or Superstitious Beliefs in the West of Scotland* (Paisley, 1879), p. 125.

[3] A. Kuhn, *Märkische Sagen und Märchen* (Berlin, 1843), p. 330.   As to the divining-rod in general, see A. Kuhn, *Die Herabkunft des Feuers und des Göttertranks*[2] (Gütersloh, 1886), pp. 181 *sqq.* ; J. Grimm, *Deutsche Mythologie*,[4] ii. 813 *sqq.* ; S. Baring-Gould, *Curious Myths of the Middle Ages* (London, 1884), pp. 55 *sqq.* Kuhn plausibly suggests that the forked shape of the divining-rod is a rude representation of the human form.   He compares the shape and magic properties of mandragora.

underground springs, but also thieves and murderers and unknown ways. In cutting it you should say, " God greet thee, thou noble twig ! With God the Father I seek thee, with God the Son I find thee, with the might of God the Holy Ghost I break thee. I adjure thee, rod and sprig, by the power of the Highest that thou shew me what I order, and that as sure and clear as Mary the Mother of God was a pure virgin when she bare our Lord Jesus, in the name of God the Father, God the Son, and God the Holy Ghost, Amen ! "[1] In Berlin and the neighbourhood they say that every seventh year there grows a wonderful branch on a hazel bush, and that branch is the divining-rod. Only an innocent child, born on a Sunday and nursed in the true faith, can find it on St. John's Night ; to him then all the treasures of the earth lie open.[2] In the Tyrol the divining-rod ought to be cut at new moon, but may be cut either on St. John's Day or on Twelfth Night. Having got it you baptize it in the name of one of the Three Holy Kings according to the purpose for which you intend to use it : if the rod is to discover gold, you name it Caspar ; if it is to reveal silver, you call it Balthasar ; and if it is to point out hidden springs of water, you dub it Melchior.[3] In Lechrain the divining-rod is a yearling shoot of hazel with two branches ; a good time for cutting it is new moon, and if the sun is rising, so much the better. As for the day of the year, you may take your choice between St. John's Day, Twelfth Night, and Shrove Tuesday. If cut with the proper form of words, the rod will as usual discover underground springs and hidden treasures.[4]

[1] F. Panzer, *Beitrag zur deutschen Mythologie* (Munich, 1848-1855), i. 296 *sq.*

[2] E. Krause, " Abergläubische Kuren und sonstiger Aberglaube in Berlin und nächster Umgebung," *Zeitschrift für Ethnologie*, xv. (1883) p. 89.

[3] J. N. Ritter von Alpenburg, *Mythen und Sagen Tirols* (Zurich, 1857), p. 393.

[4] Karl Freiherr von Leoprechting, *Aus dem Lechrain* (Munich, 1855), p. 98. Some people in Swabia say that the hazel branch which is to serve as a divining-rod should be cut at midnight on Good Friday, and that it should be laid on the altar and mass said over it. If that is done, we are told that a Protestant can use it to quite as good effect as a Catholic. See E. Meier, *Deutsche Sagen, Sitten und Gebräuche aus Schwaben* (Stuttgart, 1852), pp. 244 *sq.*, No. 268. Some of the Wends of the Spreewald agree that the divining-rod should be made of hazel-wood, and they say that it ought to

Midsummer Eve is also the favourite time for procuring the divining-rod in Sweden. Some say that it should then be cut from a mistletoe bough.[1] However, other people in Sweden are of opinion that the divining-rod (*Slag ruta*) which is obtained on Midsummer Eve ought to be compounded out of four different kinds of wood, to wit, mistletoe, mountain-ash, the aspen, and another; and they say that the mountain-ash which is employed for this purpose should, like the mistletoe, be a parasite growing from the hollow root of a fallen tree, whither the seed was carried by a bird or wafted by the wind. Armed with this fourfold implement of power the treasure-seeker proceeds at sundown to the spot where he expects to find hidden wealth; there he lays the rod on the ground in perfect silence, and when it lies directly over treasure, it will begin to hop about as if it were alive.[2]

The divining-rod in Sweden obtained on Midsummer Eve.

A mystical plant which to some extent serves the same purpose as the divining-rod is the springwort, which is sometimes supposed to be caper-spurge (*Euphorbia lathyris*). In the Harz Mountains they say that many years ago there was a wondrous flower called springwort or Johnswort, which was as rare as it was marvellous. It bloomed only on St. John's Night (some say under a fern) between the hours of eleven and twelve; but when the last stroke of twelve was struck, the flower vanished away. Only in mountainous regions, where many noble metals reposed in the bosom of the earth, was the flower seen now and then in lonely meadows among the hills. The spirits of the hills wished by means of it to shew to men where their treasures were to be found. The flower itself was yellow and shone like a lamp in the darkness of night. It never stood still, but kept

The mythical springwort supposed to bloom on Midsummer Eve.

---

be wrapt in swaddling-bands, laid on a white plate, and baptized on Easter Saturday. Many of them, however, think that it should be made of "yellow willow." See Wilibald von Schulenburg, *Wendische Volkssagen und Gebräuche aus dem Spreewald* (Leipsic, 1880), pp. 204 *sq.* A remarkable property of the hazel in the opinion of Bavarian peasants is that it is never struck by lightning; this immunity it has enjoyed ever since the day when it protected the Mother of God against a thunderstorm on her flight into Egypt. See *Bavaria, Landes- und Volkskunde des Königreichs Bayern,* i. (Munich, 1860) p. 371.

[1] J. Grimm, *Deutsche Mythologie,*[4] iii. 289, referring to Dybeck's *Runa,* 1844, p. 22, and 1845, p. 80.

[2] L. Lloyd, *Peasant Life in Sweden* (London, 1870), pp. 266 *sq.*

hopping constantly to and fro.   It was also afraid of men and fled before them, and no man ever yet plucked it unless he had been set apart by Providence for the task.   To him who was lucky enough to cull it the flower revealed all the treasures of the earth, and it made him rich, oh so rich and so happy![1]

Another way of catching the spring-wort.

However, the usual account given of the springwort is somewhat different.   They say that the way to procure it is this.   You mark a hollow in a tree where a green or black woodpecker has built its nest and hatched its young; you plug up the hole with a wooden wedge; then you hide behind the tree and wait.   The woodpecker meantime has flown away but very soon returns with the springwort in its bill.   It flutters up to the tree-trunk holding the springwort to the wedge, which at once, as if struck by a hammer, jumps out with a bang.   Now is your chance.   You rush from your concealment, you raise a loud cry, and in its fright the bird opens its bill and drops the springwort.   Quick as thought you reach out a red or white cloth, with which you have taken care to provide yourself, and catch the magic flower as it falls.   The treasure is now yours.   Before its marvellous power all doors and locks fly open; it can make the bearer of it invisible; and neither steel nor lead can wound the man who carries it in the right-hand pocket of his coat.   That is why people in Swabia say of a thief who cannot be caught, " He must surely have a springwort."[2]

[1] Heinrich Pröhle, *Harzsagen* (Leipsic, 1859), i. 99, No. 23.

[2] J. Grimm, *Deutsche Mythologie*,[4] ii. 812 *sq.*, iii. 289; A. Kuhn, *Die Herabkunft des Feuers und des Götter-tranks*[2] (Gütersloh, 1886), pp. 188-193; Walter K. Kelly, *Curiosities of Indo-European Tradition and Folk-lore* (London, 1863), pp. 174-178; J. F. L. Woeste, *Volksüberlieferungen in der Grafschaft Mark* (Iserlohn, 1848), p. 44; A. Kuhn und W. Schwartz, *Norddeutsche Sagen, Märchen und Ge-bräuche* (Leipsic, 1848), p. 459, No. 444; Ernst Meier, *Deutsche Sagen, Sitten und Gebräuche aus Schwaben* (Stuttgart, 1852), pp. 240 *sq.*, No. 265; C. Russwurm, "Aberglaube in Russland," *Zeitschrift für deutsche* *Mythologie und Sittenkunde*, iv. (Göttingen, 1859) p. 153; J. V. Groh-mann, *Aberglauben und Gebräuche aus Böhmen und Mähren* (Prague and Leipsic, 1864), p. 88, No. 623; Paul Drechsler, *Sitte, Brauch und Volks-glaube in Schlesien* (Leipsic, 1903-1906), ii. 207 *sq.*   In Swabia some people say that the bird which brings the springwort is not the woodpecker but the hoopoe (E. Meier, *op. cit.* p. 240).   Others associate the spring-wort with other birds.   See H. Pröhle, *Harzsagen* (Leipsic, 1859), ii. 116, No. 308; A. Kuhn, *Die Herabkunft des Feuers*,[2] p. 190.   It is from its power of springing or bursting open all doors and locks that the springwort derives its name (German *Springwurzel*).

The superstition which associates the springwort with the woodpecker is very ancient, for it is recorded by Pliny.   It was a vulgar belief, he tells us, that if a shepherd plugged up a woodpecker's nest in the hollow of a tree with a wedge, the bird would bring a herb which caused the wedge to slip out of the hole ; Trebius indeed affirmed that the wedge leaped out with a bang, however hard and fast you might have driven it into the tree.[1]   Another flower which possesses the same remarkable power of bursting open all doors and locks is chicory, provided always that you cut the flower with a piece of gold at noon or midnight on St. James's Day, the twenty-fifth of July.   But in cutting it you must be perfectly silent ; if you utter a sound, it is all up with you.   There was a man who was just about to cut the flower of the chicory, when he looked up and saw a millstone hovering over his head.   He fled for his life and fortunately escaped ; but had he so much as opened his lips, the millstone would have dropped on him and crushed him as flat as a pancake.   However, it is only a rare white variety of the chicory flower which can act as a picklock ; the common bright blue flower is perfectly useless for the purpose.[2]

The white bloom of chicory.

Many more examples might perhaps be cited of the marvellous virtues which certain plants have been supposed to acquire at the summer solstice, but the foregoing instances may suffice to prove that the superstition is widely spread, deeply rooted, and therefore probably very ancient in Europe. Why should plants be thought to be endowed with these wonderful properties on the longest day more than on any other day of the year ?   It seems difficult or impossible to explain such a belief except on the supposition that in some mystic way the plants catch from the sun, then at the full height of his power and glory, some fleeting effluence of radiant light and heat, which invests them for a time with powers above the ordinary for the healing of diseases and the unmasking and baffling of all the evil things that threaten the life of man. That the supposition is not purely hypothetical will appear from a folk-tale, to be noticed later on, in which the magic

The magical virtues ascribed to plants at Midsummer may be thought to be derived from the sun, then at the height of his power and glory.

---

[1] Pliny, *Nat. Hist.* x. 40.

[2] Ernst Meier, *Deutsche Sagen, Sit-* ten und Gebräuche aus Schwaben (Stutt-gart, 1852), pp. 238 *sq.*, No. 264.

bloom of the fern is directly derived from the sun at noon on

Hence it is possible that the Midsummer bonfires stand in direct relation to the sun.

Midsummer Day.   And if the magic flowers of Midsummer Eve thus stand in direct relation to the sun, which many of them resemble in shape and colour, blooming in the meadows like little yellow suns fallen from the blue sky, does it not become probable that the bonfires kindled at the same time are the artificial, as the flowers are the natural, imitations of the great celestial fire then blazing in all its strength?   At least analogy seems to favour the inference and so far to support Mannhardt's theory, that the bonfires kindled at the popular festivals of Europe, especially at the summer solstice, are intended to reinforce the waning or waxing fires of the sun.   Thus if in our enquiry into these fire-festivals the scales of judgment are loaded with the adverse theories of Mannhardt and Westermarck, we may say that the weight, light as it is, of the magic flowers of Midsummer Eve seems to incline the trembling balance back to the side of Mannhardt.

This consideration tends to bring us back to an intermediate position between the rival theories of Mannhardt and Westermarck.

Nor is it, perhaps, an argument against Mannhardt's view that the midsummer flowers and plants are so often employed as talismans to break the spells of witchcraft.[1]   For granted that employment, which is undeniable, we have still to explain it, and that we can hardly do except by reference to the midsummer sun.   And what is here said of the midsummer flowers applies equally to the midsummer bonfires. They too are used to destroy the charms of witches and warlocks ; but if they can do so, may it not be in part because fires at midsummer are thought to burn with fiercer fury than at other times by sympathy with the fiercer fervour of the sun?   This consideration would bring us back to an intermediate position between the opposing theories, namely, to the view that while the purely destructive aspect of fire is generally the most prominent and apparently the most important at these festivals, we must not overlook the additional force which by virtue of homoeopathic or imitative magic the bonfires may be supposed both to derive from and to impart to the sun, especially at the moment of the summer solstice when his strength is greatest and begins to decline, and when accordingly he can at once give and receive help to the greatest advantage.

[1] See above, pp. 45, 46, 49, 54, 55, 59, 60, 62, 64, 65, 66, 67.

To conclude this part of our subject it may not be amiss to illustrate by a few more miscellaneous examples the belief that Midsummer Eve is one of the great days of the year in which witches and warlocks pursue their nefarious calling; indeed in this respect Midsummer Eve perhaps stands second only to the famous Walpurgis Night (the Eve of May Day). For instance, in the neighbourhood of Lierre, in Belgium, the people think that on the night of Midsummer Eve all witches and warlocks must repair to a certain field which is indicated to them beforehand. There they hold their infernal Sabbath and are passed in review by a hellish magician, who bestows on them fresh powers. That is why old women are most careful, before going to bed on that night, to stop up doors and windows and every other opening in order to bar out the witches and warlocks, who but for this sage precaution might steal into the house and make the first trial of their new powers on the unfortunate inmates.[1] At Rottenburg, in Swabia, people thought that the devil and the witches could do much harm on Midsummer Eve; so they made fast their shutters and bunged up even the chinks and crannies, for wherever air can penetrate, there the devil and witches can worm their way in. All night long, too, from nine in the evening till break of day, the church bells rang to disturb the dreadful beings at their evil work, since there is perhaps no better means of putting the whole devilish crew to flight than the sound of church bells.[2] Down to the second half of the nineteenth century the belief in witches was still widespread in Voigtland, a bleak mountainous region of Central Germany. It was especially on the Eve of May Day (Walpurgis), St. Thomas's Day, St. John's Day, and Christmas Eve, as well as on Mondays, that they were dreaded. Then they would come into a neighbour's house to beg, borrow, or steal something, no matter what; but woe to the poor wretch who suffered them to carry away so much as a chip or splinter of wood; for they would certainly use it to his undoing. On these witching nights the witches rode to their Sabbath on baking-forks and the

Miscellaneous examples of the baleful activity of witches at Midsummer and of the precautions which it is necessary to take against them at that time.

Witches in Voigtland.

[1] Le Baron de Reinsberg-Dürings-feld, *Calendrier Belge* (Brussels, 1861–1862), i. 423 *sq.*

[2] Anton Birlinger, *Völksthumliches aus Schwaben* (Freiburg im Breisgau, (1861–1862), i. 278, § 437.

dashers of churns; but if when they were hurtling through the darkness any one standing below addressed one of the witches by name, she would die within the year. To counteract and undo the spells which witches cast on man and beast, people resorted to all kinds of measures. Thus on the before-mentioned days folk made three crosses on the doors of the byres or guarded them by hanging up St. John's wort, marjoram, or other equally powerful talismans. Very often, too, the village youth would carry the war into the enemy's quarters by marching out in a body, cracking whips, firing guns, waving burning besoms, shouting and making an uproar, all for the purpose of frightening and driving away

The witches' Sabbath in Prussia on Walpurgis Night and Midsummer Eve.

the witches.[1] In Prussia witches and warlocks used regularly to assemble twice a year on Walpurgis Night and the Eve of St. John. The places where they held their infernal Sabbath were various; for example, one was Pogdanzig, in the district of Schlochau. They generally rode on a baking-fork, but often on a black three-legged horse, and they took their departure up the chimney with the words, " Up and away and nowhere to stop ! " When they were all gathered on the Blocksberg or Mount of the Witches, they held high revelry, feasting first and then dancing on a tight rope lefthanded-wise to the inspiring strains which an old warlock

Midsummer Eve a witching time among the South Slavs.

drew from a drum and a pig's head.[2] The South Slavs believe that on the night of Midsummer Eve a witch will slink up to the fence of the farmyard and say, " The cheese to me, the lard to me, the butter to me, the milk to me, but the cowhide to thee ! " After that the cow will perish miserably and you will be obliged to bury the flesh and sell the hide. To prevent this disaster the thing to do is to go out into the meadows very early on Midsummer morning while the dew is on the grass, collect a quantity of dew in a waterproof mantle, carry it home, and having tethered your cow wash her down with the dew. After that you have only to place a milkpail under her udders and to milk away as hard as you can; the amount of milk that you will extract from that cow's dugs is quite surprising. Again, the

[1] Robert Eisel, *Sagenbuch des Voigt-landes* (Gera, 1871), p. 210, Nr. 551.
[2] W. J. A. von Tettau und J. D. H.

Temme, *Die Volkssagen Ostpreussens, Litthauens und Westpreussens* (Berlin, 1837), pp. 263 *sq.*

Slovenians about Görz and the Croats of Istria believe that on the same night the witches wage pitched battles with baptized folk, attacking them fiercely with broken stakes of palings and stumps of trees.   It is therefore a wise precaution to grub up all the stumps in autumn and carry them home, so that the witches may be weaponless on St. John's Night.   If the stumps are too heavy to be grubbed up, it is well to ram them down tighter into the earth, for then the witches will not be able to pull them up.[1]

[1] F. S. Krauss, *Volksglaube und religiöser Brauch der Südslaven* (Münster i. W., 1890), p. 128.

CHAPTER IX

BALDER AND THE MISTLETOE

Relation of the fire-festivals to the myth of Balder.

THE reader may remember that the preceding account of the popular fire-festivals of Europe was suggested by the myth of the Norse god Balder, who is said to have been slain by a branch of mistletoe and burnt in a great fire. We have now to enquire how far the customs which have been passed in review help to shed light on the myth. In this enquiry it may be convenient to begin with the mistletoe, the instrument of Balder's death.

Veneration of the Druids for the mistletoe.

From time immemorial the mistletoe has been the object of superstitious veneration in Europe. It was worshipped by the Druids, as we learn from a famous passage of Pliny. After enumerating the different kinds of mistletoe, he proceeds: " In treating of this subject, the admiration in which the mistletoe is held throughout Gaul ought not to pass unnoticed. The Druids, for so they call their wizards, esteem nothing more sacred than the mistletoe and the tree on which it grows, provided only that the tree is an oak. But apart from this they choose oak-woods for their sacred groves and perform no sacred rites without oak-leaves ; so that the very name of Druids may be regarded as a Greek appellation derived from their worship of the oak.[1] For

---

[1] Pliny derives the name Druid from the Greek *drus*, "oak." He did not know that the Celtic word for oak was the same (*daur*), and that therefore Druid, in the sense of priest of the oak, might be genuine Celtic, not borrowed from the Greek. This etymology is accepted by some modern scholars. See G. Curtius, *Grundzüge der Griechischen* *Etymologie* [5] (Leipsic, 1879), pp. 238 *sq.* ; A. Vaniček, *Griechisch-Lateinisch Etymologisches Wörterbuch* (Leipsic, 1877), pp. 368 *sqq.* ; (Sir) John Rhys, *Celtic Heathendom* (London and Edinburgh, 1888), pp. 221 *sqq.* However, this derivation is disputed by other scholars, who prefer to derive the name from a word meaning know-

they believe that whatever grows on these trees is sent from heaven, and is a sign that the tree has been chosen by the god himself. The mistletoe is very rarely to be met with ; but when it is found, they gather it with solemn ceremony. This they do above all on the sixth day of the moon, from whence they date the beginnings of their months, of their years, and of their thirty years' cycle, because by the sixth day the moon has plenty of vigour and has not run half its course. After due preparations have been made for a sacrifice and a feast under the tree, they hail it as the universal healer and bring to the spot two white bulls, whose horns have never been bound before. A priest clad in a white robe climbs the tree and with a golden sickle cuts the mistletoe, which is caught in a white cloth. Then they sacrifice the victims, praying that God may make his own gift to prosper with those upon whom he has bestowed it. They believe that a potion prepared from mistletoe will make barren animals to bring forth, and that the plant is a remedy against all poison. So much of men's religion is commonly concerned with trifles." [1]

---

ledge or wisdom, so that Druid would mean " wizard " or " magician." See J. Grimm, *Deutsche Mythologie*,[4] iii. 305 ; Otto Schrader, *Reallexikon der Indogermanischen Altertumskunde* (Strasburg, 1901), pp. 638 *sq.* ; H. D'Arbois de Jubainville, *Les Druides et les Dieux Celtiques à forme d'animaux* (Paris,. 1906), pp. 1, 11, 83 *sqq.* The last-mentioned scholar formerly held that the etymology of Druid was unknown. See his *Cours de Littérature Celtique*, i. (Paris, 1883) pp. 117-127.

[1] Pliny, *Nat. Hist.* xvi. 249-251. In the first edition of this book I understood Pliny to say that the Druidical ceremony of cutting the mistletoe fell in the sixth month, that is, in June ; and hence I argued that it probably formed part of the midsummer festival. But in accordance with Latin usage the words of Pliny (*sexta luna*, literally "sixth moon") can only mean "the sixth day of the month." I have to thank my friend Mr. W. Warde Fowler for courteously pointing out my mistake to me. Compare my note in the *Athenaeum*, November 21st, 1891, p. 687. I also misunderstood Pliny's words, "*et saeculi post tricesimum annum, quia jam virium abunde habeat nec sit sui dimidia*," applying them to the tree instead of to the moon, to which they really refer. After *saeculi* we must understand *principium* from the preceding *principia.* With the thirty years' cycle of the Druids we may compare the sixty years' cycle of the Boeotian festival of the Great Daedala (Pausanias, ix. 3. 5 ; see *The Magic Art and the Evolution of Kings*, ii. 140 *sq.*), which, like the Druidical rite in question, was essentially a worship, or perhaps rather a conjuration, of the sacred oak. Whether any deeper affinity, based on common Aryan descent, may be traced between the Boeotian and the Druidical ceremony, I do not pretend to determine. In India a cycle of sixty years, based on the sidereal revolution of Jupiter, has long been in use. The sidereal revolution of Jupiter is accomplished in approximately twelve solar years (more

Medical
and
magical
virtues
ascribed to
mistletoe in
ancient
Italy.
In another passage Pliny tells us that in medicine the mistletoe which grows on an oak was esteemed the most efficacious, and that its efficacy was by some superstitious people supposed to be increased if the plant was gathered on the first day of the moon without the use of iron, and if when gathered it was not allowed to touch the earth; oak-mistletoe thus obtained was deemed a cure for epilepsy; carried about by women it assisted them to conceive; and it healed ulcers most effectually, if only the sufferer chewed a piece of the plant and laid another piece on the sore.[1] Yet, again, he says that mistletoe was supposed, like vinegar and an egg, to be an excellent means of extinguishing a fire.[2]

Agreement
between
the Druids
and the
ancient
Italians as
to the valu-
able pro-
perties of
mistletoe.
If in these latter passages Pliny refers, as he apparently does, to the beliefs current among his contemporaries in Italy, it will follow that the Druids and the Italians were to some extent agreed as to the valuable properties possessed by mistletoe which grows on an oak ; both of them deemed it an effectual remedy for a number of ailments, and both of them ascribed to it a quickening virtue, the Druids believing that a potion prepared from mistletoe would fertilize barren cattle, and the Italians holding that a piece of mistletoe carried about by a woman would help her to conceive a child. Further, both peoples thought that if the plant were to exert its medicinal properties it must be gathered in a certain way and at a certain time. It might not be cut with iron, hence the Druids cut it with gold ; and it might not touch the earth, hence the Druids caught it in a white cloth. In choosing the time for gathering the plant, both peoples were determined by observation of the moon ; only they differed as to the particular day of the moon, the Italians preferring the first, and the Druids the sixth.

---

exactly 11 years and 315 days), so that five of its revolutions make a period of approximately sixty years. It seems, further, that in India a much older cycle of sixty lunar years was recognized. See Christian Lassen, *Indische Alter-thumskunde*, i.[2] (Leipsic, 1867), pp. 988 *sqq.* ; Prof. F. Kielhorn (Göttingen), "The Sixty-year Cycle of Jupiter," *The Indian Antiquary*, xviii.

(1889) pp. 193-209 ; J. F. Fleet, "A New System of the Sixty-year Cycle of Jupiter," *ibid.* pp. 221-224. In Tibet the use of a sixty-years' cycle has been borrowed from India. See W. Woodville Rockhill, "Tibet," *Journal of the Royal Asiatic Society for 1891* (London, 1891), p. 207 note [1].

[1] Pliny, *Nat. Hist.* xxiv. 11 *sq.*
[2] Pliny, *Nat. Hist.* xxxiii. 94.

With these beliefs of the ancient Gauls and Italians as to the wonderful medicinal properties of mistletoe we may compare the similar beliefs of the modern Ainos of Japan. We read that they, "like many nations of the Northern origin, hold the mistletoe in peculiar veneration. They look upon it as a medicine, good in almost every disease, and it is sometimes taken in food and at others separately as a decoction. The leaves are used in preference to the berries, the latter being of too sticky a nature for general purposes. . . . But many, too, suppose this plant to have the power of making the gardens bear plentifully. When used for this purpose, the leaves are cut up into fine pieces, and, after having been prayed over, are sown with the millet and other seeds, a little also being eaten with the food. Barren women have also been known to eat the mistletoe, in order to be made to bear children. That mistletoe which grows upon the willow is supposed to have the greatest efficacy. This is because the willow is looked upon by them as being an especially sacred tree." [1]

Thus the Ainos agree with the Druids in regarding mistletoe as a cure for almost every disease, and they agree with the ancient Italians that applied to women it helps them to bear children. A similar belief as to the fertilizing influence of mistletoe, or of similar plants, upon women is entertained by the natives of Mabuiag, an island in Torres Straits. These savages imagine that twins can be produced "by the pregnant woman touching or breaking a branch of a loranthaceous plant (*Viscum sp.*, probably *V. orientale*) parasitic on a tree, *mader*. The wood of this tree is much esteemed for making digging sticks and as firewood, no twin-producing properties are inherent in it, nor is it regarded as being infected with the properties of its twin-producing parasite." [2] Again, the Druidical notion that the mistletoe was an "all-healer" or panacea may be compared with a notion entertained by the Walos of Senegambia. These people "have much veneration for a sort of mistletoe, which they call *tob*; they carry leaves of it on their persons

---

[1] Rev. John Batchelor, *The Ainu and their Folk-lore* (London, 1901), p. 222.

[2] *Reports of the Cambridge Anthropological Expedition to Torres Straits*, v. (Cambridge, 1904) pp. 198 *sq.*

These beliefs perhaps originate in a notion that the mistletoe has fallen from heaven.

when they go to war as a preservative against wounds, just as if the leaves were real talismans (*gris-gris*)." The French writer who records this practice adds : "Is it not very curious that the mistletoe should be in this part of Africa what it was in the superstitions of the Gauls ? This prejudice, common to the two countries, may have the same origin ; blacks and whites will doubtless have seen, each of them for themselves, something supernatural in a plant which grows and flourishes without having roots in the earth. May they not have believed, in fact, that it was a plant fallen from the sky, a gift of the divinity ? "[1]

Such a notion would explain the ritual used in cutting mistletoe and other parasites.

This suggestion as to the origin of the superstition is strongly confirmed by the Druidical belief, reported by Pliny, that whatever grew on an oak was sent from heaven and was a sign that the tree had been chosen by the god himself.[2] Such a belief explains why the Druids cut the mistletoe, not with a common knife, but with a golden sickle,[3] and why, when cut, it was not suffered to touch the earth ;

[1] M. le baron Roger (ancien Gouverneur de la Colonie française du Sénégal), "Notice sur le Gouvernement, les Mœurs, et les Superstitions des Nègres du pays de Walo," *Bulletin de la Société de Géographie*, viii. (Paris, 1827) pp. 357 *sq.*

[2] Above, p. 77.

[3] Compare *The Times*, 2nd April, 1901, p. 9 : "The Tunis correspondent of the *Temps* reports that in the course of certain operations in the Belvedere Park in Tunis the workmen discovered a huge circle of enormous stumps of trees ranged round an immense square stone showing signs of artistic chisel work. In the neighbourhood were found a sort of bronze trough containing a gold sickle in perfect preservation, and a sarcophagus containing a skeleton. About the forehead of the skeleton was a gold band, having in the centre the image of the sun, accompanied by hieratic signs, which are provisionally interpreted as the monogram of Teutates. The discovery of such remains in North Africa has created a sensation." As to the Celtic god Teutates and the human sacrifices offered to him, see Lucan, *Pharsalia*, i. 444 *sq.* :

"*Et quibus immitis placatur sanguine diro*
Teutates horrensque feris altaribus Hesus."

Compare (Sir) John Rhys, *Celtic Heathendom* (London and Edinburgh, 1888), pp. 44 *sqq.*, 232. Branches of the sacred olive at Olympia, which were to form the victors' crowns, had to be cut with a golden sickle by a boy whose parents were both alive. See the Scholiast on Pindar, *Olymp.* iii. 60, p. 102, ed. Aug. Boeck (Leipsic, 1819). In Assyrian ritual it was laid down that, before felling a sacred tamarisk to make magical images out of the wood, the magician should pray to the sun-god Shamash and touch the tree with a golden axe. See C. Fossey, *La Magie Assyrienne* (Paris, 1902), pp. 132 *sq.* Some of the ancients thought that the root of the marshmallow, which was used in medicine, should be dug up with gold and then preserved from contact with the ground (Pliny, *Nat. Hist.* xx. 29). At the great horse-sacrifice in ancient India it was prescribed by ritual that the horse should be slain by a golden knife, because "gold is light" and "by

probably they thought that the celestial plant would have been profaned and its marvellous virtue lost by contact with the ground. With the ritual observed by the Druids in cutting the mistletoe we may compare the ritual which in Cambodia is prescribed in a similar case. They say that when you see an orchid growing as a parasite on a tamarind tree, you should dress in white, take a new earthenware pot, then climb the tree at noon, break off the plant, put it in the pot, and let the pot fall to the ground. After that you make in the pot a decoction which confers the gift of invulnerability.[1] Thus just as in Africa the leaves of one parasitic plant are supposed to render the wearer invulnerable, so in Cambodia a decoction made from another parasitic plant is considered to render the same service to such as make use of it, whether by drinking or washing. We may conjecture that in both places the notion of invulnerability is suggested by the position of the plant, which, occupying a place of comparative security above the ground, appears to promise to its fortunate possessor a similar security from some of the ills that beset the life of man on earth. We have already met with many examples of the store which the primitive mind sets on such vantage grounds.[2]

Whatever may be the origin of these beliefs and practices concerning the mistletoe, certain it is that some of them have their analogies in the folk-lore of modern European peasants. For example, it is laid down as a rule in various parts of Europe that mistletoe may not be cut in the ordinary way but must be shot or knocked down with stones from the tree on which it is growing. Thus, in

The ancient beliefs and practices concerning mistletoe have their analogies in modern European folk-lore.

---

means of the golden light the sacrificer also goes to the heavenly world." See *The Satapatha-Brâhmana*, translated by Julius Eggeling, Part v. (Oxford, 1900) p. 303 (*Sacred Books of the East*, vol. xliv.). It has been a rule of superstition both in ancient and modern times that certain plants, to which medical or magical virtues were attributed, should not be cut with iron. See the fragment of Sophocles's *Rootcutters*, quoted by Macrobius, *Saturn.* v. 19. 9 *sq.* ; Virgil, *Aen.* iv. 513 *sq.* ; Ovid, *Metamorph.* vii. 227 ; Pliny,

Nat. Hist. xxiv. 68, 103, 176 ; and above, p. 65 (as to purple loosestrife in Russia). On the objection to the use of iron in such cases compare F. Liebrecht, *Des Gervasius von Tilbury Otia Imperialia* (Hanover, 1856), pp. 102 *sq.* ; *Taboo and the Perils of the Soul*, pp. 225 *sqq.*

[1] Étienne Aymonier, "Notes sur les Coutumes et Croyances Superstitieuses des Cambodgiens," *Cochinchine Française, Excursions et Reconnaissance* No. 16 (Saigon, 1883), p. 136.

[2] See above, vol. i. pp. 2 *sqq.*

the Swiss canton of Aargau "all parasitic plants are esteemed in a certain sense holy by the country folk, but most particularly so the mistletoe growing on an oak. They ascribe great powers to it, but shrink from cutting it off in the usual manner. Instead of that they procure it in the following manner. When the sun is in Sagittarius and the moon is on the wane, on the first, third, or fourth day before the new moon, one ought to shoot down with an arrow the mistletoe of an oak and to catch it with the left hand as it falls. Such mistletoe is a remedy for every ailment of children."[1] Here among the Swiss peasants, as among the Druids of old, special virtue is ascribed to mistletoe which grows on an oak : it may not be cut in the usual way : it must be caught as it falls to the ground ; and it is esteemed a panacea for all diseases, at least of children. In Sweden, also, it is a popular superstition that if mistletoe is to possess its peculiar virtue, it must either be shot down out of the oak or knocked down with stones.[2] Similarly, " so late as the early part of the nineteenth century, people in Wales believed that for the mistletoe to have any power, it must be shot or struck down with stones off the tree where it grew."[3]

Medicinal virtues ascribed to mistletoe by ancients and moderns.

Again, in respect of the healing virtues of mistletoe the opinion of modern peasants, and even of the learned, has to some extent agreed with that of the ancients. The Druids appear to have called the plant, or perhaps the oak on which it grew, the " all-healer " ;[4] and " all-healer " is said to be still a name of the mistletoe in the modern Celtic speech of Brittany, Wales, Ireland, and Scotland.[5] On St. John's morning (Midsummer morning) peasants of Piedmont

---

[1] Ernst Meier, " Über Pflanzen und Kräuter," Zeitschrift für deutsche Mythologie und Sittenkunde, i. (Göttingen, 1853), pp. 443 sq. The sun enters the sign of Sagittarius about November 22nd.

[2] J. Grimm, Deutsche Mythologie,[4] iii. 533, referring to Dybeck, Runa, 1845, p. 80.

[3] Marie Trevelyan, Folk-lore and Folk-stories of Wales (London, 1909), p. 87.

[4] Pliny, Nat. Hist. xvi. 250, " Omnia sanantem appellantes suo vocabulo." See above, p. 77.

[5] J. Grimm, Deutsche Mythologie,[4] ii. 1009 : " Sonst aber wird das welsche olhiach, bretagn. ollyiach, ir. uileiceach, gal. uileice, d. i. allheiland, von ol, uile universalis, als benennung des mistels angegeben." My lamented friend, the late R. A. Neil of Pembroke College, Cambridge, pointed out to me that in N. M'Alpine's Gaelic Dictionary (Seventh Edition, Edinburgh and London, 1877, p. 432) the Gaelic word for mistletoe is given as an t' uil, which, Mr. Neil told me, means " all-healer."

and Lombardy go out to search the oak-leaves for the "oil of St. John," which is supposed to heal all wounds made with cutting instruments.[1] Originally, perhaps, the "oil of St. John" was simply the mistletoe, or a decoction made from it. For in Holstein the mistletoe, especially oak-mistletoe, is still regarded as a panacea for green wounds and as a sure charm to secure success in hunting;[2] and at Lacaune, in the south of France, the old Druidical belief in the mistletoe as an antidote to all poisons still survives among the peasantry; they apply the plant to the stomach of the sufferer or give him a decoction of it to drink.[3] Again, the ancient belief that mistletoe is a cure for epilepsy has survived in modern times not only among the ignorant but among the learned. Thus in Sweden persons afflicted with the falling sickness think they can ward off attacks of the malady by carrying about with them a knife which has a handle of oak mistletoe;[4] and in Germany for a similar purpose pieces of mistletoe used to be hung round the necks of children.[5] In the French province of Bourbonnais a popular remedy for epilepsy is a decoction of mistletoe which has been gathered on an oak on St. John's Day and boiled with rye-flour.[6] So at Bottesford in Lincolnshire a decoction of mistletoe is supposed to be a palliative for this terrible disease.[7] Indeed mistletoe was recommended as a remedy for the falling sickness by high medical authorities in England and Holland down to the eighteenth century.[8]

Mistletoe as a cure for epilepsy.

---

[1] A. de Gubernatis, *La Mythologie des Plantes* (Paris, 1878–1882), ii. 73.

[2] Rev. Hilderic Friend, *Flowers and Flower Lore*, Third Edition (London, 1886), p. 378. Compare A. Kuhn, *Die Herabkunft des Feuers und des Göttertranks* ² (Gütersloh, 1886), p. 206, referring to Keysler, *Antiq. Sept.* p. 308.

[3] A. de Nore, *Coutumes, Mythes et Traditions des Provinces de France* (Paris and Lyons, 1846), pp. 102 *sq.* The local name for mistletoe here is *besq*, which may be derived from the Latin *viscum*.

[4] A Kuhn, *Die Herabkunft des Feuers und des Göttertranks* ² (Gütersloh, 1886), p. 205 ; Walter K. Kelly, *Curiosities of Indo-European Tradition and Folk-lore* (London, 1863), p. 186.

[5] "Einige Notizen aus einem alten Kräuterbuche," *Zeitschrift für deutsche Mythologie und Sittenkunde*, iv. (Göttingen, 1859) pp. 41 *sq.*

[6] Francis Pérot, "Prières, Invocations, Formules Sacrées, Incantations en Bourbonnais," *Revue des Traditions Populaires*, xviii. (1903) p. 299.

[7] *County Folk-lore*, v. *Lincolnshire*, collected by Mrs. Gutch and Mabel Peacock (London, 1908), p. 120.

[8] Prof. P. J. Veth, "De Leer der Signatuur, iii. De Mistel en de Riembloem," *Internationales Archiv für Ethnographie*, vii. (1894) p. 111. He names Ray in England (about 1700), Boerhaave in Holland (about 1720), and Van Swieten, a pupil of Boerhaave's (about 1745).

At Kirton-in-Lindsey, in Lincolnshire, it is thought that St. Vitus's dance may be cured by the water in which mistletoe berries have been boiled.[1]   In the Scotch shires of Elgin and Moray, down to the second half of the eighteenth century, at the full moon of March people used to cut withes of mistletoe or ivy, make circles of them, keep them all the year, and profess to cure hectics and other troubles by means of them.[2]   In Sweden, apparently, for other complaints a sprig of mistletoe is hung round the patient's neck or a ring of it is worn on his finger.[3]

The medicinal virtues ascribed to mistletoe seem to be mythical, being fanciful inferences from the parasitic nature of the plant.

However, the opinion of the medical profession as to the curative virtues of mistletoe has undergone a radical alteration.   Whereas the Druids thought that mistletoe cured everything, modern doctors appear to think that it cures nothing.[4]   If they are right, we must conclude that the ancient and widespread faith in the medicinal virtue of mistletoe is a pure superstition based on nothing better than the fanciful inferences which ignorance has drawn from the parasitic nature of the plant, its position high up on the branch of a tree seeming to protect it from the dangers to which plants and animals are subject on the surface of the ground. From this point of view we can perhaps understand why mistletoe has so long and so persistently been prescribed as a cure for the falling sickness.   As mistletoe cannot fall to the ground because it is rooted on the branch of a tree high above the earth, it seems to follow as a necessary consequence that an epileptic patient cannot possibly fall down in a fit so long as he carries a piece of mistletoe in his pocket or a decoction of mistletoe in his stomach.   Such a train of reasoning would probably be regarded even now as cogent by a large portion of the human species.

Again the ancient Italian opinion that mistletoe ex-

[1] *County Folk-lore*, vol. v. *Lincolnshire*, collected by Mrs. Gutch and Mabel Peacock (London, 1908), p. 120.

[2] Rev. Mr. Shaw, Minister of Elgin, quoted by Thomas Pennant in his "Tour in Scotland, 1769," printed in J. Pinkerton's *Voyages and Travels*, iii. (London, 1809) p. 136 ; J. Brand, *Popular Antiquities of Great Britain* (London, 1882–1883), iii. 151.

[3] Walter K. Kelly, *Curiosities of Indo-European Tradition and Folk-lore* (London, 1863), p. 186.

[4] On this point Prof. P. J. Veth ("De Leer der Signatuur," *Internationales Archiv für Ethnographie*, vii. (1894) p. 112) quotes Cauvet, *Eléments d'Histoire naturelle médicale*, ii. 290 : "*La famille des Loranthacées ne nous offre aucun intéret.*"

tinguishes fire appears to be shared by Swedish peasants, who hang up bunches of oak-mistletoe on the ceilings of their rooms as a protection against harm in general and conflagration in particular.[1]   A hint as to the way in which mistletoe comes to be possessed of this property is furnished by the epithet " thunder-besom," which people of the Aargau canton in Switzerland apply to the plant.[2]   For a thunder-besom is a shaggy, bushy excrescence on branches of trees, which is popularly believed to be produced by a flash of lightning;[3] hence in Bohemia a thunder-besom burnt in the fire protects the house against being struck by a thunder-bolt.[4]   Being itself a product of lightning it naturally serves, on homoeopathic principles, as a protection against lightning, in fact as a kind of lightning-conductor. Hence the fire which mistletoe in Sweden is designed especially to avert from houses may be fire kindled by lightning; though no doubt the plant is equally effective against conflagration in general.

The belief that mistletoe extinguishes fire seems based on a fancy that it falls on the tree in a flash of lightning.

Again, mistletoe acts as a master-key as well as a lightning-conductor; for it is said to open all locks.[5]   However, in the Tyrol it can only exert this power "under certain circumstances," which are not specified.[6]   But perhaps the most precious of all the virtues of mistletoe is that it affords efficient protection against sorcery and witchcraft.[7] That, no doubt, is the reason why in Austria a twig of mistletoe is laid on the threshold as a preventive of nightmare;[8] and it may be the reason why in the north of

Other wonderful properties ascribed to mistletoe; in particular it is thought to be a protection against witchcraft.

[1] A. Kuhn, *Die Herabkunft des Feuers und des Göttertranks*[2] (Gütersloh, 1886), p. 205, referring to Dybeck, *Runa*, 1845, p. 80.

[2] A. Kuhn, *op. cit.* p. 204, referring to Rochholz, *Schweizersagen aus d. Aargau*, ii. 202.

[3] J. Grimm, *Deutsche Mythologie*,[4] i. 153.

[4] J. V. Grohmann, *Aberglauben und Gebräuche aus Böhmen und Mähren* (Prague and Leipsic, 1864), p. 37, § 218.   In Upper Bavaria the mistletoe is burned for this purpose along with the so-called palm-branches which were consecrated on Palm Sunday. See *Bavaria, Landes- und Volkskunde*

des Königreichs Bayern, i. (Munich, 1860), p. 371.

[5] A. Kuhn, *Die Herabkunft des Feuers und des Göttertranks*,[2] p. 206, referring to Albertus Magnus, p. 155; Prof. P. J. Veth, " De Leer der Signatuur," *Internationales Archiv für Ethnographie*, vii. (1904) p. 111.

[6] J. N. Ritter von Alpenburg, *Mythen und Sagen Tirols* (Zurich, 1857), p. 398.

[7] A. Wuttke, *Der deutsche Volksaberglaube*[2] (Berlin, 1869), p. 97, § 128; Prof. P. J. Veth, " De Leer der Signatuur," *Internationales Archiv für Ethnographie*, vii. (1894) p. 111.

[8] A. Wuttke, *op. cit.* p. 267, § 419.

England they say that if you wish your dairy to thrive you should give your bunch of mistletoe to the first cow that calves after New Year's Day,[1] for it is well known that nothing is so fatal to milk and butter as witchcraft. Similarly in Wales, for the sake of ensuring good luck to the dairy, people used to give a branch of mistletoe to the first cow that gave birth to a calf after the first hour of the New Year; and in rural districts of Wales, where mistletoe abounded, there was always a profusion of it in the farmhouses.   When mistletoe was scarce, Welsh farmers used to say, " No mistletoe, no luck "; but if there was a fine crop of mistletoe, they expected a fine crop of corn.[2]   In Sweden mistletoe is diligently sought after on St. John's Eve, the people " believing it to be, in a high degree, possessed of mystic qualities; and that if a sprig of it be attached to the ceiling of the dwelling-house, the horse's stall, or the cow's crib, the Troll will then be powerless to injure either man or beast." [3]

A favourite time for gathering mistletoe is Midsummer Eve.   With regard to the time when the mistletoe should be gathered opinions have varied.   The Druids gathered it above all on the sixth day of the moon, the ancient Italians apparently on the first day of the moon.[4]   In modern times some have preferred the full moon of March and others the waning moon of winter when the sun is in Sagittarius.[5] But the favourite time would seem to be Midsummer Eve or Midsummer Day.   We have seen that both in France and Sweden special virtues are ascribed to mistletoe gathered at Midsummer.[6]   The rule in Sweden is that " mistletoe must be cut on the night of Midsummer Eve when sun and moon stand in the sign of their might." [7]   Again, in Wales it was believed that a sprig of mistletoe gathered on St. John's Eve (Midsummer Eve), or at any time before the berries appeared, would induce dreams of omen, both good

---

[1] W. Henderson, *Notes on the Folk-lore of the Northern Counties of England and the Borders* (London, 1879), p. 114.

[2] Marie Trevelyan, *Folk-lore and Folk-stories of Wales* (London, 1909), p. 88.

[3] L. Lloyd, *Peasant Life in Sweden* (London, 1870), p. 269.

[4] Above, pp. 77, 78.

[5] Above, pp. 82, 84.

[6] Above, pp. 83, 86.

[7] J. Grimm, *Deutsche Mythologie*,[4] iii. 353, referring to Dybeck, *Runa*, 1844, p. 22.

and bad, if it were placed under the pillow of the sleeper.[1]
Thus mistletoe is one of the many plants whose magical
or medicinal virtues are believed to culminate with the
culmination of the sun on the longest day of the year.
Hence it seems reasonable to conjecture that in the eyes of
the Druids, also, who revered the plant so highly, the sacred
mistletoe may have acquired a double portion of its mystic
qualities at the solstice in June, and that accordingly they
may have regularly cut it with solemn ceremony on Midsummer Eve.

Be that as it may, certain it is that the mistletoe, the *The two main incidents of Balder's myth, namely the pulling of the mistletoe and the lighting of the bonfire, are reproduced in the great Midsummer celebration of Scandinavia.* instrument of Balder's death, has been regularly gathered
for the sake of its mystic qualities on Midsummer Eve in
Scandinavia, Balder's home.[2] The plant is found commonly
growing on pear-trees, oaks, and other trees in thick damp
woods throughout the more temperate parts of Sweden.[3]
Thus one of the two main incidents of Balder's myth is reproduced in the great midsummer festival of Scandinavia.
But the other main incident of the myth, the burning of
Balder's body on a pyre, has also its counterpart in the
bonfires which still blaze, or blazed till lately, in Denmark,
Norway, and Sweden on Midsummer Eve.[4] It does not
appear, indeed, that any effigy is burned in these bonfires ;
but the burning of an effigy is a feature which might
easily drop out after its meaning was forgotten. And
the name of Balder's balefires (*Balder's Bălar*), by which
these midsummer fires were formerly known in Sweden,[5]
puts their connexion with Balder beyond the reach of
doubt, and makes it probable that in former times either
a living representative or an effigy of Balder was annually
burned in them. Midsummer was the season sacred to
Balder, and the Swedish poet Tegner, in placing the burning
of Balder at midsummer,[6] may very well have followed an

[1] Marie Trevelyan, *Folk-lore and Folk-stories of Wales* (London, 1909), p. 88.

[2] See above, p. 86.

[3] G. Wahlenberg, *Flora Suecica* (Upsala, 1824–1826), ii. No. 1143 *Viscum album*, pp. 649 *sq.* : "*Hab. in sylvarum densiorum et humidiorum arboribus frondosis, ut Pyris, Quercu,* *Fago etc. per Sueciam temperatiorem passim.*"

[4] Above, vol. i. pp. 171 *sq.*

[5] L. Lloyd, *Peasant Life in Sweden* (London, 1870), p. 259.

[6] J. Grimm, *Deutsche Mythologie,*[4] iii. 78, who adds, "*Mahnen die Johann-isfeuer an Baldrs Leichenbrand?*" This pregnant hint perhaps contains in germ the solution of the whole myth.

old tradition that the summer solstice was the time when the good god came to his untimely end.

Hence the myth of Balder was probably the explanation given of a similar rite.

Thus it has been shewn that the leading incidents of the Balder myth have their counterparts in those fire-festivals of our European peasantry which undoubtedly date from a time long prior to the introduction of Christianity. The pretence of throwing the victim chosen by lot into the Beltane fire,[1] and the similar treatment of the man, the future Green Wolf, at the midsummer bonfire in Normandy,[2] may naturally be interpreted as traces of an older custom of actually burning human beings on these occasions; and the green dress of the Green Wolf, coupled with the leafy envelope of the young fellow who trod out the midsummer fire at Moosheim,[3] seems to hint that the persons who perished at these festivals did so in the character of tree-spirits or deities of vegetation. From all this we may reasonably infer that in the Balder myth on the one hand, and the fire-festivals and custom of gathering mistletoe on the other hand, we have, as it were, the two broken and dissevered halves of an original whole. In other words, we may assume with some degree of probability that the myth of Balder's death was not merely a myth, that is, a description of physical phenomena in imagery borrowed from human life, but that it was at the same time the story which people told to explain why they annually burned a human representative of the god and cut the mistletoe with solemn ceremony. If I am right, the story of Balder's tragic end formed, so to say, the text of the sacred drama which was acted year by year as a magical rite to cause the sun to shine, trees to grow, crops to thrive, and to guard man and beast from the baleful arts of fairies and trolls, of witches and warlocks. The tale belonged, in short, to that class of nature myths which are meant to be supplemented by ritual; here, as so often, myth stood to magic in the relation of theory to practice.

If a human representative of a tree-spirit was burned in the bon-

But if the victims—the human Balders—who died by fire, whether in spring or at midsummer, were put to death as living embodiments of tree-spirits or deities of vegetation, it would seem that Balder himself must have been a tree-

---

[1] Above, vol. i. p. 148.   [2] Above, vol. i. p. 186.   [3] Above, p. 26.

spirit or deity of vegetation.   It becomes desirable, therefore,
to determine, if we can, the particular kind of tree or trees,
of which a personal representative was burned at the fire-
festivals.   For we may be quite sure that it was not as
a representative of vegetation in general that the victim
suffered death.   The idea of vegetation in general is too
abstract to be primitive.   Most probably the victim at first
represented a particular kind of sacred tree.   Now of all
European trees none has such claims as the oak to be
considered as pre-eminently the sacred tree of the Aryans.
Its worship is attested for all the great branches of the
Aryan stock in Europe.   We have seen that it was not only
the sacred tree, but the principal object of worship of both
Celts and Lithuanians.[1]   The roving Celts appear to have
carried their worship of the oak with them even to Asia ;
for in the heart of Asia Minor the Galatian senate met in
a place which bore the pure Celtic name of Drynemetum or
"temple of the oak." [2]   Among the Slavs the oak seems to
have been the sacred tree of the great god Perun.[3]   According to Grimm, the oak ranked first among the holy trees of
the Germans.   It is certainly known to have been adored
by them in the age of heathendom, and traces of its worship
have survived in various parts of Germany almost to the
present day.[4]   Among the ancient Italians the oak was
sacred above all other trees.[5]   The image of Jupiter on the
Capitol at Rome seems to have been originally nothing but
a natural oak-tree.[6]   At Dodona, perhaps the oldest of all
Greek sanctuaries, Zeus was worshipped as immanent in the
sacred oak, and the rustling of its leaves in the wind was

[1] As to the worship of the oak in
Europe, see *The Magic Art and the
Evolution of Kings*, ii. 349 *sqq.*   Com-
pare P. Wagler, *Die Eiche in alter
und neuer Zeit*, in two parts (Wurzen,
N.D., and Berlin, 1891).

[2] Strabo, xii. 5. 1, p. 567.   The name
is a compound of *dryu*, "oak," and
nemed, "temple" (H. F. Tozer, *Selec-
tions from Strabo*, Oxford, 1893, p.
284).   We know from Jerome (*Com-
mentar. in Epist. ad Galat.* book ii.
praef.) that the Galatians retained
their native Celtic speech as late as

the fourth century of our era.

[3] *The Magic Art and the Evolution
of Kings*, ii. 365.

[4] J. Grimm, *Deutsche Mythologie*,[4]
i. 55 *sq.*, 58 *sq.*, ii. 542, iii. 187 *sq.* ;
P. Wagler, *Die Eiche in alter und
neuer Zeit* (Berlin, 1891), pp. 40 *sqq.* ;
*The Magic Art and the Evolution of
Kings*, ii. 363 *sqq.*, 371.

[5] L. Preller, *Römische Mythologie*[3]
(Berlin, 1881–1883), i. 108.

[6] Livy, i. 10.   Compare C. Bötticher, *Der Baumkultus der Hellenen*
(Berlin, 1856), pp. 133 *sq.*

his voice.[1] If, then, the great god of both Greeks and Romans was represented in some of his oldest shrines under the form of an oak, and if the oak was the principal object of worship of Celts, Germans, and Lithuanians, we may certainly conclude that this tree was venerated by the Aryans in common before the dispersion ; and that their primitive home must have lain in a land which was clothed with forests of oak.[2]

Hence the tree represented by the human victim who was burnt at the fire-festivals was probably the oak.

Now, considering the primitive character and remarkable similarity of the fire-festivals observed by all the branches of the Aryan race in Europe, we may infer that these festivals form part of the common stock of religious observances which the various peoples carried with them in their wanderings from their old home. But, if I am right, an essential feature of those primitive fire-festivals was the burning of a man who represented the tree-spirit. In view, then, of the place occupied by the oak in the religion of the Aryans, the presumption is that the tree so represented at the fire-festivals must originally have been the oak. So far as the Celts and Lithuanians are concerned, this conclusion will perhaps hardly be contested. But both for them and for the Germans it is confirmed by a remarkable piece of religious conservatism. The most primitive method known to man of producing fire is by rubbing two pieces of wood against each other till they ignite ; and we have seen that this method is still used in Europe for kindling sacred fires such as the need-fire, and that most probably it was formerly resorted to at all the fire-festivals under discussion. Now it is sometimes required that the need-fire, or other sacred fire, should be made by the friction of a particular kind of wood ; and when the kind of wood is prescribed, whether among Celts, Germans, or

[1] C. Bötticher, *op. cit.* pp. 111 *sqq.* ; L. Preller, *Griechische Mythologie,*[4] ed. C. Robert, i. (Berlin, 1894) pp. 122 *sqq.* ; P. Wagler, *Die Eiche in alter und neuer Zeit* (Berlin, 1891), pp. 2 *sqq.* It is noteworthy that at Olympia the only wood that might be used in sacrificing to Zeus was the white poplar (Pausanias, v. 14. 2). But it is probable that herein Zeus, who was an intruder at Olympia, merely accepted an old local custom which, long before his arrival, had been observed in the worship of Pelops (Pausanias, v. 13. 3).

[2] Without hazarding an opinion on the vexed question of the cradle of the Aryans, I may observe that in various parts of Europe the oak seems to have been formerly more common than it is now. See the evidence collected in *The Magic Art and the Evolution of Kings,* ii. 349 *sqq.*

Slavs, that wood appears to be generally the oak.[1]   Thus
we have seen that amongst the Slavs of Masuren the new
fire for the village is made on Midsummer Day by causing
a wheel to revolve rapidly round an axle of oak till the
axle takes fire.[2]   When the perpetual fire which the ancient
Slavs used to maintain chanced to go out, it was rekindled
by the friction of a piece of oak-wood, which had been
previously heated by being struck with a grey (not a red)
stone.[3]   In Germany and the Highlands of Scotland the need-
fire was regularly, and in Russia and among the South Slavs
it was sometimes, kindled by the friction of oak-wood ;[4] and
both in Wales and the Highlands of Scotland the Beltane
fires were lighted by similar means.[5]   Now, if the sacred
fire was regularly kindled by the friction of oak-wood, we
may infer that originally the fire was also fed with the same
material.   In point of fact, it appears that the perpetual fire
of Vesta at Rome was fed with oak-wood,[6] and that oak-
wood was the fuel consumed in the perpetual fire which
burned under the sacred oak at the great Lithuanian
sanctuary of Romove.[7]   Further, that oak-wood was formerly
the fuel burned in the midsummer fires may perhaps be
inferred from the custom, said to be still observed by
peasants in many mountain districts of Germany, of making

---

[1] However, some exceptions to the
rule are recorded. See above, vol. i. pp.
169, 278 (oak and fir), 220 (plane and
birch), 281, 283, 286 (limewood), 282
(poplar and fir), 286 (cornel-tree), 291
(birch or other hard wood), 278, 280
(nine kinds of wood). According to
Montanus, the need-fire, Easter, and
Midsummer fires were kindled by the
friction of oak and limewood. See
Montanus, *Die deutschen Volksfeste,
Volksbräuche und deutscher Volksglaube*
(Iserlohn, N.D.), p. 159. But elsewhere (pp. 33 *sq.*, 127) the same
writer says that the need-fire and Midsummer fires were produced by the
friction of oak and fir-wood.

[2] Above, vol. i. p. 177.

[3] M. Prätorius, *Deliciae Prussicae*,
herausgegeben von Dr. William Pierson
(Berlin, 1871), pp. 19 *sq.*   W. R. S.
Ralston says (on what authority I do
not know) that if the fire maintained

in honour of the Lithuanian god
Perkunas went out, it was rekindled
by sparks struck from a stone which
the image of the god held in his hand
(*Songs of the Russian People*, London,
1872, p. 88).

[4] See above, vol. i. pp. 148, 271,
272, 274, 275, 276, 281, 289, 294.

[5] Above, vol. i. pp. 148, 155.

[6] *The Magic Art and the Evolution
of Kings*, ii. 186.

[7] *The Magic Art and the Evolution
of Kings*, ii. 366. However, sacred
fires of other wood than oak are
not unknown among Aryan peoples.
Thus at Olympia white poplar was the
wood burnt in sacrifices to Zeus (above,
p. 90 *n.*[1]) ; at Delphi the perpetual
fire was fed with pinewood (Plutarch,
De EI apud Delphos, 2), and it was
over the glowing embers of pinewood
that the Soranian Wolves walked at
Soracte (above, p. 14).

up the cottage fire on Midsummer Day with a heavy block of oak-wood. The block is so arranged that it smoulders slowly and is not finally reduced to charcoal till the expiry of a year. Then upon next Midsummer Day the charred embers of the old log are removed to make room for the new one, and are mixed with the seed-corn or scattered about the garden. This is believed to guard the food cooked on the hearth from witchcraft, to preserve the luck of the house, to promote the growth of the crops, and to preserve them from blight and vermin.[1] Thus the custom is almost exactly parallel to that of the Yule-log, which in parts of Germany, France, England, Servia, and other Slavonic lands was commonly of oak-wood.[2] At the Boeotian festival of the Daedala, the analogy of which to the spring and midsummer festivals of modern Europe has been already pointed out, the great feature was the felling and burning of an oak.[3] The general conclusion is, that at those periodic or occasional ceremonies the ancient Aryans both kindled and fed the fire with the sacred oak-wood.[4]

If the human victims burnt at the fire-festival represented the oak, the reason But if at these solemn rites the fire was regularly made of oak-wood, it follows that any man who was burned in it as a personification of the tree-spirit could have represented no tree but the oak. The sacred oak was thus burned in duplicate ; the wood of the tree was consumed in the fire, and along with it was consumed a living man as a personi-

[1] Montanus, *Die deutschen Volksfeste, Volksbräuche und deutscher Volksglaube* (Iserlohn, N.D.), pp. 127, 159. The log is called in German *Scharholz*. The custom appears to have prevailed particularly in Westphalia, about Sieg and Lahn. Compare Montanus, *op. cit.* p. 12, as to the similar custom at Christmas. The use of the *Scharholz* is reported to be found also in Niederlausitz and among the neighbouring Saxons. See Paul Wagler, *Die Eiche in alter und neuer Zeit* (Berlin, 1891), pp. 86 *sq.*

[2] Above, vol. i. pp. 248, 250, 251, 257, 258, 260, 263. Elsewhere the Yule log has been made of fir, beech, holly, yew, crab-tree, or olive. See above, vol. i. pp. 249, 257, 263.

[3] *The Magic Art and the Evolution of Kings,* ii. 140 *sq.*

[4] A curious use of an oak-wood fire to detect a criminal is reported from Germany. If a man has been found murdered and his murderer is unknown, you are recommended to proceed as follows. You kindle a fire of dry oak-wood, you pour some of the blood from the wounds on the fire, and you change the poor man's shoes, putting the right shoe on the left foot, and *vice versa.* As soon as that is done, the murderer is struck blind and mad, so that he fancies he is riding up to the throat in water ; labouring under this delusion he returns to the corpse, when you can apprehend him and deliver him up to the arm of justice with the greatest ease. See Montanus, *op. cit.* pp. 159 *sq.*

fication of the oak-spirit.   The conclusion thus drawn for the European Aryans in general is confirmed in its special application to the Scandinavians by the relation in which amongst them the mistletoe appears to have stood to the burning of the victim in the midsummer fire.   We have seen that among Scandinavians it has been customary to gather the mistletoe at midsummer.   But so far as appears on the face of this custom, there is nothing to connect it with the midsummer fires in which human victims or effigies of them were burned.   Even if the fire, as seems probable, was originally always made with oak-wood, why should it have been necessary to pull the mistletoe ?   The last link between the midsummer customs of gathering the mistletoe and lighting the bonfires is supplied by Balder's myth, which can hardly be disjoined from the customs in question.   The myth suggests that a vital connexion may once have been believed to subsist between the mistletoe and the human representative of the oak who was burned in the fire.   According to the myth, Balder could be killed by nothing in heaven or earth except the mistletoe ; and so long as the mistletoe remained on the oak, he was not only immortal but invulnerable.   Now, if we suppose that Balder was the oak, the origin of the myth becomes intelligible.   The mistletoe was viewed as the seat of life of the oak, and so long as it was uninjured nothing could kill or even wound the oak.   The conception of the mistletoe as the seat of life of the oak would naturally be suggested to primitive people by the observation that while the oak is deciduous, the mistletoe which grows on it is evergreen.   In winter the sight of its fresh foliage among the bare branches must have been hailed by the worshippers of the tree as a sign that the divine life which had ceased to animate the branches yet survived in the mistletoe, as the heart of a sleeper still beats when his body is motionless.   Hence when the god had to be killed— when the sacred tree had to be burnt—it was necessary to begin by breaking off the mistletoe.   For so long as the mistletoe remained intact, the oak (so people might think) was invulnerable ; all the blows of their knives and axes would glance harmless from its surface.   But once tear from the oak its sacred heart—the mistletoe—and the tree nodded

for pulling the mistletoe may have been a belief that the life of the oak was in the misletoe, and that the tree could not perish either by fire or water so long as the mistletoe remained intact among its boughs.

to its fall.   And when in later times the spirit of the oak
came to be represented by a living man, it was logically
necessary to suppose that, like the tree he personated, he
could neither be killed nor wounded so long as the mistletoe
remained uninjured.   The pulling of the mistletoe was thus
at once the signal and the cause of his death.

Ancient Italian belief that mistletoe could not be destroyed by fire or water.

On this view the invulnerable Balder is neither more nor
less than a personification of a mistletoe-bearing oak.   The
interpretation is confirmed by what seems to have been an
ancient Italian belief, that the mistletoe can be destroyed
neither by fire nor water ;[1] for if the parasite is thus deemed
indestructible, it might easily be supposed to communicate
its own indestructibility to the tree on which it grows, so
long as the two remain in conjunction.   Or to put the same
idea in mythical form we might tell how the kindly god of
the oak had his life securely deposited in the imperishable
mistletoe which grew among the branches ; how accordingly
so long as the mistletoe kept its place there, the deity himself remained invulnerable ; and how at last a cunning foe,
let into the secret of the god's invulnerability, tore the mistletoe
from the oak, thereby killing the oak-god and afterwards
burning his body in a fire which could have made no impression on him so long as the incombustible parasite retained
its seat among the boughs.

Conception of a being whose life is outside himself.

But since the idea of a being whose life is thus, in a
sense, outside himself, must be strange to many readers, and
has, indeed, not yet been recognized in its full bearing on
primitive superstition, it will be worth while to illustrate it
by examples drawn both from story and custom.   The
result will be to shew that, in assuming this idea as the
explanation of Balder's relation to the mistletoe, I assume
a principle which is deeply engraved on the mind of primitive
man.

---

[1] Pliny, *Nat. Hist.* xiii. 119 :
"*Alexander Cornelius arborem leonem
appellavit ex qua facta esset Argo,
similem robori viscum ferenti, quae
neque aqua neque igni possit corrumpi,
sicuti nec viscum, nulli alii cognitam,
quod equidem sciam.*"   Here the tree
out of which the ship Argo was made
is said to have been destructible neither
by fire nor water ; and as the tree is
compared to a mistletoe-bearing oak,
and the mistletoe itself is said to be indestructible by fire and water, it seems
to follow that the same indestructibility may have been believed to attach
to the oak which bore the mistletoe,
so long at least as the mistletoe
remained rooted on the boughs.

CHAPTER X

THE EXTERNAL SOUL IN FOLK-TALES

IN a former part of this work we saw that, in the opinion of primitive people, the soul may temporarily absent itself from the body without causing death.[1]   Such temporary absences of the soul are often believed to involve considerable risk, since the wandering soul is liable to a variety of mishaps at the hands of enemies, and so forth.   But there is another aspect to this power of disengaging the soul from the body. If only the safety of the soul can be ensured during its absence, there is no reason why the soul should not continue absent for an indefinite time ; indeed a man may, on a pure calculation of personal safety, desire that his soul should never return to his body.   Unable to conceive of life abstractly as a " permanent possibility of sensation " or a " continuous adjustment of internal arrangements to external relations," the savage thinks of it as a concrete material thing of a definite bulk, capable of being seen and handled, kept in a box or jar, and liable to be bruised, fractured, or smashed in pieces.   It is not needful that the life, so conceived, should be in the man ; it may be absent from his body and still continue to animate him by virtue of a sort of sympathy or action at a distance.   So long as this object which he calls his life or soul remains unharmed, the man is well ; if it is injured, he suffers ; if it is destroyed, he dies.   Or, to put it otherwise, when a man is ill or dies, the fact is explained by saying that the material object called his life or soul, whether it be in his body or out of it, has either sustained injury or been destroyed.   But there may

Belief that a man's soul may be deposited for safety in a secure place outside his body, and that so long as it remains there intact he himself is invulnerable and immortal.

---

[1] *Taboo and the Perils of the Soul,* pp. 26 *sqq.*

be circumstances in which, if the life or soul remains in the man, it stands a greater chance of sustaining injury than if it were stowed away in some safe and secret place. Accordingly, in such circumstances, primitive man takes his soul out of his body and deposits it for security in some snug spot, intending to replace it in his body when the danger is past. Or if he should discover some place of absolute security, he may be content to leave his soul there permanently. The advantage of this is that, so long as the soul remains unharmed in the place where he has deposited it, the man himself is immortal ; nothing can kill his body, since his life is not in it.

This belief is illustrated by folk-tales told by many peoples.

Evidence of this primitive belief is furnished by a class of folk-tales of which the Norse story of " The giant who had no heart in his body " is perhaps the best-known example. Stories of this kind are widely diffused over the world, and from their number and the variety of incident and of details in which the leading idea is embodied, we may infer that the conception of an external soul is one which has had a powerful hold on the minds of men at an early stage of history. For folk-tales are a faithful reflection of the world as it appeared to the primitive mind ; and we may be sure that any idea which commonly occurs in them, however absurd it may seem to us, must once have been an ordinary article of belief. This assurance, so far as it concerns the supposed power of disengaging the soul from the body for a longer or shorter time, is amply corroborated by a comparison of the folk-tales in question with the actual beliefs and practices of savages. To this we shall return after some specimens of the tales have been given. The specimens will be selected with a view of illustrating both the characteristic features and the wide diffusion of this class of tales.[1]

[1] A number of the following examples were collected by Mr. E. Clodd in his paper, " The Philosophy of Punchkin," *Folk-lore Journal*, ii. (1884) pp. 288-303 ; and again in his *Myths and Dreams* (London, 1885), pp. 188-198. The subject of the external soul, both in folk-tales and in custom, has been well handled by G. A. Wilken in his two papers, " De betrekking tusschen men- schen- dieren- en plantenleven naar het volksgeloof," *De Indische Gids*, November 1884, pp. 595-612, and " De Simsonsage," *De Gids*, 1888, No. 5. In " De Simsonsage " Wilken has reproduced, to a great extent in the same words, most of the evidence cited by him in " De betrekking," yet without referring to that paper. When I wrote this book in 1889–1890 I was

In the first place, the story of the external soul is told, in various forms, by all Aryan peoples from Hindoostan to the Hebrides.   A very common form of it is this: A warlock, giant, or other fairyland being is invulnerable and immortal because he keeps his soul hidden far away in some secret place; but a fair princess, whom he holds enthralled in his enchanted castle, wiles his secret from him and reveals it to the hero, who seeks out the warlock's soul, heart, life, or death (as it is variously called), and, by destroying it, simultaneously kills the warlock.   Thus a Hindoo story tells how a magician called Punchkin held a queen captive for twelve years, and would fain marry her, but she would not have him.   At last the queen's son came to rescue her, and the two plotted together to kill Punchkin. So the queen spoke the magician fair, and pretended that she had at last made up her mind to marry him.   "And do tell me," she said, "are you quite immortal?   Can death never touch you?   And are you too great an enchanter ever to feel human suffering?"   "It is true," he said, "that I am not as others.   Far, far away, hundreds of thousands

Stories of an external soul common among Aryan peoples.

The external soul in Hindoo stories. Punchkin and the parrot.

---

unacquainted with "De betrekking," but used with advantage "De Simson-sage," a copy of it having been kindly sent me by the author.   I am the more anxious to express my obligations to "De Simsonsage," because I have had little occasion to refer to it, most of the original authorities cited by the author being either in my own library or easily accessible to me in Cambridge. It would be a convenience to anthropologists if Wilken's valuable papers, dispersed as they are in various Dutch periodicals which are seldom to be met with in England, were collected and published together.   After the appearance of my first anthropological essay in 1885, Professor Wilken entered into correspondence with me, and thenceforward sent me copies of his papers as they appeared; but of his papers published before that date I have not a complete set.   (Note to the Second Edition.)   The wish expressed in the foregoing note has now been happily fulfilled.   Wilken's many scattered

papers have been collected and published in a form which leaves nothing to be desired (*De verspreide Geschriften van Prof. Dr. G. A. Wilken*, verzameld door Mr. F. D. E. van Ossenbruggen, in four volumes, The Hague, 1912). The two papers "De betrekking" and "De Simsonsage" are reprinted in the third volume, pp. 289-309 and pp. 551-579.   The subject of the external soul in relation to Balder has been fully illustrated and discussed by Professor F. Kauffmann in his *Balder, Mythus und Sage* (Strasburg, 1902), pp. 136 *sqq.*   Amongst the first to collect examples of the external soul in folk-tales was the learned Dr. Reinhold Köhler (in *Orient und Occident*, ii., Göttingen, 1864, pp. 100-103; reprinted with additional references in the writer's *Kleinere Schriften*, i., Weimar, 1898, pp. 158-161).   Many versions of the tale were also cited by W. R. S. Ralston (*Russian Folk-tales*, London, 1873, pp. 109 *sqq.*).   (Note to the Third Edition.)

of miles from this, there lies a desolate country covered with thick jungle. In the midst of the jungle grows a circle of palm trees, and in the centre of the circle stand six chattees full of water, piled one above another: below the sixth chattee is a small cage, which contains a little green parrot;—on the life of the parrot depends my life;— and if the parrot is killed I must die. It is, however," he added, "impossible that the parrot should sustain any injury, both on account of the inaccessibility of the country, and because, by my appointment, many thousand genii surround the palm trees, and kill all who approach the place." But the queen's young son overcame all difficulties, and got possession of the parrot. He brought it to the door of the magician's palace, and began playing with it. Punchkin, the magician, saw him, and, coming out, tried to persuade the boy to give him the parrot. "Give me my parrot!" cried Punchkin. Then the boy took hold of the parrot and tore off one of his wings; and as he did so the magician's right arm fell off. Punchkin then stretched out his left arm, crying, "Give me my parrot!" The prince pulled off the parrot's second wing, and the magician's left arm tumbled off. "Give me my parrot!" cried he, and fell on his knees. The prince pulled off the parrot's right leg, the magician's right leg fell off; the prince pulled off the parrot's left leg, down fell the magician's left. Nothing remained of him except the trunk and the head; but still he rolled his eyes, and cried, "Give me my parrot!" "Take your parrot, then," cried the boy; and with that he wrung the bird's neck, and threw it at the magician; and, as he did so, Punchkin's head twisted round, and, with a fearful groan, he died![1] In another Hindoo tale an ogre is asked by his daughter, "Papa, where do you keep your soul?" "Sixteen miles away from this place," he said, "is a tree. Round the tree are tigers, and bears, and scorpions, and snakes; on the top of the tree is a very great fat snake; on his head is a little cage; in the cage is a bird; and my soul is in that bird." The end of the ogre is like that of the magician in the previous tale. As the bird's

The ogre whose soul was in a bird.

---

[1] Mary Frere, *Old Deccan Days*, Third Edition (London, 1881), pp. 12-16.

wings and legs are torn off, the ogre's arms and legs drop off; and when its neck is wrung he falls down dead.[1]

In another Hindoo story a princess called Sodewa Bai was born with a golden necklace about her neck, and the astrologer told her parents, "This is no common child; the necklace of gold about her neck contains your daughter's soul; let it therefore be guarded with the utmost care; for if it were taken off, and worn by another person, she would die." So her mother caused it to be firmly fastened round the child's neck, and, as soon as the child was old enough to understand, she told her its value, and warned her never to let it be taken off. In course of time Sodewa Bai was married to a prince who had another wife living. The first wife, jealous of her young rival, persuaded a negress to steal from Sodewa Bai the golden necklace which contained her soul. The negress did so, and, as soon as she put the necklace round her own neck, Sodewa Bai died. All day long the negress used to wear the necklace; but late at night, on going to bed, she would take it off and put it by till morning; and whenever she took it off, Sodewa Bai's soul returned to her and she lived. But when morning came, and the negress put on the necklace, Sodewa Bai died again. At last the prince discovered the treachery of his elder wife and restored the golden necklace to Sodewa Bai.[2]

The princess whose soul was in a golden necklace.

In another Hindoo story a holy mendicant tells a queen that she will bear a son, adding, "As enemies will try to take away the life of your son, I may as well tell you that the life of the boy will be bound up in the life of a big *boal* fish which is in your tank, in front of the palace. In the heart of the fish is a small box of wood, in the box is a necklace of gold, that necklace is the life of your son." The boy was born and received the name of Dalim. His mother was the Suo or younger queen. But the Duo or elder queen hated the child, and learning the secret of his life, she caused the *boal* fish, with which his life was bound up, to be caught. Dalim was playing near the tank at the

The prince whose soul was in a fish.

---

[1] Maive Stokes, *Indian Fairy Tales* (London, 1880), pp. 58-60. For similar Hindoo stories, see *id.*, pp. 187 *sq.* ; Lal Behari Day, *Folk-tales of Bengal* (London, 1883), pp. 121 *sq.* ;

F. A. Steel and R. C. Temple, *Wide-awake Stories* (Bombay and London, 1884), pp. 58-60.

[2] Mary Frere, *Old Deccan Days*, pp. 239 *sqq.*

time, but "the moment the *boal* fish was caught in the net, that moment Dalim felt unwell; and when the fish was brought up to land, Dalim fell down on the ground, and made as if he was about to breathe his last. He was immediately taken into his mother's room, and the king was astonished on hearing of the sudden illness of his son and heir. The fish was by the order of the physician taken into the room of the Duo queen, and as it lay on the floor striking its fins on the ground, Dalim in his mother's room was given up for lost. When the fish was cut open, a casket was found in it; and in the casket lay a necklace of gold. The moment the necklace was worn by the queen, that very moment Dalim died in his mother's room." The queen used to put off the necklace every night, and whenever she did so, the boy came to life again. But every morning when the queen put on the necklace, he died again.[1]

Cashmeer stories of ogres whose lives were in cocks, a pigeon, a starling, a spinning-wheel, and a pillar. In a Cashmeer story a lad visits an old ogress, pretending to be her grandson, the son of her daughter who had married a king. So the old ogress took him into her confidence and shewed him seven cocks, a spinning wheel, a pigeon, and a starling. "These seven cocks," said she, "contain the lives of your seven uncles, who are away for a few days. Only as long as the cocks live can your uncles hope to live; no power can hurt them as long as the seven cocks are safe and sound. The spinning-wheel contains my life; if it is broken, I too shall be broken, and must die; but otherwise I shall live on for ever. The pigeon contains your grandfather's life, and the starling your mother's; as long as these live, nothing can harm your grandfather or your mother." So the lad killed the seven cocks and the pigeon and the starling, and smashed the spinning-wheel; and at the moment he did so the ogres and ogresses perished.[2] In another story from Cashmeer an ogre cannot die unless a particular pillar in the verandah of his palace be broken. Learning the secret, a prince struck the pillar again and again till it was broken in pieces. And it was as if each

---

[1] Lal Behari Day, *Folk-tales of Bengal*, pp. 1 *sqq.* For similar stories of necklaces, see Mary Frere, *Old Deccan Days*, pp. 233 *sq.*; F. A. Steel and R. C. Temple, *Wide-awake Stories*, pp. 83 *sqq.*

[2] J. H. Knowles, *Folk-tales of Kashmir*, Second Edition (London, 1893), pp. 49 *sq.*

stroke had fallen on the ogre, for he howled lamentably and shook like an aspen every time the prince hit the pillar, until at last, when the pillar fell down, the ogre also fell down and gave up the ghost.[1]   In another Cashmeer tale an ogre is represented as laughing very heartily at the idea that he might possibly die.   He said that "he should never die.   No power could oppose him ; no years could age him ; he should remain ever strong and ever young, for the thing wherein his life dwelt was most difficult to obtain."   It was in a queen bee, which was in a honeycomb on a tree.   But the bees in the honeycomb were many and fierce, and it was only at the greatest risk that any one could catch the queen. However, the hero achieved the enterprise and crushed the queen bee ; and immediately the ogre fell stone dead to the ground, so that the whole land trembled with the shock.[2] In some Bengalee tales the life of a whole tribe of ogres is described as concentrated in two bees.   The secret was thus revealed by an old ogress to a captive princess who pretended to fear lest the ogress should die.   " Know, foolish girl," said the ogress, " that we ogres never die.   We are not naturally immortal, but our life depends on a secret which no human being can unravel.   Let me tell you what it is, that you may be comforted.   You know yonder tank ; there is in the middle of it a crystal pillar, on the top of which in deep waters are two bees.   If any human being can dive into the waters, and bring up to land the two bees from the pillar in one breath, and destroy them so that not a drop of their blood falls to the ground, then we ogres shall certainly die ; but if a single drop of blood falls to the ground, then from it will start up a thousand ogres.   But what human being will find out this secret, or, finding it, will be able to achieve the feat ?   You need not, therefore, darling, be sad ; I am practically immortal."   As usual, the princess reveals the secret to the hero, who kills the bees, and that same moment all the ogres drop down dead, each on the spot where he happened to be standing.[3]   In another Bengalee story it is

Cashmeer and Bengalee stories of ogres whose lives were in bees.

[1] J. H. Knowles, *op. cit.* p. 134.

[2] J. H. Knowles, *op. cit.* pp. 382 *sqq.*

[3] Lal Behari Day, *Folk-tales of Bengal,* pp. 85 *sq.* ; compare *id.,* pp. 253 *sqq.* ; *Indian Antiquary,* i. (1872) p. 117.   For an Indian story in which a giant's life is in five black bees, see W. A. Clouston, *Popular Tales and Fictions* (Edinburgh and London, 1887), i. 350.

said that all the ogres dwell in Ceylon, and that all their
lives are in a single lemon. A boy cuts the lemon in pieces,
and all the ogres die.[1]

The external soul in a Siamese or Cambodian story.

In a Siamese or Cambodian story, probably derived from
India, we are told that Thossakan or Ravana, the King of
Ceylon, was able by magic art to take his soul out of his
body and leave it in a box at home, while he went to the
wars. Thus he was invulnerable in battle. When he was
about to give battle to Rama, he deposited his soul with a
hermit called Fire-eye, who was to keep it safe for him. So
in the fight Rama was astounded to see that his arrows
struck the king without wounding him. But one of Rama's
allies, knowing the secret of the king's invulnerability, transformed himself by magic into the likeness of the king, and
going to the hermit asked back his soul. On receiving it
he soared up into the air and flew to Rama, brandishing the
box and squeezing it so hard that all the breath left the
King of Ceylon's body, and he died.[2]   In a Bengalee story
a prince going into a far country planted with his own hands
a tree in the courtyard of his father's palace, and said to his
parents, " This tree is my life. When you see the tree green
and fresh, then know that it is well with me ; when you see
the tree fade in some parts, then know that I am in an ill
case ; and when you see the whole tree fade, then know that
I am dead and gone." [3]   In another Indian tale a prince,
setting forth on his travels, left behind him a barley plant,
with instructions that it should be carefully tended and
watched ; for if it flourished, he would be alive and well, but
if it drooped, then some mischance was about to happen to
him. And so it fell out. For the prince was beheaded,
and as his head rolled off, the barley plant snapped in two
and the ear of barley fell to the ground.[4]   In the legend of

Indian stories of a tree and a barley plant that were life-tokens.

[1] *Indian Antiquary*, i. (1872), p.
171.
[2] A. Bastian, *Die Voelker des oestlichen Asien*, iv. (Jena, 1868) pp.
304 *sq.*
[3] Lal Behari Day, *Folk-tales of Bengal*, p. 189.
[4] F. A. Steel and R. C. Temple,
Wide-awake Stories (Bombay and London, 1884), pp. 52, 64.   In the Indian

Jataka there is a tale (book ii. No.
208) which relates how Buddha in the
form of a monkey deceived a crocodile
by pretending that monkeys kept their
hearts in figs growing on a tree. See
*The Jataka or Stories of the Buddha's
former Births* translated from the Pali
by various hands, vol. ii. translated by
W. H. D. Rouse (Cambridge, 1895),
pp. 111 *sq.*

the origin of Gilgit there figures a fairy king whose soul is in the snows and who can only perish by fire.[1]

In Greek tales, ancient and modern, the idea of an external soul is not uncommon.   When Meleager was seven days old, the Fates appeared to his mother and told her that Meleager would die when the brand which was blazing on the hearth had burnt down.   So his mother snatched the brand from the fire and kept it in a box.   But in after-years, being enraged at her son for slaying her brothers, she burnt the brand in the fire and Meleager expired in agonies, as if flames were preying on his vitals.[2]   Again, Nisus King of Megara had a purple or golden hair on the middle of his head, and it was fated that whenever the hair was pulled out the king should die.   When Megara was besieged by the Cretans, the king's daughter Scylla fell in love with Minos, their king, and pulled out the fatal hair from her father's head.   So he died.[3]   Similarly Poseidon made Pterelaus immortal by giving him a golden hair on his head.   But when Taphos, the home of Pterelaus, was besieged by Amphitryo, the daughter of Pterelaus fell in love with Amphitryo and killed her father by plucking out the golden hair with which his life was bound up.[4]   In a modern Greek folk-tale a man's strength lies in three golden hairs on his head.   When his mother pulls them out, he grows weak and timid and is slain by his enemies.[5]   Another Greek story, in which we may perhaps detect a reminiscence of Nisus and

The external soul in Greek stories.

Meleager and the firebrand.

Nisus and his purple or golden hair.

Pterelaus and his golden hair.

Modern Greek parallels.

---

[1] G. W. Leitner, *The Languages and Races of Dardistan*, Third Edition (Lahore, 1878), p. 9.

[2] Apollodorus, *Bibliotheca*, i. 8; Diodorus Siculus, iv. 34; Pausanias, x. 31. 4; Aeschylus, *Choeph.* 604 *sqq.*; Antoninus Liberalis, *Transform.* ii.; Dio Chrysostom, *Or.* lxvii. vol. ii. p. 231, ed. L. Dindorf (Leipsic, 1857); Hyginus, *Fab.* 171, 174; Ovid, *Metam.* viii. 445 *sqq.*   In his play on this theme Euripides made the life of Meleager to depend on an olive-leaf which his mother had given birth to along with the babe.   See J. Malalas, *Chronographia*, vi. pp. 165 *sq.* ed. L. Dindorf (Bonn, 1831); J. Tzetzes, *Scholia on Lycophron*, 492 *sq.* (vol. ii. pp. 646 *sq.*, ed. Chr. G. Müller, Leipsic, 1811); G. Knaack, "Zur Meleagersage," *Rhein-*

isches Museum, N.F. xlix. (1894) pp. 310-313.

[3] Apollodorus, *Bibliotheca*, iii. 15. 8; Aeschylus, *Choeph.* 612 *sqq.*; Pausanias, i. 19. 4; *Ciris*, 116 *sqq.*; Ovid, *Metam.* viii. 8 *sqq.*   According to J. Tzetzes (*Schol. on Lycophron*, 650) not the life but the strength of Nisus was in his golden hair; when it was pulled out, he became weak and was slain by Minos.   According to Hyginus (*Fab.* 198) Nisus was destined to reign only so long as he kept the purple lock on his head.

[4] Apollodorus, *Bibliotheca*, ii. 4. 5 and 7.

[5] J. G. von Hahn, *Griechische und albanesische Märchen* (Leipsic, 1864), i. 217; a similar story, *ibid.* ii. 282.

Scylla, relates how a certain king, who was the strongest man
of his time, had three long hairs on his breast. But when
he went to war with another king, and his own treacherous
wife had cut off the three hairs, he became the weakest of

The ex-
ternal soul
in doves.
men.[1] In another modern Greek story the life of an enchanter is bound up with three doves which are in the belly
of a wild boar. When the first dove is killed, the magician
grows sick ; when the second is killed, he grows very sick;
and when the third is killed, he dies.[2] In another Greek
story of the same sort an ogre's strength is in three singing
birds which are in a wild boar. The hero kills two of the
birds, and then coming to the ogre's house finds him lying
on the ground in great pain. He shews the third bird to
the ogre, who begs that the hero will either let it fly away
or give it to him to eat. But the hero wrings the bird's
neck, and the ogre dies on the spot.[3] In a variant of the
latter story the monster's strength is in two doves, and when
the hero kills one of them, the monster cries out, " Ah, woe
is me ! Half my life is gone. Something must have
happened to one of the doves." When the second dove is
killed, he dies.[4] In another Greek story the incidents of the
three golden hairs and three doves are artificially combined.
A monster has on his head three golden hairs which open
the door of a chamber in which are three doves : when the
first dove is killed, the monster grows sick ; when the second
is killed, he grows worse ; and when the third is killed, he
dies.[5] In another Greek tale an old man's strength is in a

[1] B. Schmidt, *Griechische Märchen,
Sagen und Volkslieder* (Leipsic, 1877),
pp. 91 *sq.* The same writer found in
the island of Zacynthus a belief that the
whole strength of the ancient Greeks
resided in three hairs on their breasts,
and that it vanished whenever these
hairs were cut ; but if the hairs were
allowed to grow again, their strength
returned (B. Schmidt, *Das Volksleben
der Neugriechen,* Leipsic, 1871, p.
206). The Biblical story of Samson
and Delilah (Judges xvi.) implies a
belief of the same sort, as G. A. Wilken
abundantly shewed in his paper, " De
Simsonsage," *De Gids,* 1888, No. 5
(reprinted in his *Verspreide Geschriften,*
The Hague, 1912, vol. iii. pp. 551-

579).

[2] J. G. von Hahn, *op. cit.* ii. 215
sq.

[3] *Ibid.* ii. 275 *sq.* Similar stories,
ibid. ii. 204, 294 *sq.* In an Albanian
story a monster's strength is in three
pigeons, which are in a hare, which is
in the silver tusk of a wild boar. When
the boar is killed, the monster feels ill;
when the hare is cut open, he can
hardly stand on his feet; when the
three pigeons are killed, he expires.
See Aug. Dozon, *Contes albanais* (Paris,
1881), pp. 132 *sq.*

[4] J. G. von Hahn, *op. cit.* ii. 260
sqq.

[5] *Ibid.* i. 187.

ten-headed serpent. When the serpent's heads are being
cut off, he feels unwell ; and when the last head is struck off,
he expires.[1]   In another Greek story a dervish tells a queen
that she will have three sons, that at the birth of each she
must plant a pumpkin in the garden, and that in the fruit
borne by the pumpkins will reside the strength of the
children.   In due time the infants are born and the pumpkins planted.   As the children grow up, the pumpkins grow
with them.   One morning the eldest son feels sick, and on
going into the garden they find that the largest pumpkin is
gone.   Next night the second son keeps watch in a summer-
house in the garden.   At midnight a negro appears and cuts
the second pumpkin.   At once the boy's strength goes out
of him, and he is unable to pursue the negro.   The
youngest son, however, succeeds in slaying the negro and
recovering the lost pumpkins.[2]

Ancient Italian legend furnishes a close parallel to the
Greek story of Meleager.   Silvia, the young wife of Sep-
timius Marcellus, had a child by the god Mars.   The god
gave her a spear, with which he said that the fate of the
child would be bound up.   When the boy grew up he
quarrelled with his maternal uncles and slew them.   So in
revenge his mother burned the spear on which his life depended.[3]   In one of the stories of the *Pentamerone* a certain
queen has a twin brother, a dragon.   The astrologers declared at her birth that she would live just as long as the
dragon and no longer, the death of the one involving the death
of the other.   If the dragon were killed, the only way to
restore the queen to life would be to smear her temples, breast,
pulses, and nostrils with the blood of the dragon.[4]   In a
modern Roman version of " Aladdin and the Wonderful
Lamp," the magician tells the princess, whom he holds captive
in a floating rock in mid-ocean, that he will never die.   The
princess reports this to the prince her husband, who has
come to rescue her.   The prince replies, " It is impossible

*The exter-
nal soul
in Italian
stories.
Silvia's son.*

*The dragon
twin.*

*The soul in
a gem.*

[1] *Ibid.* ii. 23 *sq.*
[2] Émile Legrand, *Contes populaires
grecs* (Paris, 1881), pp. 191 *sqq.*
[3] Plutarch, *Parallela*, 26.   In both
the Greek and Italian stories the subject of quarrel between nephew and
uncles is the skin of a boar, which the
nephew presented to his lady-love and
which his uncles took from her.
[4] G. Basile, *Pentamerone*, übertragen
von Felix Liebrecht (Breslau, 1846), ii.
60 *sq.*

but that there should be some one thing or other that is fatal to him; ask him what that one fatal thing is." So the princess asked the magician, and he told her that in the wood was a hydra with seven heads; in the middle head of the hydra was a leveret, in the head of the leveret was a bird, in the bird's head was a precious stone, and if this stone were put under his pillow he would die. The prince procured the stone, and the princess laid it under the magician's pillow. No sooner did the enchanter lay his head on the pillow than he gave three terrible yells, turned himself round and round three times, and died.[1]

Italian story of a wicked fairy whose death was in an egg.

Another Italian tale sets forth how a great cloud, which was really a fairy, used to receive a young girl as tribute every year from a certain city; and the inhabitants had to give the girls up, for if they did not, the cloud would throw things at them and kill them all. One year it fell to the lot of the king's daughter to be handed over to the cloud, and they took her in procession, to the roll of muffled drums, and attended by her weeping father and mother, to the top of a mountain, and left her sitting in a chair there all alone. Then the fairy cloud came down on the top of the mountain, set the princess in her lap, and began to suck her blood out of her little finger; for it was on the blood of girls that this wicked fairy lived. When the poor princess was faint with the loss of blood and lay like a log, the cloud carried her away up to her fairy palace in the sky. But a brave youth had seen all that happened from behind a bush, and no sooner did the fairy spirit away the princess to her palace than he turned himself into an eagle and flew after them. He lighted on a tree just outside the palace, and looking in at the window he beheld a room full of young girls all in bed; for these were the victims of former years whom the fairy cloud had half killed by sucking their blood; yet they called her mamma. When the fairy went away and left the girls, the brave young man had food drawn up for them by ropes, and he told them to ask the fairy how she might be killed and what was to become of them when she died. It was a delicate question, but the fairy answered it, saying, " I

[1] R. H. Busk, *Folk-lore of Rome* (London, 1874), pp. 164 *sqq.*

shall never die." However, when the girls pressed her, she took them out on a terrace and said, "Do you see that mountain far off there? On that mountain is a tigress with seven heads. If you wish me to die, a lion must fight that tigress and tear off all seven of her heads. In her body is an egg, and if any one hits me with it in the middle of my forehead, I shall die; but if that egg falls into my hands, the tigress will come to life again, resume her seven heads, and I shall live." When the young girls heard this they pretended to be glad and said, "Good! certainly our mamma can never die," but naturally they were discouraged. However, when she went away again, they told it all to the young man, and he bade them have no fear. Away he went to the mountain, turned himself into a lion, and fought the tigress. Meantime the fairy came home, saying, "Alas! I feel ill!" For six days the fight went on, the young man tearing off one of the tigress's heads each day, and each day the strength of the fairy kept ebbing away. Then after allowing himself two days' rest the hero tore off the seventh head and secured the egg, but not till it had rolled into the sea and been brought back to him by a friendly dog-fish. When he returned to the fairy with the egg in his hand, she begged and prayed him to give it her, but he made her first restore the young girls to health and send them away in handsome carriages. When she had done so, he struck her on the forehead with the egg, and she fell down dead.[1] Similarly in a story from the western Riviera a sorcerer called Body-without-Soul can only be killed by means of an egg which is in an eagle, which is in a dog, which is in a lion; and the egg must be broken on the sorcerer's forehead. The hero, who achieves the adventure, has received the power of changing himself into a lion, a dog, an eagle, and an ant from four creatures of these sorts among whom he had fairly divided the carcase of a dead ass.[2]

A sorcerer Body-with-out-Soul whose death was in an egg.

---

[1] T. F. Crane, *Italian Popular Tales* (London, 1885), pp. 31-34. The hero had acquired the power of turning himself into an eagle, a lion, and an ant from three creatures of these sorts whose quarrel about their shares in a dead ass he had composed. This incident occurs in other tales of the same type. See below, note [2] and pp. 120 with note,[2] 132, 133 with note.[1]

[2] J. B. Andrews, *Contes Ligures* (Paris, 1892), No. 46, pp. 213 *sqq.* In a parallel Sicilian story the hero Beppino slays a sorcerer in the same manner after he had received from an eagle, a lion, and an ant the same

The exter-
nal soul in
Slavonic
stories.

Stories of the same sort are current among Slavonic peoples. In some of them, as in the biblical story of Samson and Delilah, the warlock is questioned by a treacherous woman as to the place where his strength resides or his life or death is stowed away ; and his suspicions being roused by her curiosity, he at first puts her off with false answers, but is at last beguiled into telling her the truth, thereby incurring his doom through her treachery.

Russian
story of
Koshchei
the
Deathless,
whose
death was
in an egg.

Thus a Russian story tells how a certain warlock called Kashtshei or Koshchei the Deathless carried off a princess and kept her prisoner in his golden castle. However, a prince made up to her one day as she was walking alone and disconsolate in the castle garden, and cheered by the prospect of escaping with him she went to the warlock and coaxed him with false and flattering words, saying, " My dearest friend, tell me, I pray you, will you never die ? " " Certainly not," says he. " Well," says she, " and where is your death ? is it in your dwelling ? " " To be sure it is," says he, " it is in the broom under the threshold." Thereupon the princess seized the broom and threw it on the fire, but although the broom burned, the deathless Koshchei remained alive; indeed not so much as a hair of him was singed. Balked in her first attempt, the artful hussy pouted and said, " You do not love me true, for you have not told me where your death is ; yet I am not angry, but love you with all my heart." With these fawning words she besought the warlock to tell her truly where his death was. So he laughed and said, " Why do you wish to know ? Well then, out of love I will tell you where it lies. In a certain field there stand three green oaks, and under the roots of the largest oak is a worm, and if ever this worm is found and crushed, that instant I shall die." When the princess heard these words, she went straight to her lover and told him all ; and he searched till he found the oaks and dug up the worm and crushed it. Then he hurried to the warlock's castle, but only to learn from the princess that the warlock

gift of transformation in return for the same service. See G. Pitrè, *Fiabe, Novelle e Racconti popolari Siciliani,* ii. (Palermo, 1875) p. 215 ; and for another Sicilian parallel, Laura Gonzenbach, *Sicilianische Märchen* (Leipsic, 1870), No. 6, pp. 34-38.

was still alive. Then she fell to wheedling and coaxing Koshchei once more, and this time, overcome by her wiles, he opened his heart to her and told her the truth. "My death," said he, "is far from here and hard to find, on the wide ocean. In that sea is an island, and on the island there grows a green oak, and beneath the oak is an iron chest, and in the chest is a small basket, and in the basket is a hare, and in the hare is a duck, and in the duck is an egg ; and he who finds the egg and breaks it, kills me at the same time." The prince naturally procured the fateful egg and with it in his hands he confronted the deathless warlock. The monster would have killed him, but the prince began to squeeze the egg. At that the warlock shrieked with pain, and turning to the false princess, who stood by smirking and smiling, "Was it not out of love for you," said he, "that I told you where my death was? And is this the return you make to me?" With that he grabbed at his sword, which hung from a peg on the wall ; but before he could reach it, the prince had crushed the egg, and sure enough the deathless warlock found his death at the same moment.[1]

In another version of the same story, when the cunning warlock deceives the traitress by telling her that his death is in the broom, she gilds the broom, and at supper the warlock sees it shining under the threshold and asks her sharply, "What's that?" "Oh," says she, "you see how I honour you." "Simpleton!" says he, "I was joking. My death is out there fastened to the oak fence." So next day when the warlock was out, the prince came and gilded the whole fence ; and in the evening when the warlock was at supper he looked out of the window and saw the fence glittering like gold. "And pray what may that be?" said he to the princess. "You see," said she, "how I respect you. If you are dear to me, dear too is your death. That is why I have gilded the fence in which your death resides." The speech pleased the warlock, and in the fulness of his heart he revealed to her the fatal secret of the egg. When the prince, with the help of some friendly animals, obtained possession of the egg, he put it in his bosom and repaired to

Other versions of the story of Koshchei the Deathless.

---

[1] Anton Dietrich, *Russian Popular Tales* (London, 1857), pp. 21-24.

the warlock's house. The warlock himself was sitting at the window in a very gloomy frame of mind; and when the prince appeared and shewed him the egg, the light grew dim in the warlock's eyes and he became all of a sudden very meek and mild. But when the prince began to play with the egg and to throw it from one hand to the other, the deathless Koshchei staggered from one corner of the room to the other, and when the prince broke the egg, Koshchei the Deathless fell down and died.[1] " In one of the descriptions of Koshchei's death, he is said to be killed by a blow on the forehead inflicted by the mysterious egg—that last link in the magic chain by which his life is darkly bound. In another version of the same story, but told of a snake, the fatal blow is struck by a small stone found in the yolk of an egg, which is inside a duck, which is inside a hare, which is

Death in the blue rose-tree.

inside a stone, which is on an island." [2] In another Russian story the death of an enchantress is in a blue rose-tree in a blue forest. Prince Ivan uproots the rose-tree, whereupon the enchantress straightway sickens. He brings the rose-tree to her house and finds her at the point of death. Then he throws it into the cellar, crying, " Behold her death ! " and at once the whole building shakes, " and becomes an island, on which are people who had been sitting in Hell, and who offer up thanks to Prince Ivan." [3] In another Russian story a prince is grievously tormented by a witch who has got hold of his heart, and keeps it seething in a magic cauldron.[4]

The external soul in Bohemian and Servian stories.

In a Bohemian tale a warlock's strength lies in an egg which is in a duck, which is in a stag, which is under a tree. A seer finds the egg and sucks it. Then the warlock grows as weak as a child, " for all his strength had passed into the seer." [5] A Servian story relates how a certain warlock called

True Steel, whose strength was in a bird.

True Steel carried off a prince's wife and kept her shut up in his cave. But the prince contrived to get speech of her and told her that she must persuade True Steel to reveal to

[1] Jeremiah Curtin, *Myths and Folk-tales of the Russians, Western Slavs, and Magyars* (London, 1891), pp. 119-122. Compare W. R. S. Ralston, *Russian Folk-tales* (London, 1873), pp. 100-105.

[2] W. R. S. Ralston, *op. cit.* p. 109.

[3] W. R. S. Ralston, *Russian Folk-tales*, pp. 113 *sq.*

[4] *Id.*, p. 114.

[5] *Id.*, p. 110.

her where his strength lay.   So when True Steel came home the prince's wife said to him, " Tell me, now, where is your great strength ? "   He answered, " My wife, my strength is in my sword."   Then she began to pray and turned to his sword.   When True Steel saw that, he laughed and said, " O foolish woman ! my strength is not in my sword, but in my bow and arrows."   Then she turned towards the bow and arrows and prayed.   But True Steel said, " I see, my wife, you have a clever teacher who has taught you to find out where my strength lies.   I could almost say that your husband is living, and it is he who teaches you."   But she assured him that nobody had taught her.   When she found he had deceived her again, she waited for some days and then asked him again about the secret of his strength. He answered, " Since you think so much of my strength, I will tell you truly where it is.   Far away from here there is a very high mountain ; in the mountain there is a fox ; in the fox there is a heart; in the heart there is a bird, and in this bird is my strength.   It is no easy task, however, to catch the fox, for she can transform herself into a multitude of creatures."   So next day, when True Steel went forth from the cave, the prince came and learned from his wife the true secret of the warlock's strength.   So away he hied to the mountain, and there, though the fox, or rather the vixen, turned herself into various shapes, he managed with the help of certain friendly eagles, falcons, and dragons, to catch and kill her.   Then he took out the fox's heart, and out of the heart he took the bird and burned it in a great fire.   At that very moment True Steel fell down dead.[1]

In another Servian story we read how a dragon resided in a water-mill and ate up two king's sons, one after the other. The third son went out to seek his brothers, and coming to the water-mill he found nobody in it but an old woman. She revealed to him the dreadful character of the being that kept the mill, and how he had devoured the prince's two elder brothers, and she implored him to go away home before the same fate should overtake him.   But he was both

Servian story of the dragon of the water-mill whose strength was in a pigeon.

[1] Madam   Csedomille   Mijatovies, *Serbian Folk-lore*, edited by the Rev. W. Denton (London, 1874), pp. 167- 172 ; F. S. Krauss, *Sagen und Mär-chen der Südslaven* (Leipsic, 1883– 1884), i. 164-169.

brave and cunning, and he said to her, " Listen well to what
I am going to say to you.   Ask the dragon whither he goes
and where his strength is ; then kiss all that place where he
tells you his strength is, as if from love, till you find it out,
and afterwards tell me when I come."   So when the dragon
came in, the old woman began to question him, " Where in
God's name have you been ?   Whither do you go so far ?
You will never tell me whither you go."   The dragon
replied, " Well, my dear old woman, I do go far."   Then
the old woman coaxed him, saying, " And why do you go
so far ?   Tell me where your strength is.   If I knew where
your strength is, I don't know what I should do for love ; I
would kiss all that place."   Thereupon the dragon smiled
and said to her, " Yonder is my strength, in that fireplace."
Then the old woman began to fondle and kiss the fireplace ;
and the dragon on seeing it burst into a laugh.   " Silly old
woman," he said, " my strength is not there.   It is in the
tree-fungus in front of the house."   Then the old woman
began to fondle and kiss the tree ; but the dragon laughed
again and said to her, " Away, old woman ! my strength is
not there."   " Then where is it ? " asked the old woman.
" My strength," said he, " is a long way off, and you cannot
go thither.   Far in another kingdom under the king's city is
a lake ; in the lake is a dragon ; in the dragon is a boar ; in
the boar is a pigeon, and in the pigeon is my strength."   The
murder was now out ; so next morning when the dragon went
away from the mill to attend to his usual business of eating
people up, the prince came to the old woman and she let him
into the secret of the dragon's strength.   The prince accordingly set off to find the lake in the far country and the other
dragon that lived in it.   He found them both at last ; the lake
was a still and lonely water surrounded by green meadows,
where flocks of sheep nibbled the sweet lush grass.   The
hero tucked up his hose and his sleeves, and wading out
into the lake called aloud on the dragon to come forth
and fight.   Soon the monster emerged from the water,
slimy and dripping, his scaly back glistening in the morning sun.   The two grappled and wrestled from morning to
afternoon of a long summer day.   What with the heat of
the weather and the violence of his exertions the dragon

The fight
with the
dragon.

was quite exhausted, and said, "Let me go, prince, that I may moisten my parched head in the lake and toss you to the sky." But the prince sternly refused; so the dragon relaxed his grip and sank under the water, which bubbled and gurgled over the place where he plunged into the depths. When he had disappeared and the ripples had subsided on the surface, you would never have suspected that under that calm water, reflecting the green banks, the white, straying sheep, the blue sky, and the fleecy gold-flecked clouds of a summer evening, there lurked so ferocious and dangerous a monster. Next day the combat was renewed with the very same result. But on the third day the hero, fortified by a kiss from the fair daughter of the king of the land, tossed the dragon high in air, and when the monster fell with a most tremendous thud on the water he burst into little bits. Out of the pieces sprang a boar which ran away as fast as it could lay legs to the ground. But the prince sent sheep-dogs after it which caught it up and rent it in pieces. Out of the pieces sprang a pigeon; but the prince let loose a falcon, which stooped on the pigeon, seized it in its talons, and brought it to the prince. In the pigeon was the life of the dragon who kept the mill, so before inflicting on the monster the doom he so richly merited, the prince questioned him as to the fate of his two elder brothers who had perished at the hands, or rather under the claws and fangs, of the dragon. Having ascertained how to restore them to life and to release a multitude of other victims whom the dragon kept prisoners in a vault under the water-mill, the prince wrung the pigeon's neck, and that of course was the end of the dragon and his unscrupulous career.[1]

A Lithuanian story relates how a prince married a princess and got with her a kingdom to boot. She gave him the keys of the castle and told him he might enter every chamber except one small room, of which the key had a bit of twine tied to it. But one day, having nothing to do, he amused himself by rummaging in all the rooms of the castle, and amongst the rest he went into the little forbidden chamber.

The external soul in a Lithuanian story. The Soulless King whose soul was in a duck's egg.

---

[1] A. H. Wratislaw, *Sixty Folk-tales from exclusively Slavonic Sources* (London, 1889), pp. 224-231.

In it he found twelve heads and a man hanging on the hook of the door. The man said to the prince, " Oblige me by fetching me a glass of beer." The prince fetched it and the man drank it. Then the man said to the prince, " Oblige me by releasing me from the hook." The prince released

The Soul-less King.

him. Now the man was a king without a soul, and he at once availed himself of his liberty to come to an understanding with the coachman of the castle, and between them they put the prince's wife in the coach and drove off with her. The prince rode after them and coming up with the coach called out, " Halt, Soulless King! Step out and fight!" The King stepped out and the fight began. In a trice the King had sliced the buttons off the prince's coat and pinked him in the side. Then he stepped into the coach and drove off, The prince rode after him again, and when he came up with the coach he called out, " Halt, Soulless King! Step out and fight!" The King stepped out and they fought again, and again the King sliced off the prince's buttons and pinked him in the side. Then, after carefully wiping and sheathing his sword, he said to his discomfited adversary, " Now look here. I let you off the first time for the sake of the glass of beer you gave me, and I let you off the second time because you let me down from that infernal hook ; but if you fight me a third time, by Gad I'll make mince meat of you." Then he stepped into the coach, told the coachman to drive on, jerked up the coach window with a bang, and drove away like anything. But the prince galloped after him and coming up with the coach for the third time he called out, " Halt, Soulless King! Step out and fight!" The King did step out, and at it the two of them went, tooth and nail. But the prince had no chance. Before he knew where he was, the King ran him through the body, whisked off his head, and left him lying a heap of raw mince beside the road. His wife, or rather his widow, said to the King, " Let me gather up the fragments that remain." The King said, " Certainly." So she made up the mince into a neat parcel, deposited it on the front seat of the coach, and away

The water of life.

they drove to the King's castle. Well to cut a long story short, a brother-in-law of the deceased prince sent a hawk to fetch the water of life ; the hawk brought it in his beak ;

the brother-in-law poured the water on the fragments of the prince, and the prince came to life again at once safe and sound.   Then he went to the King's castle and played on a little pipe, and his wife heard it in the castle and said, "That is how my husband used to play, whom the King cut in bits." So she went out to the gate and said to him, "Are you my husband?"   "That I am," said he, and he told her to find out from the King where he kept his soul and then to come and tell him.   So she went to the King and said to him, "Where my husband's soul is, there must mine be too." The King was touched by this artless expression of her love, and he replied, "My soul is in yonder lake.   In that lake lies a stone; in that stone is a hare; in the hare is a duck, in the duck is an egg, and in the egg is my soul."   So the queen went and told her former husband, the prince, and gave him plenty of money and food for the journey, and off he set for the lake.   But when he came to the lake, he did not know in which part of it the stone was; so he roamed about the banks, and he was hungry, for he had eaten up all the food.   Then he met a dog, and the dog said to him, "Don't shoot me dead.   I will be a mighty helper to you in your time of need."   So he let the dog live and went on his way. Next he saw a tree with two hawks on it, an old one and a young one, and he climbed up the tree to catch the young one.   But the old hawk said to him, "Don't take my young one.   He will be a mighty helper to you in your time of need."   So the prince climbed down the tree and went on his way.   Then he saw a huge crab and wished to break off one of his claws for something to eat, but the crab said to him, "Don't break off my claw.   It will be a mighty helper to you in your time of need."   So he left the crab alone and went on his way.   And he came to people and got them to fish up the stone for him from the lake and to bring it to him on the bank.   And there he broke the stone in two and out of the stone jumped a hare.   But the dog seized the hare and tore him, and out of the hare flew a duck.   The young hawk pounced on the duck and rent it, and out of the duck fell an egg, and the egg rolled into the lake.   But the crab fetched the egg out of the lake and brought it to the prince. Then the King fell ill.   So the prince went to the King and

The soul in the duck's egg.

said, "You killed me.   Now I will kill you."   "Don't," said the King.   "I will," said the prince.   With that he threw the egg on the ground, and the King fell out of the bed as dead as a stone.   So the prince went home with his wife and very happy they were, you may take my word for it.[1]

Amongst peoples of the Teutonic stock stories of the external soul are not wanting.   In a tale told by the Saxons of Transylvania it is said that a young man shot at a witch

again and again.   The bullets went clean through her but did her no harm, and she only laughed and mocked at him. "Silly earthworm," she cried, "shoot as much as you like. It does me no harm.   For know that my life resides not in me but far, far away.   In a mountain is a pond, on the pond swims a duck, in the duck is an egg, in the egg burns a light, that light is my life.   If you could put out that light, my life would be at an end.   But that can never, never be." However, the young man got hold of the egg, smashed it, and put out the light, and with it the witch's life went out also.[2]   In this last story, as in many other stories of the same type, the hero achieves his adventure by the help of certain grateful animals whom he had met and done a service to on his travels.   The same incident occurs in another

German tale of this class which runs thus.   Once upon a time there was a young fellow called Body-without-Soul, or, for short, Soulless, and he was a cannibal who would eat nothing but young girls.   Now it was a custom in that country that the girls drew lots every year, and the one on whom the lot fell was handed over to Soulless.   In time it happened that the lot fell on the king's daughter.   The king was exceedingly sorry, but what could he do?   Law was law, and had to be obeyed.   So they took the princess to the castle where Soulless resided ; and he shut her up in the larder and fattened her for his dinner.   But a brave soldier undertook to rescue her, and off he set for the cannibal's castle.   Well, as he trudged along, what should he see but a fly, an eagle, a bear, and a lion sitting in a field by the side of the road, and quarrelling about their shares in a

---

[1] A. Leskien und K. Brugmann, *Litauische Volkslieder und Märchen* (Strasburg, 1882), pp. 423-430 ; compare *id.*, pp. 569-571.

[2] Josef Haltrich, *Deutsche Volksmärchen aus dem Sachsenlande in Siebenbürgen*[4] (Vienna, 1885), No. 34 (No. 33 of the first edition), pp. 149 *sq.*

dead horse. So he divided the carcase fairly between them, The helpful animals.
and as a reward the fly and the eagle bestowed on him the
power of changing himself at will into either of their shapes.
That evening he made himself into an eagle, and flew
up a high tree ; there he looked about, but could see nothing
but trees. Next morning he flew on till he came to a great
castle, and at the gate was a big black board with these
words chalked up on it : " Mr. Soulless lives here." When
the soldier read that he was glad, and changed himself into
a fly, and flew buzzing from window to window, looking in
at every one till he came to the one where the fair princess
sat a prisoner. He introduced himself at once and said, " I
am come to free you, but first you must learn where the soul
of Soulless really is." " I don't know," replied the princess,
" but I will ask." So after much coaxing and entreaty she
learned that the soul of Soulless was in a box, and that the
box was on a rock in the middle of the Red Sea. When
the soldier heard that, he turned himself into an eagle again,
flew to the Red Sea, and came back with the soul of
Soulless in the box. Arrived at the castle he knocked and
banged at the door as if the house was on fire. Soulless
did not know what was the matter, and he came down and
opened the door himself. When he saw the soldier standing
at it, I can assure you he was in a towering rage. " What
do you mean," he roared, " by knocking at my door like
that ? I'll gobble you up on the spot, skin and hair and all."
But the soldier laughed in his face. " You'd better not do
that," said he, " for here I've got your soul in the box." When
the cannibal heard that, all his courage went down into the
calves of his legs, and he begged and entreated the soldier
to give him his soul. But the soldier would not hear of it ;
he opened the box, took out the soul, and flung it over his
head ; and that same instant down fell the cannibal, dead as
a door-nail.[1]

Another German story, which embodies the notion of German story of flowers that were life-tokens.
the external soul in a somewhat different form, tells how
once upon a time a certain king had three sons and a
daughter, and for each of the king's four children there
grew a flower in the king's garden, which was a life-flower ;

[1] J. W. Wolf, *Deutsche Märchen und Sagen* (Leipsic, 1845), No. 20, pp. 87-93.

for it bloomed and flourished so long as the child lived, but
drooped and withered away when the child died.   Now the
time came when the king's daughter married a rich man
and went to live with him far away.   But it was not long
before her flower withered in the king's garden.   So the
eldest brother went forth to visit his brother-in-law and com-
fort him in his bereavement.   But when he came to his
brother-in-law's castle he saw the corpse of· his murdered
sister weltering on the ramparts.   And his wicked brother-
in-law set before him boiled human hands and feet for his
dinner.   And when the king's son refused to eat of them,
his brother-in-law led him through many chambers to a
murder-hole, where were all sorts of implements of murder,
but especially a gallows, a wheel, and a pot of blood.   Here
he said to the prince, " You must die, but you may choose
your kind of death."   The prince chose to die on the
gallows ; and die he did even as he had said.   So the
eldest son's flower withered in the king's garden, and the
second son went forth to learn the fate of his brother
and sister.   But it fared with him no better than with his
elder brother, for he too died on the gallows in the murder-
hole of his wicked brother-in-law's castle, and his flower also
withered away in the king's garden at home.   Now when
the youngest son was also come to his brother-in-law's castle
and saw the corpse of his murdered sister weltering on the
ramparts, and the bodies of his two murdered brothers dang-
ling from the gallows in the murder-hole, he said that for his
part he had a fancy to die by the wheel, but he was not
quite sure how the thing was done, and would his brother-
in-law kindly shew him ?   " Oh, it's quite easy," said his
brother-in-law, " you just put your head in, so," and with
that he popped his head through the middle of the wheel.
" Just so," said the king's youngest son, and he gave the
wheel a twirl, and as it spun round and round, the wicked
brother-in-law died a painful death, which he richly deserved.
And when he was quite dead, the murdered brothers and
sister came to life again, and their withered flowers bloomed
afresh in the king's garden.[1]

---

[1] L. Strackerjan, *Aberglaube und
Sagen aus dem Herzogthum Olden-* *burg* (Oldenburg, 1867), ii. 306-308,
§ 622.   In this story the flowers are

In another German story an old warlock lives with a damsel all alone in the midst of a vast and gloomy wood. She fears that being old he may die and leave her alone in the forest. But he reassures her. " Dear child," he said, " I cannot die, and I have no heart in my breast." But she importuned him to tell her where his heart was. So he said, " Far, far from here in an unknown and lonesome land stands a great church. The church is well secured with iron doors, and round about it flows a broad deep moat. In the church flies a bird and in the bird is my heart. So long as the bird lives, I live. It cannot die of itself, and no one can catch it ; therefore I cannot die, and you need have no anxiety." However the young man, whose bride the damsel was to have been before the warlock spirited her away, contrived to reach the church and catch the bird. He brought it to the damsel, who stowed him and it away under the warlock's bed. Soon the old warlock came home. He was ailing, and said so. The girl wept and said, " Alas, daddy is dying ; he has a heart in his breast after all." " Child," replied the warlock, "hold your tongue. I *can't* die. It will soon pass over." At that the young man under the bed gave the bird a gentle squeeze ; and as he did so, the old warlock felt very unwell and sat down. Then the young man gripped the bird tighter, and the warlock fell senseless from his chair. " Now squeeze him dead," cried the damsel. Her lover obeyed, and when the bird was dead, the old warlock also lay dead on the floor.[1]

In the Norse tale of " the giant who had no heart in his body," the giant tells the captive princess, " Far, far away in a lake lies an island, on that island stands a church, in that church is a well, in that well swims a duck, in that duck there is an egg, and in that egg there lies my heart." The hero of the tale, with the help of some animals to whom he had been kind, obtains the egg and squeezes it, at which

The war-lock in the wood, whose heart was in a bird.

The exter-nal soul in Norse stories. The giant whose heart was in a duck's egg.

rather life-tokens than external souls. The life-token has been carefully studied by Mr. E. S. Hartland in the second volume of his learned work *The Legend of Perseus* (London, 1895).

[1] K. Müllenhoff, *Sagen, Märchen und Lieder der Herzogthümer Schleswig Holstein und Lauenburg* (Kiel, 1845), pp. 404 *sqq.*

the giant screams piteously and begs for his life. But the hero breaks the egg in pieces and the giant at once bursts.[1] In another Norse story a hill-ogre tells the captive princess that she will never be able to return home unless she finds the grain of sand which lies under the ninth tongue of the ninth head of a certain dragon; but if that grain of sand were to come over the rock in which the ogres live, they would all burst "and the rock itself would become a gilded palace, and the lake green meadows." The hero finds the grain of sand and takes it to the top of the high rock in which the ogres live. So all the ogres burst and the rest falls out as one of the ogres had foretold.[2]

The external soul in Danish stories. The warlock whose heart was in a duck's egg.

In a Danish tale a warlock carries off a princess to his wondrous subterranean palace; and when she anxiously enquires how long he is likely to live, he assures her that he will certainly survive her. "No man," he says, "can rob me of my life, for it is in my heart, and my heart is not here; it is in safer keeping." She urges him to tell her where it is, so he says: "Very far from here, in a land that is called Poland, there is a great lake, and in the lake is a dragon, and in the dragon is a hare, and in the hare is a duck, and in the duck is an egg, and in the egg is my heart. It is in good keeping, you may trust me. Nobody is likely to stumble upon it."

The helpful animals.

However, the hero of the tale, who is also the husband of the kidnapped princess, has fortunately received the power of turning himself at will into a bear, a dog, an ant, or a falcon as a reward for having divided the carcase of a deer impartially between four animals of these species; and availing himself of this useful art he not only makes his way into the warlock's enchanted palace but also secures the egg on which the enchanter's life depends. No sooner has he

[1] P. Chr. Asbjörnsen og J. Moe, *Norske Folke - Eventyr* (Christiania, N.D.), No. 36, pp. 174-180; G. W. Dasent, *Popular Tales from the Norse* (Edinburgh, 1859), pp. 55 *sqq.*

[2] P. Chr. Asbjörnsen, *Norske Folke- Eventyr*, Ny Samling (Christiania, 1871), No. 70, pp. 35 40; G. W. Dasent, *Tales from the Fjeld* (London,

1874), pp. 223-230 ("Boots and the Beasts"). As in other tales of this type, it is said that the hero found three animals (a lion, a falcon, and an ant) quarrelling over a dead horse, and received from them the power of transforming himself into animals of these species as a reward for dividing the carcase fairly among them.

smashed the egg on the enchanter's ugly face than that miscreant drops down as dead as a herring.[1]

Another Danish story tells how a lad went out into the world to look for service. He met a man, who hired him for three years and said he would give him a bushel of money for the first year, two bushels of money for the second, and three bushels of money for the third. The lad was well content, as you may believe, to get such good wages. But the man was a magician, and it was not long before he turned the lad into a hare, by pronouncing over him some strange words. For a whole year the lad scoured the woods in the shape of a hare, and there was not a sportsman in all the country round about that had not a shot at him. But not one of them could hit him. At the end of the year the magician spoke some other words over him and turned him back into human form and gave him the bushel of money. But then the magician mumbled some other words, and the lad was turned into a raven and flew up into the sky. Again all the marksmen of the neighbourhood pointed their guns at him and banged away; but they only wasted powder and shot, for not one of them could hit him. At the end of the year the magician changed him back into a man and gave him two bushelfuls of money. But soon after he changed him into a fish, and in the form of a fish the young man jumped into the brook and swam down into the sea. There at the bottom of the ocean he saw a most beautiful castle all of glass and in it a lovely girl all alone. Round and round the castle he swam, looking into all the rooms and admiring everything. At last he remembered the words the magician had spoken when he turned him back into a man, and by repeating them he was at once transformed into a stripling again. He walked into the glass castle and introduced himself to the girl, and though at first she was nearly frightened to death, she was soon very glad to have him with her. From her he learned that she was no other than the daughter of the magician, who kept her there for safety at the bottom of the sea. The two now laid their heads together, and she told him what to do.

Danish story of the magician whose heart was in a fish.

---

[1] Svend Grundtvig, *Dänische Volks-märchen*, übersetzt von A. Strodtmann, Zweite Sammlung (Leipsic, 1879), pp. 194-218.

There was a certain king who owed her father money and had not the wherewithal to pay; and if he did not pay by such and such a day, his head was to be cut off. So the young man was to take service with the king, offer him the bushels of money which he had earned in the service of the magician, and go with him to the magician to pay his debt. But he was to dress up as the court Fool so that the magician would not know him, and in that character he was to indulge in horse-play, smashing windows and so on, till the magician would fall into such a rage that though the king had paid his debt to the last farthing he would nevertheless be condemned to instant execution unless he could answer the magician's questions. The questions would be these, " Where is my daughter ? "   " Would you know her if you saw her ? "   Now the magician would cause a whole line of phantom women to pass by, so that the young man would not be able to tell which of them was the sorcerer's daughter ; but when her turn came to pass by she would give him a nudge as a sign, and so he would know

The magician's heart.

her.   Then the magician would ask, " And where is my heart ? "   And the young man was to say, " In a fish." And the magician would ask, " Would you know the fish if you saw it ? "   And he would cause all sorts of fishes to pass by, and the young man would have to say in which of them was the heart of the magician.   He would never be able of himself to tell in which of them it was, but the girl would stand beside him, and when the right fish passed by, she would nudge him and he was to catch it and rip it up, and the magician would ask him no more questions.   Everything turned out exactly as she had said.   The king paid his debt to the last farthing ; but the young man disguised as the court Fool cut such capers and smashed so many glass windows and doors that the heaps of broken glass were something frightful to contemplate.   So there was nothing for it but that the king, who was of course responsible for the pranks of his Fool, should either answer the magician's questions or die the death.   While they were getting the axe and the block ready in the courtyard, the trembling king was interrogated by the stern magician. " Where is my daughter ? " asked the sorcerer.   Here the

court Fool cut in and said, " She is at the bottom of the sea."
" Would you know her if you saw her?" enquired the
magician. " To be sure I would," answered the Fool. So
the magician caused a whole regiment of girls to defile
before him, one after the other ; but they were mere
phantoms and apparitions. Almost the last of all came the
magician's daughter, and when she passed the young man
she pinched his arm so hard that he almost shrieked with
pain. However, he dissembled his agony and putting his
arm round her waist held her fast. The magician now
played his last trump. " Where is my heart?" said he.
" In a fish," said the Fool. " Would you know the fish if
you saw it?" asked the magician. " To be sure I would,"
answered the Fool. Then all the fishes of the sea swam
past, and when the right one came last of all, the girl
nudged her lover ; he seized the fish, and with one stroke of
his knife slit it from end to end. Out tumbled the magician's
heart ; the young man seized it and cut it in two, and at the
same moment the magician fell dead.[1]

In Iceland they say that once a king's son was out The exter-
hunting in a wood with the courtiers, when the mist came nal soul in
down so thick that his companions lost sight of the prince, stories.
and though they searched the woods till evening they could
not find him. At the news the king was inconsolable, and The king's
taking to his bed caused proclamation to be made that he son in the
who could find and bring back his lost son should have half giantesses
the kingdom. Now an old man and his old wife lived whose
together in a wretched hut, and they had a daughter. She in an egg.
resolved to seek the lost prince and get the promised reward.
So her parents gave her food for the journey and a pair of
new shoes, and off she set. Well, she walked and better
walked for days, and at last she came towards evening to a
cave and going into it she saw two beds. One of them was
covered with a cloth of silver and the other with a cloth of
gold ; and in the bed with the golden coverlet was the king's
son fast asleep. She tried to wake him, but all in vain.
Then she noticed some runes carved on the bedsteads, but
she could not read them. So she went back to the mouth

[1] Svend Grundtvig, *Dänische Volksmärchen*, übersetzt von Willibald Leo
(Leipsic, 1878), pp. 29-45.

of the cave and hid behind the door.   Hardly had she time
to conceal herself when she heard a loud noise and saw two
giantesses, two great hulking louts they were, stride into the
cave.   No sooner were they in than one said to the other,
" Ugh, what a smell of human flesh in our cave ! "   But the
other thought the smell might come from the king's son.
They went up to the bed where he was sleeping, and calling
two swans, which the girl had not perceived in the dim light
of the cave, they said :—

The swans' song.

> " *Sing, sing, my swans,*
> *That the king's son may wake.*"

So the swans sang and the king's son awoke.   The younger
of the two hags offered him food, but he refused it ; then
she asked him, if he would marry her, but he said " No,
certainly not."   Then she shrieked and said to the swans :—

> " *Sing, sing, my swans,*
> *That the king's son may sleep.*"

The swans sang and the king's son fell fast asleep.   Then
the two giantesses lay down in the bed with the silver coverlet
and slept till break of day.   When they woke in the morning, they wakened the prince and offered him food again, but
he again refused it ; and the younger hag again asked him
if he would have her to wife, but he would not hear of it.
So they put him to sleep again to the singing of the swans
and left the cave.   When they were gone a while, the girl
came forth from her hiding-place and waked the king's son
to the song of the swans, and he was glad to see her and to
get the news.   She told him that, when the hag asked him
again to marry her, he must say, " Yes, but you must first
tell me what is written on the beds, and what you do by day."
So when it drew to evening, the girl hid herself again, and
soon the giantesses came, lit a fire in the cave, and cooked at
it the game they had brought with them.   And the younger
hag wakened the king's son and asked him if he would have
something to eat.   This time he said " Yes."   And when he
had finished his supper, the giantess asked him if he would
have her to wife.   " That I will," said he, " but first you must
tell me what the runes mean that are carved on the bed."
She said that they meant :—

> " *Run, run, my little bed,*
> *Run whither I will.*"

He said he was very glad to know it, but she must also tell him what they did all day long out there in the wood.   The hag told him that they hunted beasts and birds, and that between whiles they sat down under an oak and threw their life-egg from one to the other, but they had to be careful, for if the egg were to break, they would both die. The life-egg. The king's son thanked her kindly, but next morning when the giantess asked him to go with them to the wood he said that he would rather stay at home.   So away went the giantesses by themselves, after they had lulled him to sleep to the singing of the swans.   But hardly were their backs turned when out came the girl and wakened the prince and told him to take his spear, and they would pursue the giantesses, and when they were throwing their life-egg to each other he was to hurl his spear at it and smash it to bits. " But if you miss," said she, " it is as much as your life is worth."   So they came to the oak in the wood, and there they heard a loud laugh, and the king's son climbed up the tree, and there under the oak were the two giantesses, and one of them had a golden egg in her hand and threw it to the other.   Just then the king's son hurled his spear and hit the egg so that it burst.   At the same time the two hags fell dead to the ground and the slaver dribbled out of their mouths.[1]   In an Icelandic parallel to the story of Meleager An Icelandic parallel to Meleager. the spae-wives or sibyls come and foretell the high destiny of the infant Gestr as he lies in his cradle.   Two candles were burning beside the child, and the youngest of the spae-wives, conceiving herself slighted, cried out, " I foretell that the child shall live no longer than this candle burns."   Whereupon the chief sibyl put out the candle and gave it to Gestr's

[1] J. C. Poestion, *Isländische Märchen* (Vienna, 1884), No. vii. pp. 49-55.   The same story is told with minor variations by Konrad Maurer in his *Isländische Volkssagen der Gegenwart* (Leipsic, 1860), pp. 277-280. In his version a giant and giantess, brother and sister, have their life in one stone, which they throw backwards and forwards to each other; when the stone is caught and broken by the heroine, the giant and giantess at once expire.   The tale was told to Maurer when he was crossing an arm of the sea in a small boat; and the waves ran so high and broke into the boat so that he could not write the story down at the time but had to trust to his memory in recording it afterwards.

mother to keep, charging her not to light it again until her son should wish to die. Gestr lived three hundred years; then he kindled the candle and expired.[1]

The external soul in Celtic stories. The giant whose soul was in a duck's egg.

The conception of the external soul meets us also in Celtic stories. Thus a tale, told by a blind fiddler in the island of Islay, relates how a giant carried off a king's wife and his two horses and kept them in his den. But the horses attacked the giant and mauled him so that he could hardly crawl. He said to the queen, "If I myself had my soul to keep, those horses would have killed me long ago." "And where, my dear," said she, "is thy soul? By the books I will take care of it." "It is in the Bonnach stone," said he. So on the morrow when the giant went out, the queen set the Bonnach stone in order exceedingly. In the dusk of the evening the giant came back, and he said to the queen, "What made thee set the Bonnach stone in order like that?" "Because thy soul is in it," quoth she. "I perceive," said he, "that if thou didst know where my soul is, thou wouldst give it much respect." "That I would," said she. "It is not there," said he, "my soul is; it is in the threshold." On the morrow she set the threshold in order finely, and when the giant returned, he asked her, "What brought thee to set the threshold in order like that?" "Because thy soul is in it," said she. "I perceive," said he, "that if thou knewest where my soul is, thou wouldst take care of it." "That I would," said she. "It is not there that my soul is," said he. "There is a great flagstone under the threshold. There is a wether under the flag. There is a duck in the wether's belly, and an egg in the belly of the duck, and it is in the egg that my soul is." On the morrow when the giant was gone, they raised the flagstone and out came the wether. They opened the wether and out came the duck. They split the duck, and out came the egg. And the queen took the egg and crushed it in her hands, and at that very moment the giant, who was coming home in the dusk, fell down dead.[2] In another Celtic tale, a sea beast has carried off a king's

[1] W. Mannhardt, *Germanische Mythen* (Berlin, 1858), p. 592; John Jamieson, *Etymological Dictionary of the Scottish Language*, New Edition, revised by J. Longmuir and D. Donaldson (Paisley, 1879–1882), iv. 869, *s.v.* "Yule."

[2] J. F. Campbell, *Popular Tales of the West Highlands*, New Edition (Paisley and London, 1890), i. 7·11.

daughter, and an old smith declares that there is no way of killing the beast but one. " In the island that is in the midst of the loch is Eillid Chaisthion——the white-footed hind, of the slenderest legs, and the swiftest step, and though she should be caught, there would spring a hoodie out of her, and though the hoodie should be caught, there would spring a trout out of her, but there is an egg in the mouth of the trout, and the soul of the beast is in the egg, and if the egg breaks, the beast is dead." As usual the egg is broken and the beast dies.[1]

In these Celtic tales the helpful animals reappear and assist the hero in achieving the adventure, though for the sake of brevity I have omitted to describe the parts they play in the plot. They figure also in an Argyleshire story, which seems however to be of Irish origin ; for the Cruachan of which we hear in it is not the rugged and lofty mountain Ben Cruachan which towers above the beautiful Loch Awe, but Roscommon Cruachan near Belanagare, the ancient palace of the kings of Connaught, long famous in Irish tradition.[2] The story relates how a big giant, King of Sorcha, stole away the wife and the shaggy dun filly of the herdsman or king of Cruachan. So the herdsman baked a bannock to take with him by the way, and set off in quest of his wife and the filly. He went for a long, long time, till at last his soles were blackened and his cheeks were sunken, the yellow-headed birds were going to rest at the roots of the bushes and the tops of the thickets, and the dark clouds of night were coming and the clouds of day were departing ; and he saw a house far from him, but though it was far from him he did not take long to reach it. He went in, and sat in the upper end of the house, but there was no one within ; and the fire was newly kindled, the house newly swept, and the bed newly made ; and who came in but the hawk of Glencuaich, and she said to him, " Are you here, young son of Cruachan?" " I am," said he. The hawk said to him, " Do you know who was here last night ? " " I do not," said he. " There were here,"

The herdsman of Cruachan and the helpful animals.

---

[1] J. F. Campbell, *Popular Tales of the West Highlands,* New Edition, i. 80 *sqq.*

[2] Compare *Taboo and the Perils of the Soul,* p. 12.

said she, " the big giant, King of Sorcha, your wife, and the shaggy dun filly; and the giant was threatening terribly that if he could get hold of you he would take the head off you." " I well believe it," said he. Then she gave him food and drink, and sent him to bed. She rose in the morning, made breakfast for him, and baked a bannock for him to take with him on his journey. And he went away and travelled all day, and in the evening he came to another house and went in, and was entertained by the green-headed duck, who told him that the giant had rested there the night before with the wife and shaggy dun filly of the herdsman of Cruachan. And next day the herdsman journeyed again, and at evening he came to another house and went in and was entertained by the fox of the scrubwood, who told him just what the hawk of Glencuaich and the green-headed duck had told him before. Next day the same thing happened, only it was the brown otter of the burn that entertained him at evening in a house where the fire was newly kindled, the floor newly swept, and the bed newly made. And next morning when he awoke, the first thing he saw was the hawk of Glencuaich, the green-headed duck, the fox of the scrubwood, and the brown otter of the burn all dancing together on the floor. They made breakfast for him, and partook of it all together, and said to him, " Should you be at any time in straits, think of us, and we will help you." Well, that very evening he came to the cave where the giant lived, and who was there before him but his own wife? She gave him food and hid him under clothes at the upper end of the cave. And when the giant came home he sniffed about and said, " The smell of a stranger is in the cave." But she said no, it was only a little bird she had roasted. " And I wish you would tell me," said she, " where you keep your life, that I might take good care of it." " It is in a grey stone over there," said he. So next day when he went away, she took the grey stone and dressed it well, and placed it in the upper end of the cave. When the giant came home in the evening he said to her, " What is it that you have dressed there?" " Your own life," said she, " and we must be careful of it." " I perceive that you are very fond of me, but it is not

The simple giant and the wily woman.

there," said he. " Where is it ? " said she. " It is in a grey sheep on yonder hillside," said he. On the morrow, when he went away, she got the grey sheep, dressed it well, and placed it in the upper end of the cave. When he came home in the evening he said, " What is it that you have dressed there ? " " Your own life, my love," said she. " It is not there as yet," said he. " Well ! " said she, " you are putting me to great trouble taking care of it, and you have not told me the truth these two times." He then said, " I think that I may tell it to you now. My life is below the feet of the big horse in the stable. There is a place down there in which there is a small lake. Over the lake are seven grey hides, and over the hides are seven sods from the heath, and under all these are seven oak planks. There is a trout in the lake, and a duck in the belly of the trout, an egg in the belly of the duck, and a thorn of blackthorn inside of the egg, and till that thorn is chewed small I cannot be killed. Whenever the seven grey hides, the seven sods from the heath, and the seven oak planks are touched I shall feel it wherever I shall be. I have an axe above the door, and unless all these are cut through with one blow of it the lake will not be reached ; and when it will be reached I shall feel it." Next day, when the giant had gone out hunting on the hill, the herdsman of Cruachan contrived, with the help of the friendly animals—the hawk, the duck, the fox, and the otter—to get possession of the fateful thorn and to chew it before the giant could reach him ; and no sooner had he done so than the giant dropped stark and stiff, a corpse.[1]

Another Argyleshire story relates how a certain giant, who lived in the Black Corrie of Ben Breck, carried off three daughters of a king, one after the other, at intervals of seven years. The bereaved monarch sent champions to rescue his lost daughters, but though they surprised the giant in his sleep and cut off his head, it was all to no purpose ; for as fast as they cut it off he put it on again and made after them as if nothing had happened. So the champions fled away before him as fast as they could lay legs to the ground, and the more agile of them escaped, but the shorter-winded he

Argyle-shire story of the Bare-Stripping Hangman whose soul was in a duck's egg.

[1] Rev. D. MacInnes, *Folk and Hero Tales* (London, 1890), pp. 103-121.

caught, bared them to the skin, and hanged them on hooks against the turrets of his castle. So he went by the name of the Bare-Stripping Hangman. Now this amiable man had announced his intention of coming to fetch away the fourth and last of the king's daughters, when another seven years should be up. The time was drawing near, and the king, with the natural instincts of a father, was in great tribulation, when as good luck would have it a son of the king of Ireland, by name Alastir, arrived in the king's castle and undertook to find out where the Bare-Stripping Hangman had hidden his soul. To cut a long story short, the artful Hangman had hidden his soul in an egg, which was in the belly of a duck, which was in the belly of a salmon, which was in the belly of a swift-footed hind of the cliffs. The prince wormed the secret from a little old man, and by the help of a dog, a brown otter, and a falcon he contrived to extract the egg from its various envelopes and crushed it to bits between his hands and knees. So when he came to the giant's castle he found the Bare-Stripping Hangman lying dead on the floor.[1]

Highland story of Headless Hugh

Another Highland story sets forth how Hugh, prince of Lochlin, was long held captive by a giant who lived in a cave overlooking the Sound of Mull. At last, after he had spent many years of captivity in that dismal cave, it came to pass that one night the giant and his wife had a great dispute, and Hugh overheard their talk, and learned that the giant's soul was in a precious gem which he always wore on his forehead. So the prince watched his opportunity, seized the gem, and having no means of escape or concealment, hastily swallowed it. Like lightning from the clouds, the giant's sword flashed from its scabbard and flew between Hugh's head and his body to intercept the gem before it could descend into the prince's stomach. But it was too late; and the giant fell down, sword in hand, and expired without a gasp. Hugh had now lost his head, it is true, but having the giant's soul in his body he felt none the worse for the accident. So he buckled the giant's sword at his side, mounted the grey filly, swifter than the east wind,

---

[1] Rev. J. Macdougall, *Folk and Hero Tales* (London, 1891), pp. 76 *sqq.*   (*Waifs and Strays of Celtic Tradition,* No. iii.).

that never had a bridle, and rode home.   But the want of his head made a painful impression on his friends ; indeed they maintained that he was a ghost and shut the door in his face, so now he wanders for ever in shades of darkness, riding the grey filly fleeter than the wind.   On stormy nights, when the wind howls about the gables and among the trees, you may see him galloping along the shore of the sea " between wave and sand."   Many a naughty little boy, who would not go quietly to bed, has been carried off by Headless Hugh on his grey filly and never seen again.[1]

In Sutherlandshire at the present day there is a sept of Mackays known as " the descendants of the seal," who claim to be sprung from a mermaid, and the story they tell in explanation of their claim involves the notion of the external soul.   They say that the laird of Borgie used to go down to the rocks under his castle to bathe.   One day he saw a mermaid close in shore, combing her hair and swimming about, as if she were anxious to land.   After watching her for a time, he noticed her cowl on the rocks beside him, and knowing that she could not go to sea without it, he carried the cowl up to the castle in the hope that she would follow him.   She did so, but he refused to give up the cowl and detained the sea-maiden herself and made her his wife. To this she consented with great reluctance, and told him that her life was bound up with the cowl, and that if it rotted or was destroyed she would instantly die.   So the cowl was placed for safety in the middle of a great hay-stack, and there it lay for years.   One unhappy day, when the laird was from home, the servants were working among the hay and found the cowl.   Not knowing what it was, they shewed it to the lady of the house.   The sight revived memories of her old life in the depths of the sea, so she took the cowl, and leaving her child in its cot, plunged into the sea and never

The Mackays the descendants of the seal.

---

[1] Rev. James Macdonald, *Religion and Myth* (London, 1893), pp. 187 *sq.* The writer tells us that in his youth a certain old Betty Miles used to terrify him with this tale.   For the tradition of Headless Hugh, who seems to have been the only son of Hector, first chief of Lochbuy, in the fourteenth century, see J. G. Campbell, *Witchcraft and Second Sight in the Highlands and Islands of Scotland* (Glasgow, 1902), pp. 111 *sqq.*   India also has its stories of headless horsemen.   See W. Crooke, *Popular Religion and Folk-lore of Northern India* (London, 1896), i. 256 *sqq.*

came home to Borgie any more.   Only sometimes she would swim close in shore to see her boy, and then she wept because he was not of her own kind that she might take him to sea with her.   The boy grew to be a man, and his descendants are famous swimmers.   They cannot drown, and to this day they are known in the neighbourhood as *Sliochd an roin*, that is, "the descendants of the seal." [1]

The external soul in Irish and Breton stories. The giant and the egg. In an Irish story we read how a giant kept a beautiful damsel a prisoner in his castle on the top of a hill, which was white with the bones of the champions who had tried in vain to rescue the fair captive.   At last the hero, after hewing and slashing at the giant all to no purpose, discovered that the only way to kill him was to rub a mole on the giant's right breast with a certain egg, which was in a duck, which was in a chest, which lay locked and bound at the bottom of the sea.   With the help of some obliging salmon, rams, and eagles, the hero as usual made himself master of the precious egg and slew the giant by merely striking it against the mole on his right breast. [2]   Similarly in a Breton story there figures a giant whom neither fire nor water nor steel can harm.   He tells his seventh wife, whom he has just married after murdering all her predecessors, " I am immortal, and no one can hurt me unless he crushes on my breast an egg, which is in a pigeon, which is in the belly of a hare ; this hare is in the belly of a wolf, and this wolf is in the belly of my brother, who dwells a thousand

The helpful animals. leagues from here.   So I am quite easy on that score."   A soldier, the hero of the tale, had been of service to an ant, a wolf, and a sea-bird, who in return bestowed on him the power of turning himself into an ant, a wolf, or a sea-bird at will.   By means of this magical power the soldier contrived to obtain the egg and crush it on the breast of the

Body-without-Soul. giant, who immediately expired. [3]   Another Breton story tells of a giant who was called Body-without-Soul because

---

[1] Rev. James Macdonald, *Religion and Myth*, pp. 191 *sq.*, from information furnished by the Rev. A. Mackay. In North Uist there is a sept known as "the MacCodrums of the seals," and a precisely similar legend is told to explain their descent from seals. See J. G. Campbell, *Superstitions of the* *Highlands and Islands of Scotland* (Glasgow, 1900), p. 284.

[2] Jeremiah Curtin, *Myths and Folk-tales of Ireland* (London, N.D.), pp. 71 *sqq.*

[3] P. Sébillot, *Contes populaires de la Haute-Bretagne* (Paris, 1885), pp. 63 *sqq.*

his life did not reside in his body.   He himself dwelt in
a beautiful castle which hung between heaven and earth,
suspended by four golden chains ; but his life was in an egg,
and the egg was in a dove, and the dove was in a hare, and
the hare was in a wolf, and the wolf was in an iron chest at
the bottom of the sea.   In his castle in the air he kept
prisoner a beauteous princess whom he had swooped down
upon and carried off in a magic chariot.   But her lover *The
turned himself into an ant and so climbed up one of the* *helpful
animals.*
golden chains into the enchanted castle, for he had done a
kindness to the king and queen of ants, and they rewarded
him by transforming him into an ant in his time of need.
When he had learned from the captive princess the secret of
the giant's life, he procured the chest from the bottom of the
sea by the help of the king of fishes, whom he had also
obliged ; and opening the chest he killed first the wolf, then
the hare, and then the dove, and at the death of each animal
the giant grew weaker and weaker as if he had lost a limb.
In the stomach of the dove the hero found the egg on which
the giant's life depended, and when he came with it to the
castle he found Body-without-Soul stretched on his bed at
the point of death.   So he dashed the egg against the
giant's forehead, the egg broke, and the giant straightway
expired.[1]   In another Breton tale the life of a giant resides *The giant
whose life
was in a
box-tree.*
in an old box-tree which grows in his castle garden ; and to
kill him it is necessary to sever the tap-root of the tree at a
single blow of an axe without injuring any of the lesser
roots.   This task the hero, as usual, successfully accomplishes,
and at the same moment the giant drops dead.[2]

   The notion of an external soul has now been traced in
folk-tales told by Aryan peoples from India to Brittany and

---

[1] F. M. Luzel, *Contes populaires de
Basse-Bretagne* (Paris, 1887), i. 435-
449.   Compare *id.*, *Veillées Bretonnes*
(Morlaix, 1879), pp. 133 *sq.*   For two
other French stories of the same type,
taken down in Lorraine, see E. Cosquin,
Contes populaires de Lorraine (Paris,
N.D.), Nos. 15 and 50 (vol. i. pp. 166
sqq., vol. ii. pp. 128 *sqq.*).   In both
of them there figures a miraculous beast
which can only be slain by breaking a
certain egg against its head ; but we are
not told that the life of the beast was
in the egg.   In both of them also the
hero receives from three animals, whose
dispute about the carcase of a dead
beast he has settled, the power of
changing himself into animals of the
same sort.   See the remarks and com-
parisons of the learned editor, Monsieur
E. Cosquin, *op. cit.* i. 170 *sqq.*

[2] F. M. Luzel, *Veillées Bretonnes*
pp. 127 *sqq.*

The exter-
nal soul
in stories
of non-
Aryan
peoples.
The ancient
Egyptian
story of
the Two
Brothers.
the Hebrides. We have still to shew that the same idea occurs commonly in the popular stories of peoples who do not belong to the Aryan stock. In the first place it appears in the ancient Egyptian story of "The Two Brothers." This story was written down in the reign of Rameses II., about 1300 B.C. It is therefore older than our present redaction of Homer, and far older than the Bible. The outline of the story, so far as it concerns us here, is as follows. Once upon a time there were two brethren; the name of the elder was Anpu and the name of the younger was Bata. Now Anpu had a house and a wife, and his younger brother dwelt with him as his servant. It was Anpu who made the garments, and every morning when it grew light he drove the kine afield. As he walked behind them they used to say to him, "The grass is good in such and such a place," and he heard what they said and led them to the good pasture that they desired. So his kine grew very sleek and multiplied greatly. One day when the two brothers were at work in the field the elder brother said to the younger, "Run and fetch seed from the village." So the younger brother ran and said to the wife of his elder brother, "Give me seed that I may run to the field, for my brother sent me saying, Tarry not." She said, "Go to the barn and take as much as thou wouldst." He went and filled a jar full of wheat and barley, and came forth bearing it on his shoulders. When the woman saw him her heart went out to him, and she laid hold of him and said, "Come, let us rest an hour together." But he said, "Thou art to me as a mother, and my brother is to me as a father." So he would not hearken to her, but took the load on his back and went away to the field. In the evening, when the elder brother was returning from the field, his wife feared for what she had said. So she took soot and made herself as one who had been beaten. And when her husband came home, she said, "When thy younger brother came to fetch seed, he said to me, Come, let us rest an hour together. But I would not, and he beat me." Then the elder brother became like a panther of the south; he sharpened his knife and stood behind the door of the cow-house. And when the sun set and the younger brother came laden with all the herbs of the field, as was his wont

every day, the cow that walked in front of the herd said to him, " Behold, thine elder brother stands with a knife to kill thee. Flee before him."   When he heard what the cow said, he looked under the door of the cow-house and saw the feet of his elder brother standing behind the door, his knife in his hand.   So he fled and his brother pursued him with the knife.   But the younger brother cried for help to the Sun, and the Sun heard him and caused a great water to spring up between him and his elder brother, and the water was full of crocodiles.   The two brothers stood, the one on the one side of the water and the other on the other, and the younger brother told the elder brother all that had befallen.   So the elder brother repented him of what he had done and he lifted up his voice and wept.   But he could not come at the farther bank by reason of the crocodiles.   His younger brother called to him and said, " Go home and tend the cattle thyself.   For I will dwell no more in the place where thou art.   I will go to the Valley of the Acacia.   But this is what thou shalt do for me. Thou shalt come and care for me, if evil befalls me, for I will enchant my heart and place it on the top of the flower of the Acacia ; and if they cut the Acacia and my heart falls to the ground, thou shalt come and seek it, and when thou hast found it thou shalt lay it in a vessel of fresh water.   Then I shalt come to life again.   But this is the sign that evil has befallen me ; the pot of beer in thine hand shall bubble."   So he went away to the Valley of the Acacia, but his brother returned home with dust on his head and slew his wife and cast her to the dogs.

The heart in the flower of the Acacia.

For many days afterwards the younger brother dwelt alone in the Valley of the Acacia.   By day he hunted the beasts of the field, but at evening he came and laid him down under the Acacia, on the top of whose flower was his heart.   And many days after that he built himself a house in the Valley of the Acacia.   But the gods were grieved for him ; and the Sun said to Khnumu, " Make a wife for Bata, that he may not dwell alone."   So Khnumu made him a woman to dwell with him, who was perfect in her limbs more than any woman on earth, for all the gods were in her.   So she dwelt with him.   But one day a lock of

Bata in the Valley of the Acacia.

her hair fell into the river and floated down to the land of Egypt, to the house of Pharaoh's washerwomen. The fragrance of the lock perfumed Pharaoh's raiment, and the washerwomen were blamed, for it was said, " An odour of perfume in the garments of Pharaoh ! " So the heart of Pharaoh's chief washerman was weary of the complaints that were made every day, and he went to the wharf, and there in the water he spied the lock of hair. He sent one down into the river to fetch it, and, because it smelt sweetly, he took it to Pharaoh. Then Pharaoh's magicians were sent for and they said, " This lock of hair belongs to a daughter of the Sun, who has in her the essence of all the gods. Let messengers go forth to all foreign lands to seek her." So the woman was brought from the Valley of the Acacia with chariots and archers and much people, and all the land of Egypt rejoiced at her coming, and Pharaoh loved her. But when they asked her of her husband, she said to Pharaoh, " Let them cut down the Acacia and let them destroy it." So men were sent with tools to cut down the

How Bata died and was brought to life again. Acacia. They came to it and cut the flower upon which was the heart of Bata ; and he fell down dead in that evil hour. But the next day, when the earth grew light and the elder brother of Bata was entered into his house and had sat down, they brought him a pot of beer and it bubbled, and they gave him a jug of wine and it grew turbid. Then he took his staff and his sandals and hied him to the Valley of the Acacia, and there he found his younger brother lying dead in his house. So he sought for the heart of his brother under the Acacia. For three years he sought in vain, but in the fourth year he found it in the berry of the Acacia. So he threw the heart into a cup of fresh water. And when it was night and the heart had sucked in much water, Bata shook in all his limbs and revived. Then he drank the cup of water in which his heart was, and his heart went into its place, and he lived as before.[1]

[1] (Sir) Gaston Maspero, *Contes populaires de l'Égypte ancienne*[3] (Paris, N.D.), pp. 1 *sqq.* ; W. M. Flinders Petrie, *Egyptian Tales*, Second Series (London, 1895), pp. 36 *sqq.*; Alfred Wiedemann, *Altägyptische Sagen und Märchen* (Leipsic, 1906), pp. 58-77. Compare W. Mannhardt, " Das älteste Märchen," *Zeitschrift für deutsche Mythologie und Sittenkunde,*

In the *Arabian Nights* we read how Seyf el-Mulook, The external soul in
Arabian
stories.
The jinnee
and the
sparrow. after wandering for four months over mountains and hills and deserts, came to a lofty palace in which he found the lovely daughter of the King of India sitting alone on a golden couch in a hall spread with silken carpets. She tells him that she is held captive by a jinnee, who had swooped down on her and carried her off while she was disporting herself with her female slaves in a tank in the great garden of her father the king. Seyf el-Mulook then offers to smite the jinnee with the sword and slay him. "But," she replied, "thou canst not slay him unless thou kill his soul." "And in what place," said he, "is his soul?" She answered, "I asked him respecting it many times; but he would not confess to me its place. It happened, however, that I urged him, one day, and he was enraged against me, and said to me, 'How often wilt thou ask me respecting my soul? What is the reason of thy question respecting my soul?' So I answered him, 'O Hátim, there remaineth to me no one but thee, excepting God; and I, as long as I live, would not cease to hold thy soul in my embrace; and if I do not take care of thy soul, and put it in the midst of my eye, how can I live after thee? If I knew thy soul, I would take care of it as of my right eye.' And thereupon he said to me, 'When I was born, the astrologers declared that the destruction of my soul would be effected by the hand of one of the sons of the human kings. I therefore took my soul, and put it into the crop of a sparrow, and I imprisoned the sparrow in a little box, and put this into another small box, and this I put within seven other small boxes, and I put these within seven chests, and the chests I put into a coffer of marble within the verge of this circumambient ocean; for this part is remote from the countries of mankind, and none of mankind can gain access to it.'" But Seyf el-Mulook got possession of the sparrow and strangled it, and the jinnee fell upon the ground a heap of black ashes.[1] In a modern

---

iv. (1859) pp. 232-259. The manuscript of the story, which is now in the
British Museum, belonged to an Egyptian prince, who was afterwards King
Seti II. and reigned about the year
1300 B.C. It is beautifully written

and in almost perfect condition.
    [1] *The Thousand and One Nights,*
commonly called, in England, *The
Arabian Nights' Entertainments,* translated by E. W. Lane (London, 1839–
1841), iii. 339-345.

The ogress and the bottle.

Arabian tale a king marries an ogress, who puts out the eyes of the king's forty wives.   One of the blinded queens gives birth to a son whom she names Mohammed the Prudent. But the ogress queen hated him and compassed his death. So she sent him on an errand to the house of her kinsfolk the ogres.   In the house of the ogres he saw some things hanging from the roof, and on asking a female slave what they were, she said, "That is the bottle which contains the life of my lady the queen, and the other bottle beside it contains the eyes of the queens whom my mistress blinded." A little afterwards he spied a beetle and rose to kill it. "Don't kill it," cried the slave, "for that is my life."   But Mohammed the Prudent watched the beetle till it entered a chink in the wall; and when the female slave had fallen asleep, he killed the beetle in its hole, and so the slave died. Then Mohammed took down the two bottles and carried them home to his father's palace.   There he presented himself before the ogress queen and said, "See, I have your life in my hand, but I will not kill you till you have replaced the eyes which you took from the forty queens."   The ogress did as she was bid, and then Mohammed the Prudent said, "There, take your life."   But the bottle slipped from his hand and fell, the life of the ogress escaped from it, and she died.[1]

---

[1] G. Spitta - Bey, *Contes arabes modernes* (Leyden and Paris, 1883), No. 2, pp. 12 *sqq.*   The story in its main outlines is identical with the Cashmeer story of "The Ogress Queen" (J. H. Knowles, *Folk-tales of Kashmir*, pp. 42 *sqq.*) and the Bengalee story of "The Boy whom Seven Mothers Suckled" (Lal Behari Day, *Folk-tales of Bengal*, pp. 117 *sqq.*; *Indian Antiquary*, i. 170 *sqq.*).   In another Arabian story the life of a witch is bound up with a phial; when it is broken, she dies (W. A. Clouston, *A Group of Eastern Romances and Stories*, Privately printed, 1889, p. 30).   A similar incident occurs in a Cashmeer story (J. H. Knowles, *op. cit.* p. 73).   In the Arabian story mentioned in the text, the hero, by a genuine touch of local colour, is made to drink the milk of an ogress's breasts and hence is regarded by her as her son.   The same incident occurs in Kabyle and Berber tales. See J. Rivière, *Contes populaires de la Kabylie du Djurdjura* (Paris, 1882), p. 239; R. Basset, *Nouveaux Contes Berbères* (Paris, 1897), p. 128, with the editor's note, pp. 339 *sqq.*   In a Mongolian story a king refuses to kill a lad because he has unwittingly partaken of a cake kneaded with the milk of the lad's mother (B. Jülg, *Mongolische Märchen - Sammlung, die neun Märchen des Siddhi-Kür*, Innsbruck, 1868, p. 183).   Compare W. Robertson Smith, *Kinship and Marriage in Early Arabia*, New Edition (London, 1903), p. 176; and for the same mode of creating kinship among other races, see A. d'Abbadie, *Douze ans dans la Haute Ethiopie* (Paris, 1868), pp. 272 *sq.*; Tausch, "Notices of the Circassians," *Journal of the Royal Asiatic Society*,

A Basque story, which closely resembles some of the
stories told among Aryan peoples, relates how a monster—
a Body-without-Soul—detains a princess in captivity, and is
questioned by her as to how he might be slain. With some
reluctance he tells her, "You must kill a terrible wolf which
is in the forest, and inside him is a fox, in the fox is a
pigeon ; this pigeon has an egg in his head, and whoever
should strike me on the forehead with this egg would kill
me." The hero of the story, by name Malbrouk, has learned,
in the usual way, the art of turning himself at will into
a wolf, an ant, a hawk, or a dog, and on the strength of
this accomplishment he kills the animals, one after the
other, and extracts the precious egg from the pigeon's
head. When the wolf is killed, the monster feels it and says
despondently, "I do not know if anything is going to happen
to me. I am much afraid of it." When the fox and the
pigeon have been killed, he cries that it is all over with him,
that they have taken the egg out of the pigeon, and that he
knows not what is to become of him. Finally the princess
strikes the monster on the forehead with the egg, and he falls
a corpse.[1] In a Kabyle story an ogre declares that his fate
is far away in an egg, which is in a pigeon, which is in a
camel, which is in the sea. The hero procures the egg and
crushes it between his hands, and the ogre dies.[2] In a
Magyar folk-tale, an old witch detains a young prince called
Ambrose in the bowels of the earth. At last she confided

---

i. (1834) p. 104 ; J. Biddulph, *Tribes of the Hindoo Koosh* (London, 1880), pp. 77, 83 (compare G. W. Leitner, *Languages and Races of Dardistan*, Lahore, 1878, p. 34) ; Denzil C. J. Ibbetson, *Settlement Report of the Panipat, Tahsil, and Karnal Parganah of the Karnal District* (Allahabad, 1883), p. 101 ; J. Moura, *Le Royaume du Cambodge* (Paris, 1883), i. 427; F. S. Krauss, *Sitte und Brauch der Südslaven* (Vienna, 1885), p. 14 ; J. H. Weeks, *Among Congo Cannibals* (London, 1913), p. 132. When the Masai of East Africa make peace with an enemy, each tribe brings a cow with a calf and a woman with a baby. The two cows are exchanged, and the enemy's child

is suckled at the breast of the Masai woman, and the Masai baby is suckled at the breast of the woman belonging to the enemy. See A. C. Hollis, *The Masai* (Oxford, 1905), pp. 321 *sq*.

[1] W. Webster, *Basque Legends* (London, 1877), pp. 80 *sqq*. ; J. Vinson, *Le folk-lore du pays Basque* (Paris, 1883), pp. 84 *sqq*. As so often in tales of this type, the hero is said to have received his wonderful powers of metamorphosis from animals whom he found quarrelling about their shares in a dead beast.

[2] J. Rivière, *Contes populaires de la Kabylie du Djurdjura* (Paris, 1882), p. 191.

to him that she kept a wild boar in a silken meadow, and if it were killed, they would find a hare inside, and inside the hare a pigeon, and inside the pigeon a small box, and inside the box one black and one shining beetle : the shining beetle held her life, and the black one held her power ; if these two beetles died, then her life would come to an end also. When the old hag went out, Ambrose killed the wild boar, and took out the hare ; from the hare he took the pigeon, from the pigeon the box, and from the box the two beetles ; he killed the black beetle, but kept the shining one alive. So the witch's power left her immediately, and when she came home, she had to take to her bed. Having learned from her how to escape from his prison to the upper air, Ambrose killed the shining beetle, and the old hag's spirit left her at once.[1] In another Hungarian story the safety of the Dwarf-king resides in a golden cockchafer, inside a golden cock, inside a golden sheep, inside a golden stag, in the ninety-ninth island. The hero overcomes all these golden animals and so recovers his bride, whom the Dwarf-king had carried off.[2]

The external soul in a Lapp story. The giant whose life was in a hen's egg. A Lapp story tells of a giant who slew a man and took away his wife. When the man's son grew up, he tried to rescue his mother and kill the giant, but fire and sword were powerless to harm the monster ; it seemed as if he had no life in his body. " Dear mother," at last enquired the son, " don't you know where the giant has hidden away his life ? " The mother did not know, but promised to ask. So one day, when the giant chanced to be in a good humour, she asked him where he kept his life. He said to her, " Out yonder on a burning sea is an island, in the island is a barrel, in the barrel is a sheep, in the sheep is a hen, in the hen is an egg, and in the egg is my life." When the woman's son heard this, he hired a bear, a wolf, a hawk, and a diver-bird and set off in a boat to sail to the island in the burning sea. He sat with the hawk and the diver-bird under an iron tent in the middle of the boat, and he set the bear and the wolf to row. That is why to this day the bear's hair is dark brown and the wolf has dark-brown spots ; for as they sat at the

---

[1] W. H. Jones and L. L. Kropf, *The Folk-tales of the Magyar* (London, 1889), pp. 205 *sq.*

[2] R. H. Busk, *The Folk-lore of Rome* (London, 1874), p. 168.

oars without any screen they were naturally scorched by the tossing tongues of flame on the burning sea. However, they made their way over the fiery billows to the island, and there they found the barrel. In a trice the bear had knocked the bottom out of it with his claws, and forth sprang a sheep. But the wolf soon pulled the sheep down and rent it in pieces. From out the sheep flew a hen, but the hawk stooped on it and tore it with his talons. In the hen was an egg, which dropped into the sea and sank; but the diver-bird dived after it. Twice he dived after it in vain and came up to the surface gasping and spluttering; but the third time he brought up the egg and handed it to the young man. Great was the young man's joy. At once he kindled a great bonfire on the shore, threw the egg into it, and rowed away back across the sea. On landing he went away straight to the giant's abode, and found the monster burning, just as he had left the egg burning on the island. "Fool that I was," lamented the dying giant, "to betray my life to a wicked old woman," and with that he snatched at an iron tube through which in happier days he had been wont to suck the blood of his human victims. But the woman was too subtle for him, for she had taken the precaution of inserting one end of the tube in the glowing embers of the hearth; and so, when the giant sucked hard at the other end, he imbibed only fire and ashes. Thus he burned inside as well as outside, and when the fire went out the giant's life went out with it.[1]

The helpful animals.

A Samoyed story tells how seven warlocks killed a certain man's mother and carried off his sister, whom they kept to serve them. Every night when they came home the seven warlocks used to take out their hearts and place them in a dish which the woman hung on the tent-poles. But the wife of the man whom they had wronged stole the hearts of the warlocks while they slept, and took them to her husband. By break of day he went with the hearts to the warlocks, and found them at the point of death. They all begged for their hearts; but he threw six of their hearts to the ground, and six of the warlocks died. The seventh and eldest war-

The external soul in Samoyed and Kalmuck stories.

[1] F. Liebrecht, "Lappländische Märchen," *Germania*, N.R., iii. (1870) pp. 174 *sq.*; F. C. Poestion, *Lapp-* *ländische Märchen* (Vienna, 1886), No. 20, pp. 81 *sqq.*

lock begged hard for his heart and the man said, "You killed my mother. Make her alive again, and I will give you back your heart." The warlock said to his wife, "Go to the place where the dead woman lies. You will find a bag there. Bring it to me. The woman's spirit is in the bag." So his wife brought the bag; and the warlock said to the man, "Go to your dead mother, shake the bag and let the spirit breathe over her bones; so she will come to life again." The man did as he was bid, and his mother was restored to life. Then he hurled the seventh heart to the ground, and the seventh warlock died.[1] In a Kalmuck tale we read how a certain khan challenged a wise man to shew his skill by stealing a precious stone on which the khan's life depended. The sage contrived to purloin the talisman while the khan and his guards slept; but not content with this he gave a further proof of his dexterity by bonneting the slumbering potentate with a bladder. This was too much for the khan. Next morning he informed the sage that he could overlook everything else, but that the indignity of being bonneted with a bladder was more than he could stand; and he ordered his facetious friend to instant execution. Pained at this exhibition of royal ingratitude, the sage dashed to the ground the talisman which he still held in his hand; and at the same instant blood flowed from the nostrils of the khan, and he gave up the ghost.[2]

The external soul in Tartar poems.

In a Tartar poem two heroes named Ak Molot and Bulat engage in mortal combat. Ak Molot pierces his foe through and through with an arrow, grapples with him, and dashes him to the ground, but all in vain, Bulat could not die. At last when the combat has lasted three years, a friend of Ak Molot sees a golden casket hanging by a white thread from the sky, and bethinks him that perhaps this casket contains Bulat's soul. So he shot through the white thread with an arrow, and down fell the casket. He opened it, and in the casket sat ten white birds, and one of the birds was Bulat's soul. Bulat wept when he saw that his soul was found in the casket. But one after the other the birds were

---

[1] A. Castren, *Ethnologische Vorlesungen über die altaischen Völker* (St. Petersburg, 1857), pp. 173 *sqq.*

[2] B. Jülg, *Kalmückische Märchen* (Leipsic, 1866), No. 12, pp. 58 *sqq.*

killed, and then Ak Molot easily slew his foe.[1] In another Tartar poem, two brothers going to fight two other brothers take out their souls and hide them in the form of a white herb with six stalks in a deep pit. But one of their foes sees them doing so and digs up their souls, which he puts into a golden ram's horn, and then sticks the ram's horn in his quiver. The two warriors whose souls have thus been stolen know that they have no chance of victory, and accordingly make peace with their enemies.[2] In another Tartar poem a terrible demon sets all the gods and heroes at defiance. At last a valiant youth fights the demon, binds him hand and foot, and slices him with his sword. But still the demon is not slain. So the youth asked him, "Tell me, where is your soul hidden? For if your soul had been hidden in your body, you must have been dead long ago." The demon replied, "On the saddle of my horse is a bag. In the bag is a serpent with twelve heads. In the serpent is my soul. When you have killed the serpent, you have killed me also." So the youth took the saddle-bag from the horse and killed the twelve-headed serpent, whereupon the demon expired.[3] In another Tartar poem a hero called Kök Chan deposits with a maiden a golden ring, in which is half his strength. Afterwards when Kök Chan is wrestling long with a hero and cannot kill him, a woman drops into his mouth the ring which contains half his strength. Thus inspired with fresh force he slays his enemy.[4]

In a Mongolian story the hero Joro gets the better of his enemy the lama Tschoridong in the following way. The lama, who is an enchanter, sends out his soul in the form of a wasp to sting Joro's eyes. But Joro catches the wasp in his hand, and by alternately shutting and opening his hand

The external soul in a Mongolian story and Tartar poems.

---

[1] Anton Schiefner, *Heldensagen der Minussinschen Tataren* (St. Petersburg, 1859), pp. 172-176.

[2] A. Schiefner, *op. cit.* pp. 108-112.

[3] A. Schiefner, *op. cit.* pp. 360-364; A. Castren, *Vorlesungen über die finnische Mythologie* (St. Petersburg, 1857), pp. 186 *sq.*

[4] A. Schiefner, *op. cit.* pp. 189-193. In another Tartar poem (Schiefner, *op. cit.* pp. 390 *sq.*) a boy's soul is shut up by his enemies in a box. While the soul is in the box, the boy is dead; when it is taken out, he is restored to life. In the same poem (p. 384) the soul of a horse is kept shut up in a box, because it is feared the owner of the horse will become the greatest hero on earth. But these cases are, to some extent, the converse of those in the text.

he causes the lama alternately to lose and recover consciousness.[1]   In a Tartar poem two youths cut open the body of an old witch and tear out her bowels, but all to no purpose, she still lives.   On being asked where her soul is, she answers that it is in the middle of her shoe-sole in the form of a seven-headed speckled snake.   So one of the youths slices her shoe-sole with his sword, takes out the speckled snake, and cuts off its seven heads.   Then the witch dies.[2] Another Tartar poem describes how the hero Kartaga grappled with the Swan - woman.   Long they wrestled. Moons waxed and waned and still they wrestled; years came and went, and still the struggle went on.   But the piebald horse and the black horse knew that the Swan-woman's soul was not in her.   Under the black earth flow nine seas ; where the seas meet and form one, the sea comes to the surface of the earth.   At the mouth of the nine seas rises a rock of copper ; it rises to the surface of the ground, it rises up between heaven and earth, this rock of copper. At the foot of the copper rock is a black chest, in the black chest is a golden casket, and in the golden casket is the soul of the Swan-woman.   Seven little birds are the soul of the Swan-woman ; if the birds are killed the Swan-woman will die straightway.   So the horses ran to the foot of the copper rock, opened the black chest, and brought back the golden casket.   Then the piebald horse turned himself into a bald-headed man, opened the golden casket, and cut off the heads of the seven birds.   So the Swan-woman died.[3]   In a Tartar story a chief called Tash Kan is asked where his soul is. He answers that there are seven great poplars, and under the poplars a golden well ; seven *Maralen* (?) come to drink the water of the well, and the belly of one of them trails on the ground ; in this *Maral* is a golden box, in the golden box is a silver box, in the silver box are seven quails, the head of one of the quails is golden and its tail silver ; that quail is Tash Kan's soul.   The hero of the story gets possession of the seven quails and wrings the necks of six of them.

---

[1] Schott, "Ueber die Sage von Geser-Chan," *Abhandlungen der königlichen Akademie der Wissenschaften zu Berlin*, 1851, p. 269.

[2] W. Radloff, *Proben der Volks-* *litteratur der türkischen Stämme Süd-Sibiriens*, ii. (St. Petersburg, 1868), pp. 237 *sq.*

[3] W. Radloff, *op. cit.* ii. 531 *sqq.*

Then Tash Kan comes running and begs the hero to let his soul go free. But the hero wrings the last quail's neck, and Tash Kan drops dead.[1] In another Tartar poem the hero, pursuing his sister who has driven away his cattle, is warned to desist from the pursuit because his sister has carried away his soul in a golden sword and a golden arrow, and if he pursues her she will kill him by throwing the golden sword or shooting the golden arrow at him.[2]

A modern Chinese story tells how an habitual criminal used to take his soul out of his own body for the purpose of evading the righteous punishment of his crimes. This bad man lived in Khien (Kwei-cheu), and the sentences that had been passed on him formed a pile as high as a hill. The mandarins had flogged him to death with sticks and flung his mangled corpse into the river, but three days afterwards the scoundrel got his soul back again, and on the fifth day he resumed his career of villainy as if nothing had happened. The thing occurred again and again, till at last it reached the ears of the Governor of the province, who flew into a violent passion and proposed to the Governor-General to have the rascal beheaded. And beheaded he was; but in three days the wretch was alive again with no trace of decapitation about him except a slender red thread round his neck. And now, like a giant refreshed, he began a fresh series of enormities. He even went so far as to beat his own mother. This was more than she could bear, and she brought the matter before the magistrate. She produced in court a vase and said, " In this vase my refractory son has hidden his soul. Whenever he was conscious of having committed a serious crime, or a misdeed of the most heinous kind, he remained at home, took his soul out of his body, purified it, and put it in the vase. Then the authorities only punished or executed his body of flesh and blood, and not his soul. With his soul, refined by a long process, he then cured his freshly mutilated body, which thus became able in three days to recommence in the old way. Now, however, his crimes have reached a climax, for he has beaten me, an old woman, and I cannot bear it. I pray you, smash this vase, and

The external soul in a Chinese story.

---

[1] W. Radloff, *op. cit.* iv. (St. Peters-burg, 1872) pp. 88 *sq.*

[2] W. Radloff, *op. cit.* i. (St. Peters-burg, 1866) pp. 345 *sq.*

scatter his soul by fanning it away with a windwheel; and if then you castigate his body anew, it is probable that bad son of mine will really die." The mandarin took the hint. He had the rogue cudgelled to death, and when they examined the corpse they found that decay had set in within ten days.[1]

The Khasis of Assam tell of a certain Kyllong, king of Madur, who pursued his conquests on a remarkable principle. He needed few or no soldiers, because he himself was a very strong man and nobody could kill him permanently; they could, it is true, put him to death, but then he came to life again immediately. The king of Synteng, who was much afraid of him, once chopped him in pieces and threw the severed hands and feet far away, thinking thus to get rid of him for good and all; but it was to no purpose. The very next morning Kyllong came to life again and stalked about as brisk as ever. So the king of Synteng was very anxious to learn how his rival contrived thus to rise from the dead; and he hit on a plan for worming out the secret. He chose the fairest girl of the whole country, clad her in royal robes, put jewels of gold and silver upon her, and said, "All these will I give thee and more besides, if thou canst obtain for me King Kyllong's secret, and canst inform me how he brings himself to life again after being killed." So he sent the girl to the slave-market in King Kyllong's country; and the king saw and loved her and took her to wife. So she caressed him and coaxed him to tell her his secret, and in a fatal hour he was beguiled into revealing it. He said, "My life depends upon these things. I must bathe every day and must wash my entrails. After that, I take my food, and there is no one on earth who can kill me unless he obtains possession of my entrails. Thus my life hangs only on my entrails." His treacherous wife at once sent word to the king of Synteng, who caused men to lie in wait while Kyllong was bathing. As usual, Kyllong had laid his entrails on one side of the bathing-place, while he disported himself in the water, intending afterwards to wash them and replace them in his body. But before he could do so,

---

[1] J. J. M. de Groot, *The Religious System of China*, iv. (Leyden, 1901) pp. 105 *sq.*

one of the liers-in-wait had seized the entrails and killed him. The entrails he cut in pieces and gave to the dogs to eat. That was the end of King Kyllong. He was never able to come to life again ; his country was conquered, and the members of the royal family were scattered far and wide. Seven generations have passed since then.[1]

A Malay poem relates how once upon a time in the city of Indrapoora there was a certain merchant who was rich and prosperous, but he had no children. One day as he walked with his wife by the river they found a baby girl, fair as an angel. So they adopted the child and called her Bidasari. The merchant caused a golden fish to be made, and into this fish he transferred the soul of his adopted daughter. Then he put the golden fish in a golden box full of water, and hid it in a pond in the midst of his garden. In time the girl grew to be a lovely woman. Now the King of Indrapoora had a fair young queen, who lived in fear that the king might take to himself a second wife. So, hearing of the charms of Bidasari, the queen resolved to put her out of the way. She lured the girl to the palace and tortured her cruelly ; but Bidasari could not die, because her soul was not in her. At last she could stand the torture no longer and said to the queen, " If you wish me to die, you must bring the box which is in the pond in my father's garden." So the box was brought and opened, and there was the golden fish in the water. The girl said, " My soul is in that fish. In the morning you must take the fish out of the water, and in the evening you must put it back into the water. Do not let the fish lie about, but bind it round your neck. If you do this, I shall soon die." So the queen took the fish out of the box and fastened it round her neck ; and no sooner had she done so, than Bidasari fell into a swoon. But in the evening, when the fish was put back into the water, Bidasari came to herself again. Seeing that she thus had the girl in her power, the queen sent her home to her adopted parents. To save her from further persecution her parents resolved to remove their daughter from the city. So in a lonely and desolate spot they built a house and brought Bidasari thither. There she dwelt alone, under-

[1] Major P. R. T. Gurdon, *The Khasis* (London, 1907), pp. 181-184.

going vicissitudes that corresponded with the vicissitudes of the golden fish in which was her soul. All day long, while the fish was out of the water, she remained unconscious ; but in the evening, when the fish was put into the water, she revived. One day the king was out hunting, and coming to the house where Bidasari lay unconscious, was smitten with her beauty. He tried to waken her, but in vain. Next day, towards evening, he repeated his visit, but still found her unconscious. However, when darkness fell, she came to herself and told the king the secret of her life. So the king returned to the palace, took the fish from the queen, and put it in water. Immediately Bidasari revived, and the king took her to wife.[1]

The external soul in a story told in Nias.

Another story of an external soul comes from Nias, an island to the west of Sumatra. Once on a time a chief was captured by his enemies, who tried to put him to death but failed. Water would not drown him nor fire burn him nor steel pierce him. At last his wife revealed the secret. On his head he had a hair as hard as a copper wire ; and with this wire his life was bound up. So the hair was plucked out, and with it his spirit fled.[2]

The external soul in a Hausa story. The king whose life was in a box.

A Hausa story from Northern Nigeria closely resembles some of the European tales which we have noticed ; for it contains not only the incident of the external soul, but also the incident of the helpful animals, by whose assistance the hero is able to slay the Soulless King and obtain possession of the kingdom. The story runs thus. A certain man and his wife had four daughters born to them in succession, but

[1] G. A. Wilken, "De betrekking tusschen menschen- dieren- en plantenleven naar het volksgeloof," *De Indische Gids*, November 1884, pp. 600-602 ; *id.*, "De Simsonsage," *De Gids*, 1888, No. 5, pp. 6 *sqq.* (of the separate reprint); *id.*, *Verspreide Geschriften* (The Hague, 1912), iii. 296-298, 559-561. Compare L. de Backer, *L'Archipel Indien* (Paris, 1874), pp. 144-149. The Malay text of the long poem was published with a Dutch translation and notes by W. R. van Hoëvell ("Sjaïr Bidasari, een oorspronkelijk Maleisch Gedicht, uitgegeven en van eene Vertaling en Aanteekeningen voorzien,"

Verhandelingen van het Bataviaasch Genootschap van Kunsten en Wetenschappen, xix. (Batavia, 1843) pp. 1-421).

[2] J. T. Nieuwenhuisen en H. C. B. von Rosenberg, "Verslag omtrent het eiland Nias," *Verhandelingen van het Bataviaasch Genootschap van Kunsten en Wetenschappen*, xxx. (Batavia, 1863) p. 111 ; H. Sundermann, "Die Insel Nias," *Allgemeine Missions-Zeitschrift*, xi. (1884) p. 453 ; *id.*, *Die Insel Nias und die Mission daselbst* (Barmen, 1905), p. 71. Compare E. Modigliani, *Un Viaggio a Nias* (Milan, 1890), p. 339.

every one of the baby girls mysteriously disappeared on the day when she was to be weaned ; so the parents fell under the suspicion of having devoured them.   Last of all there was born to them a son, who to avoid accidents was left to wean himself.   One day, as he grew up, the son received a magic lotion from an old woman, who told him to rub his eyes with it.   He did so, and immediately he saw a large house and entering it he found his eldest sister married to a bull.   She bade him welcome and so did her husband the bull ; and when he went away, the bull very kindly presented him with a lock of his hair as a keepsake.   In like manner the lad discovered his other three sisters, who were living in wedlock with a ram, a dog, and a hawk respectively.   All of them welcomed him and from the ram, the dog, and the hawk he received tokens of regard in the shape of hair or feathers. Then he returned home and told his parents of his adventure and how he had found his sisters alive and married.   Next day he went to a far city, where he made love to the Queen and persuaded her to plot with him against the life of the King her husband.   So she coaxed the King to shew his affection for her by " taking his own life, and joining it to hers."   The unsuspecting husband, as usual, fell into the trap set for him by his treacherous wife.   He confided to her the secret of his life.   " My life," said he, " is behind the city, behind the city in a thicket.   In this thicket there is a lake ; in the lake is a rock ; in the rock is a gazelle ; in the gazelle is a dove ; and in the dove is a small box."   The *The helpful* Queen divulged the secret to her lover, who kindled a fire *animals.* behind the city and threw into it the hair and feathers which he had received from the friendly animals, his brothers-in-law. Immediately the animals themselves appeared and readily gave their help in the enterprise.   The bull drank up the lake ;   the ram broke up the rock ;   the dog caught the gazelle ;   the hawk captured the dove.   So the youth extracted the precious box from the dove and repaired to the palace, where he found the King already dead.   His Majesty had been ailing from the moment when the young man left the city, and he grew steadily worse with every fresh success of the adventurer who was to supplant him.   So the hero became King and married the false Queen ; and his sisters' husbands were changed from animals into men and received subordinate posts in the government. The hero's parents, too, came to live in the city over which he reigned.[1]

The external soul in a South Nigerian story.

A West African story from Southern Nigeria relates how a king kept his soul in a little brown bird, which perched on a tall tree beside the gate of the palace. The king's life was so bound up with that of the bird that whoever should kill the bird would simultaneously kill the king and succeed to the kingdom. The secret was betrayed by the queen to her lover, who shot the bird with an arrow and thereby slew the king and ascended the vacant throne.[2] A tale told by the Ba-Ronga of South Africa sets forth how the lives of a whole family were contained in one cat. When a girl of the family, named Titishan, married a husband, she begged her parents to let her take the precious cat with her to her new home. But they refused, saying, "You know that our life is attached to it"; and they offered to give her an antelope or even an elephant instead of it. But nothing would satisfy her but the cat. So at last she carried it off with her and shut it up in a place where nobody saw it; even her husband knew nothing about it. One day, when she went to work in the fields, the cat escaped from its place of concealment, entered the hut, put on the warlike trappings of the husband, and danced and sang. Some children, attracted by the noise, discovered the cat at its antics, and when they expressed their astonishment, the animal only capered the more and insulted them besides. So they went to the owner and said, "There is somebody dancing in your house, and he insulted us." "Hold your tongues," said he, "I'll soon put a stop to your lies." So he went and hid behind the door and peeped in, and there sure enough was the cat prancing about and singing. He fired at it, and the animal dropped down dead. At the same moment his wife fell to the ground in the field where she was at work; said she, "I have been killed at home." But she had strength enough left to ask her husband to go with her to her parents' village, taking with him the

The external soul in a story told by the Ba-Ronga of South Africa. The Clan of the Cat.

[1] Major A. J. N. Tremearne, *Hausa Superstitions and Customs* (London, 1913), pp. 131 *sq.* The original Hausa text of the story appears to be printed in Major Edgar's *Lîtafi na Tatsuniyoyi* na Hausa (ii. 27), to which Major Tremearne refers (p. 9).

[2] Major A. G. Leonard, *The Lower Niger and its Tribes* (London, 1906), pp. 319-321.

dead cat wrapt up in a mat. All her relatives assembled, and bitterly they reproached her for having insisted on taking the animal with her to her husband's village. As soon as the mat was unrolled and they saw the dead cat, they all fell down lifeless one after the other. So the Clan of the Cat was destroyed ; and the bereaved husband closed the gate of the village with a branch, and returned home, and told his friends how in killing the cat he had killed the whole clan, because their lives depended on the life of the cat. In another Ronga story the lives of a whole clan are attached to a buffalo, which a girl of the clan in like manner insists on taking with her.[1]

Ideas of the same sort meet us in stories told by the North American Indians. Thus in one Indian tale the hero pounds his enemy to pieces, but cannot kill him because his heart is not in his body. At last the champion learns that his foe's heart is in the sky, at the western side of the noon-day sun ; so he reaches up, seizes the heart, and crushes it, and straightway his enemy expires. In another Indian myth there figures a personage Winter whose song brings frost and snow, but his heart is hidden away at a distance. However, his foe finds the heart and burns it, and so the Snow-maker perishes.[2] A Pawnee story relates how a wounded warrior was carried off by bears, who healed him of his hurts. When the Indian was about to return to his village, the old he-bear said to him, " I shall look after you. I shall give you a part of myself. If I am killed, you shall be killed. If I grow old, you shall be old." And the bear gave him a cap of bearskin, and at parting he put his arms round the Indian and hugged him, and put his mouth against the man's mouth and held the man's hands in his paws. The Indian who told the tale conjectured that when the man died, the old bear died also.[3] The Navajoes tell of a certain mythical being called " the Maiden that becomes a

The external soul in stories told by the North American Indians.

[1] Henri A. Junod, *Les Chants et les Contes des Ba-ronga* (Lausanne, N.D.), pp. 253-256; *id.*, *The Life of a South African Tribe* (Neuchatel, 1912–1913), i. 338 *sq.*

[2] J. Curtin, *Myths and Folk-tales of the Russians, Western Slavs, and Magyars* (London, 1891), p. 551. The writer does not mention his authorities.

[3] G. B. Grinnell, *Pawnee Hero Stories and Folk-tales* (New York, 1889), pp. 121 *sqq.*, " The Bear Man."

Bear," who learned the art of turning herself into a bear from the prairie wolf. She was a great warrior and quite invulnerable; for when she went to war she took out her vital organs and hid them, so that no one could kill her; and when the battle was over she put the organs back in their places again.[1] The Kwakiutl Indians of British Columbia tell of an ogress, who could not be killed because her life was in a hemlock branch. A brave boy met her in the woods, smashed her head with a stone, scattered her brains, broke her bones, and threw them into the water. Then, thinking he had disposed of the ogress, he went into her house. There he saw a woman rooted to the floor, who warned him, saying, " Now do not stay long. I know that you have tried to kill the ogress. It is the fourth time that somebody has tried to kill her. She never dies; she has nearly come to life. There in that covered hemlock branch is her life. Go there, and as soon as you see her enter, shoot her life. Then she will be dead." Hardly had she finished speaking when sure enough in came the ogress, singing as she walked :—

The ogress whose life was in a hemlock branch.

> " *I have the magical treasure,*
> *I have the supernatural power,*
> *I can return to life.*"

Such was her song. But the boy shot at her life, and she fell dead to the floor.[2]

---

[1] Washington Matthews, " The Mountain Chant: a Navajo Ceremony," *Fifth Annual Report of the Bureau of Ethnology* (Washington, 1887), pp. 406 *sq.*

[2] Franz Boas, "The Social Organization and the Secret Societies of the Kwakiutl Indians," *Report of the United States National Museum for 1895* (Washington, 1897), p. 373.

CHAPTER XI

THE EXTERNAL SOUL IN FOLK-CUSTOM

§ 1. *The External Soul in Inanimate Things*

THUS the idea that the soul may be deposited for a longer The exter- or shorter time in some place of security outside the body, nal soul in folk- or at all events in the hair, is found in the popular tales of custom. many races. It remains to shew that the idea is not a mere figment devised to adorn a tale, but is a real article of primitive faith, which has given rise to a corresponding set of customs.

We have seen that in the tales the hero, as a prepara- The soul tion for battle, sometimes removes his soul from his body, in removed from the order that his body may be invulnerable and immortal in body as a the combat. With a like intention the savage removes his precaution in seasons soul from his body on various occasions of real or imaginary of danger. peril. Thus among the people of Minahassa in Celebes, Souls of people when a family moves into a new house, a priest collects the collected souls of the whole family in a bag, and afterwards restores in a bag at a house- them to their owners, because the moment of entering a new warming. house is supposed to be fraught with supernatural danger.[1] In Southern Celebes, when a woman is brought to bed, the messenger who fetches the doctor or the midwife always carries with him something made of iron, such as a chopping-knife, which he delivers to the doctor. The doctor must keep the thing in his house till the confinement is over, when he gives it back, receiving a fixed sum of money for doing so. The chopping-knife, or whatever it is, represents the woman's soul, which at this critical time is believed to be safer out of

---

[1] *Taboo and the Perils of the Soul*, pp. 63 *sq.*

Soul of a woman put in a chopping-knife at childbirth. her body than in it. Hence the doctor must take great care of the object; for were it lost, the woman's soul would assuredly, they think, be lost with it.[1] But in Celebes the convenience of occasionally depositing the soul in some external object is apparently not limited to human beings. The Alfoors, or Toradjas, who inhabit the central district of that island, and among whose industries the working of iron occupies a foremost place, attribute to the metal a soul which would be apt to desert its body under the blows of the hammer, if some means were not found to detain it. Accordingly in every smithy of Poso—for that is the name of the country of these people—you may see hanging up a bundle of wooden instruments, such as chopping-knives, swords, spear-heads, and so forth. This bundle goes by the name of *lamoa*, which is the general word for "gods," and in it the soul of the iron that is being wrought in the smithy is, according to one account, supposed to reside. "If we did not hang the *lamoa* over the anvil," they say, "the iron would flow away and be unworkable," on account of the absence of the soul.[2] However, according to another interpretation these wooden models are substitutes offered to the gods in room of the iron, whose soul the covetous deities might otherwise abstract for their own use, thus making the metal unmalleable.[3]

Among the Dyaks of Pinoeh, a district of South-Eastern Borneo, when a child is born, a medicine-man is sent for, who conjures the soul of the infant into half a coco-nut,

[1] B. F. Matthes, *Bijdragen tot de Ethnologie van Zuid-Celebes* (The Hague, 1875), p. 54.

[2] A. C. Kruijt, "Een en ander aangaande het geestelijk en maatschappelijk leven van den Poso-Alfoer," *Mededeelingen van wege het Nederlandsche Zendelinggenootschap*, xxxix. (1895) pp. 23 *sq.*; *id.*, "Van Paloppo naar Posso," *Mededeelingen van wege het Nederlandsche Zendelinggenootschap*, xlii. (1898) p. 72. As to the *lamoa* in general, see A. C. Kruijt, *op. cit.* xl. (1896) pp. 10 *sq.*

[3] A. C. Kruijt, "Het koppensnellen der Toradja's van Midden-Celebes, en zijne beteekenis," *Verslagen en Mededeelingen der koninklijke Akademie der Wetenschappen*, Afdeeling Letterkunde, iv. Reeks, iii. (Amsterdam, 1899) pp. 201 *sq.*; *id.*, "Het ijzer in Midden-Celebes," *Bijdragen tot de Taal- Land- en Volkenkunde van Nederlandsch-Indië*, liii. (1901) pp. 156 *sq.* Both the interpretations in the text appear to be inferences drawn by Mr. Kruijt from the statement of the natives, that, if they did not hang up these wooden models in the smithy, "the iron would flow away and be unworkable" ("*zou het ijzer vervloeien en onbewerkbaar worden*").

which he thereupon covers with a cloth and places on a
square platter or charger suspended by cords from the roof.
This ceremony he repeats at every new moon for a year.[1]
The intention of the ceremony is not explained by the
writer who describes it, but we may conjecture that it is to
place the soul of the child in a safer place than its own frail
little body. This conjecture is confirmed by the reason
assigned for a similar custom observed elsewhere in the
Indian Archipelago. In the Kei Islands, when there is a
newly-born child in a house, an empty coco-nut, split and
spliced together again, may sometimes be seen hanging
beside a rough wooden image of an ancestor. The soul of
the infant is believed to be temporarily deposited in the
coco-nut in order that it may be safe from the attacks of
evil spirits ; but when the child grows bigger and stronger,
the soul will take up its permanent abode in its own body.
Similarly among the Esquimaux of Alaska, when a child is
sick, the medicine-man will sometimes extract its soul from
its body and place it for safe-keeping in an amulet, which
for further security he deposits in his own medicine-bag.[2]
It seems probable that many amulets have been similarly
regarded as soul-boxes, that is, as safes in which the souls
of the owners are kept for greater security.[3]   An old

Soul of a child put for safety in an empty coco-nut or a bag.

[1] A. H. B. Agerbeek, "Enkele
gebruiken van de Dajaksche bevolking
der Pinoehlanden," *Tijdschrift voor
Indische Taal- Land- en Volkenkunde*,
li. (1909) pp. 447 *sq.*

[2] J. A. Jacobsen, *Reisen in die
Inselwelt des Banda-Meeres* (Berlin,
1896), p. 199.

[3] In a long list of female ornaments
the prophet Isaiah mentions (iii. 20)
"houses of the soul" (בָּתֵּי הַנֶּפֶשׁ), which
modern scholars suppose to have been
perfume boxes, as the Revised English
Version translates the phrase. The
name, literally translated "houses of
the soul," suggests that these trinkets
were amulets of the kind mentioned in
the text. See my article, "Folk-lore
in the Old Testament," *Anthropological Essays presented to E. B. Tylor*
(Oxford, 1907), pp. 148 *sqq.* In
ancient Egyptian tombs there are often

found plaques or palettes of schist
bearing traces of paint ; some of them
are decorated with engravings of animals or historical scenes, others are
modelled in the shape of animals of
various sorts, such as antelopes, hippopotamuses, birds, tortoises, and fish.
As a rule only one such plaque is
found in a tomb, and it lies near the
hands of the mummy. It has been
conjectured by M. Jean Capart that
these plaques are amulets or soul-
boxes, in which the external souls of
the dead were supposed to be preserved. See Jean Capart, *Les Palettes
en schiste de l'Égypte primitive* (Brussels, 1908), pp. 5 *sqq.*, 19 *sqq.*
(separate reprint from the *Revue des
Questions Scientifiques*, avril, 1908).
For a full description of these plaques
or palettes, see Jean Capart, *Les Débuts
de l'Art en Égypte* (Brussels, 1904),
pp 76 *sqq.*, 221 *sqq.*

Souls of
people in
ornaments,
horns, a
column,
and so
forth.
Mang'anje woman in the West Shire district of British
Central Africa used to wear round her neck an ivory ornament, hollow, and about three inches long, which she called
her life or soul (*moyo wanga*). Naturally, she would not
part with it; a planter tried to buy it of her, but in vain.[1]
When Mr. James Macdonald was one day sitting in the house
of a Hlubi chief, awaiting the appearance of that great man,
who was busy decorating his person, a native pointed to a
pair of magnificent ox-horns, and said, " Ntame has his soul
in these horns." The horns were those of an animal which
had been sacrificed, and they were held sacred. A magician
had fastened them to the roof to protect the house and its
inmates from the thunder-bolt. " The idea," adds Mr.
Macdonald, " is in no way foreign to South African thought.
A man's soul there may dwell in the roof of his house, in a
tree, by a spring of water, or on some mountain scaur." [2]
Among the natives of the Gazelle Peninsula in New Britain
there is a secret society which goes by the name of Ingnict
or Ingiet. On his entrance into it every man receives a stone
in the shape either of a human being or of an animal, and
henceforth his soul is believed to be knit up in a manner
with the stone. If it breaks, it is an evil omen for him;
they say that the thunder has struck the stone and that he
who owns it will soon die. If nevertheless the man survives
the breaking of his soul-stone, they say that it was not a
proper soul-stone and he gets a new one instead.[3] The
emperor Romanus Lecapenus was once informed by an
astronomer that the life of Simeon, prince of Bulgaria, was

---

[1] Miss Alice Werner, in a letter to
the author, dated 25th September
1899. Miss Werner knew the old
woman. Compare *Contemporary Review*, lxx. (July–December 1896), p.
389, where Miss Werner describes the
ornament as a rounded peg, tapering
to a point, with a neck or notch at
the top.

[2] Rev. James Macdonald, *Religion
and Myth* (London, 1893), p. 190.
Compare Dudley Kidd, *The Essential
Kafir* (London, 1904), p. 83 : " The
natives occasionally fix ox-horns in
their roofs and say that the spirit of
the chief lives in these horns and pro-

tects the hut; these horns also protect
the hut from lightning, though not in
virtue of their spiritual connections.
(They are also used simply as ornaments.)" No doubt amulets often
degenerate into ornaments.

[3] R. Thurnwald, "Im Bismarck-
archipel und auf den Salomo-inseln,"
Zeitschrift für Ethnologie, xiii. (1910)
p. 136. As to the Ingniet, Ingiet, or
Iniet Society see P. A. Kleintitschen,
*Die Küstenbewohner der Gazellehalb-
insel* (Hiltrup bei Münster, N.D.),
pp. 354 *sqq.*; R. Parkinson, *Dreissig
Jahre in der Südsee* (Stuttgart, 1907),
pp. 598 *sqq.*

bound up with a certain column in Constantinople, so that if the capital of the column were removed, Simeon would immediately die. The emperor took the hint and removed the capital, and at the same hour, as the emperor learned by enquiry, Simeon died of heart disease in Bulgaria.[1] The deified kings of ancient Egypt appear to have enjoyed the privilege of depositing their spiritual doubles or souls (*ka*) during their lifetime in a number of portrait statues, properly fourteen for each king, which stood in the chamber of adoration (*pa douaït*) of the temple and were revered as the equivalents or representatives of the monarchs themselves.[2] Among the Karens of Burma " the knife with which the navel string is cut is carefully preserved for the child. The life of the child is supposed to be in some way connected with it, for, if lost or destroyed, it is said the child will not be long lived."[3] Among the Shawnee Indians of North America it once happened that an eminent man was favoured with a special revelation by the Great Spirit. Wisely refusing to hide the sacred light of revelation under a bushel, he generously communicated a few sparks of the illumination to John Tanner, a white man who lived for many years as an Indian among the Indians. "Henceforth," said the inspired sage, "the fire must never be suffered to go out in your lodge. Summer and winter, day and night, in the storm, or when it is calm, you must remember that the life in your body, and the fire in your lodge, are the same, and of the same date. If you suffer your fire to be extinguished, at that moment your life will be at its end."[4]

Again, we have seen that in folk-tales a man's soul or

The souls of Egyptian kings in portrait statues.

A man's life bound up with the fire in his lodge.

[1] G. Cedrenus, *Historiarum Compendium*, p. 625B, vol. ii. p. 308, ed. Im. Bekker (Bonn, 1838–1839).

[2] Alexandre Moret, *Du caractère religieux de la Royauté Pharaonique* (Paris, 1902), pp. 224 *sqq.* As to the Egyptian doctrine of the spiritual double or soul (*ka*), see A. Wiedemann, *The Ancient Egyptian Doctrine of the Immortality of the Soul* (London, 1895), pp. 10 *sqq.* ; A. Erman, *Die ägyptische Religion* (Berlin, 1905), p. 88 ; A. Moret, *Mystères Égyptiens* (Paris, 1913), pp. 199 *sqq.*

[3] F. Mason, " Physical Character of the Karens," *Journal of the Asiatic Society of Bengal*, 1866, Part ii. No. 1, p. 9.

[4] *A Narrative of the Captivity and Adventures of John Tanner, during Thirty Years' Residence among the Indians*, prepared for the press by Edwin James, M.D. (London, 1830), pp. 155 *sq.* The passage has been already quoted by Sir John Lubbock (Lord Avebury) in his *Origin of Civilisation*[4] (London, 1882), p. 241.

Strength
of people
supposed
to reside in
their hair.
strength is sometimes represented as bound up with his hair,
and that when his hair is cut off he dies or grows weak.
So the natives of Amboyna used to think that their strength
was in their hair and would desert them if it were shorn.
A criminal under torture in a Dutch Court of that island
persisted in denying his guilt till his hair was cut off, when
he immediately confessed.   One man, who was tried for
murder, endured without flinching the utmost ingenuity of
his torturers till he saw the surgeon standing with a pair of
shears.   On asking what this was for, and being told that
it was to cut his hair, he begged they would not do it, and
made a clean breast.   In subsequent cases, when torture
failed to wring a confession from a prisoner, the Dutch
authorities made a practice of cutting off his hair.[1]   In
Ceram it is still believed that if young people have their hair
cut they will be weakened and enervated thereby.[2]

Witches
and
wizards
shaved to
deprive
them of
their
power.
Here in Europe it used to be thought that the maleficent
powers of witches and wizards resided in their hair, and that
nothing could make any impression on these miscreants so
long as they kept their hair on.   Hence in France it was
customary to shave the whole bodies of persons charged with
sorcery before handing them over to the torturer.   Millaeus
witnessed the torture of some persons at Toulouse, from
whom no confession could be wrung until they were stripped
and completely shaven, when they readily acknowledged the
truth of the charge.   A woman also, who apparently led a
pious life, was put to the torture on suspicion of witchcraft,
and bore her agonies with incredible constancy, until complete depilation drove her to admit her guilt.   The noted
inquisitor Sprenger contented himself with shaving the head
of the suspected witch or wizard ; but his more thorough-
going colleague Cumanus shaved the whole bodies of forty-
one women before committing them all to the flames.   He
had high authority for this rigorous scrutiny, since Satan
himself, in a sermon preached from the pulpit of North
Berwick church, comforted his many servants by assuring

---

[1] François Valentyn, *Oud en Nieuw
Oost-Indiën* (Dordrecht and Amsterdam, 1724–1726), ii. 143 *sq.* ; G. A.
Wilken, " De Simsonsage," *De Gids*,
1888, No. 5, pp. 15 *sq.* (of the separate

reprint) ; *id.*, *Verspreide Geschriften*
(The Hague, 1912), iii. 569 *sq.*
[2] J. G. F. Riedel, *De sluik- en
kroesharige rassen tusschen Selebes en
Papua* (The Hague, 1886), p. 137.

them that no harm could befall them "sa lang as their hair wes on, and sould newir latt ane teir fall fra thair ene."[1] Similarly in Bastar, a province of India, "if a man is adjudged guilty of witchcraft, he is beaten by the crowd, his hair is shaved, the hair being supposed to constitute his power of mischief, his front teeth are knocked out, in order, it is said, to prevent him from muttering incantations. . . . Women suspected of sorcery have to undergo the same ordeal; if found guilty, the same punishment is awarded, and after being shaved, their hair is attached to a tree in some public place."[2] So among the Bhils of India, when a woman was convicted of witchcraft and had been subjected to various forms of persuasion, such as hanging head downwards from a tree and having pepper put into her eyes, a lock of hair was cut from her head and buried in the ground, "that the last link between her and her former powers of mischief might be broken."[3] In like manner among the Aztecs of Mexico, when wizards and witches "had done their evil deeds, and the time came to put an end to their detestable life, some one laid hold of them and cropped the hair on the crown of their heads, which took from them all their power of sorcery and enchantment, and then it was that by death they put an end to their odious existence."[4]

§ 2. *The External Soul in Plants*

Further it has been shewn that in folk-tales the life of a person is sometimes so bound up with the life of a plant that the withering of the plant will immediately follow or be followed by the death of the person.[5] Similarly among the natives of the Pennefather River in Queensland, when a visiter has made himself very agreeable and taken his departure, an effigy of him about three or four feet long is cut on some soft tree, such as the *Canarium australasicum*,

(margin note: Life of a person supposed to be bound up with that of a tree or plant.)

---

[1] J. G. Dalyell, *The darker Superstitions of Scotland* (Edinburgh, 1834), pp. 637-639; C. de Mensignac, *Recherches ethnographiques sur la Salive et le Crachat* (Bordeaux, 1892), p. 49 note.

[2] W. Crooke, *Popular Religion and Folk-lore of Northern India* (Westminster, 1896), ii. 281.

[3] W. Crooke, *op. cit.* ii. 281 *sq.*

[4] B. de Sahagun, *Histoire des choses de la Nouvelle Espagne*, traduite par D. Journdanet et R. Siméon (Paris, 1880), p. 274.

[5] Above, pp. 102, 110, 117 *sq.*, 135, 136.

so as to face in the direction taken by the popular stranger. Afterwards from observing the state of the tree the natives infer the corresponding state of their absent friend, whose illness or death are apparently supposed to be portended by the fall of the leaves or of the tree.[1]   In Uganda, when a new royal enclosure with its numerous houses was built for a new king, barkcloth trees used to be planted at the main entrance by priests of each principal deity and offerings were laid under each tree for its particular god.   Thenceforth " the trees were carefully guarded and tended, because it was believed that as they grew and flourished, so the king's life and power would increase." [2]   Among the M'Bengas in Western Africa, about the Gaboon, when two children are born on the same day, the people plant two trees of the same kind and dance round them.   The life of each of the children is believed to be bound up with the life of one of the trees ; and if the tree dies or is thrown down, they are sure that the child will soon die.[3]   In Sierra Leone also it is customary at the birth of a child to plant a shoot of a *malep*-tree, and they think that the tree will grow with the child and be its god.   If a tree which has been thus planted withers away, the people consult a sorcerer on the subject.[4]   Among the Wajagga of German East Africa, when a child is born, it is usual to plant a cultivated plant of some sort behind the house.   The plant is thenceforth carefully tended, for they believe that were it to wither away the child would die. When the navel-string drops from the infant, it is buried under the plant.   The species of birth-plant varies with the clan ; members of one clan, for example, plant a particular sort of banana, members of another clan plant a sugar-cane, and so on.[5]   Among the Swahili of East Africa, when a child is born, the afterbirth and navel-string are buried in

Birth-trees in Africa.

---

[1] Walter E. Roth, *North Queensland Ethnography, Bulletin, No. 5, Superstition, Magic, and Medicine* (Brisbane, 1903), p. 27.

[2] Rev. J. Roscoe, *The Baganda* (London, 1911), p. 202.

[3] G. Duloup, " Huit jours chez les M'Bengas," *Revue d'Ethnographie,* ii. (1883), p. 223 ; compare P. Barret, *L'Afrique Occidentale* (Paris, 1888),

ii. 173.

[4] Fr. Kunstmann, " Valentin Ferdinand's Beschreibung der Serra Leoa," *Abhandlungen der histor. Classe der könig. Bayer. Akad. der Wissenschaften,* ix. (1866) pp. 131 *sq.*

[5] Bruno Gutmann, " Feldbausitten und Wachstumsbräuche der Wadschagga," *Zeitschrift für Ethnologie,* xlv. (1913), p. 496.

the courtyard and a mark is made on the spot.   Seven
days afterwards, the hair of the child is shaved and
deposited, along with the clippings of its nails, in the
same place.   Then over all these relics of the infant's
person a coco-nut is planted.   As the tree grows up from
the nut, the child likes to point it out to his playfellows
and tell them, " This coco-nut palm is my navel."   In
planting the coco-nut the parents say, " May God cause our
child to grow up, that he or she may one day enjoy the
coco-nut milk of the tree which we plant here." [1]   Though
it is not expressly affirmed, we may perhaps assume that
such a birth-tree is supposed to stand in a sympathetic
relation with the life of the person.   In the Cameroons, also,
the life of a person is believed to be sympathetically bound
up with that of a tree.[2]   The chief of Old Town in Calabar
kept his soul in a sacred grove near a spring of water.
When some Europeans, in frolic or ignorance, cut down part
of the grove, the spirit was most indignant and threatened
the perpetrators of the deed, according to the king, with all
manner of evil.[3]   Among the Fans of the French Congo,
when a chief's son is born, the remains of the navel-string
are buried under a sacred fig-tree, and " thenceforth great
importance is attached to the growth of the tree ; it is strictly
forbidden to touch it.   Any attempt on the tree would be
considered as an attack on the human being himself." [4]
Among the Boloki of the Upper Congo a family has a plant
with red leaves (called *nkungu*) for its totem.   When a
woman of the family is with child for the first time, one of
the totemic plants is planted near the hearth outside the
house and is never destroyed, otherwise it is believed that
the child would be born thin and weak and would remain
puny and sickly.   " The healthy life of the children and
family is bound up with the healthiness and life of the totem

---

[1] C. Velten, *Sitten und Gebräuche
der Suaheli* (Göttingen, 1903), pp.
8 *sq.*   In Java it is customary to plant
a tree, for example, a coco-nut palm,
at the birth of a child, and when he
grows up he reckons his age by the
age of the tree.   See *Annales de la
Propagation de la Foi,* iii. (Lyons and

Paris, 1830) pp. 400 *sq.*
   [2] A. Bastian, *Die deutsche Expedition an der Loango-Küste* (Jena, 1874–
1875), i. 165.
   [3] Rev. J. Macdonald, *Religion and
Myth* (London, 1893), p. 178.
   [4] H. Trilles, *Le Totémisme chez les
Fâṅ* (Münster i. W., 1912), p. 570.

tree as respected and preserved by the family."[1]   Among
the Baganda of Central Africa a child's afterbirth was called
the second child and was believed to be animated by a spirit,
which at once became a ghost.   The afterbirth was usually
buried at the root of a banana tree, and afterwards the tree
was carefully guarded by old women, who prevented any
one from going near it ; they tied ropes of fibre from tree
to tree to isolate it, and all the child's excretions were
thrown into this enclosure.   When the fruit ripened, it was
cut by the old woman in charge.   The reason for guarding
the tree thus carefully was a belief that if any stranger were
to eat of the fruit of the tree or to drink beer brewed from
it, he would carry off with him the ghost of the child's afterbirth, which had been buried at the root of the banana-tree,
and the living child would then die in order to follow its
twin ghost.   Whereas a grandparent of the child, by eating
the fruit or drinking the beer, averted this catastrophe and
ensured the health of the child.[2]   Among the Wakondyo,

[1] Rev. John H. Weeks, *Among Congo Cannibals* (London, 1913), p. 295.

[2] Rev. J. Roscoe, *The Baganda* (London, 1911), pp. 52, 54 *sq.* Compare *The Magic Art and the Evolution of Kings*, i. 295 *sq.* ; and for other examples of burying the afterbirth or navel-string at the foot of a tree or planting a young tree over these remains, see *id.*, pp. 182 *sqq.* In Kiziba, a district to the west of Lake Victoria Nyanza, the afterbirth is similarly regarded as a sort of human being. Hence when twins are born the people speak of four children instead of two, reckoning the two afterbirths as two children. See H. Rehse, *Kiziba, Land und Leute* (Stuttgart, 1910), p. 117. The conception of the afterbirth and navel-string as spiritual doubles of the child with whom they are born is held very firmly by the Kooboos, a primitive tribe of Sumatra. We are told that among these people "a great vital power is ascribed to the navel-string and afterbirth ; because they are looked upon as brother or sister of the infant, and though their bodies have not come to perfection, yet their soul and spirit are just as normal as those of the child and indeed have even reached a much higher stage of development. The navel-string (*oeri*) and afterbirth (*tĕmboeni*) visit the man who was born with them thrice a day and thrice by night till his death, or they hover near him ('*zweven voorbij hem heen*'). They are the good spirits, a sort of guardian angels of the man who came into the world with them and who lives on earth ; they are said to guard him from all evil. Hence it is that the Kooboo always thinks of his navel-string and afterbirth (*oeri-tĕmboeni*) before he goes to sleep or to work, or undertakes a journey, and so on. Merely to think of them is enough ; there is no need to invoke them, or to ask them anything, or to entreat them. By not thinking of them a man deprives himself of their good care." Immediately after the birth the navel-string and afterbirth are buried in the ground close by the spot where the birth took place ; and a ceremony is performed over it, for were the ceremony omitted, the navel-string and afterbirth, "instead of being a good spirit for the newly born child,

at the north-western corner of Lake Albert Nyanza, it is customary to bury the afterbirth at the foot of a young banana-tree, and the fruit of this particular tree may be eaten by no one but the woman who assisted at the birth.[1] The reason for the custom is not mentioned, but probably, as among the Baganda, the life of the child is supposed to be bound up with the life of the tree, since the afterbirth, regarded as a spiritual double of the infant, has been buried at the root of the tree.

Some of the Papuans unite the life of a new-born child sympathetically with that of a tree by driving a pebble into the bark of the tree. This is supposed to give them complete mastery over the child's life; if the tree is cut down, the child will die.[2] After a birth the Maoris used to bury the navel-string in a sacred place and plant a young sapling over it. As the tree grew, it was a *tohu oranga* or sign of life for the child; if it flourished, the child would prosper; if it withered and died, the parents augured the worst for their child.[3] In the Chatham Islands, when the child of a leading man received its name, it was customary to plant a tree, " the growth of which was to be as the growth of the child," and during the planting priests chanted a spell.[4] In some parts of Fiji the navel-string of a male child is planted together with a coco-nut or the slip of a breadfruit-tree, and the child's life is supposed to be intimately connected with that of the tree.[5] With certain Malayo-Siamese families of

Birth-trees among the Papuans, Maoris, Fijians, Dyaks, and others.

might become an evil spirit for him and visit him with all sorts of calamities out of spite for this neglect." The nature of the ceremony performed over the spot is not described by our authority. The navel-string and afterbirth are often regarded by the Kooboos as one; their names are always mentioned together. See G. J. van Dongen, "De Koeboe in de Onderafdeeling Koeboe-streken der Residentie Palembang," *Bijdragen tot de Taal-Land- en Volkenkunde van Nederlandsch-Indië*, lxiii. (1910) pp. 229 *sq.*

[1] Franz Stuhlmann, *Mit Emin Pascha ins Herz von Afrika* (Berlin, 1894), p. 653.

[2] A. Bastian, *Ein Besuch in San Salvador* (Bremen, 1859), pp. 103 *sq.* ; *id.*, *Der Mensch in der Geschichte* (Leipsic, 1860), iii. 193.

[3] R. Taylor, *Te Ika a Maui, or New Zealand and its Inhabitants* [2] (London, 1870), p. 184; Dumont D'Urville, *Voyage autour du monde et à la recherche de La Pérouse sur la corvette Astrolabe*, ii. 444.

[4] W. T. L. Travers, "Notes of the traditions and manners and customs of the Mori-oris," *Transactions and Proceedings of the New Zealand Institute*, ix. (1876) p. 22.

[5] The late Rev. Lorimer Fison, in a letter to me dated May 29th, 1901. Compare *The Magic Art and the Evolution of Kings*, i. 184.

the Patani States it is customary to bury the afterbirth
under a banana-tree, and the condition of the tree is afterwards regarded as ominous of the child's fate for good or
evil.[1]   In Southern Celebes, when a child is born, a coco-nut
is planted and watered with the water in which the afterbirth and navel-string have been washed.   As it grows up,
the tree is called the "contemporary" of the child.[2]   So in
Bali a coco-palm is planted at the birth of a child.   It is
believed to grow up equally with the child, and is called its
"life-plant."[3]   On certain occasions the Dyaks of Borneo
plant a palm-tree, which is believed to be a complete index
of their fate.   If it flourishes, they reckon on good fortune;
but if it withers or dies, they expect misfortune.[4]   Amongst
the Dyaks of Landak and Tajan, districts of Dutch
Borneo, it is customary to plant a fruit-tree for a child,
and henceforth in the popular belief the fate of the child
is bound up with that of the tree.   If the tree shoots up
rapidly, it will go well with the child; but if the tree is
dwarfed or shrivelled, nothing but misfortune can be expected for its human counterpart.[5]   According to another
account, at the naming of children and certain other festivals
the Dyaks are wont to set a *sawang*-plant, roots and all,
before a priestess; and when the festival is over, the plant
is replaced in the ground.   Such a plant becomes thenceforth a sort of prophetic index for the person in whose
honour the festival was held.   If the plant thrives, the
man will be fortunate; if it fades or perishes, some evil
will befall him.[6]   The Dyaks also believe that at the birth
of every person on earth a flower grows up in the spirit
world and leads a life parallel to his.   If the flower flourishes,

[1] N. Annandale, "Customs of the
Malayo - Siamese," *Fasciculi Malay-
enses*, Anthropology, part ii. (a) (May,
1904), p. 5.

[2] B. F. Matthes, *Bijdragen tot de
Ethnologie van Zuid-Celebes* (The
Hague, 1875), p. 59.

[3] R. van Eck, "Schetsen van het
eiland Bali," *Tijdschrift voor Nederlandsch Indië*, N.S., ix. (1880) pp.
417 *sq.*

[4] G. A. Wilken, "De Simsonsage,"

De Gids, 1888, No. 5, p. 26 (of the
separate reprint); *id.*, *Verspreide Geschriften* (The Hague, 1912), iii. 562.

[5] M. C. Schadee, "Het familie-
leven en familierecht der Dajaks van
Landak en Tajan," *Bijdragen tot de
Taal- Land- en Volkenkunde van
Nederlandsch-Indië*, lxiii. (1910) p.
416.

[6] F. Grabowsky, "Die Theogenie
der Dajaken auf Borneo," *Internationales Archiv für Ethnographie*, v.
(1892) p. 133.

the man enjoys good health, but if it droops, so does he. Hence when he has dreamed bad dreams or has felt unwell for several days, he infers that his flower in the other world is neglected or sickly, and accordingly he employs a medicine-man to tend the precious plant, weed the soil, and sweep it up, in order that the earthly and unearthly life may prosper once more.[1]

It is said that there are still families in Russia, Germany, England, France, and Italy who are accustomed to plant a tree at the birth of a child. The tree, it is hoped, will grow with the child, and it is tended with special care.[2] The custom is still pretty general in the canton of Aargau in Switzerland ; an apple-tree is planted for a boy and a pear-tree for a girl, and the people think that the child will flourish or dwindle with the tree.[3] In Mecklenburg the afterbirth is thrown out at the foot of a young tree, and the child is then believed to grow with the tree.[4] In Bosnia, when the children of a family have died one after the other, the hair of the next child is cut with some ceremony by a stranger, and the mother carries the shorn tresses into the garden, where she ties them to a fine young tree, in order that her child may grow and flourish like the tree.[5] At Muskau, in Lausitz, it used to be customary for bride and bridegroom on the morning of their wedding-day to plant a pair of young oaks side by side, and as each of the trees flourished or withered, so the good luck of the person who planted it was believed to wax or wane.[6] On a promontory in Lake Keitele, in Finland, there used to stand an old fir-tree, which according to tradition had been planted by the first colonists to serve as a symbol or token of their fortune. First-fruits of the harvest used to be offered to the tree

[margin notes:] Birth-trees in Europe.

Marriage oaks.

Trees with which the fate of families or individuals is thought to be bound up.

[1] J. Perham, "Manangism in Borneo," *Journal of the Straits Branch of the Royal Asiatic Society*, No. 19 (Singapore, 1887), p. 97 ; *id.*, in H. Ling Roth, *The Natives of Sarawak and British North Borneo* (London, 1896), i. 278.

[2] Angelo de Gubernatis, *Mythologie des Plantes* (Paris, 1878–1882), i. pp. xxviii. *sq.*

[3] W. Mannhardt, *Baumkultus*, p. 50 ; H. Ploss, *Das Kind*[2] (Leipsic,

1884), i. 79.

[4] K. Bartsch, *Sagen, Märchen und Gebräuche aus Mecklenburg* (Vienna, 1879–1880), ii. p. 43, § 63.

[5] F. S. Krauss, "Haarschurgodschaft bei den Südslaven," *Internationales Archiv für Ethnographie*, vii. (1894) p. 193.

[6] Karl Haupt, *Sagenbuch der Lausitz* (Leipsic, 1862–1863), ii. 129, No. 207.

before any one would taste of the new crop ; and whenever a branch fell, it was deemed a sign that some one would die. More and more the crown of the tree withered away, and in the same proportion the family whose ancestors had planted the fir dwindled away, till only one old woman was left. At last the tree fell, and soon afterwards the old woman departed this life.[1]   When Lord Byron first visited his ancestral estate of Newstead " he planted, it seems, a young oak in some part of the grounds, and had an idea that as *it* flourished so should *he*." [2]   On a day when the cloud that settled on the later years of Sir Walter Scott lifted a little, and he heard that *Woodstock* had sold for over eight thousand pounds, he wrote in his journal: " I have a curious fancy ; I will go set two or three acorns, and judge by their success in growing whether I shall succeed in clearing my way or

The Edge-
well oak.

not." [3]   Near the Castle of Dalhousie, not far from Edinburgh, there grows an oak-tree, called the Edgewell Tree, which is popularly believed to be linked to the fate of the family by a mysterious tie ; for they say that when one of the family dies, or is about to die, a branch falls from the Edgewell Tree.   Thus, on seeing a great bough drop from the tree on a quiet, still day in July 1874, an old forester exclaimed, " The laird's deid noo ! " and soon after news came that Fox Maule, eleventh Earl of Dalhousie, was

The old
tree at
Howth
Castle.

dead.[4]   At Howth Castle in Ireland there is an old tree with which the fortunes of the St. Lawrence family are supposed to be connected.   The branches of the tree are propped on strong supports, for tradition runs that when the tree falls the direct line of the Earls of Howth will become

The oak
of the
Guelphs.

extinct.[5]   On the old road from Hanover to Osnabrück, at the village of Oster-Kappeln, there used to stand an ancient oak, which put out its last green shoot in the year 1849.   The

[1] " Heilige Haine und Bäume der Finnen," *Globus*, lix. (1891) p. 350. Compare K. Rhamm, " Der heidenische Gottesdienst des finnischen Stammes," *Globus*, lxvii. (1891) p. 344.

[2] Thomas Moore, *Life of Lord Byron*, i. 101 (i. 148, in the collected edition of Byron's works, London, 1832–1833).

[3] J. G. Lockhart, *Life of Sir Walter Scott* (First Edition), vi. 283 (viii. 317, Second Edition, Edinburgh, 1839).

[4] Sir Walter Scott's *Journal* (First Edition, Edinburgh, 1890), ii. 282, with the editor's note.

[5] Letter of Miss A. H. Singleton to me, dated Rathmagle House, Abbey Leix, Ireland, 24th February, 1904.

tree was conjecturally supposed to be contemporary with the Guelphs ; and in the year 1866, so fatal for the house of Hanover, on a calm summer afternoon, without any visible cause, the veteran suddenly fell with a crash and lay stretched across the highroad.   The peasants regarded its fall as an ill omen for the reigning family, and when King George V. heard of it he gave orders that the giant trunk should be set up again, and it was done with much trouble and at great expense, the stump being supported in position by iron chains clamped to the neighbouring trees.   But the king's efforts to prop the falling fortunes of his house were vain ; a few months after the fall of the oak Hanover formed part of the Prussian monarchy.[1]

In the midst of the " Forbidden City " at Peking there is a tiny private garden, where the emperors of the now fallen Manchu dynasty used to take the air and refresh themselves after the cares of state.   In accordance with Chinese taste the garden is a labyrinth of artificial rockeries, waterfalls, grottoes, and kiosks, in which everything is as unlike nature as art can make it.   The trees in particular (*Arbor vitae*), the principal ornament of the garden, exhibit the last refinement of the gardener's skill, being clipped and distorted into a variety of grotesque shapes.   Only one of the trees remained intact and had been spared these deformations for centuries.   Far from being stunted by the axe or the shears, the tree was carefully tended and encouraged to shoot up to its full height.   " It was the ' Life-tree of the Dynasty,' and according to legend the prosperity or fall of the present dynasty went hand in hand with the welfare or death of the tree.   Certainly, if we accept the tradition, the days of the present reigning house must be numbered, for all the care and attention lavished on the tree have been for some years in vain.   A glance at our illustration shews the tree as it still surpasses all its fellows in height and size ; but it owes its pre-eminence only to the many artificial props which hold it up.   In reality the ' Life-tree of the Dynasty ' is dying, and might fall over night, if one of its artificial props were suddenly to give way.   For the

The Life-tree of the Manchu dynasty.

[1] P. Wagler, *Die Eiche in alter und neuer Zeit*, ii. (Berlin, 1891) pp. 85 *sq.*

superstitious Chinese—and superstitious they certainly are—it is a very, very evil omen." [1] Some twelve years have passed since this passage was written, and in the interval the omen has been fulfilled — the Manchu dynasty has fallen. We may conjecture that the old tree in the quaint old garden has fallen too. So vain are all human efforts to arrest the decay of royal houses by underpropping trees on which nature herself has passed a sentence of death.

The myrtle-trees of the patricians and plebeians at Rome.

At Rome in the ancient sanctuary of Quirinus there grew two old myrtle-trees, one named the Patrician and the other the Plebeian. For many years, so long as the patricians were in the ascendant, their myrtle-tree flourished and spread its branches abroad, while the myrtle of the plebeians was shrivelled and shrunken ; but from the time of the Marsian war, when the power of the nobles declined, their myrtle in like manner drooped and withered, whereas that of the popular party held up its head and grew strong.[2]

The oak of the Vespasian family.

Thrice when Vespasia was with child, an old oak in the garden of the Flavian family near Rome suddenly put forth branches. The first branch was puny and soon withered away, and the girl who was born accordingly died within the year ; the second branch was long and sturdy ; and the third was like a tree. So on the third occasion the happy father reported to his mother that a future emperor was born to her as a grandchild. The old lady only laughed to think that at her age she should keep her wits about her, while her son had lost his ; yet the omen of the oak came true, for the grandson was afterwards the emperor Vespasian.[3]

Life of persons supposed to be bound up with that of the cleft trees through which in their youth they were

In England children are sometimes passed through a cleft ash-tree as a cure for rupture or rickets, and thenceforward a sympathetic connexion is supposed to exist between them and the tree. An ash-tree which had been used for this purpose grew at the edge of Shirley Heath, on the road from Hockly House to Birmingham. "Thomas Chillingworth, son of the owner of an adjoining farm, now about thirty-four, was, when an infant of a year old,

---

[1] *Die Woche*, Berlin, 31 August, 1901, p. 3, with an illustration shewing the garden and the tree.

[2] Pliny, *Natur. Hist.* xv. 120 *sq.*

[3] Suetonius, *Divus Vespasianus*, 5.

passed through a similar tree, now perfectly sound, which he preserves with so much care that he will not suffer a single branch to be touched, for it is believed the life of the patient depends on the life of the tree, and the moment that is cut down, be the patient ever so distant, the rupture returns, and a mortification ensues, and terminates in death, as was the case in a man driving a waggon on the very road in question." " It is not uncommon, however," adds the writer, " for persons to survive for a time the felling of the tree." [1]   The ordinary mode of effecting the cure is to split a young ash-sapling longitudinally for a few feet and pass the child, naked, either three times or three times three through the fissure at sunrise.   In the West of England it is said that the passage should be " against the sun."   As soon as the ceremony has been performed, the tree is bound tightly up and the fissure plastered over with mud or clay. The belief is that just as the cleft in the tree closes up, so the rupture in the child's body will be healed ; but that if the rift in the tree remains open, the rupture in the child will remain too, and if the tree were to die, the death of the child would surely follow.[2]

Down to the second half of the nineteenth century the remedy was still in common use at Fittleworth and many other places in Sussex.   The account of the

passed as a cure for rupture. In England ruptured children are passed through cleft ash- trees.

The practice in Sussex.

[1] *The Gentleman's Magazine*, 1804, p. 909; John Brand, *Popular Antiquities of Great Britain* (London, 1882–1883), iii. 289.

[2] Gilbert White, *The Natural History of Selborne*, Part II. Letter 28 (Edinburgh, 1829), pp. 239 *sq.* ; Francis Grose, *A Provincial Glossary* (London, 1811), p. 290 ; J. Brand, *op. cit.* iii. 287-292 ; R. Hunt, *Popular Romances of the West of England*[3] (London, 1881), pp. 415, 421 ; W. G. Black, *Folk-medicine* (London, 1883), pp. 67 *sq.* ; W. Wollaston Groome, "Suffolk Leechcraft," *Folk-lore*, vi. (1895) pp. 123 *sq.* ; E. S. Hartland, in *Folk-lore*, vii. (1896) pp. 303-306 ; *County Folk-lore, Suffolk*, edited by Lady E. C. Gurdon (London, 1893) pp. 26-28 ; Beatrix A. Wherry, " Mis- cellaneous Notes from Monmouth- shire," *Folk-lore*, xvi. (1905) p. 65 ; Marie Trevelyan, *Folk-lore and Folk- stories of Wales* (London, 1909), p. 320.   Sometimes the tree was an oak instead of an ash (M. Trevelyan, *l.c.*). To ensure the success of the cure various additional precautions are some- times recommended, as that the ash should be a maiden, that is a tree that has never been topped or cut ; that the split should be made east and west ; that the child should be passed into the tree by a maiden and taken out on the other side by a boy ; that the child should always be passed through head foremost (but according to others feet foremost), and so forth.   In Surrey we hear of a holly-tree being used instead of an ash (*Notes and Queries*, Sixth Series, xi. Jan.-Jun. 1885, p. 46).

Sussex practice and belief is notable because it brings out very clearly the sympathetic relation supposed to exist between the ruptured child and the tree through which it has been passed. We are told that the patient " must be passed nine times every morning on nine successive days at sunrise through a cleft in a sapling ash-tree, which has been so far given up by the owner of it to the parents of the child, as that there is an understanding it shall not be cut down during the life of the infant who is to be passed through it. The sapling must be sound at heart, and the cleft must be made with an axe. The child on being carried to the tree must be attended by nine persons, each of whom must pass it through the cleft from west to east. On the ninth morning the solemn ceremony is concluded by binding the tree lightly with a cord, and it is supposed that as the cleft closes the health of the child will improve. In the neighbourhood of Petworth some cleft ash-trees may be seen, through which children have very recently been passed. I may add, that only a few weeks since, a person who had lately purchased an ash-tree standing in this parish, intending to cut it down, was told by the father of a child, who had some time before been passed through it, that the infirmity would be sure to return upon his son if it were felled. Whereupon the good man said, he knew that such would be the case ; and therefore he would not fell it for the world." [1]

Sick children passed through cleft trees, especially oaks, as a cure in Germany, France, Denmark, Sweden, and Greece.

A similar cure for various diseases, but especially for rupture and rickets, has been commonly practised in other parts of Europe, as Germany, France, Denmark, and Sweden ; but in these countries the tree employed for the purpose is usually not an ash but an oak ; sometimes a willow-tree is allowed or even prescribed instead. With these exceptions the practice and the belief are nearly the same on the Continent as in England : a young oak is split longitudinally and the two sides held forcibly apart while the sick child is passed through the cleft ; then the opening in the tree is closed, and bound up, and it is believed that as the cleft in the tree heals by the parts

[1] " Some West Sussex superstitions lingering in 1868, collected by Charlotte Latham, at Fittleworth," *Folk-lore Record*, i. (1878) pp. 40 *sq.*

growing together again, so the rupture in the child will be simultaneously cured. It is often laid down that the ceremony must be performed in the strictest silence; sometimes the time prescribed is before sunrise, and sometimes the child must be passed thrice through the cleft.[1] In Oldenburg and Mecklenburg they say that the cure should be performed on St. John's Eve (Midsummer Eve) by three men named John, who assist each other in holding the split

[1] For the custom in Germany and Austria, see J. Grimm, *Deutsche Mythologie*,[4] ii. 975 *sq.* ; A. Wuttke, *Der deutsche Volksaberglaube* [2] (Berlin, 1869), p. 317, § 503; A. Kuhn und W. Schwartz, *Nord-deutsche Sagen, Märchen und Gebräuche* (Leipsic, 1848), pp. 443 *sq.* ; J. F. L. Woeste, *Volksüberlieferungen in der Grafschaft Mark* (Iserlohn, 1848), p. 54; E. Meier, *Deutsche Sagen, Sitten und Gebräuche aus Schwaben* (Stuttgart, 1852), p. 390, § 56; F. Panzer, *Beitrag zur deutschen Mythologie* (Munich, 1848-1855), ii. 301 ; *Bavaria, Landes- und Volkskunde des Königreichs Bayern*, ii. (Munich, 1863) p. 255 ; J. A. E. Köhler, *Volksbrauch, Aberglauben, Sagen und andre alte Ueberlieferungen im Voigtlande* (Leipsic, 1867), pp. 415 *sq.* ; L. Strackerjan, *Aberglaube und Sagen aus dem Herzogthum Oldenburg* (Oldenburg, 1867), i. 72 *sq.*, § 88; K. Bartsch, *Sagen, Märchen und Gebräuche aus Mecklenburg* (Vienna, 1879-1880), ii. 290 *sq.*, § 1447 ; J. Haltrich, *Zur Volkskunde der Siebenbürger Sachsen* (Vienna, 1885), p. 264 ; P. Wagler, *Die Eiche in alter und neuer Zeit*, i. (Wurzen, 1891) pp. 21-23. As to the custom in France, see Marcellus, *De medicamentis*, xxxiii. 26 (where the tree is a cherry) ; J. B. Thiers, *Traité des Superstitions* (Paris, 1679), pp. 333 *sq.* ; A. de Nore, *Coutumes, Mythes et Traditions des Provinces de France* (Paris and Lyons, 1846), p. 231; L. J. B. Bérenger-Féraud, in *Bulletins de la Société d'Anthropologie de Paris*, iv. série, i. (1890) pp. 895-902; *id., Superstitions et Survivances* (Paris, 1896), i. 523 *sqq.* As to the custom in Denmark and Sweden, see J. Grimm, *Deutsche Mythologie*,[4] ii. 976 ; H. F. Feilberg, "Zwieselbäume nebst verwandtem Aberglauben in Skandinavien," *Zeitschrift des Vereins für Volkskunde*, vii. (1897) pp. 42 *sqq.* In Mecklenburg it is sometimes required that the tree should have been split by lightning (K. Bartsch, *l.c.*). The whole subject of passing sick people through narrow apertures as a mode of cure has been well handled in an elegant little monograph (*Un Vieux Rite médical*, Paris, 1892) by Monsieur H. Gaidoz, who rightly rejects the theory that all such passages are symbols of a new birth. But I cannot agree with him in thinking that the essence of the rite consists in the transference of the disease from the person to the tree ; rather, it seems to me, the primary idea is that of interposing an impassable barrier between a fugitive and his pursuing foe, though no doubt the enemy thus left behind is apparently supposed to adhere to the further side of the obstacle (whether tree, stone, or what not) through which he cannot pass. However, the sympathetic relation supposed to exist between the sufferer and the tree through which he has been passed certainly favours the view that he has left some portion of himself attached to the tree. But in this as in many similar cases, the ideas in the minds of the persons who practise the custom are probably vague, confused, and inconsistent ; and we need not attempt to define them precisely. Compare also R. Andree, *Ethnographische Parallelen und Vergleiche* (Stuttgart, 1878), pp. 31 *sq.* ; E. S. Hartland, *The Legend of Perseus* (London, 1894-1896), ii. 146 *sq.* ; L. J. B. Bérenger-Féraud, *Superstitions et Survivances* (Paris, 1896), i. 523-540.

oak-sapling open and passing the child through it.[1]   Some people, however, prefer Good Friday or Christmas Eve as the season for the performance of the ceremony.[2]   In Denmark copper coins are laid as an offering at the foot of the tree through which sick persons have been passed ; and threads, ribbons, or bandages which have been worn by the sufferers are tied to a branch of the tree.[3]   In the Greek island of Ceos, when a child is sickly, the parents carry it out into the country " and the father selects a young oak ; this they split up from the root, then the father is assisted by another man in holding the tree open whilst the mother passes the child three times through, and then they bind up the tree well, cover it all over with manure, and carefully water it for forty days.   In the same fashion they bind up the child for a like period, and after the lapse of this time they expect that it will be quite well." [4]

Sympathetic relation thought to exist between the child and the tree through which it has been passed.

In Mecklenburg, as in England, the sympathetic relation thus established between the tree and the child is so close that if the tree is cut down the child will die.[5]   In the island of Rügen people believe that when a person who has been thus cured of rupture dies, his soul passes into the same oak-tree through which his body was passed in his youth.[6]   Thus it seems that in ridding himself of the disease the sufferer is supposed to transfer a certain vital part of his person to the tree so that it is impossible to injure the tree without at the same time injuring the man ; and in Rügen this partial union is thought to be completed by the transmigration of the man's soul at death into the tree.

The disease is apparently thought to be left behind on the farther side of the cleft tree.

Apparently the disease is conceived as something physical, which clings to the patient but can be stripped off him and left behind on the farther side of the narrow aperture through which he has forced his way ; when the aperture is closed by the natural growth of the tree, the door is as it

[1] L. Strackerjan, *l.c.* ; K. Bartsch, *l.c.*

[2] E. Meier, *l.c.* ; *Bavaria, Landes- und Volkskunde des Königreichs Bayern*, ii. 255 ; A. Wuttke, *l.c.*

[3] H. F. Feilberg, "Zwieselbäume nebst verwandtem Aberglauben in Skandinavien," *Zeitschrift des Vereins für Volkskunde*, vii. (1897) p. 44.

[4] J. Theodore Bent, *The Cyclades* (London, 1885), pp. 457 *sq.*

[5] H. Ploss, *Das Kind* [2] (Leipsic, 1884), ii. 221.

[6] R. Baier, "Beiträge von der Insel Rügen," *Zeitschrift für deutsche Mythologie und Sittenkunde*, ii. (1855) p. 141.

were shut against the disease, which is then unable to pursue and overtake the sufferer. Hence the idea at the root of the custom is not so much that the patient has transferred his ailment to the tree, as that the tree forms an impervious barrier between him and the malady which had hitherto afflicted him. This interpretation is confirmed by the following parallels.

In those parts of Armenia which are covered with forests, many great and ancient trees are revered as sacred and receive marks of homage. The people burn lights before them, fumigate them with incense, sacrifice cocks and wethers to them, and creep through holes in their trunks or push lean and sickly children through them "in order to put a stop to the influence of evil spirits."[1] Apparently, they think that evil spirits cannot creep through the cleft in the holy tree, and therefore that the sick who have effected the passage are safe from their demoniacal pursuers. The same conception of a fissure in a tree as an obstacle placed in the path of pursuing spirits meets us in a number of savage customs. Thus in the island of Nias, when a man is in training for the priesthood, he has to be introduced to the various spirits between whom and mankind it will be his office to mediate. A priest takes him to an open window, and while the drums are beating points out to him the great spirit in the sun who calls away men to himself through death ; for it is needful that the future priest should know him from whose grasp he will often be expected to wrest the sick and dying. In the evening twilight he is led to the graves and shewn the envious spirits of the dead, who also are ever drawing away the living to their own shadowy world. Next day he is conducted to a river and shewn the spirit of the waters ; and finally they take him up to a mountain and exhibit to him the spirits of the mountains, who have diverse shapes, some appearing like swine, others like buffaloes, others like goats, and others again like men with long hair on their bodies. When he has seen all this, his education is complete, but on his return from the mountain the new priest may not at once enter his own house. For the people think that, were he to do so, the

[marginal note: Creeping through cleft trees to get rid of spirits in Armenia and Nias.]

[1] Manuk Abeghian, *Der armenische Volksglaube* (Leipsic, 1899), p. 58.

dangerous spirits by whom he is still environed would stay in the house and visit both the family and the pigs with sickness. Accordingly he betakes himself to other villages and passes several nights there, hoping that the spirits will leave him and settle on the friends who receive him into their houses; but naturally he does not reveal the intention of his visits to his hosts. Lastly, before he enters his own dwelling, he looks out for some young tree by the way, splits it down the middle, and then creeps through the fissure, in the belief that any spirit which may still be clinging to him will thus be left sticking to the tree.[1] Again, among the Bilqula or Bella Coola Indians of British Columbia "the bed of a mourner must be protected against the ghost of the deceased. His male relatives stick a thorn-bush into the ground at each corner of their beds. After four days these are thrown into the water. Mourners must rise early and go into the woods, where they stick four thorn-bushes into the ground, at the corners of a square, in which they cleanse themselves by rubbing their bodies with cedar branches. They also swim in ponds. After swimming they cleave four small trees and creep through the clefts, following the course of the sun. This they do on four subsequent mornings, cleaving new trees every day. Mourners cut their hair short. The hair that has been cut off is burnt. If they should not observe these regulations, it is believed that they would dream of the deceased."[2] To the savage, who fails to distinguish the visions of sleep from the

(marginal note:) Among the Bella Coola Indians mourners creep through cleft trees to get rid of the ghost.

---

[1] Fr. Kramer, "Der Götzendienst der Niasser," *Tijdschrift voor Indische Taal- Land- en Volkenkunde,* xxxiii. (1890) pp. 478-480; H. Sundermann, *Die Insel Nias und die Mission daselbst* (Barmen, 1905), pp. 81-83. According to the latter writer the intention of passing through the cleft stick is "to strip off from himself (*von sich abzustreifen*) the last spirit that may have followed him." The notion that the sun causes death by drawing away the souls of the living is Indian. See *The Satapatha Brâhmana,* ii. 3. 3. 7-8, translated by Julius Eggeling, Part I. (Oxford, 1882) p. 343 (*Sacred Books of the East,* vol. xii.): "Now yonder burning (sun) doubtless is no

other than Death; and because he is Death, therefore the creatures that are on this side of him die. But those that are on the other side of him are the gods, and they are therefore immortal. . . . And the breath of whomsoever he (the sun) wishes he takes and rises, and that one dies."

[2] Fr. Boas, in *Seventh Report on the North-Western Tribes of Canada,* p. 13 (separate reprint from the *Report of the British Association,* Cardiff meeting, 1891). The Shuswap Indians of the same region also fence their beds against ghosts with a hedge of thorn bushes. See *Taboo and the Perils of the Soul,* p. 142.

appearances of waking life, the apparition of a dead man in a dream is equivalent to the actual presence of the ghost; and accordingly he seeks to keep off the spiritual intruder, just as he might a creature of flesh and blood, by fencing his bed with thorn-bushes. Similarly the practice of creeping through four cleft trees is clearly an attempt to shake off the clinging ghost and leave it adhering to the trees, just as in Nias the future priest hopes to rid himself in like manner of the dangerous spirits who have dogged his steps from the mountains and the graves.

This interpretation of the custom is strongly confirmed by a funeral ceremony which Dr. Charles Hose witnessed at the chief village of the Madangs, a tribe of Kayans who occupy a hitherto unexplored district in the heart of Borneo. "Just across the river from where we were sitting," says Dr. Hose, "was the graveyard, and there I witnessed a funeral procession as the day was drawing to a close. The coffin, which was a wooden box made from a tree-trunk, was decorated with red and black patterns in circles, with two small wooden figures of men placed at either end; it was lashed with rattans to a long pole, and by this means was lifted to the shoulders of the bearers, who numbered thirteen in all, and who then carried it to the burying-ground. After the mourners had all passed over to the graveyard, a man quickly cut a couple of small sticks, each five feet long and about an inch in diameter. One of these he split almost the whole way down, and forced the unsplit end into the ground, when the upper part opened like a V, leaving sufficient room for each person to pass through. He next split the top of the other stick, and, placing another short stick in the cleft, made a cross, which he also forced into the ground. The funeral procession climbed the mound on which the cemetery was situated, passing through the V of the cleft stick in single file. As soon as the coffin had been placed on the stage erected for the purpose, the people commenced their return, following on one another's heels as quickly as possible, each spitting out the words, '*Pit balli krat balli jat tesip bertatip !*' ('Keep back, and close out all things evil, and sickness') as they passed through the V-shaped stick. The whole party having

The Madangs of Borneo creep through a cleft stick after a funeral in order to rid themselves of the ghost.

left the graveyard, the gate was closed by the simple process of tying the cleft ends of the stick together, and a few words were then said to the cross-stick, whick they call *ngring*, or the wall that separates the living from the dead. All who had taken part in the ceremony then went and bathed before returning to their homes, rubbing their skins with rough pebbles, the old Mosaic idea of the uncleanness of the dead, as mentioned in Numbers (chap. xix.), evidently finding a place among their religious beliefs. It is apparently a great relief to their minds to think that they can shut out the spirit of the deceased. They believe that the spirit of the dead is not aware that life has left the body until a short time after the coffin has been taken to the graveyard, and then not until the spirit has had leisure to notice the clothes, weapons, and other articles belonging to its earthly estate, which are placed with the coffin. But before this takes place the gate has been closed." [1]

The cleft stick or tree through which a person passes is a barrier to part him from a dangerous foe ; the closing of the cleft is like shutting the door in the face of a pursuer. But combined with this in the case of ruptured

Here the words uttered by the mourners in passing through the cloven stick shew clearly that they believe the stick to act as a barrier or fence, on the further side of which they leave behind the ghost or other dangerous spirit whose successful pursuit might entail sickness and death on the survivors. Thus the passage of these Madang mourners through the cleft stick is strictly analogous to the passage of ruptured English children through a cleft ash-tree. Both are simply ways of leaving an evil thing behind. Similarly the subsequent binding up of the cloven stick in Borneo is analogous to the binding up of the cloven ash-tree in England. Both are ways of barricading the road against the evil which is dogging your steps ; having passed through the doorway you slam the door in the face of your pursuer. Yet it seems probable that the intention of binding up the cleft in a tree through which a ruptured patient has been

---

[1] C. Hose, "In the heart of Borneo," *The Geographical Journal*, xvi. (1900) pp. 45 *sq.* Compare C. Hose and W. McDougall, *The Pagan Tribes of Borneo* (London, 1912), ii. 36 *sq.*, where, after describing the ceremony of passing through the cloven stick, the writers add : "In this way the Kayans symbolically prevent any of the un- canny influences of the graveyard following the party back to the house ; though they do not seem to be clear as to whether it is the ghosts of the dead, or the *Toh* of the neighbourhood, or those which may have contributed to his death, against whom these precautions are taken."

passed is not merely that of shutting the door on the malady
conceived as a personal being ; combined with this idea is
perhaps the notion that in virtue of the law of magical homoeo-
pathy the rupture in the body of the sufferer will close up
exactly in the same measure as the cleft in the tree closes up
through the force of bandages and of natural growth.   That
this shade of meaning attaches to the custom is rendered
probable by a comparison of an ancient Roman cure for
dislocation, which has been preserved for us by the grave
authority of the elder Cato.   He recommended that a green
reed, four or five feet long, should be taken, split down the
middle, and held by two men to the dislocated bones while
a curious and now unintelligible spell was recited ; then,
when the spell had been recited and the aperture in the reed
had closed, the reed was to be tied to the dislocated limb,
and a perfect cure might be expected.   Apparently it was
supposed that just as the two sides of the split reed came
together and coalesced after being held apart, so the dislocated
bones would come together and fit into their proper places.[1]

But the usual idea in passing through a narrow aperture as a cure or preventive of evil would seem to be
simply that of giving the slip to a dangerous pursuer.   With
this intention, doubtless, the savage Thays of Tonquin
repair after a burial to the banks of a stream and there
creep through a triangle formed by leaning two reeds
against each other, while the sorcerer souses them with dirty
water.   All the relations of the deceased must wash their
garments in the stream before they return home, and they
may not set foot in the house till they have shorn their hair

(marginal notes:) patients seems to be the idea that the rupture heals sympathetically as the cleft in the tree closes. Analogous Roman cure for dislocation.

Other examples of creeping through narrow openings after a death.

---

[1] Cato, *De agri cultura*, 159 (pp.
106 *sq.* ed. H. Keil, Leipsic, 1884) :
"*Luxum siquod est, hac cantione sanum
fiet. Harundinem prende tibi viridem
P. III. aut quinque longam, mediam
diffinde, et duo homines teneant ad
coxendices. Incipe cantare in alio s. f.
moetas vaeta daries dardaries asia-
darides una petes, usque dum coeant.
Motas vaeta daries dardares astataries
dissunapiter, usque dum coeant. Fer-
rum insuper jactato. Ubi coierint et
altera alteram tetigerint, id manu pre-
hende et dextera sinistra praecide, ad
luxum aut ad fracturam alliga, sanum*
fiet." The passage is obscure and perhaps corrupt.   It is not clear whether
"*usque dum coeant*" and "*ubi coierint*"
refer to the drawing together of the
bones or of the split portions of the
reed, but apparently the reference is
to the reed.   The charm is referred to
by Pliny, *Nat. Hist.*, xvii. 267 :
"*Quippe cum averti grandines carmine
credant plerique, cujus verba inserere
non equidem serio ausim, quamquam a
Catone proditis contra luxata membra
jungenda harundinum fissurae.*" Compare J. Grimm, *Deutsche Mythologie,*[4]
i. 186, ii. 1031 *sq.*

at the foot of the ladder. Afterwards the sorcerer comes
and sprinkles the whole house with water for the purpose of
expelling evil spirits.[1] Here again we cannot doubt that
the creeping through the triangle of reeds is intended to
rid the mourners of the troublesome ghost. So when the
Kamtchatkans had disposed of a corpse after their usual
fashion by throwing it to the dogs to be devoured, they
purified themselves as follows. They went into the forest
and cut various roots which they bent into rings, and through
these rings they crept twice. Afterwards they carried the
rings back to the forest and flung them away westward.
The Koryaks, a people of the same region, burn their dead
and hold a festival in honour of the departed a year after
the death. At this festival, which takes place on the spot
where the corpse was burned, or, if that is too far off, on a
neighbouring height, they sacrifice two young reindeer which
have never been in harness, and the sorcerer sticks a great
many reindeer horns in the earth, believing that thereby
he is dispatching a whole herd of these animals to their
deceased friend in the other world. Then they all hasten
home, and purify themselves by passing between two poles
planted in the ground, while the sorcerer strikes them with
a stick and adjures death not to carry them off.[2] The
Tokoelawi in the interior of Central Celebes hold a great
sacrificial festival on the eighth day after the death of a man
or the ninth day after the death of a woman. When the
guests return homewards after the festival they pass under
two poles placed in a slanting direction against each other,
and they may not look round at the house where the death
occurred. " In this way they take a final leave of the soul
of the deceased. Afterwards no more sacrifices are offered
to the soul." [3] Among the Toboengkoe, another tribe in the
interior of Central Celebes, when a man buries his wife, he
goes to the grave by a different road from that along which

[1] Pinabel, "Notes sur quelques
peuplades dépendant du Tong-King,"
Bulletin de la Société de Géographie,
Septième Série, v. (Paris, 1884) p.
430 ; A. Bourlet, "Funérailles chez
les Thay," *Anthropos*, viii. (1913) p.
45.

[2] S. Krascheninnikow, *Beschreibung*

des Landes Kamtschatka (Lemgo,
1766), pp. 268, 282.

[3] N. Adriani en Alb. C. Kruijt,
"Van Posso naar Parigi, Sigi en
Lindoe," *Mededeelingen van wege het
Nederlandsche Zendelinggenootschap*,
xlii. (1898) p. 502. The poles are of
a certain plant or tree called *bomba*.

the corpse is carried; and on certain days afterwards he bathes, and on returning from the bath must pass through a Λ-shaped erection, which is formed by splitting a pole up the middle and separating the two split pieces except at the top. "This he must do in order that his second wife, if he has one, may not soon die."[1]   Here the notion probably is that the jealous ghost of the dead wife seeks to avenge herself on her living rival by carrying off her soul with her to deadland.   Hence to prevent this catastrophe the husband tries to evade the ghost, first by going to the grave along a different path, and second by passing under a cleft stick, through which as usual the spirit cannot follow him.

In the light of the foregoing customs, as well as of a multitude of ceremonies observed for a similar purpose in all parts of the world,[2] we may safely assume that when people creep through rings after a death or pass between poles after a sacrifice to the dead, their intention simply is to interpose a barrier between themselves and the ghost; they make their way through a narrow pass or aperture through which they hope that the ghost will not be able to follow them. To put it otherwise, they conceive that the spirit of the dead is sticking to them like a burr, and that like a burr it may be rubbed or scraped off and left adhering to the sides of the opening through which they have squeezed themselves. *The intention of the custom probably is to escape from the ghost of the dead.*

Similarly, when a pestilence is raging among the Koryaks, they kill a dog, wind its guts about two poles, and pass between the poles,[3] doubtless for the sake of giving the slip to the demon of the plague in the same way that they give the slip to the ghost.   When the Kayans of Borneo have been dogged by an evil spirit on a journey and are nearing their destination, they fashion a small archway of boughs, light a fire under it, and pass in single file under the archway and over the fire, spitting into the fire as they pass.   By this ceremony, we are told, "they thoroughly exorcise the *Passing through an archway in order to escape from demons.*

---

[1] Alb. C. Kruijt, "Eenige ethnografische aanteekeningen omtrent de Toboengkoe en de Tomori," *Mededeelingen van wege het Nederlandsche Zendelinggenootschap,* xliv. (1900) p. 223.

[2] For examples of these ceremonies I may refer to my article, "On certain burial customs as illustrative of the primitive theory of the soul," *Journal of the Anthropological Institute,* xv. (1886) pp. 64 *sqq.*

[3] S. Krascheninnikow, *Beschreibung des Landes Kamtschatka* (Lemgo, 1766), pp. 277 *sq.*

evil spirits and emerge on the other side free from all baleful influences."[1]   Here, to make assurance doubly sure, a fire as well as an archway is interposed between the travellers and the dreadful beings who are walking unseen behind.   To crawl under a bramble which has formed an arch by sending down a second root into the ground, is an English and Welsh cure for whooping-cough, rheumatism, boils, and other complaints. In some parts of the west of England they say that to get rid of boils the thing to do is to crawl through such a natural arch nine times against the sun ; but in Devonshire the patient should creep through the arch thrice with the sun, that is from east to west.   When a child is passed through it for whooping-cough, the operators ought to say :

Crawling under an arch of bramble as a cure for various maladies.

> " *In bramble, out cough,*
> *Here I leave the whooping-cough.*"[2]

Crawling under arches of various sorts as a cure or preventive of sickness.

In Perigord and other parts of France the same cure is employed for boils.[3]   In Bulgaria, when a person suffers from a congenital malady such as scrofula, a popular cure is to take him to a neighbouring village and there make him creep naked thrice through an arch, which is formed by inserting the lower ends of two vine branches in the ground and joining their upper ends together.   When he has done so, he hangs his clothes on a tree, and dons other garments.   On his way home the patient must also crawl under a ploughshare, which is held high enough to let him pass.[4]   Further, when

---

[1] W. H. Furness, *Folk-lore in Borneo, a Sketch*, p. 28 (Wallingford, Pennsylvania, 1899, privately printed). Compare *id.*, *The Home-life of Borneo Head-hunters* (Philadelphia, 1902), p. 28 : "Here a halt for final purification was made.   An arch of boughs about five feet high was erected on the beach, and beneath it a fire was kindled, and then Tama Bulan, holding a young chicken, which he waved and brushed over every portion of the arch, invoked all evil spirits which had been accompanying us, and forbade them to follow us further through the fire.   The fowl was then killed, its blood smeared all over the archway and sprinkled in the fire ; then, led by Tama Bulan, the whole party filed under the arch, and as they

stepped over the fire each one spat in it vociferously and immediately took his place in the boats."

[2] T. F. Thiselton Dyer, *English Folk-lore* (London, 1884), pp. 171 *sq.* ; W. G. Black, *Folk-medicine* (London, 1883), p. 70 ; R. Hunt, *Popular Romances of the West of England*, Third Edition (London, 1881), pp. 412, 415 ; Marie Trevelyan, *Folk-lore and Folk-stories of Wales* (London, 1909), p. 320.

[3] A. de Nore, *Coutumes, Mythes et Traditions des Provinces de France* (Paris and Lyons, 1846), p. 152 ; H. Gaidoz, *Un Vieux Rite médical* (Paris, 1892), pp. 7 *sq.*

[4] A. Strausz, *Die Bulgaren* (Leipsic, 1898), p. 414.

whooping-cough is prevalent in a Bulgarian village, an old woman will scrape the earth from under the root of a willow-tree.   Then all the children of the village creep through the opening thus made, and a thread from the garment of each of them is hung on the willow.   Adults sometimes go through the same ceremony after recovering from a dangerous illness.[1]   Similarly, when sickness is rife among some of the villages to the east of Lake Nyassa, the inhabitants crawl through an arch formed by bending a wand and inserting the two ends in the ground.   By way of further precaution they wash themselves on the spot with medicine and water, and then bury the medicine and the evil influence together in the earth.   The same ceremony is resorted to as a means of keeping off evil spirits, wild beasts, and enemies.[2]

In Uganda "sometimes a medicine-man directed a sick man to provide an animal, promising that he would come and transfer the sickness to the animal.   The medicine-man would then select a plantain-tree near the house, kill the animal by it, and anoint the sick man with its blood, on his forehead, on each side of his chest, and on his legs above the knees.   The plantain-tree selected had to be one that was about to bear fruit, and the medicine-man would split the stem from near the top to near the bottom, leaving a few inches not split both at the top and at the bottom ; the split stem would be held open so that the sick man could step through it, and in doing so he would leave his clothing at the plantain-tree, and would run into the house without looking back.   When he entered the house, new clothes would be given him to wear.   The plantain, the clothing, and meat would be carried away by the medicine-man, who would deposit the plantain-tree on waste land, but would take the meat and clothing for himself.   Sometimes the medicine-man would kill the animal near the hut, lay a stout stick across the threshold, and narrow the doorway by partially filling it with branches of trees ; he would then put some of the blood on either side of the narrow entrance, and some on the stick across the threshold, and

Custom in Uganda of causing a sick man to pass through a cleft stick or a narrow opening in the door-way.

---

[1] A. Strausz, *op. cit.* p. 404.   As to the Bulgarian custom of creeping through a tunnel in a time of epidemic, see above, vol. i. pp. 282-284.

[2] *Last Journals of David Livingstone in Central Africa* (London, 1874), i. 60.

would also anoint with it the sick man, who would be taken outside for the purpose. The patient would then re-enter the house, letting his clothing fall off, as he passed through the doorway. The medicine-man would carry away the branches, the stick, the clothing, and the meat. The branches and the stick he would cast upon waste land, but the meat and the clothing he would keep for himself." [1] Here the notion of transferring the sickness to the animal is plainly combined with, we may almost say overshadowed by the notion that the ailment is left behind adhering to the cleft plantain-stem or to the stick and branches of the narrow opening through which the patient has made his way. That obviously is why the plantain-stem or the stick and branches are thrown away on waste land, lest they should infect other people with the sickness which has been transferred to them.

Similar custom practised by the Kai of New Guinea and the Looboos of Sumatra for the purpose of giving the slip to spiritual pursuers.   The Kai of German New Guinea attribute sickness to the agency either of ghosts or of sorcerers, but suspicion always falls at first on ghosts, who are deemed even worse than the sorcerers. To cure a sick man they will sometimes cleave a stick in the middle, leaving the two ends intact, and then oblige the sufferer to insert his head through the cleft. After that they stroke his whole body with the stick from head to foot. "The stick with the soul-stuff of the ghosts is then hurled away or otherwise destroyed, whereupon the sick man is supposed to recover." [2] Here the ghosts who cause the sickness are clearly supposed to be scraped from the patient's body by means of the cleft stick, and to be thrown away or destroyed with the implement. The Looboos, a primitive tribe in the Mandailing district of Sumatra, stand in great fear of the wandering spirits of the dead (*soemangots*). But "they know all sorts of means of protecting themselves against the unwelcome visits of the spirits. For example, if a man has lost his way in the forest, he thinks that this is the work of such a spirit (*soemangot*), who dogs the

---

[1] Rev. J. Roscoe, *The Baganda* (London, 1911), p. 343. Compare *id.*, "Notes on the Manners and Customs of the Baganda," *Journal of the Anthropological Institute*, xxxi. (1901) p. 126; *id.*, "Further Notes on the Manners and Customs of the Baganda," *Journal of the Anthropological Institute*, xxxii. (1902) pp. 42 *sq.*

[2] Ch. Keysser, "Aus dem Leben der Kaileute," in R. Neuhauss's *Deutsch Neu-Guinea*, iii. (Berlin, 1911) pp. 141 *sq.*

wanderer and bedims his sight. So in order to throw the malignant spirit off the track he takes a rattan and splits it through the middle. By bending the rattan an opening is made, through which he creeps. After that the rattan is quickly stretched and the opening closes. By this procedure the spirit (so they think) cannot find the opening again and so cannot further follow his victim."[1] Here therefore, the passage through a cleft stick is conceived in the clearest way as an escape from a spiritual pursuer, and the closing of the aperture when the fugitive has passed through it is nothing but the slamming of the door in the face of his invisible foe.

A similar significance is probably to be attached to other cases of ceremonially passing through a cleft stick even where the intention of the rite is not expressly alleged. Thus among the Ovambo of German South-West Africa young women who have become marriageable perform a variety of ceremonies; among other things they dance in the large and the small cattle-kraal. On quitting the large cattle-kraal after the dance, and on entering and quitting the small cattle-kraal, they are obliged to pass, one after the other, through the fork of a cleft stick, of which the two sides are held wide open by an old man.[2] Among the Washamba of German East Africa, when a boy has been circumcised, two women bring a long sugar-cane, which still bears its leaves. The cane is split at some distance from its upper and lower ends and the two sides are held apart so as to form a cleft or opening; at the lower end of the cleft a *danga* ring is fastened. The father and mother of the circumcised youth now place the sugar-cane between them, touch the ring with their feet, and then slip through the cleft; and after them the lad's aunt must also pass through the cleft sugar-cane.[3] In both these cases the passage through the cleft stick is probably intended to give

Passing through cleft sticks in connexion with puberty and circumcision.

---

[1] J. Kreemer, "De Loeboes in Mandailing," *Bijdragen tot de Taal- Land- en Volkenkunde van Neder- landsch- Indie*, lxvi. (1912) p. 327.

[2] Hermann Tönjes, *Ovamboland, Land, Leute, Mission* (Berlin, 1911), pp. 139 *sq.* The writer was unable to

ascertain the meaning of the rite ; the natives would only say that it was their custom.

[3] A. Karasek, "Beiträge zur Kenntnis der Waschambo," *Baessler- Archiv*, i. (Leipsic and Berlin, 1911) p. 192.

the slip to certain dangerous spirits, which are apt to molest people at such critical seasons as puberty and circumcision.

Crawling through a ring or hoop as a cure or preventive of disease.

Again, the passage through a ring or hoop is resorted to for like reasons as a mode of curing or preventing disease. Thus in Sweden, when a natural ring has been found in a tree, it is carefully removed and treasured in the family ; for sick and especially rickety children are healed by merely passing through it.[1]   A young married woman in Sweden, who suffered from an infirmity, was advised by a wise woman to steal three branches of willow, make them into a hoop, and creep through it naked, taking care not to touch the hoop and to keep perfectly silent.   The hoop was afterwards to be burnt.   She carried out the prescription faithfully, and her faith was rewarded by a perfect cure.[2]   No doubt her infirmity was thought to adhere to the hoop and to be burnt with it.   Similarly in Scotland children who suffered from hectic fever and consumptive patients used to be healed by passing thrice through a circular wreath of woodbine, which was cut during the increase of the March moon and was let down over the body of the sufferer from the head to the feet. Thus Jonet Stewart cured sundry women by "taking ane garland of grene woodbynd, and causing the patient pas thryis throw it, quhilk thairefter scho cut in nyne pieces, and cast in the fyre."   Another wise woman transmitted the sick "throw ane girth of woodbind thryis thre times, saying, ' I do this in name of the Father, the Sone, and the Halie Ghaist.' "[3]   The Highlanders of Strathspey used to force all their sheep and lambs to pass through a hoop of rowan-tree on All Saints' Day and Beltane (the first of November and the first of May),[4] probably as a means of

Passing sheep through a hoop of rowan.

[1] H. F. Feilberg, "Zwieselbäume nebst verwandtem Aberglauben in Skandinavien," *Zeitschrift des Vereins für Volkskunde*, vii. (1897) pp. 49 sq.

[2] H. F. Feilberg, *op. cit.* p. 44.

[3] J. G. Dalyell, *The Darker Superstitions of Scotland* (Edinburgh, 1834), p. 121 ; Ch. Rogers, *Social Life in Scotland* (Edinburgh, 1884-1886), iii. 239.

[4] John Ramsay of Ochtertyre, *Scotland and Scotsmen in the Eighteenth*

Century, edited by A. Allardyce, (Edinburgh and London, 1888), ii. 454.   Immediately after mentioning this custom the writer adds : " And in Breadalbane it is the custom for the dairymaid to drive the cattle to the sheals with a wand of that tree [the rowan] cut upon the day of removal, which is laid above the door until the cattle be going back again to the wintertown.   This was reckoned a preservative against witchcraft."   As to the activity of witches and fairies on Hallowe'en and

warding off the witches and fairies, who are especially
dreaded at these seasons, and against whose malignant arts
the rowan-tree affords an efficient protection.   In Oldenburg   Milking
when a cow gives little or no milk, they milk her through a   a cow
                                                               through
hole in a branch.   In Eversten they say that this should be   a natural
done through a ring which an oak-tree has formed round the   wooden
                                                             ring or a
scar where a branch has been sawn off.   Others say the   "witch's
beast should be milked through a "witch's nest," that is,   nest."
through the boughs of a birch-tree which have grown in a
tangle.   Such a " witch's nest " is also hung up in a pig's stye
to protect the pig against witchcraft.[1]   Hence the aim of
milking a cow through a "witch's nest" or through a natural
wooden ring is no doubt to deliver the poor creature from
an artful witch who has been draining away the milk into
her own pail, as witches are too apt to do.   Again, in   Passing
Oldenburg sick children, and also adults and animals, are   sick
                                                            persons
passed through a ring of rough unwashed yarn, just as it   or animals
comes from the reel.   To complete the cure you should   through
                                                          a ring
throw a hot coal thrice through the ring, then spit through   of yarn.
it thrice, and finally bury the yarn under a stone, where you
leave it to rot.   The writer who reports these remedies explains them as intended to strip the witchcraft, as you might
say, from the bodies of the victims, whether human or animal,
on whom the witch has cast her spell.[2]   Among the Lushais   Passing
of Assam " five to ten days after the child is born its body   diseased
                                                               children
is said to be covered with small pimples, its lips become   through
black and its strength decreases.   The family then obtain   a coil.
a particular kind of creeping plant called *vawm*, which they
make into a coil.   In the evening everything in the house
that has a lid or covering is uncovered, and the child is thrice
passed through this coil, which act is supposed to clear the

---

the first of May, see above, vol. i. pp.
226 *sqq.*, 295 ; *The Magic Art and the
Evolution of Kings*, ii. 52 *sqq.* ; J. G.
Campbell, *Superstitions of the Highlands and Islands of Scotland* (Glasgow,
1900), p. 18 ; *id.*, *Witchcraft and
Second Sight in the Highlands and
Islands of Scotland* (Glasgow, 1902),
p. 270.   As to the power of the
rowan-tree to counteract their spells,
see W. Gregor, *Notes on the Folk-lore*

of the North-East of Scotland (London,
1881), p. 188 ; J. C. Atkinson, *Forty
Years in a Moorland Parish* (London,
1891), pp. 97 *sqq.* ; *The Scapegoat*, pp.
266 *sq.*

[1] L. Strackerjan, *Aberglaube und
Sagen aus dem Herzogthum Oldenburg*
(Oldenburg, 1867), i. p. 364, § 241.

[2] L. Strackerjan, *op. cit.* i. p. 364,
§ 240.

child's skin and restore its strength.   After this is finished, the parents go to bed and the pots or other receptacles are covered again by any of the other members of the family. The parents themselves must not replace any of these lids for fear that they might shut up the spirit of the child in

Passing through a hemlock ring during an epidemic.

them."[1]   When the Kwakiutl Indians of British Columbia fear the outbreak of an epidemic, a medicine-man takes a large ring of hemlock branches and causes every member of the tribe to pass through it.   Each person puts his head through the ring and then moves the ring downwards over his body till it has almost reached his feet, when he steps out of it, right foot first.   They think that this prevents the

Passing through a ring of red-hot iron to escape an evil spirit.

epidemic from breaking out.[2]   In Asia Minor, "if a person is believed to be possessed by an evil spirit, one form of treatment is to heat an iron-chain red-hot, form it into a ring and pass the afflicted person through the opening, on the theory that the evil spirit cannot pass the hot chain, and so is torn from his victim and left behind."[3]   Here the intention of the passage through the aperture is avowedly to shake off a spiritual pursuer, who is deterred from further pursuit not only by the narrowness of the opening but by the risk of burning himself in the attempt to make his way through it.

Crawling through holed stones as a cure in Scotland and Cornwall.

But if the intention of these ceremonies is essentially to rid the performer of some harmful thing, whether a disease or a ghost or a demon, which is supposed to be clinging to him, we should expect to find that any narrow hole or opening would serve the purpose as well as a cleft tree or stick, an arch or ring of boughs, or a couple of posts fixed in the ground.   And this expectation is not disappointed. On the coast of Morven and Mull thin ledges of rock may be seen pierced with large holes near the sea.   Consumptive people used to be brought thither, and after the tops of nine

[1] Lieutenant-Colonel H. W. G. Cole, "The Lushais," in *Census of India, 1911*, vol. iii. *Assam*, Part i. *Report* (Shillong, 1912), p. 140.

[2] Franz Boas, in *Eleventh Report on the North-Western Tribes of Canada*, pp. 3 *sq.* (separate reprint from the *Report of the British Association for* the *Advancement of Science*, Liverpool meeting, 1896).

[3] Rev. G. E. White, Dean of Anatolia College, *Survivals of Primitive Religion among the People of Asia Minor*, p. 12 (paper read before the Victoria Institute or Philosophical Society of Great Britain, 6 Adelphi Terrace, Strand, London).

waves had been caught in a dish and thrown on the patient's head, he was made to pass through one of the rifted rocks thrice in the direction of the sun.[1] "On the farm of Crossapol in Coll there is a stone called *Clach Thuill*, that is, the Hole Stone, through which persons suffering from consumption were made to pass three times in the name of the Father, Son, and Holy Ghost. They took meat with them each time, and left some on the stone. The bird that took the food away had the consumption laid upon it. Similar stones, under which the patient can creep, were made use of in other islands."[2] Here it is manifest that the patient left his disease behind him on the stone, since the bird which carried off the food from the stone caught the disease. In the Aberdeenshire river Dee, at Cambus o' May, near Ballater, there is a rock with a hole in it large enough to let a person pass through. Legend runs that childless women used to wade out to the stone and squeeze themselves through the hole. It is said that a certain noble lady tried the effect of the charm not very many years ago with indifferent success.[3] In the parish of Madern in Cornwall, near the village of Lanyon, there is a perforated stone called the *Mên-an-tol* or "holed stone," through which people formerly crept as a remedy for pains in the back and limbs ; and at certain times of the year parents drew their children through the hole to cure them of the rickets.[4] The passage through the stone was also deemed a cure for scrofula, provided it was made against the sun and repeated three times or three times three.[5]

Near the little town of Dourgne, not far from Castres, in Southern France, there is a mountain, and on the top of the mountain is a tableland, where a number of large stones may be seen planted in the ground about a cross and rising to a height of two to five feet above the

Crawling through holed stones as a cure in France.

---

[1] John Ramsay, *Scotland and Scotsmen in the Eighteenth Century*, edited by Alex. Allardyce (Edinburgh, 1888), ii. 451 *sq.*

[2] J. G. Campbell, *Witchcraft and Second Sight in the Highlands and Islands of Scotland* (Glasgow, 1902), p. 100.

[3] Mr. James S. Greig, in a letter to me dated Lindean, Perth Road, Dundee, 17th August, 1913.

[4] W. Borlase, *Antiquities, historical and monumental, of the County of Cornwall* (London, 1769), pp. 177 *sq.*

[5] Robert Hunt, *Popular Romances of the West of England*, Third Edition (London, 1881), pp. 176, 415.

ground. Almost all of them are pierced with holes of different sizes. From time immemorial people used to assemble at Dourgne and the neighbourhood every year on the sixth of August, the festival of St. Estapin. The palsied, the lame, the blind, the sick of all sorts, flocked thither to seek and find a cure for their various infirmities. Very early in the morning they set out from the villages where they had lodged or from the meadows where for want of better accommodation they had been forced to pass the night, and went on pilgrimage to the chapel of St. Estapin, which stands in a gorge at the southern foot of the mountain. Having gone nine times in procession round the chapel, they hobbled, limped, or crawled to the tableland on the top of the mountain. There each of them chose a stone with a hole of the requisite size and thrust his ailing member through the hole. For there are holes to suit every complaint ; some for the head, some for the arm, some for the leg, and so on. Having performed this simple ceremony they were cured ; the lame walked, the blind saw, the palsied recovered the use of their limbs, and so on. The chapel of the saint is adorned with the crutches and other artificial aids, now wholly superfluous, which the joyful pilgrims left behind them in token of their gratitude and devotion.[1] About two miles from Gisors, in the French department of Oise, there is a dolmen called Trie or Trie- Chateau, consisting of three upright stones with a fourth and larger stone laid horizontally on their tops. The stone which forms the back wall of the dolmen is pierced about the middle by an irregularly shaped hole, through which the people of the neighbourhood used from time immemorial to pass their sickly children in the firm belief that the passage through the stone would restore them to health.[2]

In the church of St. Corona at the village of Koppenwal, in Lower Bavaria, there is a hole in the stone on which the

[1] Thomas-de-Saint-Mars, " Fête de Saint Estapin," *Mémoires de la Société Royale des Antiquaires de France*, i. (1817) pp. 428-430.

[2] J. Deniker, "Dolmen et superstitions," *Bulletins et Mémoires de la Société d'Anthropologie de Paris*, v. série, i. (1900) p. 111. Compare H. Gaidoz, *Un Vieux Rite médical* (Paris, 1892), pp. 26 *sq.*; G. Fouju, " Légendes et Superstitions préhistoriques," *Revue des Traditions Populaires*, xiv. (1899) pp. 477 *sq.*

altar rests.   Through this hole, while service was going on,
the peasants used to creep, believing that having done so
they would not suffer from pains in their back at harvest.[1]
In the crypt of the old cathedral at Freising in Bavaria
there is a tomb which is reputed to contain the relics of
St. Nonnosius.   Between a pillar of the tomb and the
wall there is a narrow opening, through which persons
afflicted with pains in the back creep in order to obtain
thereby some mitigation of their pangs.[2]   In Upper Austria,
above the Lake of Aber, which is a sheet of dark-green
water nestling among wooded mountains, there stands
the Falkenstein chapel of St. Wolfgang built close to the
face of a cliff that rises from a little green dale.   A
staircase leads up from the chapel to a narrow, dark,
dripping cleft in the rock, through which pilgrims creep
in a stooping posture " in the belief that they can strip
off their bodily sufferings or sins on the face of the rock." [3]
Women with child also crawl through the hole, hoping
thus to obtain an easy delivery.[4]   In the Greek island
of Cythnos, when a child is sickly, the mother will take
it to a hole in a rock about half an hour distant from
Messaria.   There she strips the child naked and pushes it
through the hole in the rock, afterwards throwing away the
old garments and clothing the child in new ones.[5]

Near Everek, on the site of the ancient Caesarea in Asia
Minor, there is a rifted rock through which persons pass to rid
themselves of a cough.[6]   A writer well acquainted with Asia
Minor has described how he visited " a well-known pool of
water tucked away in a beautiful nook high up among the
Anatolian mountains, and with a wide reputation for sanctity
and healing powers.   We arrived just as the last of a flock
of three hundred sheep were being passed through a peculiar
hole in the thin ledge of a huge rock to deliver them
from a disease of the liver supposed to prevent the proper

[1] F. Panzer, *Beitrag zur deutschen Mythologie* (Munich, 1848–1855), ii. 48 § 61.

[2] F. Panzer, *op. cit.* ii. 431 *sq.*

[3] Marie Andree-Eysn, *Volkskundliches aus dem bayrisch-österreichischen Alpengebiet* (Brunswick, 1910), pp. 1, 9, with the illustrations on pp. 10, 11.

[4] F. Panzer, *Beitrag zur deutschen Mythologie*, ii. 431.

[5] J. Theodore Bent, *The Cyclades* (London, 1885), p. 437.

[6] E. H. Carnoy et J. Nicolaides, *Traditions populaires de l'Asie Mineure* (Paris, 1889), p. 338.

Passing through various narrow openings as a cure or preventive in India and Ireland.

laying on of fat."[1]   Among the Kawars of the Central Provinces in India a man who suffers from intermittent fever will try to cure it by walking through a narrow passage between two houses.[2]   In a ruined church of St. Brandon, about ten miles from Dingle, in the west of Ireland, there is a narrow window, through which sick women pass thrice in order to be cured.[3]   The Hindoos of the Punjaub think that the birth of a son after three girls is unlucky for the parents, and in order to avert the ill-luck they resort to a number of devices.   Amongst other things they break the centre of a bronze plate and remove all but the rim ; then they pass the luckless child through the bronze rim.   Moreover, they make an opening in the roof of the room where the birth took place, and then pull the infant out through the opening ; and further they pass the child under the sill of the door.[4]   By these passages through narrow apertures they apparently hope to rid the child of the ill-luck which is either pursuing it or sticking to it like a burr.   For in this case, as in many similar ones, it might be hard to say whether the riddance is conceived as an escape from the pursuit of a maleficent spirit or as the abrasion of a dangerous substance which adheres to the person of the sufferer.

Crawling through holes in the ground as a cure for disease.

Another way of ridding man and beast of the clinging infection of disease is to pass them through a hole dug in the ground.   This mode of cure was practised in Europe during the Middle Ages, and has survived in Denmark down to modern times.   In a sermon preached by St. Eloi, Bishop of Noyon, in the sixth century, he forbade the faithful to practise lustrations and to drive their sheep through hollow trees and holes in the earth, " because by this they seem to consecrate them to the devil."[5]   Theodore, Archbishop of Canterbury, who died in 690 A.D., decreed that " if any one for the health of his little son shall pass through a hole in the ground and then close it behind him with thorns, let him

[1] Rev. George E. White (of Marsovan, Turkey), *Present Day Sacrifices in Asia Minor*, p. 3 (reprinted from *The Hartford Seminary Record*, February 1906).

[2] *Central Provinces, Ethnographic Survey*, vii. *Draft Articles on Forest Tribes* (Allahabad, 1911), p. 46.

[3] So my friend Dr. G. W. Prothero informs me in a letter.

[4] *Census of India, 1911*, vol. xiv. *Punjab*, Part i. *Report*, by Pandit Harikishan Kaul (Lahore, 1912), p. 302.

[5] H. Gaidoz, *Un Vieux Rite médical* (Paris, 1892), p. 10.

do penance for eleven days on bread and water."[1]   Here
the closing of the hole with thorns after the patient or his
representative has passed through is plainly intended to
barricade the narrow way against the pursuit of sickness
personified as a demon; hence it confirms the general
interpretation here given of these customs.   Again, Burchard,
Bishop of Worms, who died in A.D. 1025, repeated the same
condemnation: "Hast thou done what certain women are
wont to do?   I mean those who have squalling babes;
they dig the earth and pierce it, and through that hole they
drag the babe, and they say that thus the squalling babe
ceases to squall.   If thou has done this or consented unto
it, thou shalt do penance for fifteen days on bread and
water."[2]   At Fünen in Denmark, as late as the latter part of
the nineteenth century, a cure for childish ailments was to
dig up several sods, arrange them so as to form a hole,
and then to pass the sick child through it.[3]   A simplified
form of this cure is adopted in Jutland.   At twelve o'clock
on a Thursday night you go to a churchyard, dig up a
circular piece of turf, and make a hole in it large enough
to permit the passage through it of your infant progeny.
Taking the sod with you, go home, salute nobody on the
way, and speak to nobody.   On getting to your house,
take the child and pass it thrice through the turf from right
to left; then take the turf back to the churchyard and
replace it in position.   If the turf takes root and grows
afresh, the child will recover; but if the turf withers, there is
no hope.   Elsewhere it is at the hour of sunset rather than
of midnight that people cut the turf in the churchyard.   The
same cure is applied to cattle which have been bewitched;
though naturally in that case you must cut a much bigger
turf and make a much bigger hole in it to let a horse or a
cow through than is necessary for an infant.[4]   Here, again,
the conception of a sympathetic relation, established between

---

[1] H. Gaidoz, *op. cit.* p. 21.

[2] H. Gaidoz, *Un Vieux Rite médical*
(Paris, 1892), p. 21.   Compare J.
Grimm, *Deutsche Mythologie,*[4] ii. 975
sq.

[3] H. F. Feilberg, "Zwieselbäume

nebst verwandtem Aberglaube in
Skandinavien," *Zeitschrift des Vereins
für Volkskunde,* vii. (1897) p. 45.

[4] H. Gaidoz, *Un Vieux Rite médical*
(Paris, 1892), pp. 22 *sq.,* referring to
Nyrop, in *Dania,* i. No. 1 (Copen-
hagen, 1890), pp. 5 *sqq.*

the sufferer and the thing which has rid him of his ailment, comes out clearly in the belief, that if the turf through which the child has been passed thrives, the child will thrive also, but that if the turf withers, the child will die. Among the Corannas, a people of the Hottentot race on the Orange River, "when a child recovers from a dangerous illness, a trench is dug in the ground, across the middle of which an arch is thrown, and an ox made to stand upon it; the child is then dragged under the arch. After this ceremony the animal is killed, and eaten by married people who have children, none else being permitted to participate of the feast." [1] Here the attempt to leave the sickness behind in the hole, which is probably the essence of the ceremony, may perhaps be combined with an endeavour to impart to the child the strength and vigour of the animal. Ancient India seems also to have been familiar with the same primitive notion that sickness could, as it were, be stripped off the person of the sufferer by passing him through a narrow aperture; for in the Rigveda it is said that Indra cured Apala of a disease of the skin by drawing her through the yoke of the chariot; "thus the god made her to have a golden skin, purifying her thrice." [2]

Passing through the yoke of a chariot as a cure for skin disease.

[1] Rev. John Campbell, *Travels in South Africa, Second Journey* (London, 1822), ii. 346. Among the same people "when a person is ill, they bring an ox to the place where he is laid. Two cuts are then made in one of its legs, extending down the whole length of it. The skin in the middle of the leg being raised up, the operator thrusts in his hand, to make way for that of the sick person, whose whole body is afterwards rubbed over with the blood of the animal. The ox after enduring this torment is killed, and those who are married and have children, as in the other case, are the only partakers of the feast" (J. Campbell, *op. cit.* ii. 346 *sq.*). Here the intention seems to be not so much to transfer the disease to the ox, as to transfuse the healthy life of the beast into the veins of the sick man. The same is perhaps true of the Welsh and French cure for whooping-cough, which consists in passing the little sufferer several times under an ass. See J. Brand, *Popular Antiquities of Great Britain* (London, 1882–1883), iii. 288; L. J. B. Bérenger-Féraud, in *Bulletins de la Société d'Anthropologie de Paris*, Quatrième Série, i. (1890) p. 897; *id., Superstitions et Survivances* (Paris, 1896), i. 526. The same cure for whooping-cough "is also practised in Ireland; only here the sufferer is passed round, that is, over and under, the body of an ass" (letter of Miss A. H. Singleton to me, dated Rathmagle House, Abbey-Leix, Ireland, 24th February 1904). But perhaps the intention rather is to give the whooping-cough to the animal; for it might reasonably be thought that the feeble whoop of the sick child would neither seriously impair the lungs, nor perceptibly augment the stentorian bray, of the donkey.

[2] H. Oldenberg, *Die Religion des Veda* (Berlin, 1894), p. 495. According to a fuller account, Indra drew her through three holes, that of a war-

At the small village of Damun, on the Kabenau river, in German New Guinea, a traveller witnessed the natives performing a ceremony of initiation, of which the following rite formed part. The candidates for initiation, six in number, were boys and lads of various ages from about four years of age to sixteen or seventeen. The company betook themselves to the bed of a small stream, where at the end of a gully a hollow in the rocks formed a natural basin. At the entrance to the gully a sort of yoke, so the traveller calls it, was erected by means of some poles, and from the cross-piece plants were hung so as to make an arch. One of the men took up his station in front of the arch, and as each candidate came up, the man seized him, spat on his breast and back a clot of red spittle, and gave him several severe blows with the stock of a plant. After that the candidate, who had previously stripped himself naked, passed under the leafy arch and bathed in the rocky pool at the other end of the gully. All the time that this solemnity was proceeding another man sat perched on a neighbouring rock, beating a drum and singing. Only men took part in the ceremony.[1] Though no explanation of the ceremony is given by the observer who witnessed it, we may suppose that by passing under the yoke or arch the novices were supposed to rid themselves of certain evil influences, whether conceived as spiritual or not, which they left behind them on the further side of the barrier. This interpretation is confirmed by the bath which each candidate took immediately afterwards. In short the whole purpose of the rite would seem to have been purificatory.

With the preceding examples before us, it seems worth while to ask whether the ancient Italian practice of making conquered enemies to pass under a yoke may not in its

Passing under a yoke or arch as a rite of initiation.

The ancient Roman custom

---

chariot, that of a cart, and that of a yoke. See W. Caland, *Altindisches Zauberritual* (Amsterdam, 1900), p. 31 note [6].

[1] Dr. E. Werner, "Im westlichen Finsterregebirge und an der Nordküste von Deutsch-Neuginea," *Petermanns Mitteilungen*, lv. (1909) pp. 74 *sq.* Among some tribes of South-Eastern Australia it was customary at the

ceremonies of initiation to bend growing saplings into arches and compel the novices to pass under them; sometimes the youths had to crawl on the ground to get through. See A. W. Howitt, "On some Australian ceremonies of Initiation," *Journal of the Anthropological Institute*, xiii. (1884) p. 445; *id.*, *Native Tribes of South-East Australia* (London, 1904), p. 536.

of passing enemies under a yoke was probably in origin a ceremony of purification rather than of degradation.

origin have been a purificatory ceremony, designed to rid the foe of some uncanny powers before dismissing him to his home. For apparently the ceremony was only observed with prisoners who were about to be released;[1] had it been a mere mark of ignominy, there seems to be no reason why it should not have been inflicted also on men who were doomed to die. This conjectural explanation of the ceremony is confirmed by the tradition that the Roman Horatius was similarly obliged by his fellow-countrymen to pass under a yoke as a form of purification for the murder of his sister. The yoke by passing under which he cleansed himself from his sister's blood was still to be seen in Rome when Livy was writing his history under the emperor Augustus. It was an ancient wooden beam spanning a narrow lane in an old quarter of the city, the two ends of the beam being built into the masonry of the walls on either side; it went by the name of the Sister's Beam, and whenever the wood decayed and threatened to fall, the venerable monument, which carried back the thoughts of passers-by to the kingly age of Rome, was repaired at the public expense.[2] If our interpretation of these customs is right, it was the ghost of his murdered sister whom the Roman hero gave the slip to by passing under the yoke; and it may have been the angry ghosts of slaughtered

---

[1] Livy iii. 28, ix. 6, x. 36; Dionysius Halicarnasensis, *Antiquit. Roman.* iii. 22. 7. The so-called yoke in this case consisted of two spears or two beams set upright in the ground, with a third spear or beam laid transversely across them. See Livy iii. 28; Dionysius Halicarnasensis, *l.c.*

[2] Livy i. 26: "*Itaque, ut caedes manifesta aliquo tamen piaculo lueretur, imperatum patri, ut filium expiaret pecunia publica. Is quibusdam piacularibus sacrificiis factis, quae deinde genti Horatiae tradita sunt, transmisso per viam tigillo capite adoperto velut sub jugum misit juvenem. Id hodie quoque publice semper refectum manet; sororium tigillum vocant;*" Festus, *s.v.* "Sororium Tigillum," pp. 297, 307, ed. C. O. Müller (Leipsic, 1839); Dionysius Halicarnasensis, *Antiquit.*

Roman. iii. 22. The position of the beam is described exactly by the last of these writers, who had evidently seen it. According to Festus, the yoke under which Horatius passed was composed of three beams, two uprights, and a cross-piece. The similarity of the ceremony to that which was exacted from conquered foes is noted by Dionysius Halicarnasensis as well as by Livy. The tradition of the purification has been rightly explained by Dr. W. H. Roscher with reference to the custom of passing through cleft trees, holed stones, and so on. See W. H. Roscher, *Ausführliches Lexikon der griech. und röm. Mythologie*, ii. (Leipsic, 1890–1897) col. 21. Compare G. Wissowa, *Religion und Kultus der Römer* [2] (Munich, 1912), p. 104.

Romans from whom the enemy's soldiers were believed to be delivered when they marched under the yoke before being dismissed by their merciful conquerors to their homes.

In a former part of this work we saw that homicides in general and victorious warriors in particular are often obliged to perform a variety of ceremonies for the purpose of ridding them of the dangerous ghosts of their victims.[1] If the ceremony of passing under the yoke was primarily designed, as I have suggested, to free the soldiers from the angry ghosts of the men whom they had slain, we should expect to find that the victorious Romans themselves observed a similar ceremony after a battle for a similar purpose. Was this the original meaning of passing under a triumphal arch? In other words, may not the triumphal arch have been for the victors what the yoke was for the vanquished, a barrier to protect them against the pursuit of the spirits of the slain? That the Romans felt the need of purification from the taint of bloodshed after a battle appears from the opinion of Masurius, mentioned by Pliny, that the laurel worn by soldiers in a triumphal procession was intended to purge them from the slaughter of the enemy.[2] A special gate, the *Porta Triumphalis*, was reserved for the entrance of a victorious army into Rome;[3] and it would be in accordance with ancient religious views if this distinction was originally not so much an honour conferred as a precaution enforced to prevent the ordinary gates from being polluted by the passage of thousands of blood-guilty men.[4]

Similarly the passage of a victorious Roman army under a triumphal arch may have been intended to purify the men from the stain of bloodshed by interposing a barrier between the slayers and the angry ghosts of the slain.

[1] *Taboo and the Perils of the Soul,* pp. 165 *sqq.*

[2] Pliny, *Natur. Histor.* xv. 135: "*Quia suffimentum sit caedis hostium et purgatio.*"

[3] Cicero, *In Pisonem,* xxiii. 55; Josephus, *Bellum Judaicum,* vii. 5. 4.

[4] It was not till after I had given this conjectural explanation of the "Sister's Beam" and the triumphal arch at Rome that I read the article of Mr. W. Warde Fowler, "Passing under the Yoke" (*The Classical Review,* March 1913, pp. 48-51), in which he quite independently suggests practically the same explanation of both these Roman structures. I have left my exposition, except for one or two trivial verbal changes, exactly as it stood before I was aware that my friend had anticipated me in both conjectures. The closeness of the coincidence between our views is a welcome confirmation of their truth. As to the *Porta Triumphalis,* the exact position of which is uncertain, Mr. Warde Fowler thinks that it was not a gate in the walls, but an archway standing by itself in the Campus Martius outside the city walls. He points out that in the oldest existing triumphal arch, that of Augustus at

§ 3. *The External Soul in Animals*

But in practice, as in folk-tales, it is not merely with inanimate objects and plants that a person is occasionally believed to be united by a bond of physical sympathy. The same bond, it is supposed, may exist between a man and an animal, so that the welfare of the one depends on the welfare of the other, and when the animal dies the man dies also. The analogy between the custom and the tales is all the closer because in both of them the power of thus removing the soul from the body and stowing it away in an animal is often a special privilege of wizards and witches.

Thus the Yakuts of Siberia believe that every shaman or wizard keeps his soul, or one of his souls, incarnate in an animal which is carefully concealed from all the world. "Nobody can find my external soul," said one famous wizard, "it lies hidden far away in the stony mountains of Edzhigansk." Only once a year, when the last snows melt and the earth turns black, do these external souls of wizards appear in the shape of animals among the dwellings of men. They wander everywhere, yet none but wizards can see them. The strong ones sweep roaring and noisily along, the weak steal about quietly and furtively. Often they fight, and then the wizard whose external soul is beaten, falls ill or dies. The weakest and most cowardly wizards are they whose souls are incarnate in the shape of dogs, for the dog gives his human double no peace, but gnaws his heart and tears his body. The most powerful wizards are they whose external souls have the shape of stallions, elks, black bears, eagles, or boars. Again, the Samoyeds of the Turukhinsk region hold that every shaman has a familiar spirit in the shape of a boar, which he leads about by a magic belt. On the death of the boar the shaman himself dies ; and stories are told of battles between

---

Ariminum, the most striking part of the structure consists of two upright Corinthian pillars with an architrave laid horizontally across them ; and he ingeniously conjectures that we have here a reminiscence of the two uprights and the cross-piece, which, if our theory is correct, was the original form both of the triumphal arch and of the yoke.

wizards, who send their spirits to fight before they encounter each other in person.[1]   In Yorkshire witches are thought to stand in such peculiarly close relations to hares, that if a particular hare is killed or wounded, a certain witch will at the same moment be killed or receive a hurt in her body exactly corresponding to the wound in the hare.[2] However, this fancy is probably a case of the general European belief that witches have the power of temporarily transforming themselves into certain animals, particularly hares and cats, and that any hurts inflicted on such transformed animals are felt by the witches who are concealed in the animals.[3]   But the notion that a person can temporarily transform himself into an animal differs from the notion that he can deposit his soul for a longer or shorter period in an animal, while he himself retains the human form ; though in the cloudy mind of the peasant and the savage the two ideas may not always be sharply distinguished.   The Malays believe that " the soul of a person may pass into another person or into an animal, or rather that such a mysterious relation can arise between the two that the fate of the one is wholly dependent on that of the other." [4]

Sympathetic relation between witches and hares.

Among the Melanesians of Mota, one of the New Hebrides islands, the conception of an external soul is carried out in the practice of daily life.   The Mota word for soul is *atai.*   " The use of the word *atai* in Mota seems properly and originally to have been to signify something peculiarly and intimately connected with a person and sacred to him, something that he has set his fancy upon when he has seen it in what has seemed to him a wonderful manner, or some one has shewn it to him as such.   Whatever the thing might be the man believed it to be the reflection of his own personality ; he and his *atai* flourished, suffered, lived, and died together.   But the word must not be supposed to have been borrowed from this use and

Melanesian conception of the *tamaniu,* a person's external soul lodged in an animal or other object.

1 Professor V. M. Mikhailoviskij, "Shamanism in Siberia and European Russia," *Journal of the Anthropological Institute,* xxiv. (1895) pp. 133, 134.

2 Th. Parkinson, *Yorkshire Legends and Traditions,* Second Series (London, 1889), pp. 160 *sq.*

3 See above, vol. i. pp. 315 *sqq.*

4 B. F. Matthes, *Makassaarsch-Hollandsch Woordenboek* (Amsterdam, 1859), *s.v.* soemǎñgǎ, p. 569 ; G. A. Wilken, " Het animisme bij de volken van den Indischen Archipel," *De Indische Gids,* June 1884, p. 933 ; *id., Verspreide Geschriften* (The Hague, 1912), iii. 12.

applied secondarily to describe the soul; the word carries a sense with it which is applicable alike to that second self, the visible object so mysteriously connected with the man, and to this invisible second self which we call the soul. There is another Mota word, *tamaniu*, which has almost if not quite the same meaning as *atai* has when it describes something animate or inanimate which a man has come to believe to have an existence intimately connected with his own. The word *tamaniu* may be taken to be properly 'likeness,' and the noun form of the adverb *tama*, as, like. It was not every one in Mota who had his *tamaniu*; only some men fancied that they had this relation to a lizard, a snake, or it might be a stone; sometimes the thing was sought for and found by drinking the infusion of certain leaves and heaping together the dregs; then whatever living thing was first seen in or upon the heap was the *tamaniu*. It was watched but not fed or worshipped; the natives believed that it came at call, and that the life of the man was bound up with the life of his *tamaniu*, if a living thing, or with its safety; should it die, or if not living get broken or be lost, the man would die. Hence in case of sickness they would send to see if the *tamaniu* was safe and well. This word has never been used apparently for the soul in Mota; but in Aurora in the New Hebrides it is the accepted equivalent. It is well worth observing that both the *atai* and the *tamaniu*, and it may be added the Motlav *talegi*, is something which has a substantial existence of its own, as when a snake or stone is a man's *atai* or *tamaniu*; a soul then when called by these names is conceived of as something in a way substantial." [1]

Sympathetic relation between a man and his *tamaniu* (external soul).

From this account, which we owe to the careful and accurate researches of the Rev. Dr. Codrington, we gather that while every person in Mota has a second self or external soul in a visible object called an *atai*, only some people have, it may be, a second external soul in another visible object called a *tamaniu*. We may conjecture that persons who have a *tamaniu* in addition to an *atai* are more than

[1] R. H. Codrington, D.D., *The Melanesians* (Oxford, 1891), pp. 250 *sq.* Compare *id.*, "Notes on the Customs of Mota, Banks Islands,"   *Transactions and Proceedings of the Royal Society of Victoria*, xvi. (1880) p. 136.

usually anxious as to the state of their soul, and that they seek to put it in perfect security by what we may call a system of double insurance, calculating that if one of their external souls should die or be broken, they themselves may still survive by virtue of the survival of the other.   Be that as it may, the *tamaniu* discharges two functions, one of them defensive and the other offensive.   On the one hand, so long as it lives or remains unbroken, it preserves its owner in life; and on the other hand it helps him to injure his enemies. In its offensive character, if the *tamaniu* happens to be an eel, it will bite its owner's enemy; if it is a shark, it will swallow him.   In its defensive character, the state of the *tamaniu* is a symptom or life-token of the state of the man; hence when he is ill he will visit and examine it, or if he cannot go himself he will send another to inspect it and report.   In either case the man turns the animal, if animal it be, carefully over in order to see what is the matter with it; should something be found sticking to its skin, it is removed, and through the relief thus afforded to the creature the sick man recovers.   But if the animal should be found dying, it is an omen of death for the man; for whenever it dies he dies also.[1]

In Melanesia a native doctor was once attending to a sick man.   Just then "a large eagle-hawk came soaring past the house, and Kaplen, my hunter, was going to shoot it; but the doctor jumped up in evident alarm, and said, 'Oh, don't shoot; that is my spirit' (*niog*, literally, my shadow); 'if you shoot that, I will die.'   He then told the old man, 'If you see a rat to-night, don't drive it away, 'tis my spirit (*niog*), or a snake which will come to-night, that also is my spirit.'"[2]   It does not appear whether the doctor in this case, like the giant or warlock in the tales, kept his spirit

Soul of a Melanesian doctor in an eagle-hawk and a rat.

---

[1] W. H. R. Rivers, "Totemism in Polynesia and Melanesia," *Journal of the Royal Anthropological Institute,* xxxix. (1909) p. 177.   Dr. Rivers cites a recent case of a man who had a large lizard for his *tamaniu*.   The animal lived in the roots of a big banyan-tree; when the man was ill, the lizard also seemed unwell; and when the man died, the tree fell, which was deemed a sign that the lizard also was dead.

[2] George Brown, D.D., *Melanesians and Polynesians* (London, 1910), p. 177.   The case was known to Dr. Brown, who made notes of it.   The part of Melanesia where it happened was probably the Duke of York Island or New Britain.

permanently in the bird or in the animal, or whether he only transferred it temporarily to the creature for the purpose of enabling him the better to work the cure, perhaps by sending out his own soul in a bird or beast to find and bring back the lost soul of the patient. In either case he seems to have thought, like the giant or warlock in the stories, that the death of the bird or the animal would simultaneously entail his own. A family in Nauru, one of the Marshall Islands, apparently imagine that their lives are bound up with a species of large fish, which has a huge mouth and devours human beings ; for when one of these fish was killed, the members of the family cried, " Our guardian spirit is killed, now we must all die ! " [1]

The theory of an external soul lodged in an animal is very prevalent in West Africa.

The theory of an external soul deposited in an animal appears to be very prevalent in West Africa, particularly in Nigeria, the Cameroons, and the Gaboon.[2] In the latter part of the nineteenth century two English missionaries, established at San Salvador, the capital of the King of Congo, asked the natives repeatedly whether any of them had seen the strange, big, East African goat which Stanley had given to a chief at Stanley Pool in 1877. But their enquiries were fruitless ; no native would admit that he had seen the goat. Some years afterwards the missionaries discovered why they could obtain no reply to their enquiry. All the people, it turned out, imagined that the missionaries believed the spirit of the King of Salvador to be contained in the goat, and that they wished to obtain possession of the animal in order to exercise an evil influence on his majesty.[3] The belief from the standpoint of the Congo savages was natural enough, since in that region some chiefs regularly link their fate to that of an animal.

The soul of a chief in a hippopotamus or a black snake.

Thus the Chief Bankwa of Ndolo, on the Moeko River, had conferred this honour on a certain hippopotamus of the neighbourhood, at which he would allow nobody to shoot.[4] At the village of Ongek, in the Gaboon, a French missionary slept in the hut of an old Fan chief. Awakened about two

---

[1] " Totemismus auf den Marshall-Inseln (Südsee)," *Anthropos*, viii. (1913) p. 251.

[2] Much of the following evidence has already been cited by me in *Totemism and Exogamy*, ii. 593 *sqq.*

[3] Herbert Ward, *Five Years with the Congo Cannibals* (London, 1890), p. 53.

[4] *Notes Analytiques sur les Collections ethnographiques du Musée du Congo*, i. (Brussels, 1902–1906) p. 150.

in the morning by a rustling of dry leaves, he lit a torch,
when to his horror he perceived a huge black serpent of the
most dangerous sort, coiled in a corner, with head erect,
shining eyes, and hissing jaws, ready to dart at him. In-
stinctively he seized his gun and pointed it at the reptile,
when suddenly his arm was struck up, the torch was
extinguished, and the voice of the old chief said, "Don't
fire! don't fire! I beg of you. In killing the serpent, it is
me that you would kill. Fear nothing. The serpent is my
elangela." So saying he flung himself on his knees beside
the reptile, put his arms about it, and clasped it to his breast.
The serpent received his caresses quietly, manifesting neither
anger nor fear, and the chief carried it off and laid it down
beside him in another hut, exhorting the missionary to have
no fear and never to speak of the subject.[1] His curiosity
being excited by this adventure, the missionary, Father
Trilles, pursued his enquiries and ascertained that among
the Fans of the Gaboon every wizard is believed at initiation to unite his life with that of some particular wild animal
by a rite of blood-brotherhood ; he draws blood from the ear
of the animal and from his own arm, and inoculates the
animal with his own blood, and himself with the blood of the
beast. Henceforth such an intimate union is established
between the two that the death of the one entails the death
of the other. The alliance is thought to bring to the wizard
or sorcerer a great accession of power, which he can turn to
his advantage in various ways. In the first place, like the
warlock in the fairy tales who has deposited his life outside
of himself in some safe place, the Fan wizard now deems
himself invulnerable. Moreover, the animal with which he
has exchanged blood has become his familiar, and will obey
any orders he may choose to give it ; so he makes use of it
to injure and kill his enemies. For that reason the creature
with whom he establishes the relation of blood-brotherhood
is never a tame or domestic animal, but always a ferocious
and dangerous wild beast, such as a leopard, a black serpent,
a crocodile, a hippopotamus, a wild boar, or a vulture. Of

Belief of the Fans that every wizard unites his life to that of a wild animal by a rite of blood brother-hood.

---

[1] Father H. Trilles, " Chez les
Fangs," *Les Missions Catholiques*, xxx.
(1898) p. 322 ; *id., Le Totémisme*
chez les Fân (Münster i. W. 1912),
pp. 473 *sq.*

all these creatures the leopard is by far the commonest familiar of Fan wizards, and next to it comes the black serpent; the vulture is the rarest. Witches as well as wizards have their familiars; but the animals with which the lives of women are thus bound up generally differ from those to which men commit their external souls. A witch never has a panther for her familiar, but often a venomous species of serpent, sometimes a horned viper, sometimes a black serpent, sometimes a green one that lives in banana-trees; or it may be a vulture, an owl, or other bird of night. In every case the beast or bird with which the witch or wizard has contracted this mystic alliance is an individual, never a species; and when the individual animal dies the alliance is naturally at an end, since the death of the animal is supposed to entail the death of the man.[1]

Belief of the natives of the Cross River that they stand in a vital relation to certain wild animals, so that when the animal dies the man dies also.

Similar beliefs are held by the natives of the Cross River valley within the German provinces of the Cameroons. Groups of people, generally the inhabitants of a village, have chosen various animals, with which they believe themselves to stand on a footing of intimate friendship or relationship. Amongst such animals are hippopotamuses, elephants, leopards, crocodiles, gorillas, fish, and serpents, all of them creatures which are either very strong or can easily hide themselves in the water or a thicket. This power of concealing themselves is said to be an indispensable condition of the choice of animal familiars, since the animal friend or helper is expected to injure his owner's enemy by stealth; for example, if he is a hippopotamus, he will bob up suddenly out of the water and capsize the enemy's canoe. Between the animals and their human friends or kinsfolk such a sympathetic relation is supposed to exist that the moment the animal dies the man dies also, and similarly the instant the man

---

[1] Father H. Trilles, *Le Totémisme chez les Fân* (Münster i. W. 1912), pp. 167 *sq.*, 438 *sq.*, 484-489. The description of the rite of blood-brotherhood contracted with the animal is quoted by Father Trilles (pp. 486 *sq.*) from a work by Mgr. Buléon, *Sous le ciel d'Afrique, Récits d'un Missionnaire*, pp. 88 *sqq.* Father Trilles's own observations and enquiries confirm the account given by Mgr. Buléon. But the story of an alliance contracted between a man or woman and a ferocious wild beast and cemented by the blood of the high contracting parties is no doubt a mere fable devised by wizards and witches in order to increase their reputation by imposing on the credulity of the simple.

perishes so does the beast. From this it follows that the animal kinsfolk may never be shot at or molested for fear of injuring or killing the persons whose lives are knit up with the lives of the brutes. This does not, however, prevent the people of a village, who have elephants for their animal friends, from hunting elephants. For they do not respect the whole species but merely certain individuals of it, which stand in an intimate relation to certain individual men and women ; and they imagine that they can always distinguish these brother elephants from the common herd of elephants which are mere elephants and nothing more. The recognition indeed is said to be mutual. When a hunter, who has an elephant for his friend, meets a human elephant, as we may call it, the noble animal lifts up a paw and holds it before his face, as much as to say, " Don't shoot." Were the hunter so inhuman as to fire on and wound such an elephant, the person whose life was bound up with the elephant would fall ill.[1]

The Balong of the Cameroons think that every man has several souls, of which one is in his body and another in an animal, such as an elephant, a wild pig, a leopard, and so forth. When a man comes home, feeling ill, and says, " I shall soon die," and dies accordingly, the people aver that one of his souls has been killed in a wild pig or a leopard, and that the death of the external soul has caused the death of the soul in his body. Hence the corpse is cut open, and a diviner determines, from an inspection of the inwards, whether the popular surmise is correct or not.[2]

A similar belief in the external souls of living people is entertained by the Ibos, an important tribe of the Niger delta, who inhabit a country west of the Cross River. They think that a man's spirit can quit his body for a time during life and take up its abode in an animal. This is called *ishi anu*, " to turn animal." A man who wishes to acquire this power procures a certain drug from a wise man and mixes it with his food. After that his soul goes out and enters

Similar belief of the Balong in the Cameroons.

Belief of the Ibos in external human souls which are lodged in animals.

[1] Alfred Mansfeld, *Urwald-Dokumente, vier Jahre unter den Crossfluss-negern Kameruns* (Berlin, 1908), pp. 220 *sq.*

[2] J. Keller (missionary), " Ueber das Land und Volk der Balong," *Deutsches Kolonialblatt*, 1 Oktober 1895, p. 484 ; H. Seidel, " Ethnographisches aus Nordost Kamerun," *Globus*, lxix. (1896) p. 277.

into the animal.   If it should happen that the animal is killed while the man's soul is lodged in it, the man dies; and if the animal be wounded, the man's body will presently be covered with boils.   This belief instigates to many deeds of darkness ; for a sly rogue will sometimes surreptitiously administer the magical drug to his enemy in his food, and having thus smuggled the other's soul into an animal will destroy the creature, and with it the man whose soul is lodged in it.[1]   A like belief is reported to prevail among the tribes of the Obubura Hill district on the Cross River in Southern Nigeria.   Once when Mr. Partridge's canoe-men wished to catch fish near a town of the Assiga tribe, the people objected, saying, " Our souls live in those fish, and if you kill them we shall die." [2]

Belief of the negroes of Calabar that every person has an external or bush soul lodged in a wild beast.   The negroes of Calabar, at the mouth of the Niger, believe that every person has four souls, one of which always lives outside of his or her body in the form of a wild beast in the forest.   This external soul, or bush soul, as Miss Kingsley calls it, may be almost any animal, for example, a leopard, a fish, or a tortoise ; but it is never a domestic animal and never a plant.   Unless he is gifted with second sight, a man cannot see his own bush soul, but a diviner will often tell him what sort of creature his bush soul is, and after that the man will be careful not to kill any animal of that species, and will strongly object to any one else doing so. A man and his sons have usually the same sort of animals for their bush souls, and so with a mother and her daughters. But sometimes all the children of a family take after the bush soul of their father ; for example, if his external soul is a leopard, all his sons and daughters will have leopards for their external souls.   And on the other hand, sometimes they all take after their mother ; for instance, if her external soul is a tortoise, all the external souls of her sons and daughters will be tortoises too.   So intimately bound up is the life of the man with that of the animal which he regards as his external or bush soul, that the death or injury of the animal necessarily entails the death or injury of the man.

[1] John Parkinson, "Note on the Asaba People (Ibos) of the Niger," *Journal of the Anthropological Institute*, xxxvi. (1906) pp. 314 *sq.*

[2] Charles Partridge, *Cross River Natives* (London, 1905), pp. 225 *sq.*

And, conversely, when the man dies, his bush soul can no longer find a place of rest, but goes mad and rushes into the fire or charges people and is knocked on the head, and that is an end of it. When a person is sick, the diviner will sometimes tell him that his bush soul is angry at being neglected ; thereupon the patient will make an offering to the offended spirit and deposit it in a tiny hut in the forest at the spot where the animal, which is his external soul, was last seen. If the bush soul is appeased, the patient recovers ; but if it is not, he dies. Yet the foolish bush soul does not understand that in injuring the man it injures itself, and that it cannot long survive his decease.[1]

Such is the account which Miss Kingsley gives of the bush souls of the Calabar negroes. Some fresh particulars are furnished by Mr. Richard Henshaw, Agent for Native Affairs at Calabar. He tells us that a man may only marry a woman who has the same sort of bush soul as himself ; for example, if his bush soul is a leopard, his wife also must have a leopard for her bush soul. Further, we learn from Mr. Henshaw that a person's bush soul need not be that either of his father or of his mother. For example, a child with a hippopotamus for his bush soul may be born into a family, all the members of which have wild pigs for their bush souls ; this happens when the child is a reincarnation of a man whose external soul was a hippopotamus. In such a case, if the parents object to the intrusion of an alien soul, they may call in a medicine-man to check its growth and finally abolish it altogether, after which they will give the child their own bush soul. Or they may leave the matter over till the child comes of age, when he will choose a bush soul for himself with the help of a medicine-man, who will also select the piece of bush or water in which the chosen animal lives. When a man dies, then the animal which contains his

Further particulars as to the Calabar belief in bush souls.

---

[1] Miss Mary H. Kingsley, *Travels in West Africa* (London, 1897), pp. 459-461. The lamented authoress was kind enough to give me in conversation (1st June 1897) some details which do not appear in her book ; among these are the statements, which I have embodied in the text, that the bush soul is never a domestic animal, and that when a man knows what kind of creature his bush soul is, he will not kill an animal of that species and will strongly object to any one else doing so. Miss Kingsley was not able to say whether persons who have the same sort of bush soul are allowed or forbidden to marry each other.

external soul "becomes insensible and quite unconscious of the approach of danger. Thus a hunter can capture or kill him with perfect ease." Sacrifices are often offered to prevent other people from killing the animal in which a man's bush soul resides. The tribes of Calabar which hold these beliefs as to the bush soul are the Efik and Ekoi.[1] The belief of the Calabar negroes in the external soul has been described as follows by a missionary: "*Ukpong* is the native word we have taken to translate our word *soul*. It primarily signifies the shadow of a person. It also signifies that which dwells within a man on which his life depends, but which may detach itself from the body, and visiting places and persons here and there, again return to its abode in the man. . . . Besides all this, the word is used to designate an animal possessed of an *ukpong*, so connected with a person's *ukpong*, that they mutually act upon each other. When the leopard, or crocodile, or whatever animal may be a man's *ukpong*, gets sick or dies, the like thing happens to him. Many individuals, it is believed, have the power of changing themselves into the animals which are their *ukpong*."[2]

Belief of the Ekoi of Southern Nigeria in external souls lodged in animals.

Among the Ekoi of the Oban district, in Southern Nigeria, it is usual to hear a person say of another that he or she "possesses" such and such an animal, meaning that the person has the power to assume the shape of that particular creature. It is their belief that by constant practice and by virtue of certain hereditary secrets a man can quit his human body and put on that of a wild beast. They say that in addition to the soul which animates his human body

---

[1] John Parkinson, "Notes on the Efik Belief in 'Bush-soul,'" *Man*, vi. (1906) pp. 121 *sq.*, No. 80. Mr. Henshaw is a member of the highest grade of the secret society of Egbo.

[2] Rev. Hugh Goldie, *Calabar and its Mission*, New Edition (Edinburgh and London, 1901), pp. 51 *sq.* Compare Major A. G. Leonard, *The Lower Niger and its Tribes* (London, 1906), p. 217 : "When Efik or waterside Ibo see a dead fish floating in the water of the kind called *Edidim* by the former and *Elili* by the latter—a variety of the electric species—they believe it to be a bad omen, generally signifying that some one belonging to the house will die, the man who first sees it becoming the victim according to Ibo belief. The only reason that is assigned for this lugubrious forecast is the fact that one of the souls of the departed is in the dead fish—that, in fact, the relationship or affinity existing between the soul essence that had animated the fish and that of one of the members of the household was so intimate that the death of the one was bound to effect the death of the other."

everybody has a bush soul which at times he can send forth
to animate the body of the creature which he "possesses."
When he wishes his bush soul to go out on its rambles, he
drinks a magic potion, the secret of which has been handed
down from time immemorial, and some of which is always
kept ready for use in an ancient earthen pot set apart for the
purpose. No sooner has he drunk the mystic draught than
his bush soul escapes from him and floats away invisible
through the town into the forest. There it begins to swell
and, safe in the shadow of the trees, takes on the shape of
the man's animal double, it may be an elephant, a leopard, a
buffalo, a wild boar, or a crocodile. Naturally the potion
differs according to the kind of animal into which a man is
temporarily converted. It would be absurd, for example, to
expect that the dose which turns you into an elephant should
also be able to turn you into a crocodile ; the thing is mani-
festly impossible. A great advantage of these temporary
conversions of a man into a beast is that it enables the
convert in his animal shape to pay out his enemy without
being suspected. If, for example, you have a grudge at a
man who is a well-to-do farmer, all that you have to do is to
turn yourself by night into a buffalo, an elephant, or a wild
boar, and then, bursting into his fields, stamp about in them
till you have laid the standing crops level with the ground.
That is why in the neighbourhood of large well-tilled farms,
people prefer to keep their bush souls in buffaloes, elephants,
and wild boars, because these animals are the most convenient
means of destroying a neighbour's crops. Whereas where
the farms are small and ill-kept, as they are round about
Oban, it is hardly worth a man's while to take the trouble
of turning into a buffalo or an elephant for the paltry satis-
faction of rooting up a few miserable yams or such like trash.
So the Oban people keep their bush souls in leopards and
crocodiles, which, though of little use for the purpose of
destroying a neighbour's crops, are excellent for the purpose
of killing the man himself first and eating him afterwards.
But the power of turning into an animal has this serious dis-
advantage that it lays you open to the chance of being
wounded or even slain in your animal skin before you have
time to put it off and scramble back into your human integu-

Case of a
chief whose
external
soul was in
a buffalo. ment.   A remarkable case of this sort happened only a few miles from Oban not long ago.   To understand it you must know that the chiefs of the Ododop tribe, who live about ten miles from Oban, keep their bush souls, whenever they are out on a ramble, in the shape of buffaloes.   Well, one day the District Commissioner at Oban saw a buffalo come down to drink at a stream which runs through his garden.   He shot at the beast and hit it, and it ran away badly wounded.   At the very same moment the head chief of the Ododop tribe, ten miles away, clapped his hand to his side and said, "They have killed me at Oban."   Death was not instantaneous, for the buffalo lingered in pain for a couple of days in the forest, but an hour or two before its dead body was discovered by the trackers the chief expired.   Just before he died, with touching solicitude he sent a message warning all people who kept their external souls in buffaloes to profit by his sad fate and beware of going near Oban, which was not a safe place for them.   Naturally, when a man keeps his external soul from time to time in a beast, say in a wild cow, he is not so foolish as to shoot an animal of that particular sort, for in so doing he might perhaps be killing himself.   But he may kill animals in which other people keep their external souls.   For example, a wild cow man may freely shoot an antelope or a wild boar ; but should he do so and then have reason to suspect that the dead beast is the animal double of somebody with whom he is on friendly terms, he must perform certain ceremonies over the carcase and then hurry home, running at the top of his speed, to administer a particular medicine to the man whom he has unintentionally injured.   In this way he may possibly be in time to save the life of his friend from the effects of the deplorable accident.[1]

[1] P. Amaury Talbot, *In the Shadow of the Bush* (London, 1912), pp. 80-87. The Ekoi name for a man who has the power of sending out his spirit into the form of some animal is *efumi* (*id.*, p. 71 note *). A certain chief named Agbashan, a great elephant hunter, is believed to have the power of transforming himself into an elephant ; and "a man of considerable intelligence, educated in England, the brother of a member of the Legislative Council for one of the West African Colonies, offered to take oath that he had seen Agbashan not only in his elephant form, but while actually undergoing the metamorphosis" (*id.*, pp. 82 *sq.*).   In this case, therefore, the man seems to have felt no scruples at hunting the animals in one of which his own bush soul might be lodged.

Near Eket in North Calabar there is a sacred lake, the fish of which are carefully preserved because the people believe that their own souls are lodged in the fish, and that with every fish killed a human life would be simultaneously extinguished.[1] In the Calabar River not very many years ago there used to be a huge old crocodile, popularly supposed to contain the external soul of a chief who resided in the flesh at Duke Town.   Sporting vice-consuls used from time to time to hunt the animal, and once a peculiarly energetic officer contrived to hit it.   Forthwith the chief was laid up with a wound in his leg.   He gave out that a dog had bitten him, but no doubt the wise shook their heads and refused to be put off with so flimsy a pretext.[2]   Again, among several tribes on the banks of the Niger between Lokoja and the delta there prevails " a belief in the possibility of a man possessing an *alter ego* in the form of some animal such as a crocodile or a hippopotamus.   It is believed that such a person's life is bound up with that of the animal to such an extent that, whatever affects the one produces a corresponding impression upon the other, and that if one dies the other must speedily do so too.   It happened not very long ago that an Englishman shot a hippopotamus close to a native village; the friends of a woman who died the same night in the village demanded and eventually obtained five pounds as compensation for the murder of the woman." [3]   Among the Montols of Northern Nigeria, " in many of the compounds there will be found a species of snake, of a non-poisonous sort, which, when full grown, attains a length of about five feet and a girth of eight or nine inches.   These snakes live in and about the compound.   They are not specially fed by the people of the place, nor are places provided for them to nest in.   They live generally in the roofs of the small granaries and huts that make up the compound.   They feed upon small mammals, and no doubt serve a useful purpose in destroying vermin which might otherwise eat the stored grain.   They are not kept for the purpose of destroying vermin, however.   The Montols believe that at the birth of

Belief of other tribes of Nigeria in external souls lodged in animals.

---

[1] Letter of Mr. P. Amaury Talbot to me, dated Eket, North Calabar, Southern Nigeria, April 3d, 1913.

[2] Miss Mary H. Kingsley, *Travels* *in West Africa* (London, 1897), pp. 538 *sq.*

[3] C. H. Robinson, *Hausaland* (London, 1896), pp. 36 *sq.*

every individual of their race, male and female, one of these snakes, of the same sex, is also born. If the snake be killed, his human partner in life dies also and at the same time. If the wife of a compound-owner gives birth to a son, shortly after the interesting event, the snake of the establishment will be seen with a young one of corresponding sex. From the moment of birth, these two, the snake and the man, share a life of common duration, and the measure of the one is the measure of the other. Hence every care is taken to protect these animals from injury, and no Montol would in any circumstances think of injuring or killing one. It is said that a snake of this kind never attempts any injury to a man. There is only one type of snake thus regarded."[1]   Among the Angass, of the Kanna District in Northern Nigeria, "when a man is born, he is endowed with two distinct entities, life and a *kurua* (Arabic *rin*) . . . When the *rin* enters a man, its counterpart enters some beast or snake at the same time, and if either dies, so also does the body containing the counterpart. This, however, in no wise prevents a man from killing any game, etc., he may see, though he knows full well that he is causing thereby the death of some man or woman. When a man dies, his life and *rin* both leave him, though the latter is asserted sometimes to linger near the place of death for a day or two."[2]   Again, at the town of Paha, in the northern territory of the Gold Coast, there are pools inhabited by crocodiles which are worshipped by the people. The natives believe that for every death or birth in the town a similar event takes place among the crocodiles.[3]

The conception of an external soul lodged in an animal appears to be absent in South Africa.
In South Africa the conception of an external soul deposited in an animal, which is so common in West Africa, appears to be almost unknown ; at least I have met with no clear traces of it in literature. The Bechuanas, indeed, commonly believe that if a man wounds a crocodile, the man will be ill as long as the crocodile is ill of its wound, and

[1] J. F. J. Fitzpatrick (Assistant Resident, Northern Nigeria), "Some Notes on the Kwolla District and its Tribes," *Journal of the African Society*, No. 37, October, 1910, p. 30.

[2] Extract from a Report by Captain Foulkes to the British Colonial Office.

My thanks are due to Mr. N. W. Thomas for sending me the extract and to the authorities of the Colonial Office for their permission to publish it.

[3] *The Daily Graphic*, Tuesday, October 7th, 1902, p. 3.

that if the crocodile dies, the man dies too.   This belief is
not, apparently, confined to the Bechuana clan which has
the crocodile for its totem, but is shared by all the other
clans ; all of them certainly hold the crocodile in respect.[1] It
does not appear whether the sympathetic relation between a
man and a crocodile is supposed by the Bechuanas to be
lifelong, or only to arise at the moment when the man
wounds the animal ; in the latter case the shedding of the
crocodile's blood might perhaps be thought to establish a
relationship of affinity or sympathy between the two.   The
Zulus believe that every man is attended by an ancestral
spirit (*ihlozi*, or rather *idhlozi*) in the form of a serpent,
"which specially guards and helps him, lives with him, wakes
with him, sleeps and travels with him, but always under
ground.   If it ever makes its appearance, great is the joy,
and the man must seek to discover the meaning of its
appearance.   He who has no *ihlozi* must die.   Therefore if
any one kills an *ihlozi* serpent, the man whose *ihlozi* it was
dies, but the serpent comes to life again."[2]   But the concep-

[1] Rev. W. C. Willoughby, "Notes
on the Totemism of the Becwana,"
Journal of the Anthropological Institute,
xxxv. (1905) p. 300.   The writer adds
that he found a similar belief as to
the sympathetic relation between a
wounded crocodile and the man who
wounded it very general among the
Wanyamwezi, who, in 1882, were
living under Mirambo about two
hundred miles south of Lake Victoria
Nyanza and a hundred miles east of
Lake Tanganyika.

[2] F. Speckmann, *Die Hermanns-
burger Mission in Africa* (Hermanns-
burg, 1876) p. 167.   Compare David
Leslie, *Among the Zulus and Amaton-
gas*, Second Edition (Edinburgh, 1875)
pp. 47 *sq.* ; "The Kaffirs believe that
after death their spirits turn into a
snake, which they call *Ehlose*, and that
every living man has two of these
familiar spirits—a good and a bad.
When everything they undertake goes
wrong with them, such as hunting,
cattle - breeding, etc., they say they
know that it is their enemies who are
annoying them, and that they are only
to be appeased by sacrificing an animal;
but when everything prospers, they
ascribe it to their good *Ehlose* being in
the ascendant" ; *id.*, *op. cit.* p. 148 :
"When in battle two men are fighting,
their snakes (*Mahloze*) are poetically
said to be twisting and biting each
other overhead.   One 'softens' and
goes down, and the man, whose attendant it is, goes down with it.   Everything is ascribed to *Ehlose*.   If he
fails in anything, his *Ehlose* is bad ; if
successful, it is good. . . . It is this
thing which is the inducing cause of
everything.   In fact, nothing in Zulu
is admitted to arise from natural
causes ; everything is ascribed to
witchcraft or the *Ehlose*."
   It is not all serpents that are *amad-
hlozi* (plural of *idhlozi*), that is, are the
transformed spirits of the dead.   Serpents which are dead men may easily
be distinguished from common snakes,
for they frequent huts ; they do not
eat mice, and they are not afraid of
people.   If a man in his life had a
scar, his serpent after his death will
also have a scar ; if he had only one
eye, his serpent will have only one
eye ; if he was lame, his serpent

tion of a dead ancestor incarnate in a snake, on which the welfare or existence of one of his living descendants depends, is rather that of a guardian spirit than of an external soul.

The conception of an external soul lodged in an animal occurs among the Indians of Central America, some of whom call such a soul a *nagual*.

Amongst the Zapotecs of Central America, when a woman was about to be confined, her relations assembled in the hut, and began to draw on the floor figures of different animals, rubbing each one out as soon as it was completed. This went on till the moment of birth, and the figure that then remained sketched upon the ground was called the child's *tona* or second self. "When the child grew old enough, he procured the animal that represented him and took care of it, as it was believed that health and existence were bound up with that of the animal's, in fact that the death of both would occur simultaneously," or rather that when the animal died the man would die too.[1]   Among the

will be lame too. That is how you can recognise So-and-So in his serpent form. Chiefs do not turn into the same kind of snakes as ordinary people. For common folk become harmless snakes with green and white bellies and very small heads; but kings become boa-constrictors or the large and deadly black *mamba*. See Rev. Henry Callaway, M.D., *The Religious System of the Amazulu*, Part ii. (Capetown, London, etc., 1869) pp. 134 *sq.*, 140, 196-202, 205, 208-211, 231. "The *Ehlose* of Chaka and other dead kings is the Boa-constrictor, or the large and deadly black Mamba, whichever the doctors decide. That of dead Queens is the tree Iguana" (David Leslie, *op. cit.* p. 213). Compare Rev. Joseph Shooter, *The Kafirs of Natal and the Zulu Country* (London, 1857), pp. 161 *sq.*; W. R. Gordon, "Words about Spirits," (*South African*) *Folk-lore Journal*, ii. (Cape Town, 1880) pp. 101-103; W. Grant, "Magato and his Tribe," *Journal of the Anthropological Institute*, xxxv. (1905) p. 270. A word which is sometimes confounded with *idhlozi* is *itongo* (plural *amatongo*); but the natives themselves when closely questioned distinguish between the two. See Dudley Kidd, *Savage Childhood*, a *Study of Kafir Children* (London, 1906), pp. 14 *sq.*, 281-286. The notion that the spirits of the dead appear in the form of serpents is widespread in Africa. See *Adonis, Attis, Osiris*, Second Edition, pp. 73 *sqq.* Dr. F. B. Jevons has suggested that the Roman *genius*, the guardian-spirit which accompanied a man from birth to death (Censorinus, *De die natali*, 3) and was commonly represented in the form of a snake, may have been an external soul. See F. B. Jevons, *Plutarch's Romane Questions* (London, 1892) pp. xlvii. *sq.*; *id.*, *Introduction to the History of Religion* (London, 1896), pp. 186 *sq.*; L. Preller, *Römische Mythologie*[3] (Berlin, 1881-1883), ii. 195 *sqq.*; G. Wissowa, *Religion und Kultus der Römer*[2] (Munich, 1912), pp. 176 *sq.*

[1] H. H. Bancroft, *The Native Races of the Pacific Coast* (London, 1875-1876), i. 661. The words quoted by Bancroft (p. 662, note), "*Consérvase entre ellos la creencia de que su vida está unida à la de un animal, y que es forzoso que mueran ellos cuando éste muere,*" are not quite accurately represented by the statement of Bancroft in the text. Elsewhere (vol. ii. p. 277) the same writer calls the "second self" of the Zapotecs a

Indians of Guatemala and Honduras the *nagual* or *naual* is
"that animate or inanimate object, generally an animal,
which stands in a parallel relation to a particular man, so
that the weal and woe of the man depend on the fate of the
nagual." [1]   According to an old writer, many Indians of
Guatemala "are deluded by the devil to believe that their
life dependeth upon the life of such and such a beast (which
they take unto them as their familiar spirit), and think that
when that beast dieth they must die ; when he is chased,
their hearts pant ; when he is faint, they are faint ; nay, it
happeneth that by the devil's delusion they appear in the
shape of that beast (which commonly by their choice is a
buck, or doe, a lion, or tigre, or dog, or eagle) and in that
shape have been shot at and wounded." [2]   Herrera's account
of the way in which the Indians of Honduras acquired their
naguals, runs thus : " The devil deluded them, appearing in
the shape of a lion or a tiger, or a coyte, a beast like a
wolf, or in the shape of an alligator, a snake, or a bird, that
province abounding in creatures of prey, which they called
naguales, signifying keepers or guardians, and when the bird
died the Indian that was in league with him died also,
which often happened and was looked upon as infallible.
The manner of contracting this alliance was thus.   The
Indian repaired to the river, wood, hill, or most obscure

"*nagual*, or tutelary genius," adding
that the fate of the child was supposed
to be so intimately bound up with the
fortune of the animal that the death
of the one involved the death of the
other.   Compare Daniel G. Brinton,
" Nagualism, a Study in American
Folk-lore and History," *Proceedings of
the American Philosophical Society
held at Philadelphia*, vol. xxxiii. No.
144 (Philadelphia, January, 1894), pp.
11 - 73.   According to Professor E.
Seler the word *nagual* is akin to the
Mexican *naualli*, " a witch or wizard,"
which is derived from a word meaning
"hidden" with reference to the power
attributed to sorcerers of transforming
themselves into animals.   See E. Seler,
" Altmexikanische Studien, II." *Veröf-
fentlichungen aus dem Königlichen
Museum für Völkerkunde*, vi. heft 2/4

(Berlin, 1899), pp. 52-57.
   [1] Otto Stoll, *Die Ethnologie der
Indianerstämme von Guatemala* (Leyden, 1889), p. 57.
   [2] Thomas Gage, *A New Survey of
the West Indies*, Third Edition (London,
1677), p. 334.   The same writer
relates how a certain Indian named
Gonzalez was reported to have the
power of turning himself into a lion or
rather a puma.   Once when a Spaniard
had shot a puma in the nose, Gonzalez
was found with a bruised face and
accused the Spaniard of having shot
him.   Another Indian chief named
Gomez was said to have transformed
himself into a puma, and in that shape
to have fought a terrific battle with a
rival chief named Lopez, who had
changed himself into a jaguar.   See
Gage, *op. cit.* pp. 383-389.

place, where he called upon the devils by such names as he thought fit, talked to the rivers, rocks, or woods, said he went to weep that he might have the same his predecessors had, carrying a cock or a dog to sacrifice. In that melancholy fit he fell asleep, and either in a dream or waking saw some one of the aforesaid birds or other creatures, whom he entreated to grant him profit in salt, cacao, or any other commodity, drawing blood from his own tongue, ears, and other parts of his body, making his contract at the same time with the said creature, the which either in a dream or waking told him, ' Such a day you shall go abroad asporting, and I will be the first bird or other animal you shall meet, and will be your *nagual* and companion at all times.' Whereupon such friendship was contracted between them, that when one of them died the other did not survive, and they fancied that he who had no *nagual* could not be rich." [1] The Indians were persuaded that the death of their *nagual* would entail their own. Legend affirms that in the first battles with the Spaniards on the plateau of Quetzaltenango the *naguals* of the Indian chiefs fought in the form of serpents. The *nagual* of the highest chief was especially conspicuous, because it had the form of a great bird, resplendent in green plumage. The Spanish general Pedro de Alvarado killed the bird with his lance, and at the same moment the Indian chief fell dead to the ground. [2]

In some tribes of South-Eastern Australia the lives of

In many tribes of South-Eastern Australia each sex used to regard a particular species of animals in the same way that a Central American Indian regarded his *nagual*, but with this difference, that whereas the Indian apparently knew the indi-

---

[1] Antonio de Herrera, *General History of the Vast Continent and Islands of America*, translated by Capt. John Stevens (London, 1725–1726), iv. 138 *sq.* The Spanish original of Herrera's history, a work based on excellent authorities, was first published at Madrid in 1601–1615. The Indians of Santa Catalina Istlavacan still receive at birth the name of some animal, which is commonly regarded as their guardian spirit for the rest of their life. The name is bestowed by the heathen priest, who usually hears of a birth in the village sooner than his Catholic colleague. See K. Scherzer, "Die Indianer von Santa Catalina Istlávacana (Frauenfuss), ein Beitrag zur Culturgeschichte der Urbewohner Central-Amerikas," *Sitzungsberichte der philos. histor. Classe der kais. Akademie der Wissenschaften* (Vienna), xviii. (1856) p. 235.

[2] Otto Stoll, *Die Ethnologie der Indianerstämme von Guatemala* (Leyden, 1889), pp. 57 *sq.*; *id.*, *Suggestion und Hypnotism* [2] (Leipsic, 1904), p. 170.

vidual animal with which his life was bound up, the Australians only knew that each of their lives was bound up with some one animal of the species, but they could not say with which. The result naturally was that every man spared and protected all the animals of the species with which the lives of the men were bound up ; and every woman spared and protected all the animals of the species with which the lives of the women were bound up; because no one knew but that the death of any animal of the respective species might entail his or her own ; just as the killing of the green bird was immediately followed by the death of the Indian chief, and the killing of the parrot by the death of Punchkin in the fairy tale. Thus, for example, the Wotjobaluk tribe of South-Eastern Australia " held that 'the life of Ngŭnŭngŭnŭt (the Bat) is the life of a man, and the life of Yártatgŭrk (the Nightjar) is the life of a woman,' and that when either of these creatures is killed the life of some man or of some woman is shortened. In such a case every man or every woman in the camp feared that he or she might be the victim, and from this cause great fights arose in this tribe. I learn that in these fights, men on one side and women on the other, it was not at all certain which would be victorious, for at times the women gave the men a severe drubbing with their yamsticks, while often women were injured or killed by spears." The Wotjobaluk said that the bat was the man's " brother " and that the nightjar was his " wife." [1]

---

[1] A. W. Howitt, "Further Notes on the Australian Class Systems," *Journal of the Anthropological Institute*, xviii. (1889) pp. 57 *sq.* Compare *id.*, *Native Tribes of South-East Australia* (London, 1904), pp. 148, 150. It is very remarkable that among the Kurnai these fights had a special connexion with marriage. When young men were backward of taking wives, the women used to go out into the forest and kill an emu-wren, which was the men's "brother"; then returning to the camp they shewed the dead bird to the men. The result was a fight between the young men and the young women, in which, however, lads who were not yet marriageable might not take part. Next day the marriageable young men went out and killed a superb warbler, which was the women's "sister," and this led to a worse fight than before. Some days afterwards, when the wounds and bruises were healed, one of the marriageable young men met one of the marriageable young women, and said, " Superb warbler ! " She answered, " Emu-wren ! What does the emu-wren eat ? " To which the young man answered, " He eats so-and-so," naming kangaroo, opossum, emu, or some other game. Then they laughed, and she ran off with him without telling any one. See L. Fison and A. W. Howitt, *Kamilaroi and Kurnai* (Melbourne, Sydney, Adelaide, and Brisbane, 1880), pp. 201 *sq.*; A. W. Howitt, *Native Tribes of South-East*

The particular species of animals with which the lives of the sexes were believed to be respectively bound up varied somewhat from tribe to tribe. Thus whereas among the Wotjobaluk the bat was the animal of the men, at Gunbower Creek on the Lower Murray the bat seems to have been the animal of the women, for the natives would not kill it for the reason that " if it was killed, one of their lubras [women] would be sure to die in consequence." [1]   In the Kurnai tribe of Gippsland the emu-wren (*Stipiturus malachurus*) was the " man's brother " and the superb warbler (*Malurus cyaneus*) was the " woman's sister " ; at the initiation of young men into the tribal mysteries the name of the emu-wren was invoked over the novices for the purpose of infusing manly virtue into them.[2]   Among the Yuin on the south-eastern coast of Australia, the " woman's sister " was the tree-creeper (*Climacteris scandens*), and the men had both the bat and the emu-wren for their " brothers." [3]   In the Kulin nation each sex had a pair of " brothers " and " sisters " ; the men had the bat and the emu-wren for their " brothers," and the women had the superb warbler and the small nightjar for their " sisters." [4]   It is notable that in South-Eastern Australia the animals thus associated with the lives of men and women were generally flying creatures, either birds or bats. However, in the Port Lincoln tribe of South Australia the man's " brother " and the woman's " sister " seem to have been identified with the male and female respectively of a species of lizard ; for we read that " a small kind of lizard, the male of which is called *ibirri*, and the female *waka*, is said to have divided the sexes in the human species ; an event that would appear not to be much approved of by the natives, since either sex has a mortal hatred against the

---

Australia, pp. 149, 273 *sq.* Perhaps this killing of the sex-totem before marriage may be related to the pretence of killing young men and bringing them to life again at puberty. See below, pp. 225 *sqq.*

[1] Gerard Krefft, "Manners and Customs of the Aborigines of the Lower Murray and Darling," *Transactions of the Philosophical Society of New South Wales*, 1862–65, pp. 359 *sq.*

[2] A. W. Howitt, " Further Notes on the Australian Class Systems," *Journal of the Anthropological Institute*, xviii. (1889) pp. 56 *sq.*

[3] A. W. Howitt, *op. cit.* p. 57 ; *id.*, *Native Tribes of South-East Australia*, p. 150.

[4] A. W. Howitt, " On the Migrations of the Kurnai Ancestors," *Journal of the Anthropological Institute*, xv. (1886) p. 416.

opposite sex of these little animals, the men always destroying the *waka* and the women the *ibirri*."[1]   But whatever
the particular sorts of creature with which the lives of men
and women were believed to be bound up, the belief itself
and the fights to which it gave rise are known to have
prevailed over a large part of South-Eastern Australia, and
probably they extended much farther.[2]   The belief was a very
serious one, and so consequently were the fights which sprang
from it.   Thus among some tribes of Victoria " the common
bat belongs to the men, who protect it against injury, even
to the half-killing of their wives for its sake.   The fern owl,
or large goatsucker, belongs to the women, and, although a
bird of evil omen, creating terror at night by its cry, it is
jealously protected by them.   If a man kills one, they are
as much enraged as if it was one of their children, and will
strike him with their long poles."[3]

The jealous protection thus afforded by Australian men
and women to bats and owls respectively (for bats and
owls seem to be the creatures usually allotted to the two
sexes)[4] is not based upon purely selfish considerations.
For each man believes that not only his own life but the
lives of his father, brothers, sons, and so on are bound up with
the lives of particular bats, and that therefore in protecting the
bat species he is protecting the lives of all his male relations
as well as his own.   Similarly, each woman believes that the
lives of her mother, sisters, daughters, and so forth, equally
with her own, are bound up with the lives of particular owls,

[marginal note: Bats regarded as the brothers of men, and owls as the sisters of women.*]*

[1] C. W. Schürmann, "The Aboriginal
Tribes of Port Lincoln," in *Native
Tribes of South Australia* (Adelaide,
1879), p. 241. Compare G. F. Angas,
*Savage Life and Scenes in Australia
and New Zealand* (London, 1847), i.
109.

[2] A. W. Howitt, " Further Notes on
the Australian Class Systems," *Journal
of the Anthropological Institute*, xviii.
(1889) p. 58. Compare *id., Native
Tribes of South-East Australia* (London,
1904), pp. 148-151.

[3] James Dawson, *Australian Aborigines* (Melbourne, Sydney, and Adelaide, 1881), p. 52.

[4] See *Totemism and Exogamy*, i.
47 *sq.* It is at least remarkable that

both the creatures thus assigned to the
two sexes should be nocturnal in their
habits. Perhaps the choice of such
creatures is connected with the belief
that the soul is absent from the body
in slumber. On this hypothesis bats
and owls would be regarded by these
savages as the wandering souls of
sleepers. Such a belief would fully
account for the reluctance of the natives
to kill them. The Kiowa Indians of
North America think that owls and
other night birds are animated by the
souls of the dead. See James Mooney,
"Calendar History of the Kiowa
Indians," *Seventeenth Annual Report
of the Bureau of American Ethnology*,
Part i. (Washington, 1898) p. 237.

and that in guarding the owl species she is guarding the lives of all her female relations besides her own. Now, when men's lives are thus supposed to be contained in certain animals, it is obvious that the animals can hardly be distinguished from the men, or the men from the animals. If my brother John's life is in a bat, then, on the one hand, the bat is my brother as well as John; and, on the other hand, John is in a sense a bat, since his life is in a bat. Similarly, if my sister Mary's life is in an owl, then the owl is my sister and Mary is an owl. This is a natural enough conclusion, and the Australians have not failed to draw it. When the bat is the man's animal, it is called his brother; and when the owl is the woman's animal, it is called her sister. And conversely a man addresses a woman as an owl, and she addresses him as a bat.[1] So with the other animals allotted to the sexes respectively in other tribes. For example, among the Kurnai all emu-wrens were " brothers " of the men, and all the men were emu-wrens; all superb warblers were " sisters " of the women, and all the women were superb warblers.[2]

§ 4. *A Suggested Theory of Totemism* [3]

But when a savage names himself after an animal, calls

[1] A. L. P. Cameron, "Notes on some Tribes of New South Wales," *Journal of the Anthropological Institute*, xiv. (1885) p. 350 note[1]; A. W. Howitt, "On the Migrations of the Kurnai Ancestors," *Journal of the Anthropological Institute*, xv. (1886) p. 416; *id.*, "Further Notes on the Australian Class Systems," *Journal of the Anthropological Institute*, xviii. (1889) p. 57.

[2] L. Fison and A. W. Howitt, *Kamilaroi and Kurnai*, pp. 194, 201, *sq.*, 215; *Journal of the Anthropological Institute*, xv. 416, xviii. 56 *sq.*; A. W. Howitt, *Native Tribes of South-East Australia* (London, 1904), pp. 148-151.

[3] The following suggestion as to the origin of totemism was made in the first edition of this book (published in 1890) and is here reprinted without any substantial change. In the mean-

time much additional evidence as to the nature and prevalence of totemism has come to light, and with the new evidence my opinions, or rather conjectures, as to the origin of the institution have repeatedly changed. If I here reprint my earliest conjecture, it is partly because I still think it may contain an element of truth, and partly because it serves as a convenient peg on which to hang a collection of facts which are much more valuable than any theories of mine. The reader who desires to acquaint himself more fully with the facts of totemism and with the theories that have been broached on the subject, will find them stated at length in my *Totemism and Exogamy* (London, 1910). Here I will only call attention to the Arunta legend that the ancestors of the tribe kept their spirits in certain sacred sticks

it his brother, and refuses to kill it, the animal is said to be his totem.   Accordingly in the tribes of South-Eastern Australia which we have been considering the bat and the owl, the emu-wren and the superb warbler, may properly be described as totems of the sexes.   But the assignation of a totem to a sex is comparatively rare, and has hitherto been discovered nowhere but in Australia.   Far more commonly the totem is appropriated not to a sex, but to a clan, and is hereditary either in the male or female line.   The relation of an individual to the clan totem does not differ in kind from his relation to the sex totem ; he will not kill it, he speaks of it as his brother, and he calls himself by its name. Now if the relations are similar, the explanation which holds good of the one ought equally to hold good of the other. Therefore the reason why a clan revere a particular species of animals or plants (for the clan totem may be a plant) and call themselves after it, would seem to be a belief that the life of each individual of the clan is bound up with some one animal or plant of the species, and that his or her death would be the consequence of killing that particular animal, or destroying that particular plant.   This explanation of totemism squares very well with Sir George Grey's definition of a totem or *kobong* in Western Australia.   He says : " A certain mysterious connection exists between a family and its *kobong*, so that a member of the family will never kill an animal of the species to which his *kobong* belongs, should he find it asleep ; indeed he always kills it reluctantly, and never without affording it a chance to escape.   This arises from the family belief that some one individual of the species is their nearest friend, to kill whom would be a great crime, and to be carefully avoided.   Similarly, a native who has a vegetable for his *kobong* may not gather it under certain

Sex totems and clan totems may both be based on the notion that men and women keep their external souls in their totems, whether these are animals, plants, or what not.

---

and stones (*churinga*), which bear a close resemblance to the well-known bull-roarers, and that when they went out hunting they hung these sticks or stones on certain sacred poles (*nurtunjas*) which represented their totems.   See Baldwin Spencer and F. J. Gillen, *Native Tribes of Central Australia* (London, 1899), pp. 137 *sq.*, 629.

This tradition appears to point to a custom of transferring a man's soul or spirit temporarily to his totem.   Conversely when an Arunta is sick he scrapes his *churinga* and swallows the scrapings, as if to restore to himself the spiritual substance deposited in the instrument.   See Baldwin Spencer and F. J. Gillen, *op. cit.* p. 135 note[1].

circumstances, and at a particular period of the year."[1]   Here
it will be observed that though each man spares all the
animals or plants of the species, they are not all equally
precious to him ; far from it, out of the whole species there
is only one which is specially dear to him ; but as he does
not know which the dear one is, he is obliged to spare them
all from fear of injuring the one.   Again, this explanation
of the clan totem harmonizes with the supposed effect of
killing one of the totem species.   " One day one of the
blacks killed a crow.   Three or four days afterwards a
Boortwa (crow) [*i.e.* a man of the   Crow clan] named
Larry died.   He had been ailing for some days, but the
killing of his *wingong* [totem] hastened his death."[2]   Here
the killing of the crow caused the death of a man of the
Crow clan, exactly as, in the case of the sex-totems, the
killing of a bat causes the death of a Bat-man or the killing
of an owl causes the death of an Owl-woman.   Similarly,
the killing of his *nagual* causes the death of a Central
American Indian, the killing of his bush soul causes the
death of a Calabar negro, the killing of his *tamaniu* causes
the death of a Banks Islander, and the killing of the animal
in which his life is stowed away causes the death of the giant
or warlock in the fairy tale.

The savage may imagine his life to be bound up with that of more animals than one at the same time ; for many savages think that

Thus it appears that the story of " The giant who had no
heart in his body " may perhaps furnish the key to the relation
which is supposed to subsist between a man and his totem.
The totem, on this theory, is simply the receptacle in which
a man keeps his life, as Punchkin kept his life in a parrot,
and Bidasari kept her soul in a golden fish.   It is no
valid objection to this view that when a savage has both
a sex totem and a clan totem his life must be bound up
with two different animals, the death of either of which

[1] (Sir) George Grey, *Journals of Two Expeditions of Discovery in North-West and Western Australia* (London, 1841), ii. 228 *sq.*

[2] L. Fison and A. W. Howitt, *Kamilaroi and Kurnai*, p. 169.   According to Dr. Howitt, it is a serious offence to kill the totem of another person "with intent to injure him" (*Journal of the Anthropological Institute*, xviii. (1889) p. 53).   Such an

intention seems to imply a belief in a sympathetic connexion between the man and the animal.   Similarly the Siena of the Ivory Coast, in West Africa, who have totemism, believe that if a man kills one of his totemic animals, a member of his totemic clan dies instantaneously.   See Maurice Delafosse, " Le peuple Siéna ou Sénoufo," *Revue des Etudes Ethnographiques et Sociologiques*, i. (1908) p. 452.

would entail his own. If a man has more vital places than one in his body, why, the savage may think, should he not have more vital places than one outside it? Why, since he can put his life outside himself, should he not transfer one portion of it to one animal and another to another? The divisibility of life, or, to put it otherwise, the plurality of souls, is an idea suggested by many familiar facts, and has commended itself to philosophers like Plato,[1] as well as to savages. It finds favour also with the sages of China, who tell us that every human being is provided with what may be called a male soul (*shen*) and a female soul (*kwei*), which by their harmonious co-operation compose an organic unity. However, some Chinese philosophers will have it that each of the five viscera has its own separate male soul (*shen*); and a Taoist treatise written about the end of the tenth or beginning of the eleventh century has even enriched science with a list of about three dozen souls distributed over the various parts of the human frame; indeed, not content with a bare catalogue of these souls, the learned author has annexed to the name and surname of each a brief description of its size and stature, of the kind of dress in which it is clothed and the shape of hat it wears.[2] It is only when the notion of a soul, from being a quasi-scientific hypothesis, becomes a theological dogma that its unity and indivisibility are insisted upon as essential. The savage, unshackled by dogma, is free to explain the facts of life by the assumption of as many souls as he thinks necessary. Hence, for example, the Caribs supposed that there was one soul in the head, another in the heart, and other souls at all the places where an artery is felt pulsating.[3] Some of the Hidatsa Indians explain the phenomena of gradual death, when the extremities appear dead first, by supposing that man has four

every person has more souls than one.

---

[1] According to Plato, the different parts of the soul were lodged in different parts of the body (*Timaeus*, pp. 69C-72D), and as only one part, on his theory, was immortal, Lucian seems not unnaturally to have interpreted the Platonic doctrine to mean that every man had more than one soul (*Demonax*, 33).

[2] J. J. M. de Groot, *The Religious System of China*, iv. (Leyden, 1901) pp. 3 *sq.*, 70-75.

[3] Le sieur de la Borde, "Relation de l'Origine, Mœurs, Coustumes, Religion, Guerres et Voyages des Caraibes sauvages des Isles Antilles de l'Amerique," p. 15, in *Recueil de divers Voyages faits en Afrique et en l'Amerique* (Paris, 1684).

souls, and that they quit the body, not simultaneously, but one after the other, dissolution being only complete when all four have departed.[1]   Some of the Dyaks of Borneo and the Malays of the Peninsula believe that every man has seven souls.[2]   The Alfoors of Poso in Celebes are of opinion that he has three.[3]   The natives of Laos suppose that the body is the seat of thirty spirits, which reside in the hands, the feet, the mouth, the eyes, and so on.[4]   Hence, from the primitive point of view, it is perfectly possible that a savage should have one soul in his sex totem and another in his clan totem.   However, as I have observed, sex totems have been found nowhere but in Australia ; so that as a rule the savage who practises totemism need not have more than one soul out of his body at a time.[5]

The Battas of Sumatra, who have totemism, believe that every person has a soul which is always outside of his body.

If this explanation of the totem as a receptacle in which a man keeps his soul or one of his souls is correct, we should expect to find some totemic people of whom it is expressly said that every man amongst them is believed to keep at least one soul permanently out of his body, and that the destruction of this external soul is supposed to entail the death of its owner.   Such a people are the Battas of Sumatra.   The Battas are divided into exogamous clans (*margas*) with descent in the male line ; and each clan is forbidden to eat

---

[1] Washington Matthews, *The Hidatsa Indians* (Washington, 1877), p. 50.

[2] H. Ling Roth, " Low's Natives of Borneo," *Journal of the Anthropological Institute*, xxi. (1892) p. 117 ; W. W. Skeat, *Malay Magic* (London, 1900), p. 50.

[3] A. C. Kruijt, " Een en ander aangaande het geestelijk en maatschappelijk leven van den Poso-Alfoer," *Mededeelingen van wege het Nederlandsche Zendelinggenootschap*, xxxix. (1895) pp. 3 *sq.*

[4] A. Bastian, *Die Völker des östlichen Asien*, iii. (Jena, 1867) p. 248.

[5] In some tribes, chiefly of North American Indians, every man has an individual or personal totem in addition to the totem of his clan.   This personal totem is usually the animal of which he dreamed during a long and solitary fast at puberty.   See *Totemism and Exogamy*, i. 49-52, iii. 370-456, where the relation of the individual or personal totem (if we may call it so) to the clan totem is discussed.   It is quite possible that, as some good authorities incline to believe, the clan totem has been developed out of the personal totem by inheritance.   See Miss Alice C. Fletcher, *The Import of the Totem*, pp. 3 *sqq.* (paper read before the American Association for the Advancement of Science, August 1887, separate reprint) ; Fr. Boas, " The Social Organization and the Secret Societies of the Kwakiutl Indians," *Report of the United States National Museum for 1895* (Washington, 1897), pp. 323 *sq.*, 336-338, 393.   In the bush souls of the Calabar negroes (see above, pp. 204 *sqq.*) we seem to have something like the personal totem on its way to become hereditary and so to grow into the totem of a clan.

the flesh of a particular animal. One clan may not eat the tiger, another the ape, another the crocodile, another the dog, another the cat, another the dove, another the white buffalo, and another the locust. The reason given by members of a clan for abstaining from the flesh of the particular animal is either that they are descended from animals of that species, and that their souls after death may transmigrate into the animals, or that they or their forefathers have been under certain obligations to the creatures. Sometimes, but not always, the clan bears the name of the animal.[1] Thus the Battas have totemism in full. But, further, each Batta believes that he has seven or, on a more moderate computation, three souls. One of these souls is always outside the body, but nevertheless whenever it dies, however far away it may be at the time, that same moment the man dies also.[2] The writer who mentions this belief says nothing

---

[1] J. B. Neumann, "Het Pane- en Bila - stroomgebied op het eiland Sumatra," *Tijdschrift van het Nederlandsch Aardrijkskundig Genootschap,* Tweede Serie, dl. iii. Afdeeling, meer uitgebreide artikelen, No. 2 (1886), pp. 311 *sq.* ; *id.,* dl. iv. No. 1 (1887), pp. 8 *sq.* ; Van Hoëvell, "Iets over 't oorlogvoeren der Batta's," *Tijdschrift voor Nederlandsch Indië,* N.S., vii. (1878) p. 434 ; G. A. Wilken, *Verspreide Geschriften* (The Hague, 1912), i. 296, 306 *sq.,* 309, 325 *sq.* ; L. de Backer, *L'Archipel Indien* (Paris, 1874), p. 470 ; Col. Yule, in *Journal of the Anthropological Institute,* ix. (1880) p. 295 ; Joachim Freiherr von Brenner, *Besuch bei den Kannibalen Sumatras* (Würzburg, 1894), pp. 197 *sqq.* ; P. A. L. E. van Dijk, "Eenige aanteekeningen omtrent de verschillenden stammen (*Margas*) en de stamverdeling bij de Battaks," *Tijdschrift voor Indische Taal- Land- en Volkenkunde,* xxxviii. (1895) pp. 296 *sq.* ; M. Joustra, "Naar het landschap Goenoeng," *Mededeelingen van wege het Nederlandsche Zendelinggenootschap,* xlv. (1901) pp. 80 *sq.* ; *id.,* "Het leven, de zeden en gewoonten der Bataks," *Mededeelingen van wege het Nederlandsche Zendelinggenootschap,* xlvi. (1902) pp. 387 *sqq.* ; J. E. Neu-

mann, "Kemali, Pantang, en Rĕboe bij de Karo-Bataks," *Tijdschrift voor Indische Taal- Land- en Volkenkunde,* xlviii. (1906) p. 512. See further *Totemism and Exogamy,* ii. 185 *sqq.*

[2] B. Hagen, "Beiträge zur Kenntniss der Battareligion," *Tijdschrift voor Indische Taal- Land- en Volkenkunde,* xxviii. (1883) p. 514. J. B. Neumann (*op. cit.* dl. iii. No. 2, pp. 299) is the authority for the seven souls. According to another writer, six out of the seven souls reside outside of the body ; one of them dwells in heaven, the remaining five have no definite place of abode, but are so closely related to the man that were they to abandon him his health would suffer. See J. Freiherr von Brenner, *Besuch bei den Kannibalen Sumatras,* pp. 239 *sq.* A different account of Batta psychology is given by Mr. Westenberg. According to him, each Batta has only one *tendi* (not three or seven of them) ; and the *tendi* is something between a soul and a guardian spirit. It always resides outside of the body, and on its position near, before, behind, above, or below, the welfare of its owner is supposed in great measure to depend. But in addition each man has two invisible guardian spirits (his *kaka* and *agi*) whose help he invokes in great danger ;

about the Batta totems; but on the analogy of the Australian, Central American, and African evidence we may conjecture that the external soul, whose death entails the death of the man, is housed in the totemic animal or plant.

If a totem is the receptacle in which a man keeps his external soul, it is no wonder that savages should conceal the secret from strangers. Against this view it can hardly be thought to militate that the Batta does not in set terms affirm his external soul to be in his totem, but alleges other grounds for respecting the sacred animal or plant of his clan. For if a savage seriously believes that his life is bound up with an external object, it is in the last degree unlikely that he will let any stranger into the secret. In all that touches his inmost life and beliefs the savage is exceedingly suspicious and reserved; Europeans have resided among savages for years without discovering some of their capital articles of faith, and in the end the discovery has often been the result of accident.[1] Above all, the savage lives in an intense and perpetual dread of assassination by sorcery; the most trifling relics of his person—the clippings of his hair and nails, his spittle, the remnants of his food, his very name [2]—all these may, he fancies, be turned by the

---

one is the seed by which he was begotten, the other is the afterbirth, and these he calls respectively his elder and his younger brother. Mr. Westenberg's account refers specially to the Karo-Battas. See C. J. Westenberg, "Aanteekeningen omtrent de godsdienstige begrippen der Karo-Bataks," *Bijdragen tot de Taal- Land- en Volkenkunde van Nederlandsch Indië*, xli. (1892) pp. 228 *sq.*

[1] Compare Ch. Hose and W. McDougall, *The Pagan Tribes of Borneo* (London, 1912), ii. 90 *sqq.* : "An important institution among some of the Ibans, which occurs but in rare instances among the other peoples, is the *ngarong* or secret helper. The *ngarong* is one of the very few topics in regard to which the Ibans display any reluctance to speak freely. So great is their reserve in this connection that one of us lived for fourteen years on friendly terms with Ibans of various districts without ascertaining the meaning of the word *ngarong*, or suspecting the great importance of the part played

by the notion in the lives of some of these people. The *ngarong* seems to be usually the spirit of some ancestor or dead relative, but not always so, and it is not clear that it is always conceived as the spirit of a deceased human being. This spirit becomes the special protector of some individual Iban, to whom in a dream he manifests himself, in the first place in human form, and announces that he will be his secret helper. . . . When, as is most commonly the case, the secret helper takes on the form of some animal, all individuals of that species become objects of especial regard to the fortunate Iban; he will not kill or eat any such animal, and he will as far as possible restrain others from doing so." Thus the *ngarong* or secret helper of the Ibans closely resembles what I have called the individual or personal totem.

[2] It is not merely the personal name which is often shrouded in mystery (see *Taboo and the Perils of the Soul*, pp. 318 *sqq.*); the names of the clans and

sorcerer to his destruction, and he is therefore anxiously careful to conceal or destroy them. But if in matters such as these, which are but the outposts and outworks of his life, he is so shy and secretive, how close must be the concealment, how impenetrable the reserve in which he enshrouds the inner keep and citadel of his being ! When the princess in the fairy tale asks the giant where he keeps his soul, he often gives false or evasive answers, and it is only after much coaxing and wheedling that the secret is at last wrung from him. In his jealous reticence the giant resembles the timid and furtive savage ; but whereas the exigencies of the story demand that the giant should at last reveal his secret, no such obligation is laid on the savage ; and no inducement that can be offered is likely to tempt him to imperil his soul by revealing its hiding-place to a stranger. It is therefore no matter for surprise that the central mystery of the savage's life should so long have remained a secret, and that we should be left to piece it together from scattered hints and fragments and from the recollections of it which linger in fairy tales.

§ 5. *The Ritual of Death and Resurrection*

This view of totemism throws light on a class of religious rites of which no adequate explanation, so far as I am aware, has yet been offered. Amongst many savage tribes, especially such as are known to practise totemism, it is customary for lads at puberty to undergo certain initiatory rites, of which one of the commonest is a pretence of killing the lad and bringing him to life again. Such rites become intelligible if we suppose that their substance consists in extracting the youth's soul in order to transfer it to his totem. For the

This view of totemism may help to explain the rite of death and resurrection which forms part of many initiatory ceremonies among savages.

---

their subdivisions are objects of mysterious reverence among many, if not all, of the Siouan tribes of North America, and are never used in ordinary conversation. See J. Owen Dorsey, " Osage Traditions," *Sixth Annual Report of the Bureau of Ethnology* (Washington, 1888), p. 396. Among the Yuin of South-Eastern Australia " the totem name was called *Budjan*, and it was

said to be more like *Joïa*, or magic, than a name ; and it was in one sense a secret name, for with it an enemy might cause injury to its bearer by magic. Thus very few people knew the totem names of others, the name being told to a youth by his father at his initiation " (A. W. Howitt, *Native Tribes of South-East Australia*, London, 1904, p. 133).

extraction of his soul would naturally be supposed to kill the youth or at least to throw him into a death-like trance, which the savage hardly distinguishes from death. His recovery would then be attributed either to the gradual recovery of his system from the violent shock which it had received, or, more probably, to the infusion into him of fresh life drawn from the totem. Thus the essence of these initiatory rites, so far as they consist in a simulation of death and resurrection, would be an exchange of life or souls between the man and his totem. The primitive belief in the possibility of such an exchange of souls comes clearly out in the story of the Basque hunter who affirmed that he had been killed by a bear, but that the bear had, after killing him, breathed its own soul into him, so that the bear's body was now dead, but he himself was a bear, being animated by the bear's soul.[1] This revival of the dead hunter as a bear is exactly analogous to what, on the theory here suggested, is supposed to take place in the ceremony of killing a lad at puberty and bringing him to life again. The lad dies as a man and comes to life again as an animal; the animal's soul is now in him, and his human soul is in the animal. With good right, therefore, does he call himself a Bear or a Wolf, etc., according to his totem; and with good right does he treat the bears or the wolves, etc., as his brethren, since in these animals are lodged the souls of himself and his kindred.

Examples of this supposed death and resurrection at

---

[1] Theodor Benfey, *Pantschatantra* (Leipsic, 1859), i. 128 *sq.* Similarly a man of the Kulin tribe in Victoria was called Kurburu, that is, "native bear," because the spirit of a native bear was supposed to have entered into him when he killed the animal, and to have endowed him with its wonderful cleverness. This I learn from Miss E. B. Howitt's *Folklore and Legends of some Victorian Tribes* (chapter vi.), which I have been privileged to see in manuscript. Among the Chiquites Indians of Paraguay sickness was sometimes accounted for by supposing that the soul of a deer or a turtle had entered into the patient. See *Lettres Edifiantes et Curieuses*, Nouvelle Édition, viii. (Paris, 1781) p. 339. We have seen (pp. 213 *sq.*) that the Indians of Honduras made an alliance with the animal that was to be their *nagual* by offering some of their own blood to it. Conversely the North American Indian kills the animal which is to be his personal totem, and thenceforth wears some part of the creature as an amulet (*Totemism and Exogamy*, i. 50). These facts seem to point to the establishment of a blood covenant, involving an interchange of life between a man and his personal totem or *nagual*; and among the Fans of West Africa, as we saw (above, p. 201), such a covenant is actually supposed to exist between a sorcerer and his *elangela*.

initiation are as follows.   In the Wonghi or Wonghibon
tribe of New South Wales "the youths on approaching
manhood attend a meeting of the tribe.   The ceremonies
of initiation are secret, and at them none but the men of the
tribe who have been initiated attend with the novices.   At
the spot where the ceremonies are to be performed, a large
oval space is cleared.   The old men of the tribe conduct the
ceremonies, and the 'medicine man' of the tribe is the master
of them.   Part of the proceedings consists in knocking out
a tooth and giving a new designation to the novice, indicating
the change from youth to manhood.   When the tooth is
knocked out, a loud humming noise is heard, which is made
with an instrument of the following description : a flat piece
of wood is made with serrated edges, and having a hole at
one end, to which a string is attached, and this swung round
produces a humming noise.   The uninitiated are not even
allowed to see this instrument.   Women are forbidden to be
present at these ceremonies, and should one, by accident or
otherwise, witness them, the penalty is death.   The penalty
for revealing the secrets is probably the same.   When everything is prepared the women and children are covered with
boughs, and the men retire, with the young fellows who are
to be initiated, to a little distance.   It is said that the youths
are sent away a short distance one by one, and that they are
each met in turn by a Being, who, so far as I can understand,
is believed to be something between a blackfellow and a spirit.
This Being, called Thuremlin, it is said, takes the youth to a
distance, kills him, and in some instances cuts him up, after
which he restores him to life and knocks out a tooth.   Their
belief in the power of Thuremlin is undoubted." [1]

The foregoing account, while it applies strictly to one
tribe only, may be regarded as typical of the initiation ceremonies performed on young men throughout the tribes of
South-Eastern and Central Australia, except that among the
Central tribes the practice of knocking out a tooth on these
occasions is replaced by the equally mysterious and much
severer bodily mutilations of circumcision and subincision,

[1] A. L. P. Cameron, "Notes on some Tribes of New South Wales," *Journal of the Anthropological Insti- tute*, xiv. (1885) pp. 357 *sq.* Com pare A. W. Howitt, *Native Tribes of South-East Australia* (London, 1904), pp. 588 *sq.*

which are not practised by the tribes of the South-East.[1] The instrument whose humming or booming sound accompanies the critical operation of knocking out the tooth of the novice, is the now well-known bull-roarer, which figures in many savage rites of initiation. Its true nature is concealed from the women and uninitiated lads, who are taught to believe that its sonorous and long-drawn notes are the voice of the mythical being, often called Daramulun, who lives in the sky, instituted the rites, and superintends their performance. The hollow roar of the slat of wood, as it is swung round and round, " represents the muttering of thunder, and the thunder is the voice of Daramulun, and therefore its sound is of the most sacred character. Umbara once said to me, ' Thunder is the voice of him (pointing upward to the sky) calling on the rain to fall and make everything grow up new.'"[2] This supposed resemblance of the sound to

The sound of the bull-roarer compared to thunder.

---

[1] Baldwin Spencer and F. J. Gillen, *Native Tribes of Central Australia* (London, 1899), pp. 213, 453.

[2] A. W. Howitt, *Native Tribes of South-East Australia* (London, 1904), p. 538. As to Daramulun (of whose name Thuremlin is no doubt only a dialectical variation) see *id.*, pp. 407, 493, 494 *sq.*, 497, 499, 500, 507, 523 *sq.*, 526, 528, 529 *sq.*, 535, 540, 541, 585 *sq.*, 587 ; *id.*, " On some Australian Ceremonies of Initiation," *Journal of the Anthropological Institute*, xiii. (1884) pp. 442, 443, 446, 447, 448, 450, 451, 452, 455, 456, 459. On the bull-roarer see Andrew Lang, *Custom and Myth* (London, 1884), pp. 29-44 ; J. D. E. Schmeltz, *Das Schwirrholz* (Hamburg, 1896) ; A. C. Haddon, *The Study of Man* (London and New York, 1898), pp. 277-327 ; J. G. Frazer, " On some Ceremonies of the Central Australian Aborigines," *Proceedings of the Australasian Association for the Advancement of Science for the Year 1900* (Melbourne, 1901), pp. 317-322. The religious or magical use of the bull-roarer is best known in Australia. See, for example, L. Fison and A. W. Howitt, *Kamilaroi and Kurnai* (Melbourne, Sydney, Adelaide, and Brisbane, 1880), pp. 267-269 ; A. W. Howitt, *Native Tribes*

of South-East Australia, pp. 354, 509 *sq.*, 514, 515, 517, 569, 571, 575, 578, 579, 582, 583, 584, 589, 592, 594, 595, 606, 659 *sq.*, 670, 672, 696, 715 ; Baldwin Spencer and F. J. Gillen, *Native Tribes of Central Australia* (London, 1899), pp. 246, 344, 347 ; W. Baldwin Spencer, *Introduction to the Study of Certain Native Tribes of the Northern Territory* (*Bulletin of the Northern Territory*, No. 2) (Melbourne, 1912), pp. 19 *sq.*, 23, 24, 31 *sq.*, 37 *sqq.* ; A. R. Brown, " Three Tribes of Western Australia," *Journal of the Royal Anthropological Institute*, xliii. (1913) pp. 168, 174 ; R. Pettazzoni, " Mythologie Australienne du Rhombe," *Revue de l'Histoire des Religions*, lxv. (1912) pp. 149-170. But in the essay just referred to Mr. Andrew Lang shewed that the instrument has been similarly employed not only by savages in various parts of the world, but also by the ancient Greeks in their religious mysteries. In the Torres Straits Islands it is used both at the initiation of young men and as a magical instrument. See *Reports of the Cambridge Anthropological Expedition to Torres Straits*, v. (Cambridge, 1904) pp. 217, 218, 219, 328, 330-333, 346, 352. In various parts of New Guinea it is

thunder probably explains a certain use which the Dieri, a
tribe of Central Australia, made of the instrument.   When

sounded at the initiation of young men
and is carefully concealed from women;
the sound is thought to be the voice of a
spirit.   See Rev. J. Chalmers, *Pioneering in New Guinea* (London, 1887),
p. 85; *id.*, "Toaripi," *Journal of the
Anthropological Institute*, xxvii. (1898)
p. 329; Rev. J. Holmes, "Initiation
Ceremonies of Natives of the Papuan
Gulf," *Journal of the Anthropological
Institute*, xxxii. (1902) pp. 420, 424
sq.; O. Schellong, "Das Barlum-fest
der Gegend Finsch-hafens," *Internationales Archiv für Ethnographie*, ii.
(1889) pp. 150 *sq.*, 154 *sq.*; F.
Grabowsky, "Der Bezirk von Hatz-
feldthafen und seine Bewohner," *Petermanns Mitteilungen*, xli. (1895) p.
189; B. Hagen, *Unter den Papua's*
(Wiesbaden, 1899), pp. 188 *sq.*; Max
Krieger, *Neu-Guinea* (Berlin, preface
dated 1899), pp. 168 *sqq.*; J. Vetter,
in *Mitteilungen der Geographischen
Gesellschaft zu Jena*, xi. (1892) p.
105; K. Vetter, in *Nachrichten über
Kaiser Wilhelms-Land und den Bismarck-Archipel, 1897* (Berlin), p. 93;
R. Neuhauss, *Deutsch Neu-Guinea*
(Berlin, 1911), pp. 36, 297, 403, 406
sq., 410-412, 494 *sqq.*; Otto Reche,
Der Kaiserin-Augusta-Fluss (Hamburg, 1913), pp. 349 *sqq.* (*Ergebnisse
der Südsee-Expedition 1908–1910*, herausgegeben von G. Thilenius).   It is
similarly used at the circumcision-
festivals in the French Islands, to the
west of New Britain (R. Parkinson,
Dreissig Jahre in der Südsee, Stuttgart,
1907, pp. 640 *sq.*), and it is employed
at mysteries or mourning ceremonies
in Bougainville and other Melanesian
Islands.   See R. Parkinson, *op. cit.*
pp. 658 *sq.*; *id.*, *Zur Ethnographie
der Nordwestlichen Salomo Inseln* (Berlin, 1899), p. 11; R. H. Codrington,
The Melanesians (Oxford, 1891), pp.
98 *sq.*, 342.   Among the Minangkabauers of Sumatra the bull-roarer
(*gasiěng*) is used by a rejected lover
to induce the demons to carry off the
soul of the jilt and so drive her mad.
It is made of the frontal bone of a
brave or skilful man, and some of the

intended victim's hair is attached to it.
See J. L. van der Toorn, "Het animisme bij den Minangkabauer in der
Padangsche Bovenlanden," *Bijdragen
tot de Taal- Land- en Volkenkunde van
Nederlandsch Indië*, xxxix. (1890) pp.
55 *sq.*   Among the Yoruba-speaking
negroes of the Slave Coast in West
Africa, particularly at Abeokuta, the
sound of the bull-roarer is supposed to
be the voice of a great bogey named
Oro, whose votaries compose a secret
society under the name of Ogboni.
When the sound of the bull-roarer is
heard in the streets, every woman must
shut herself up in her house and not
look out of the window under pain of
death.   See R. F. Burton, *Abeokuta
and the Cameroons Mountains* (London,
1863), i. 197 *sq.*; Missionary Chautard,
in *Annales de la Propagation de la Foi*,
lv. (Lyons, 1883) pp. 192-198; Missionary Baudin, "Le Fétichisme," *Les
Missions Catholiques*, xvi. (1884) p.
257; P. Bouche, *La Côte des Esclaves
et le Dahomey* (Paris, 1885), p. 124;
Mrs. R. B. Batty and Governor Mol-
oney, "Notes on the Yoruba Country,"
Journal of the Anthropological Institute,
xix. (1890) pp. 160-164; A. B. Ellis,
*The Yoruba-speaking Peoples of the
Slave Coast of West Africa* (London,
1894), pp. 110 *sq.*; R. H. Stone, *In
Afric's Forest and Jungle* (Edinburgh
and London, 1900), p. 88; L. Frobenius, *Die Masken und Geheimbünde
Afrikas* (Halle, 1898), pp. 95 *sqq.*
(*Nova Acta, Abh. der Kaiserl. Leop.-
Carol. Deutschen Akademie der Naturforscher*, vol. lxxiv. No. 1).   Among
the Nandi of British East Africa and
the Bushongo of the Congo region bull-
roarers are sounded by men to frighten
novices at initiation.   See A. C. Hollis,
The Nandi (Oxford, 1909), pp. 40,
56; E. Torday and T. A. Joyce, *Les
Bushongo* (Brussels, 1910), p. 82.
Among the Caffres of South Africa
and the Boloki of the Upper Congo
the bull-roarer is a child's toy, but yet
is thought to be endowed with magical
virtue.   See below, p. 232 note[3].   Among
the Koskimo Indians of British Col-

Belief of the Dieri that by sounding a bull-roarer a newly initiated young man produces a supply of edible snakes and lizards.

a young man had passed through an initiatory rite, which consisted in cutting a row of gashes in his back, he was given a bull-roarer, and when he went out in search of game, he used to twirl the implement in the belief that by doing so, while his wounds were still unhealed, he created a good harvest of snakes, lizards, and other reptiles, which the natives employ as food ; but on the contrary they imagined that these supplies of food would be cut off for ever, if a woman were to see a bull-roarer which had been swung at the rites of initiation.[1]   No doubt these savages, living in a parched wilderness where the existence of plants and animals depends on rare and irregular showers,[2] have observed that

---

umbia the sound of the bull-roarers is supposed to be the voice of a spirit who comes to fetch away the novices. See Franz Boas, " The Social Organization and the Secret Societies of the Kwakiutl Indians," *Report of the United States National Museum* (Washington, 1897), p. 610. The bull-roarer is used as a sacred or magical instrument for the making of rain by the Zuñi and other Pueblo Indians of Arizona and New Mexico, also by the Navajos and Apaches of the same region, and by the Utes of Nevada and Utah. See Dr. Washington Matthews, " The Mountain Chant, a Navajo Ceremony," *Fifth Annual Report of the Bureau of Ethnology* (Washington, 1887), pp. 435, 436 ; Captain J. G. Bourke, "The Medicine-men of the Apache," *Ninth Annual Report of the Bureau of Ethnology* (Washington, 1892), pp. 476-479 ; Mrs. Matilda Coxe Stevenson, " The Zuñi Indians," *Twenty-third Report of the Bureau of American Ethnology* (Washington, 1904), pp. 115, 117, 128 *sq.*, 175, 177, 355. The Guatusos of Costa Rica ascertain the will of the deity by listening to the humming sound of the bull-roarer. See Dr. C. Sapper, " Ein Besuch bei den Guatusos in Costarica," *Globus*, lxxvi. (1899) p. 352 ; *id.*, " Beiträge zur Ethnographie des südlichen Mittelamerika," *Petermanns Mitteilungen*, xlvii. (1901) p. 36. The Caripunas Indians of the Madeira River, in Brazil, sound bull-roarers in

lamentations for the dead. See Franz Keller, *The Amazon and Madeira Rivers* (London, 1874), p. 124. The Bororo of Brazil also swing bull-roarers at their festivals of the dead ; the sound of them is the signal for the women to hide themselves ; it is believed that women and children would die if they saw a bull-roarer. See K. von den Steinen, *Unter den Naturvölkern Zentral-Brasiliens* (Berlin, 1894), pp. 497-499. The Nahuqua and other Brazilian tribes use bull-roarers in their masked dances, but make no mystery of them. See K. von den Steinen, *op. cit.* pp. 327 *sq.* As to the magical use of the bull-roarer, see pp. 230 *sqq.*

[1] A. W. Howitt, "The Dieri and other Kindred Tribes of Central Australia," *Journal of the Anthropological Institute*, xx. (1891) p. 83 ; *id.*, *Native Tribes of South-East Australia*, p. 660. In the latter passage Dr. Howitt omits the not unimportant particular that the bull-roarer is swung for this purpose by the young man *before his wounds are healed.*

[2] On the desert nature of Central Australia and the magical-like change wrought in its fauna and flora by heavy rain, see Baldwin Spencer and F. J. Gillen, *Native Tribes of Central Australia* (London, 1899), pp. 4 *sq.* ; *Totemism and Exogamy*, i. 170 *sqq.*, 316 *sqq.*, 341 *sq.* ; J. G. Frazer, " Howitt and Fison," *Folk-lore*, xx. (1909) pp. 160, 162 *sq.*, 164.

the fall of rain is regularly followed by a great and sudden increase in the food supply, and that this increase is most marked after violent thunder-storms.   Hence by making a noise like thunder with the help of bull-roarers they probably hope, on the principle of imitative magic, to bring on a thunder-storm and with it a fertilizing deluge of rain.

For the same reason in the parched and torrid regions of Arizona and New Mexico the Indians make great use of the bull-roarer in their ceremonies for procuring rain.   For example, when Captain Bourke was at the Pueblo Indian village of Walpi in the month of August, 1881, he saw the instrument in use at the snake dance.   "The medicine-men twirled it rapidly, and with a uniform motion, about the head and from front to rear, and succeeded in faithfully imitating the sound of a gust of rain-laden wind.   As explained to me by one of the medicine-men, by making this sound they compelled the wind and rain to come to the aid of the crops.   At a later date I found it in use among the Apache, and for the same purpose." [1]   The Zuñi Indians of New Mexico whirl bull-roarers "to create enthusiasm" among the mythical beings who are supposed to cause rain, or for the purpose of making them gather in the air over the village.[2]   In a Zuñi rain-making ceremony, while one medicine-man whirls a bull-roarer, another whips up a mixture of water and meal into frothy suds symbolic of clouds, and a third plays a flute. "All this is an invocation to the gods for rain—the one great and perpetual prayer of the people of this arid land." [3]   This supposed connexion of the instrument with thunder-storms explains why the Navajos of the same torrid country say that the bull-roarer should always be made of wood from a pine-tree that has been struck by lightning; [4] and why the Bakairi of Brazil call the unpretentious

The bull-roarer used by the Indians of New Mexico and Arizona to procure rain.

[1] Captain J. G. Bourke, "The Medicine-men of the Apache," *Ninth Annual Report of the Bureau of Ethnology* (Washington, 1892), pp. 476 *sq.*

[2] Mrs. Matilda Coxe Stevenson, "The Zuñi Indians," *Twenty-third Annual Report of the Bureau of American Ethnology* (Washington, 1904), pp. 115, 355.

[3] Mrs. Matilda Coxe Stevenson, *op. cit.* p. 175; compare *id.*, pp. 128 *sq.*, 177.

[4] Dr. Washington Matthews, "The Navajo Chant," *Fifth Annual Report of the Bureau of Ethnology* (Washington, 1887), p. 436; compare *id.*, p. 435, where the sound of the bull-roarer is said to be "like that of a rain storm."

instrument by a name that means "thunder and lightning."[1]
The resemblance of the sound of the bull-roarer to the
roaring of the wind is doubtless the reason why in the Torres
Straits Islands wizards whirled bull-roarers in order to make
the wind to blow,[2] and why, when Caffres wish for calm
weather, they forbid boys to play with bull-roarers, because
they think that the booming noise attracts a gale of wind.[3]
Hence, as an instrument whose sound resembles the rumbling
of thunder, the roar of wind, and the patter of rain, the bull-
roarer is naturally swung by agricultural savages as a powerful means of promoting the growth of the crops.   In the
island of Kiwai, off the mouth of the Fly River in British
New Guinea, bull-roarers are whirled in order to ensure a
good crop of yams, sweet potatoes, and bananas.[4]   Similarly
the Yabim of German New Guinea imagine that by twirling
bull-roarers while they mention the names of the dead they
produce a fine crop of taro.[5]

But why among the Dieri of Central Australia should
the power of attracting rain and so ensuring a supply of
food be specially attributed to a young man whose back has
just been scored and whose wounds are still raw?   Perhaps
the reason may be that the blood dripping from the gashes
is thought to resemble rain and therefore to be endowed with
a magical potency of drawing showers from the clouds.   The
conjecture is confirmed by the observation that the Dieri
actually do bleed themselves avowedly for the purpose of
making rain, and they are not the only people in Australia
and elsewhere who have resorted to this singular mode of

The bull-roarer used in Torres Straits Islands to produce wind and good crops.

The whirling of bull-roarers by young men with bleeding backs in Australia seems to have been a rain-making ceremony.

[1] Karl von den Steinen, *Unter den Naturvölkern Zentral-Brasiliens* (Berlin, 1894), p. 328.

[2] *Reports of the Cambridge Anthropological Expedition to Torres Straits*, v. (Cambridge, 1904) p. 352.

[3] G. McCall Theal, *Kaffir Folk-lore* (London, 1886), pp. 222 *sq.*; *id.*, *Records of South-Eastern Africa*, vii. (1901) p. 456; Dudley Kidd, *The Essential Kafir* (London, 1904), p. 333.   For an analogous reason among the Boloki of the Upper Congo the elders do not like when boys play with bull-roarers, because the sound resembles the growl of a leopard and will attract these ferocious animals. See Rev. John H. Weeks, *Among Congo Cannibals* (London, 1913), p. 157.

[4] A. C. Haddon, *Head-hunters, Black, White, and Brown* (London, 1901), p. 104; *Reports of the Cambridge Anthropological Expedition to Torres Straits*, v. (Cambridge, 1904) pp. 218, 219; Rev. J. Chalmers, "Notes on the Natives of Kiwai Island," *Journal of the Anthropological Institute*, xxxiii. (1903) p. 119.

[5] H. Zahn, "Die Jabim," in R. Neuhauss's *Deutsch Neu-Guinea* (Berlin, 1911), iii. 333.

putting an end to a drought. Altogether the foregoing evidence seems to hint that the whole virtue of the bull-roarer resides, as its English name implies, in its voice, and that its original significance was simply that of a magical instrument for causing thunder, wind, and rain.[2] When these natural phenomena came to be personified as spirits, the sound of the bull-roarer was naturally interpreted as their voice.

Among the tribes on the Brisbane River in Queensland the weird sound of the bull-roarers swung at initiation was believed by the women and children to be made by the wizards in swallowing the boys and bringing them up again as young men. The Ualaroi of the Upper Darling River said that the boy met a ghost, who killed him and brought him to life again as a young man. Among the natives on the Lower Lachlan and Murray Rivers it was Thrumalun (Daramulun) who was thought to slay and resuscitate the novices.[8] In the Arunta tribe of Central Australia, at the moment when the lads are being circumcised, the bull-roarer sounds in the darkness all round the ceremonial ground ; and the awestruck women, listening in the distance, believe that it is the voice of a spirit called Twanyirika, who lives in wild and inaccessible regions and only comes out when a youth is initiated. They think that the spirit enters the body of the lad after the operation of circumcision has been performed and carries him away into the bush, keeping him there till his wound is healed. While the newly circumcised youth is out in the wilds, carefully secluded from the sight of the women and children, he constantly sounds the bull-roarer. When he has recovered from the wound, the spirit leaves him and he returns to camp an initiated, or rather partially initiated, man. He has learned, at all events, the secret of Twanyirika ; for no sooner is he circumcised than an elder brother comes up to him, and placing in his hands a bundle

[1] *The Magic Art and the Evolution of Kings*, i. 256-258.

[2] This appears to be the view also of Professor K. von den Steinen (*Unter den Naturvölkern Zentral-Brasiliens*, pp. 327 *sq.*), who is probably right in thinking that the primary intention of the instrument is to make thunder, and that the idea of making rain is secondary.

[3] A. W. Howitt, "On Australian Medicine Men," *Journal of the Anthropological Institute*, xvi. (1887) pp. 47 *sq.* ; compare *id.*, *Native Tribes of South-East Australia*, p. 596.

of sacred sticks or stones (*churinga*), says, "Here is Twanyirika, of whom you have heard so much. They are *churinga* and will help you to heal quickly; guard them well, or else you and your mothers and sisters will be killed."[1]

In some Australian tribes the women believe that lads at initiation are killed and brought to life again by a spirit, whose voice is heard in the sound of the bull-roarer.

In this account nothing is said about killing the lad and bringing him to life again; but a belief in the death and resurrection of the novices at initiation is expressly affirmed to be part of the feminine creed in other tribes of Central Australia. Thus in the Unmatjera tribe both women and children believe that Twanyirika kills the youth and afterwards brings him to life again during the period of initiation. The rites of initiation in this tribe, as in the other Central tribes, comprise the operations of circumcision and sub-incision; and as soon as the second of these has been performed on him, the young man receives from his father a sacred stick (*churinga*), with which, he is told, his spirit was associated in the remotest past. While he is out in the bush recovering from his wounds, he must swing the bull-roarer, or a being who lives up in the sky will swoop down and carry him off.[2] In the Urabunna tribe of Central Australia a lad at initiation receives a bull-roarer, the very name of which (*chimbaliri*) is never heard by women and children. They are taught to believe that the sound of it is the voice of a spirit called Witurna, who takes the boy away, cuts out all his bowels, provides him with a new set, and brings him back an initiated youth. The lad is warned that on no account may he allow a woman or a child to see the sacred stick, else he and his mother and sisters will fall down as dead as stones.[3] In the Binbinga tribe, on the western coast of the Gulf of Carpentaria, the women and children believe that the noise of the bull-roarer at initiation is made by a spirit named Katajalina, who lives in an ant-hill and comes

[1] Baldwin Spencer and F. J. Gillen, *Native Tribes of Central Australia*, p. 246 note [1]; *id.*, *Northern Tribes of Central Australia* (London, 1904), p. 497. According to the classificatory system of relationship, which prevails among all the aborigines of Australia, a man may have, and generally has, a number of women who stand to him in the relation of mother as well as of sister, though there need not be a drop of blood in common between them, as we count kin. This explains the reference in the text to a boy's "mothers."

[2] B. Spencer and F. J. Gillen, *Northern Tribes of Central Australia*, pp. 342 *sq.*, 498.

[3] Spencer and Gillen, *op. cit.* p. 498.

out and eats up the boy, afterwards restoring him to life.[1] Similarly among their neighbours the Anula the women imagine that the droning sound of the bull-roarer is produced by a spirit called Gnabaia, who swallows the lads at initiation and afterwards disgorges them in the form of initiated men.   In this tribe, after a lad has been subincised as well as circumcised, he is presented with a bull-roarer and informed that the instrument was originally made by the whirlwind, that it is sacred or tabooed, and that it may on no account be shewn to women or children.[2]

Among the tribes settled on the southern coast of New South Wales, of which the Coast Murring tribe may be regarded as typical, the drama of resurrection from the dead was exhibited in a graphic form to the novices at initiation. Before they were privileged to witness this edifying spectacle they had been raised to the dignity of manhood by an old man, who promoted them to their new status by the simple process of knocking a tooth out of the mouth of each with the help of a wooden chisel and hammer.   The ceremony of the resurrection has been described for us in detail by an eye-witness, the late Dr. A. W. Howitt, one of the best authorities on the customs of the Australian aborigines. The scene selected for the sacred drama was the bottom of a deep valley, where a sluggish stream wound through a bed of tall sharp-edged sedge.   Though the hour was between ten and eleven o'clock in the morning, the sun had but just peeped over the mountains which enclosed the valley like a wall on the east ; and while the upper slopes, clothed with a forest of tall rowan trees, looked warm and bright in sunshine, which shot between the grey stems and under the light feathery foliage of the trees, all the bottom of the dell was still in deep shadow and dank with the moisture of the night's rain.   While the novices rested and warmed themselves at a crackling fire, the initiated men laid their heads together, prepared a stock of decorations made of stringy bark, and dug a grave.   There was some discussion as to the shape of the grave, but the man who was to be buried in it decided the question by declaring that he

A drama of resurrection from the dead used to be shewn to novices at initiation in some tribes of New South Wales.

Dr. Howitt's description of the scene.

<hr>

[1] Spencer and Gillen, *op. cit.* pp. 366 *sq.*, 501.

[2] Spencer and Gillen, *op. cit.* pp. 373, 501.

would be laid in it on his back at full length.   He was a
man of the eagle-hawk totem and belonged to the tribal
subdivision called Yibai.   So while two men under his
directions were digging the grave with sticks in the friable
granitic soil, he superintended the costume of the other
actors in the drama.   Sheets of bark were beaten out into
fleeces of stringy fibre, and in these garments six performers were clothed from head to foot so that not even
a glimpse could be obtained of their faces.   Four of them
were tied together by a cord which was fastened to the back
of their heads, and each of them carried two pieces of bark
in his hands.   The other two walked free, but hobbled along
bent double and supporting their tottery steps on staves to
mark the weight of years ; for they played the part of two
medicine-men of venerable age and great magical power.

The seem-
ing dead
man in
the grave.
By this time the grave was ready, and the eagle-hawk man
stretched himself in it at full length on a bed of leaves, his
head resting on a rolled-up blanket, just as if he were a
corpse.   In his two hands, crossed on his chest, he held the
stem of a young tree (*Persoonia linearis*), which had been
pulled up by the roots and now stood planted on his chest,
so that the top of it rose several feet above the level of the
ground.   A light covering of dried sticks filled the grave, and
dead leaves, tufts of grass, and small plants were artistically
arranged over them so as to complete the illusion.   All
being now ready, the novices were led by their sisters'
husbands to the grave and placed in a row beside it, while
a singer, perched on the trunk of a fallen tree at the head of
the grave, crooned a melancholy ditty, the song of Yibai.
Though the words of the song consisted merely of a monot-
onous repetition of the words *Burrin-burrin Yibai*, that is,
Stringy-bark Yibai, they were understood to refer to the
eagle-hawk totem, as well as to the tribal subdivision of the
buried man.   Then to the slow, plaintive but well-marked
air of the song the actors began to move forward, winding
among the trees, logs, and rocks.   On came the four disguised
men, stepping in time to the music, swaying from side to
side, and clashing their bark clappers together at every step,
while beside them hobbled the two old men keeping a little
aloof to mark their superior dignity.   They represented a

party of medicine-men, guided by two reverend seniors, who had come on pilgrimage to the grave of a brother medicine-man, him of the eagle-hawk totem, who lay buried here in the lonely valley, now illumined by the warm rays of the sun ; for by this time the morning was wearing on to noon.   When the little procession, chanting an invocation to Daramulun, had defiled from among the rocks and trees into the open, it drew up on the side of the grave opposite to the novices, the two old men taking up a position in the rear of the dancers.   For some time the dance and song went on till the tree that seemed to grow from the grave began to quiver.   " Look there ! " cried the sisters' husbands to the novices, pointing to the trembling leaves. As they looked, the tree quivered more and more, then was violently agitated and fell to the ground, while amid the excited dancing of the dancers and the chanting of the tuneful choir the supposed dead man spurned from him the superincumbent mass of sticks and leaves, and springing to his feet danced his magic dance in the grave itself, and exhibited in his mouth the magic substances which he was supposed to have received from Daramulun in person.[1]

The resurrection from the grave.

In some tribes of Central and Northern Australia the initiation of a medicine-man into the mysteries of his craft is supposed to be accomplished by certain spirits, who kill him, cut out his internal organs, and having provided him with a new set bring him to life again.   Sometimes the spirits kindly replace the man's human organs by their own spiritual organs ; sometimes along with the new organs they insert magical stones in his body or even a serpent, and the stones or the serpents naturally endow the new wizards with marvellous powers.   In some tribes the initiation takes place in a cave, where the spirits dwell. After the man has been restored to life with a new heart, a new pair of lungs, and so forth, he returns to his people in a more or less dazed condition, which his friends may at first mistake for insanity, though afterwards they recognize

In some Australian tribes a medicine-man at his initiation is thought to be killed and raised again from the dead.

---

[1] A. W. Howitt, *Native Tribes of South-East Australia*, pp. 554-556. Compare *id.*, " On some Australian Ceremonies of Initiation," *Journal of the Anthropological Institute*, xiii. (1884) pp. 453 *sq.*

its true character as inspiration.[1]   One eminent medical
practitioner in the Unmatjera tribe assured Messrs. Spencer
and Gillen that when he came to himself after the operation,
which in his case was performed by an aged doctor, he had
completely forgotten who he was and all about his past life.
After a time his venerable friend led him back to the camp
and shewed it to him, and said, " That woman there is your
wife," for she had gone clean out of his head.[2]   We shall
see presently that this temporary oblivion, a natural effect
of the shock to the nervous system produced by resuscita-
tion from the dead, is characteristic of novices under similar
circumstances in other lands.   Among the Arunta of Alice
Springs the cave where the mystic initiation takes place is
a limestone cavern in a range of hills which rises to the
north of the wide level expanse known as the Emily plain.
None of the ordinary natives would dare to set foot in the
awful grotto, which they believe to extend for miles into the
bowels of the earth and to be tenanted by certain ancestral
spirits, who live there in perpetual sunshine and amid streams
of running water, an earthly paradise by contrast with the
arid sun-scorched steppes and barren mountains outside.
White men have explored the cave, and if they perceived
no spirits, they found bats in plenty.   The man who aspires
to the rank of a wizard lies down at the mouth of the
cave and falls asleep ; and as he sleeps one of the ancestral
spirits steals up to him and drives an invisible spear through
his neck from back to front.   The point of the spear comes
out through the man's tongue, leaving a hole through which
you could put your little finger, and this hole the man
retains for the rest of his natural life, or at least so long as
he retains his magical powers ; for if the hole should close
up, these spiritual gifts and graces would depart from him.
A second thrust from the invisible spear transfixes the man's
head from ear to ear; he drops down dead, and is immediately transported into the depths of the cavern, where the
spirits dissect his dead body, extract the old viscera, and

---

[1] B. Spencer and F. J. Gillen,
Native Tribes of Central Australia,
pp. 523-525 ; *id., Northern Tribes of
Central Australia,* 480 *sq.,* 484, 485,
487, 488 ; *id., Across Australia* (London, 1912), ii. 334 *sqq.*

[2] Spencer and Gillen, *Northern
Tribes of Central Australia,* pp. 480 *sq.*

replace them with a new set in the manner already described.[1]

In this account of the manner in which medicine-men obtain their magical powers not only are the supposed death and resurrection of the novice worthy of attention, but also the exchange of internal organs which in the Binbinga and Mara tribes is supposed to be effected between the man and the spirit;[2] for this exchange resembles that which, on the theory I have suggested, may be thought to take place between a lad and his totem at the ceremonies of initiation which mark the momentous transition from boyhood to manhood. Further, the bodily mutilation which is the visible sign of the medicine-man's initiation (for however the hole may be made it certainly exists in the tongues of regular Arunta practitioners) corresponds to the bodily mutilations of other sorts, which in many savage tribes attest to the world that the mutilated persons are fullgrown men. What the precise meaning of such mutilations may be, still remains very obscure; but they seem in some cases to be directly associated with the conception of death and resurrection.

Notable features in the initiation of Australian medicine-men.

This association certainly comes out plainly in the rites of initiation through which in some parts of New Guinea all lads must pass before they attain to the status of adults. The rites are observed by a group of tribes who occupy contiguous territories about Finsch Harbour and Huon Gulf in German New Guinea. The tribes in question are the Yabim, the Bukaua, the Kai, and the Tami. All of them except the Kai belong to the Melanesian stock and are therefore presumably immigrants from the adjoining islands; but the Kai, who inhabit the rugged, densely wooded, and rainy mountains inland from Finsch Harbour, belong to the aboriginal Papuan stock and differ from their neighbours in speech as well as in appearance. Yet the

Rites of initiation in some tribes of German New Guinea.

[1] F. J. Gillen, "Notes on some Manners and Customs of the Aborigines of the McDonnel Ranges belonging to the Arunta Tribe," in *Report on the Work of the Horn Scientific Expedition to Central Australia*, Part iv. *Anthropology* (London and Melbourne, 1896), pp. 180 *sq.*; B. Spencer and

F. J. Gillen, *Native Tribes of Central Australia* (London, 1899), pp. 523 *sq.*; *id.*, *Across Australia* (London, 1912), ii. 335.

[2] B. Spencer and F. J. Gillen, *Northern Tribes of Central Australia*, pp. 487, 488; *id.*, *Across Australia*, ii. 481 *sq.*

rites of initiation which all these tribes celebrate and the beliefs which they associate with them are so similar that a single description will apply accurately enough to them all.

The novices thought to be swallowed and dis- gorged by a monster, whose voice is heard in the hum of the bull- roarers.

All of them, like many Australian tribes, require every male member of the tribe to be circumcised before he ranks as a full-grown man ; and the tribal initiation, of which circum- cision is the central feature, is conceived by them, as by some Australian tribes, as a process of being swallowed and disgorged by a mythical monster, whose voice is heard in the humming sound of the bull-roarer. Indeed the New Guinea tribes not only impress this belief on the minds of women and children, but enact it in a dramatic form at the actual rites of initiation, at which no woman or un- initiated person may be present. For this purpose a hut about a hundred feet long is erected either in the village or in a lonely part of the forest. It is modelled in the shape of the mythical monster ; at the end which represents his head it is high, and it tapers away at the other end. A betel-palm, grubbed up with the roots, stands for the back- bone of the great being and its clustering fibres for his hair ; and to complete the resemblance the butt end of the building is adorned by a native artist with a pair of goggle eyes and a gaping mouth. When after a tearful parting from their mothers and women folk, who believe or pretend to believe in the monster that swallows their dear ones, the awe-struck novices are brought face to face with this im- posing structure, the huge creature emits a sullen growl, which is in fact no other than the humming note of bull- roarers swung by men concealed in the monster's belly. The actual process of deglutition is variously enacted. Among the Tami it is represented by causing the candi- dates to defile past a row of men who hold bull-roarers over their heads ; among the Kai it is more graphically set forth by making them pass under a scaffold on which stands a man, who makes a gesture of swallowing and takes in fact a gulp of water as each trembling novice passes beneath him. But the present of a pig, opportunely offered for the redemption of the youth, induces the monster to relent and disgorge his victim ; the man who represents the monster accepts the gift vicariously, a gurgling sound is heard, and the water which had just been swallowed descends in a jet on the novice. This signifies that the young man has been released from the monster's belly. However, he has now to undergo the more painful and dangerous operation of circumcision. It follows immediately, and the cut made by the knife of the operator is explained to be a bite or scratch which the monster inflicted on the novice in spewing him out of his capacious maw. While the operation is proceeding, a prodigious noise is made by the swinging of bull-roarers to represent the roar of the dreadful being who is in the act of swallowing the young men.

When, as sometimes happens, a lad dies from the effect of the operation, he is buried secretly in the forest, and his sorrowing mother is told that the monster has a pig's stomach as well as a human stomach, and that unfortunately her son slipped into the wrong stomach, from which it was impossible to extricate him. After they have been circumcised the lads must remain for some months in seclusion, shunning all contact with women and even the sight of them. They live in the long hut which represents the monster's belly; among the Yabim they beguile the tedium of this enforced leisure by weaving baskets and playing on certain sacred flutes, which are never used except on these occasions. The instruments are of two patterns. One is called the male and the other the female; and they are believed to be married to each other. No woman may see these mysterious flutes; if she did, she would die. When the long seclusion is over, the lads, now ranking as initiated men, are brought back with great pomp and ceremony to the village, where they are received with sobs and tears of joy by the women, as if the grave had given up its dead. At first the young men keep their eyes rigidly closed or even sealed with a plaster of chalk, and they appear not to understand the words of command which are given them by an elder. Gradually, however, they come to themselves as if awaking from a stupor, and next day they bathe and wash off the crust of white chalk with which their bodies had been coated.[1]

The return of the novices after initiation.

[1] As to the initiatory rites among the Yabim, see K. Vetter, in *Nach-* *richten über Kaiser Wilhelms - Land und den Bismarck-Archipel*, 1897,

The monster who is supposed to swallow the novices is apparently conceived as a ghost or ancestral spirit.

It is highly significant that all these tribes of New Guinea apply the same word to the bull-roarer and to the monster, who is supposed to swallow the novices at circumcision, and whose fearful roar is represented by the hum of the harmless wooden instruments. The word in the speech of the Yabim and Bukaua is *balum*; in that of the Kai it is *ngosa*; and in that of the Tami it is *kani*. Further, it deserves to be noted that in three languages out of the four the same word which is applied to the bull-roarer and to the monster means also a ghost or spirit of the dead, while in the fourth language (the Kai) it signifies "grandfather." From this it seems to follow that the being who swallows and disgorges the novices at initiation is believed to be a powerful ghost or ancestral spirit, and that the bull-roarer, which bears his name, is his material representative. That would explain the jealous secrecy with which the sacred implement is kept from the sight of women. While they are not in use, the bull-roarers are stowed away in the men's clubhouses, which no woman may enter; indeed no woman or uninitiated person may set eyes on a bull-roarer under pain of death.[1] Similarly among the Tugeri or Kaya-Kaya, a large Papuan tribe on the south coast of Dutch New

---

pp. 92 *sq.*; *id.*, in *Mitteilungen der Geographischen Gesellschaft zu Jena*, xi. (1892) p. 105; *id.*, *Komm herüber und hilf uns!* ii. (Barmen, 1898) p. 18; *id.*, cited by M. Krieger, *Neu-Guinea* (Berlin, preface dated 1899), pp. 167-170; O. Schellong, "Das Barlum-fest der Gegend Finschhafens," *Internationales Archiv für Ethnographie*, ii. (1889) pp. 145-162; H. Zahn, "Die Jabim," in R. Neuhauss's *Deutsch Neu-Guinea* (Berlin, 1911), iii. 296-298. As to the initiatory rites among the Bukaua, see S. Lehner, "Bukaua," in R. Neuhauss's *Deutsch Neu-Guinea*, iii. 402-410; among the Kai, see Ch. Keysser, "Aus dem Kai-Leute," *ibid.* pp. 34-40; among the Tami, see G. Bamler, "Tami," *ibid.* pp. 493-507. I have described the rites of the various tribes more in detail in *The Belief in Immortality and the Worship of the Dead*, i. 250-255, 260 *sq.*, 290 *sq.*, 301 *sq.* In the Bukaua and Tami tribes the initiation ceremonies are performed not in the forest but in a special house built for the purpose in the village, which the women are obliged to vacate till the rites are over.

[1] *The Belief in Immortality and the Worship of the Dead*, i. 250, 251, 255, 261, 290 *sq.*, 301. Among the Bukaua not only does the bull-roarer bear the general name for a ghost (*balum*), but each particular bull-roarer bears in addition the name of a particular dead man, and varies in dignity and importance with the dignity and importance of the deceased person whom it represents. And besides the big bull-roarers with gruff voices there are little bull-roarers with shrill voices, which represent the shrill-voiced wives of the ancient heroes. See S. Lehner, "Bukaua," in R. Neuhauss's *Deutsch Neu-Guinea*, iii. 410-412.

Guinea, the name of the bull-roarer, which they call *sosom*, is given to a mythical giant, who is supposed to appear every year with the south-east monsoon. When he comes, a festival is held in his honour and bull-roarers are swung. Boys are presented to the giant, and he kills them, but considerately brings them to life again.[1]

In certain districts of Viti Levu, the largest of the Fijian Islands, the drama of death and resurrection used to be acted with much solemnity before the eyes of young men at initiation. The ceremonies were performed in certain sacred precincts of oblong shape, enclosed by low walls or rows of stones but open to the sky. Such a precinct was called a *Nanga*, and it might be described as a temple dedicated to the worship of ancestors ; for in it sacrifices and prayers were offered to the ancestral spirits. For example, the first-fruits of the yam harvest were regularly presented with great ceremony to the souls of the dead in the temple before the bulk of the crop was dug for the people's use, and no man might taste of the new yams until this solemn offering had been made. The yams so offered were piled up in the sacred enclosure and left to rot there ; if any man were so bold as to eat of these dedicated fruits, it was believed that he would go mad.[2] Any initiated man had the right of approaching the ancestral spirits at any time in their holy place, where he would pray to them for help and protection and propitiate them by laying down his offering of a pig, or yams, or eels, or cloth, or what not.[3] Of these offerings perhaps the most curious was that of the foreskins of young men, who were circumcised as a sort of vicarious sacrifice or atonement for

The drama of death and resurrection used to be enacted before young men at initiation in some parts of Fiji.

[1] R. Pöch, "Vierter Bericht über meine Reise nach Neu-Guinea," *Sitzungsberichte der mathematisch-naturwissenschaftlichen Klasse der Kaiserlichen Akademie der Wissenschaften* (Vienna), cxv. (1906) Abteilung i. pp. 901, 902.

[2] Rev. Lorimer Fison, "The *Nanga* or Sacred Stone Enclosure of Wainimala, Fiji," *Journal of the Anthropological Institute*, xiv. (1885) p. 27. The *Nanga* or sacred enclosure of stones, with its sacred rites, was known only to certain tribes of Fiji (the Nuyaloa, Vatusila, Mbatiwai, and Mdavu-

tukia), who inhabited a comparatively small area, barely a third, of the island of Viti Levu. As to the institution in general, see Rev. Lorimer Fison, *op. cit.* pp. 14-31 ; A. B. Joske, "The Nanga of Viti-levu," *Internationales Archiv für Ethnographie*, ii. (1889) pp. 254-266 ; Basil Thomson, *The Fijians* (London, 1908), pp. 146-157. Compare *The Belief in Immortality and the Worship of the Dead*, i. 427-438.

[3] Rev. Lorimer Fison, *op. cit.* p. 26 ; Basil Thomson, *op. cit.* 147.

the recovery of a sick relative, it might be either their father
or one of their father's brothers. The bloody foreskins, stuck
in the cleft of a split reed, were presented to the ancestral
gods in the temple by the chief priest, who prayed for the
sick man's recovery.[1]   The temple or sacred enclosure was
divided into two or three compartments by cross walls of
stones, and the inmost of these compartments was the *Nanga-
tambu-tambu*, or Holy of Holies.[2]

Description
tion of the
rite.

In these open-air temples of the dead the ceremony of
initiating young men was performed as a rule every year at
the end of October or the beginning of November, which
was the commencement of the Fijian New Year; hence the
novices who were initiated at that season went by the name
of *Vilavou* or New Year's Men.   The exact time for cele-
brating the rite was determined by the flowering of the
ndrala tree (*Erythrina*); but it roughly coincided with the
New Year of the Tahitians and Hawaiians, who dated the
commencement of the year by observation of the Pleiades.
The highlanders of Fiji, who alone celebrated these rites, did
not trouble their heads about the stars.[3]   As a preparation

---

[1] Rev. Lorimer Fison, *op. cit.* pp. 27
sq. The phrase "the ancestral gods"
is used by Mr. Fison, one of our best
authorities on Fijian religion. Mr.
Basil Thomson (*op. cit.* p. 157)
questions the accuracy of Mr. Fison's
account of this vicarious sacrifice on
the ground that every youth was regularly circumcised as a matter of course.
But there seems to be no inconsistency
between the two statements. While
custom required that every youth should
be circumcised, the exact time for performing the ceremony need not have
been rigidly prescribed; and if a sav-
ing or atoning virtue was attributed to
the sacrifice of foreskins, it might be
thought desirable in cases of emergency,
such as serious illness, to anticipate it
for the benefit of the sufferer.

[2] According to Mr. Fison, the enclosure was divided into three compartments; Mr. Basil Thomson describes only two, though by speaking
of one of them as the "Middle
Nanga" he seems to imply that there
were three. The structure was a rough

parallelogram lying east and west,
about a hundred feet long by fifty feet
broad, enclosed by walls or rows of
stone slabs embedded endwise in the
earth. See Basil Thomson, *op. cit.*
pp. 147 *sq.*

[3] A. B. Joske, "The Nanga of Viti-
levu," *Internationales Archiv für Ethnographie*, ii. (1889) p. 259; Basil
Thomson, *The Fijians*, pp. 150 *sq.*
According to Mr. Fison (*op. cit.* p. 19)
the initiatory ceremonies were held as
a rule only every second year; but he
adds: "This period, however, is not
necessarily restricted to two years.
There are always a number of youths
who are growing to the proper age,
and the length of the interval depends
upon the decision of the elders." Perhaps the seeming discrepancy between
our authorities on this point may be explained by Mr. Joske's statement (p.
259) that the rites are held in alternate
years by two different sets of men, the
Kai Vesina and the Kai Rukuruku,
both of whom claim to be descended
from the original founders of the rites.

XI THE RITUAL OF DEATH AND RESURRECTION 245

for the solemnity the heads of the novices were shaved and
their beards, if they had any, were carefully eradicated. On
four successive days they went in procession to the temple
and there deposited in the Holy of Holies their offerings of
cloth and weapons to the ancestral spirits. But on the fifth
and great day of the festival, when they again entered the
sacred ground, they beheld a sight which froze their souls
with horror. Stretched on the ground was a row of dead or
seemingly dead and murdered men, their bodies cut open
and covered with blood, their entrails protruding. At the
further end sat the High Priest, regarding them with a
stony glare, and to reach him the trembling novices had
to crawl on hands and knees over the ghastly blood-
bedabbled corpses that lay between. Having done so they
drew up in a line before him. Suddenly he blurted out a
piercing yell, at which the counterfeit dead men started to
their feet and ran down to the river to cleanse themselves
from the blood and guts of pigs with which they were
beslobbered. The High Priest now unbent his starched
dignity, and skipping from side to side cried in stridulous
tones, " Where are the people of my enclosure ? Are they
gone to Tonga Levu ? Are they gone to the deep sea ? "
He was soon answered by a deep-mouthed chant, and back
from the river marched the dead men come to life, clean,
fresh, and garlanded, swaying their bodies in time to the
music of their solemn hymn. They took their places in
front of the novices and a religious silence ensued. Such
was the drama of death and resurrection. It was immediately followed by a sacramental meal. Four old men of
the highest order of initiates now entered the Holy of
Holies. The first bore a cooked yam carefully wrapt up in
leaves so that no part of it should touch the hands of the
bearer : the second carried a piece of baked pork similarly
enveloped : the third held a drinking-cup full of water and
wrapt round with native cloth ; and the fourth bore a
napkin of the same stuff. The first elder passed along the
row of novices putting the end of the yam into each of their

The mimic
death.

The mimic
resurrec-
tion.

The sacra-
mental
meal.

The custom of dating the New Year
by observation of the Pleiades was
apparently universal among the Polynesians. See *The Spirits of the Corn
and of the Wild*, i. 312 *sq.*

mouths, and as he did so each of them nibbled a morsel of the sacred food : the second elder did the same with the hallowed pork : the third elder followed with the holy water, with which each novice merely wetted his lips ; and the fourth elder wiped all their mouths with his napkin. Then the high priest or one of the elders addressed the young men, warning them solemnly against the sacrilege of betraying to the profane vulgar any of the high mysteries which they had witnessed, and threatening all such traitors with the vengeance of the gods. The general intention of the initiatory rites seems to have been to introduce the young men to the worshipful spirits of the dead at their temple, and to cement the bond between them by a sacramental meal.[1]

The intention of the rite.

Initiatory rite in the island of Rook: pretence that the novices are swallowed by the devil.

The people of Rook, an island between New Guinea and New Britain, hold festivals at which one or two disguised men, their heads covered with wooden masks, go dancing through the village, followed by all the other men. They demand that the circumcised boys who have not yet been swallowed by Marsaba (the devil) shall be given up to them. The boys, trembling and shrieking, are delivered to them, and must creep between the legs of the disguised men. Then the procession moves through the village again, and announces that Marsaba has eaten up the boys, and will not disgorge them till he receives a present of pigs, taro, and so forth. So all the villagers, according to their means, contribute provisions, which are then consumed in the name of Marsaba.[2] In New Britain all males are members of an association called the Duk-duk. The boys are admitted to it very young, but are not fully initiated till their fourteenth year, when they receive from the Tubuvan or Tubuan a

Secret society of the Dukduk in New Britain.

---

[1] Rev. Lorimer Fison, *op. cit.* pp. 20-23 ; A. B. Joske, *op. cit.* pp. 264 *sq.* ; Basil Thomson, *The Fijians*, pp. 150-153. The sacramental character of the meal is recognized by Mr. Fison, who says (p. 23) that after the performance of the rites the novices " are now *Vilavóu*, accepted members of the *Nanga*, qualified to take their place among the men of the community, though still only on probation. As children—their childhood being indi-

cated by their shaven heads—they were presented to the ancestors, and their acceptance was notified by what (looking at the matter from the natives' standpoint) we might, without irreverence, almost call the *sacrament* of food and water, too sacred even for the elders' hands to touch."

[2] Paul Reina, " Ueber die Bewohner der Insel Rook," *Zeitschrift für allgemeine Erdkunde*, N.F., iv. (1858) pp. 356 *sq.*

terrible blow with a cane, which is supposed to kill them. Novices supposed to be killed. The Tubuan and the Duk-duk are two disguised men who represent cassowaries. They dance with a short hopping step in imitation of the cassowary. Each of them wears a huge hat like an extinguisher, woven of grass or palm-fibres; it is six feet high, and descends to the wearer's shoulders, completely concealing his head and face. From the neck to the knees the man's body is hidden by a crinoline made of the leaves of a certain tree fastened on hoops, one above the other. The Tubuan is regarded as a female, the Duk-duk as a male. The former is supposed to breed The new birth. and give birth to the novices, who are accordingly looked upon as newly born. The female masks are very plain compared with the male masks. Two of them are regularly kept from year to year in order that they may annually breed new Duk-duks. When they are wanted for this purpose they are brought forth, decorated afresh, and provided with new leaf dresses to match. According to one account, women and children may not look upon one of these disguised men or they would die. So strong is this superstition among them that they will run away and hide as soon as they hear him coming, for they are aware of his approach through a peculiar shrieking noise he utters as he goes along. In the district of Berara, where red is the Duk-duk colour, the mere sight of a red cloth is enough to make the women take to their heels. The common herd are not allowed to know who the masker is. If he stumbles and his hat falls to the ground, disclosing his face, or his crinoline is torn to tatters by the bushes, his attendants immediately surround him to hide his person from the vulgar eye. According to one writer, indeed, the performer who drops his mask, or lets it fall so that the sharp point at the top sticks in the ground, is put to death. The institution of the Duk-duk is common to the neighbouring islands of New Ireland and the Duke of York.[1]

[1] R. Parkinson, *Im Bismarck Archipel* (Leipsic, 1887), pp. 129-134; id. *Dreissig Jahre in der Südsee* (Stuttgart, 1907), pp. 567 *sqq.*; Rev. G. Brown, "Notes on the Duke of York Group, New Britain, and New Ireland," *Journal of the Royal Geographical Society*, xlvii. (1878) pp. 148 *sq.*; H. H. Romilly, "The Islands of the New Britain Group," *Proceedings of the Royal Geographical Society*, N.S., ix. (1887) pp. 11 *sq.*; Rev. G. Brown,

Initiatory
rite in
Halma-
hera : pre-
tence of
begetting
the novices
anew.
Among the Galelareese and Tobelorese of Halmahera, an island to the west of New Guinea, boys go through a form of initiation, part of which seems to consist in a pretence of begetting them anew. When a number of boys have reached the proper age, their parents agree to celebrate the ceremony at their common expense, and they invite others to be present at it. A shed is erected, and two long tables are placed in it, with benches to match, one for the men and one for the women. When all the preparations have been made for a feast, a great many skins of the rayfish, and some pieces of a wood which imparts a red colour to water, are taken to the shed. A priest or elder causes a vessel to be placed in the sight of all the people, and then begins, with significant gestures, to rub a piece of the wood with the ray-skin. The powder so produced is put in the vessel, and at the same time the name of one of the boys is called out. The same proceeding is repeated for each boy. Then the vessels are filled with water, after which the feast begins. At the third cock-crow the priest smears the faces and bodies of the boys with the red water, which represents the blood shed at the perforation of the *hymen*. Towards daybreak the boys are taken to the wood, and must hide behind the largest trees. The men, armed with sword and shield, accompany them, dancing and singing. The priest knocks thrice on each of the trees behind which a boy is hiding. All day the boys stay in the wood, exposing themselves to the heat of the sun as much as possible. In the evening they bathe and return to the shed, where the women supply them with food.[1]

---

ibid. p. 17 ; *id., Melanesians and Poly-
nesians* (London, 1910), pp. 60 *sqq.* ;
W. Powell, *Wanderings in a Wild
Country* (London, 1883), pp. 60-66 ;
C. Hager, *Kaiser Wilhelm's Land und
der Bismarck Archipel* (Leipsic, N.D.),
pp. 115-128 ; Hubner, quoted by W.
H. Dall, "On masks, labrets, and
certain aboriginal customs," *Third
Annual Report of the Bureau of Eth-
nology* (Washington, 1884), p. 100 ;
P. A. Kleintitschen, *Die Küstenbewoh-
ner der Gazellehalbinsel* (Hiltrup bei
Münster, N.D.), pp. 350 *sqq.* ; H.
Schurtz, *Altersklassen und Männer-
bünde* (Berlin, 1902), pp. 369-377.

The inhabitants of these islands are
divided into two exogamous classes,
which in the Duke of York Island have
two insects for their totems. One of
the insects is the *mantis religiosus* ; the
other is an insect that mimics the leaf
of the horse-chestnut tree very closely.
See Rev. B. Danks, "Marriage Customs
of the New Britain Group," *Journal of
the Anthropological Institute,* xviii.
(1889) pp. 281 *sq.* ; *Totemism and
Exogamy,* ii. 118 *sqq.*

[1] J. G. F. Riedel, "Galela und
Tobeloresen," *Zeitschrift für Ethnologie,* xvii. (1885) pp. 81 *sq.*

In the west of Ceram boys at puberty are admitted to the Kakian association.[1] Modern writers have commonly regarded this association as primarily a political league instituted to resist foreign domination.   In reality its objects are purely religious and social, though it is possible that the priests may have occasionally used their powerful influence for political ends.   The society is in fact merely one of those widely-diffused primitive institutions, of which a chief object is the initiation of young men.   In recent years the true nature of the association has been duly recognized by the distinguished Dutch ethnologist, J. G. F. Riedel.   The Kakian house is an oblong wooden shed, situated under the darkest trees in the depth of the forest, and is built to admit so little light that it is impossible to see what goes on in it.   Every village has such a house.   Thither the boys who are to be initiated are conducted blindfold, followed by their parents and relations.   Each boy is led by the hand by two men, who act as his sponsors or guardians, looking after him during the period of initiation.   When all are assembled before the shed, the high priest calls aloud upon the devils. Immediately a hideous uproar is heard to proceed from the shed.   It is made by men with bamboo trumpets, who have been secretly introduced into the building by a back door, but the women and children think it is made by the devils,

---

[1] The Kakian association and its initiatory ceremonies have often been described.   See François Valentyn, *Oud en nieuw Oost-Indiën* (Dordrecht and Amsterdam, 1724–1726), iii. 3 *sq.* ; Von Schmid, "Het Kakihansch Verbond op het eiland Ceram," *Tijdschrift voor Neêrlands Indië* (Batavia, 1843), dl. ii. pp. 25-38 ; A. van Ekris, "Het Ceramsche Kakianverbond," *Mededeelingen van wege het Nederlandsche Zendelinggenootschap*, ix. (1865) pp. 205-226 (repeated with slight changes in *Tijdschrift voor Indische Taal- Land- en Volkenkunde*, xvi. (1867) pp. 290-315) ; P. Fournier, "De Zuidkust van Ceram," *Tijdschrift voor Indische Taal- Land- en Volkenkunde*, xvi. (1867) pp. 154-156 ; W. A. van Rees, *Die Pionniers der Beschaving in Neêrlands Indië* (Arnheim, 1867), pp. 92-106 ; G. W. W. C. Baron van Hoëvell, *Ambon en meer bepaaldelijk de Oeliasers* (Dordrecht, 1875), pp. 153 *sqq.* ; Schulze, "Ueber Ceram und seine Bewohner," *Verhandlungen der Berliner Gesellschaft für Anthropologie, Ethnologie, und Urgeschichte* (1877), p. 117 ; W. Joest, "Beiträge zur Kenntniss der Eingebornen der Insel Formosa und Ceram," *ibid.* (1882) p. 64 ; H. von Rosenberg, *Der Malayische Archipel* (Leipsic, 1878), p. 318 ; A. Bastian, *Indonesien*, i. (Berlin, 1884) pp. 145-148 ; J. G. F. Riedel, *De sluik- en kroesharige rassen tusschen Selebes en Papua* (The Hague, 1886), pp. 107-111 ; O. D. Tauern, "Ceram," *Zeitschrift für Ethnologie*, xlv. (1913) pp. 167 *sq.* The best accounts are those of Valentyn, Von Schmid, Van Ekris, Van Rees, and Riedel, which are accordingly followed in the text.

and are much terrified. Then the priests enter the shed, followed by the boys, one at a time. As soon as each boy has disappeared within the precincts, a dull chopping sound is heard, a fearful cry rings out, and a sword or spear, dripping with blood, is thrust through the roof of the shed. This is a token that the boy's head has been cut off, and that the devil has carried him away to the other world, there to regenerate and transform him. So at sight of the bloody sword the mothers weep and wail, crying that the devil has murdered their children. In some places, it would seem, the boys are pushed through an opening made in the shape of a crocodile's jaws or a cassowary's beak, and it is then said that the devil has swallowed them. The boys remain in the shed for five or nine days. Sitting in the dark, they hear the blast of the bamboo trumpets, and from time to time the sound of musket shots and the clash of swords. Every day they bathe, and their faces and bodies are smeared with a yellow dye, to give them the appearance of having been swallowed by the devil. During his stay in the Kakian house each boy has one or two crosses tattooed with thorns on his breast or arm. When they are not sleeping, the lads must sit in a crouching posture without moving a muscle. As they sit in a row cross-legged, with their hands stretched out, the chief takes his trumpet, and placing the mouth of it on the hands of each lad, speaks through it in strange tones, imitating the voice of the spirits. He warns the lads, under pain of death, to observe the rules of the Kakian society, and never to reveal what has passed in the Kakian house. The novices are also told by the priests to behave well to their blood relations, and are taught the traditions and secrets of the tribe.

The resurrection of the novices. Meantime the mothers and sisters of the lads have gone home to weep and mourn. But in a day or two the men who acted as guardians or sponsors to the novices return to the village with the glad tidings that the devil, at the intercession of the priests, has restored the lads to life. The men who bring this news come in a fainting state and daubed with mud, like messengers freshly arrived from the nether world. Before leaving the Kakian house, each lad receives from the priest a stick adorned at both ends with cock's or cassowary's feathers.   The sticks are supposed to have been given to the lads by the devil at the time when he restored them to life, and they serve as a token that the youths have been in the spirit land.   When they return to their homes they totter in their walk, and enter the house backward, as if they had forgotten how to walk properly ; or they enter the house by the back door.   If a plate of food is given to them, they hold it upside down.   They remain dumb, indicating their wants by signs only.   All this is to shew that they are still under the influence of the devil or the spirits.   Their sponsors have to teach them all the common acts of life, as if they were new-born children.   Further, upon leaving the Kakian house the boys are strictly forbidden to eat of certain fruits until the next celebration of the rites has taken place.   And for twenty or thirty days their hair may not be combed by their mothers or sisters. At the end of that time the high priest takes them to a lonely place in the forest, and cuts off a lock of hair from the crown of each of their heads.   After these initiatory rites the lads are deemed men, and may marry; it would be a scandal if they married before.

In the region of the Lower Congo a simulation of death and resurrection is, or rather used to be, practised by the members of a guild or secret society called *ndembo*.   The society had nothing to do with puberty or circumcision, though the custom of circumcision is common in the country. Young people and adults of both sexes might join the guild ; after initiation they were called "the Knowing Ones" (*nganga*).   To found a branch of the society it was necessary to have an albino, who, whether a child, lad, or adult, was the acknowledged head of the society.[1]   The ostensible reason for starting a branch of the guild in a district was commonly an epidemic of sickness, "and the

The secret society of Ndembo in the valley of the Lower Congo.

---

[1] No reason is assigned for this curious choice of a president. Can it have been that, because negro children are born pale or nearly white, an albino was deemed a proper president for a society, all the initiated members of which claimed to have been born again ?   Speaking of the people of the Lower Congo the old English traveller Andrew Battel observes that "the children of this country are born white, but change their colour in two days' time to a perfect black" ("Adventures of Andrew Battel," in J. Pinkerton's *Voyages and Travels*, xvi. London, 1814, p. 331).

idea was to go into *ndembo* to die, and after an indefinite period, from a few months to two or three years, to be resurrected with a new body not liable to the sickness then troubling the countryside.   Another reason for starting a *ndembo* was a dearth of children in a district.   It was believed that good luck in having children would attend those who entered or died *ndembo*.   But the underlying idea was the same, *i.e.* to get a 'new body' that would be healthy and perform its functions properly."   The quarters of the society were always a stockaded enclosure in a great thick forest ; a gate of planks painted yellow and red gave access to it, and within there was an assemblage of huts. The place was fenced to keep intruders from prying into the mysteries of the guild, and it was near water.   Un-initiated persons might walk on the public roads through the forest, but if they were caught in bye-paths or hunting in the woods, they were flogged, fined, and sometimes killed. They might not even look upon the persons of those who had "died *ndembo*"; hence when these sanctified persons were roving about the forest or going to the river, the boom-ing notes of a drum warned the profane vulgar to keep out of their way.

Pretence of death as a preliminary to resurrec-tion.

When the stockade and the huts in the forest were ready to receive all who wished to put off the old man or woman and to put on the new, one of the initiates gave the sign and the aspirant after the higher life dropped down like dead in some public place, it might be the market or the centre of the town where there were plenty of people to witness the edifying spectacle.   The initiates immediately spread a pall over him or her, beat the earth round about the pretended corpse with plantain stalks, chanted incanta-tions, fired guns, and cut capers.   Then they carried the seemingly dead body away into the forest and disappeared with it into the stockade.   The spectacle proved infectious ; one after another in the emotional, excitable crowd of negroes followed the example, dropped down like dead, and were carried off, sometimes in a real cataleptic state.   In this way fifty to a hundred or more novices might feign death and be transported into the sacred enclosure.   There they were supposed not only to die but to rot till only a single bone of their body remained, of which the initiated had to take the greatest care in expectation of the joyful resurrection that was soon to follow. However, though they were both dead and rotten, they consumed a large quantity of food, which their credulous relatives brought to them in baskets, toiling with the loads on their backs over the long paths through the forest in the sweltering heat of the tropical day. If the relations failed to discharge this pious and indispensable duty, their kinsman in the sacred enclosure ran a risk of dying in good earnest, or rather of being spirited away to a distant town and sold as a slave.

Shut up within the stockade for months or years, the men and women, boys and girls, dispensed with the superfluity of clothes, rubbed their naked bodies with red ochre or powdered camwood instead, and gave themselves up to orgies of unbridled lust. Some feeble attempts were made to teach them the rudiments of a secret language, but the vocabulary was small and its principles lacking in ingenuity. The time during which this seclusion lasted might vary from three months to three years. When the circumstances which had furnished the pretext for instituting the society had passed away, whether it was that the epidemic had died out or that the birth-rate had sensibly increased, murmurs would begin to be heard among friends and relatives in the town, who did not see why they should be taxed any longer to support a set of idle and dissolute ruffians in the forest, and why they should trudge day after day in the sweat of their brow to carry provisions to them. So the supplies would begin to run short, and whenever that happened the mystery of the resurrection was sure to follow very soon after.

Accordingly it would be announced that on a certain market-day the new initiates, now raised from the dead, would reveal themselves in all their glory to the astonished gaze of the public. The glad tidings were received with enthusiasm, and crowds assembled from all the country round about to welcome those who had come back from the world beyond the grave. When all were gathered in eager expectancy in the market-place, the sounds of distant music would be heard, and soon the gay procession would defile into the open square and march round it, while the dusky skins, reddened with cam-

Seclusion of the novices.

Resurrection of the novices.

wood powder, glistened in the sunshine, the gay garments
fluttered in the wind, and the tassels of palm-leaf fibre
dangled at every arm.   In the crowd of spectators many
parents would recognize their children in the marching
figures of the procession, and girls and boys would point
out their brothers and sisters and eagerly call out their
names.   But in the stolid faces of the initiates not an eye
would gleam with recognition, not a muscle would twitch
with an involuntary expression of delight ; for having just
been raised from the dead they were supposed to know
nothing of their former life, of friends and relations, of home
and country.   There might be in the crowd a mother or a
sister not seen for years ; or, more moving still, the novice
might look in vain for loved and remembered faces that
would never be seen in the market-place again.   But whatever his feelings might be, he must rigidly suppress them
under pain of a flogging, a fine, or even death.   At last the
parade was over and the procession broke up.   Then the
old hands introduced the new hands to their own parents
and brothers and sisters, to their old homes and haunts.

Pretence
of the
novices
that they
have for-
gotten
everything.

For still the novices kept up the pretence that everything
was new and strange to them, that they could not speak
their mother tongue, that they did not know their own
fathers and mothers, their own town and their own houses ;
nay that they had forgotten even how to eat their food.   So
everything and everybody had to be shewn to them and
their names and meanings explained.   Their guides would
lead them about the town, pointing out the various roads
and telling where they led to—this one to the watering-
place on the river, this to the forest, that to the farms, and
so on : they would take up the commonest domestic utensils
and shew what they were used for : they would even chew
the food and put it into the mouths of the novices, like
mother birds feeding their callow young.   For some time
afterwards the resuscitated persons, attended by their mentors,
would go about the town and the neighbourhood acting in a
strange way like children or mad folk, seizing what they
wanted and trying to beat or even kill such as dared to
refuse them anything.   Their guardian would generally
restrain these sallies ; but sometimes he would arrange with

his hopeful pupils to be out of sight when two or three of them clubbed together to assault and rob an honest man, and would only return in time to share the booty. After a while, however, the excitement created by the resurrection would wear off; the dead folk come to life were expected to have learned their lessons, and if they forgot themselves, their memory was promptly refreshed by the law.[1]

[1] Rev. J. H. Weeks, "Notes on some Customs of the Lower Congo People," *Folk - lore*, xx. (1909) pp. 189-198; Rev. W. H. Bentley, *Life on the Congo* (London, 1887), pp. 78 *sq.*; *id.*, *Pioneering on the Congo* (London, 1900), i. 284 - 287. Mr. Weeks's description of the institution is the fullest and I have followed it in the text. The custom was in vogue down to recent years, but seems to have been suppressed chiefly by the exertions of the missionaries. Besides the *ndembo* guild there is, or was, in these regions another secret society known as the *nkimba*, which some writers have confused with the *ndembo*. The *nkimba* was of a more harmless character than the other; indeed it seems even to have served some useful purposes, partly as a kind of free-masonry which encouraged mutual help among its members, partly as a system of police for the repression of crime, its professed object being to put down witchcraft and punish witches. Only males were admitted to it. Candidates for initiation were stupefied by a drug, but there was apparently no pretence of killing them and bringing them to life again. Members of the society had a home in the jungle away from the town, where the novices lived together for a period varying from six months to two years. They learned a secret language, and received new names; it was afterwards an offence to call a man by the name of his childhood. Instead of the red dye affected by members of the *ndembo* guild, members of the *nkimba* guild whitened their bodies with pipe clay and wore crinolines of palm frondlets. See Rev. W. H. Bentley, *Life on the Congo*, pp. 80-83; *id.*, *Pioneering on the Congo*, i. 282-284; Rev. J. H.

Weeks, *op. cit.* pp. 198-201; (Sir) H. H. Johnston, "A Visit to Mr. Stanley's Stations on the River Congo," *Proceedings of the Royal Geographical Society*, N.S. v. (1883) pp. 572 *sq.*; E. Delmar Morgan, "Notes on the Lower Congo," *id.*, N.S. vi. (1884) p. 193. As to these two secret societies on the Lower Congo, see further (Sir) H. H. Johnston, "On the Races of the Congo," *Journal of the Anthropological Institute*, xiii. (1884) pp. 472 *sq.*; É. Dupont, *Lettres sur le Congo* (Paris, 1889), pp. 96-100; Herbert Ward, *Five Years with the Congo Cannibals* (London, 1890), pp. 54 *sq.*; *id.* "Ethnographical Notes relating to the Congo Tribes," *Journal of the Anthropological Institute*, xxiv. (1895) pp. 288 *sq.*; E. J. Glave, *Six Years of Adventure in Congo Land* (London, 1893), pp. 80-83; L. Frobenius, *Die Masken und Geheimbünde Afrikas* (Halle, 1898), pp. 43 - 54 (*Nova Acta, Abh. der Kaiserl. Leop. Carol. Deutschen Akademie der Naturforscher*, vol. lxxiv. No. 1); H. Schurtz, *Altersklassen und Männerbünde* (Berlin, 1902), pp. 433-437; *Notes Annalytiques sur les Collections Ethnographiques du Musée du Congo* (Brussels, 1902–1906), pp. 199-206; Ed. de Jonghe, *Les Sociétés Secrètes au Bas-Congo* (Brussels, 1907), pp. 15 *sqq.* (extract from the *Revue des Questions Scientifiques*, October 1907). Some of these writers do not discriminate between the two societies, the *ndembo* and the *nkimba*. According to our best authorities (Messrs. Bentley and Weeks) the two societies are quite distinct and neither of them has anything to do with circumcision, which is, however, prevalent in the region. See Rev. J. H. Weeks, "Notes on some Customs of the

Bastian's
account of
the ritual
of death
and resur-
rection in
West
Africa.
The following account of the rites, as practised in this part of Africa, was given to Adolf Bastian by an interpreter. "The great fetish lives in the interior of the forest-land, where nobody sees him and nobody can see him. When he dies, the fetish priests carefully collect his bones in order to bring them to life again, and they nourish them, that he may be clothed anew in flesh and blood. But it is not good to speak of it. In the land of Ambamba every one must die once, and when the fetish priest shakes his calabash against a village, all the men and lads whose hour is come fall into a state of lifeless torpidity, from which they generally arise after three days. But if the fetish loves a man he carries him away into the bush and buries him in the fetish house, often for many years. When he comes to life again, he begins to eat and drink as before, but his understanding is gone and the fetish man must teach him and direct him in every motion, like the smallest child. At first this can only be done with a stick, but gradually his senses return, so that it is possible to talk with him, and when his education is complete, the priest brings him back to his parents. They would seldom recognize their son but for the express assur- ances of the fetish priest, who moreover recalls previous events to their memory. He who has not gone through the ceremony of the new birth in Ambamba is universally looked down upon and is not admitted to the dances." [1]

Acquisition
of a patron
animal or
guardian
spirit in a
dream.
In the same part of Africa we hear of a fetish called Malassi, the votaries of which form a secret order of the usual sort with a variety of ranks to which the initiates are promoted. "The candidate is plunged into a magic sleep within the temple-hut, and while he sleeps he beholds a bird or other object with which his existence is henceforth

---

Lower Congo People," *Folk-lore*, xx. (1909) pp. 304 *sqq.* A secret society of the Lower Congo which Adolf Bastian has described under the name of *quimba* is probably identical with the *nkimba.* He speaks of a "Secret Order of those who have been born again," and tells us that the candidates "are thrown into a death- like state and buried in the fetish house. When they are wakened to life again, they have (as in the Belli-

paro) lost their memory of everything that is past, even of their father and mother, and they can no longer re- member their own name. Hence new names are given them according to the titles or ranks to which they are advanced." See A. Bastian, *Die deutsche Expedition an der Loango- Küste* (Jena, 1874–1875), ii. 15 *sqq.*

[1] A. Bastian, *Ein Besuch in San Salvador* (Bremen, 1859), pp. 82 *sq.*

sympathetically bound up, just as the life of the young
Indian is bound up with the animal which he sees in his
dream at puberty. All who have been born again at
initiation, after their return to a normal state, bear the name
of Swamie (a sacred designation also in India) or, if they are
women, Sumbo (Tembo), and wear as a token the ring called
sase, which consists of an iron hoop with a fruit attached to
it."[1]   Similarly among the Fans of the Gaboon a young
warrior acquires his guardian spirit by dreaming. He is
secluded in the forest, drinks a fermented and intoxicating
liquor, and smokes hemp. Then he falls into a heavy sleep,
and next morning he must describe exactly to the fetish
priest the animal, tree, mineral, or whatever it may have
been which he saw in his dream. This magical dream is
repeated on three successive nights ; and after that the young
man is sent forth by the priest to seek and bring back the
beast, bird, reptile, or whatever it was of which he dreamed.
The youth obeys, reduces the animal or thing to cinders or
ashes, and preserves these calcined remains as a talisman
which will protect him against many dangers.[2]   However,
in these rites there is no clear simulation of dying and coming
to life again.

Rites of death and resurrection were formerly observed in
Quoja, on the west coast of Africa, to the north of the Congo.
They are thus described by an old writer :—" They have
another ceremony which they call Belli-Paaro, but it is not for
everybody. For it is an incorporation in the assembly of
the spirits, and confers the right of entering their groves,
that is to say, of going and eating the offerings which the
simple folk bring thither. The initiation or admission to
the Belli-Paaro is celebrated every twenty or twenty-five
years. The initiated recount marvels of the ceremony,
saying that they are roasted, that they entirely change their

Dapper's account of the ritual of death and resurrection in the Belli-Paaro society.

---

[1] A. Bastian, *Die deutsche Expedition an der Loango-Küste*, ii. 183.
Elsewhere Bastian says that about San Salvador lads at puberty are secluded in the forest and circumcised, and during their seclusion " each of them is mystically united to the fetish by which his life is henceforth determined, as the Brahman whispers the secret charm in

the ear of him who has been born again." See A. Bastian, *Ein Besuch in San Salvador* (Bremen, 1859), pp. 85 *sq.*
[2] H. Trilles, *Le Totémisme chez les Fân* (Münster i. W., 1912), pp. 479 *sq.* The writer speaks of the guardian spirit as the individual totem of the young warrior.

habits and life, and that they receive a spirit quite different from that of other people and quite new lights.   The badge of membership consists in some lines traced on the neck between the shoulders ; the lines seem to be pricked with a needle.   Those who have this mark pass for persons of spirit, and when they have attained a certain age they are allowed a voice in all public assemblies ; whereas the uninitiated are regarded as profane, impure, and ignorant persons, who dare not express an opinion on any subject of importance.   When the time for the ceremony has come, it is celebrated as follows.   By order of the king a place is appointed in the forest, whither they bring the youths who have not been marked, not without much crying and weeping ; for it is impressed upon the youths that in order to undergo this change it is necessary to suffer death.   So they dispose of their property, as if it were all over with them. There are always some of the initiated beside the novices to instruct them.   They teach them to dance a certain dance called *killing*, and to sing verses in praise of Belli.   Above all, they are very careful not to let them die of hunger, because if they did so, it is much to be feared that the spiritual resurrection would profit them nothing.   This manner of life lasts five or six years, and is comfortable enough, for there is a village in the forest, and they amuse themselves with hunting and fishing.   Other lads are brought thither from time to time, so that the last comers have not long to stay.   No woman or uninitiated person is suffered to pass within four or five leagues of the sacred wood. When their instruction is completed, they are taken from the wood and shut up in small huts made for the purpose.   Here they begin once more to hold communion with mankind and to talk with the women who bring them their food.   It is amusing to see their affected simplicity.   They pretend to know no one, and to be ignorant of all the customs of the country, such as the customs of washing themselves, rubbing themselves with oil, and so forth.   When they enter these huts, their bodies are all covered with the feathers of birds, and they wear caps of bark which hang down before their faces. But after a time they are dressed in clothes and taken to a great open place, where all the people of the neighbourhood are assembled.   Here the novices give the first proof of their capacity by dancing a dance which is called the dance of Belli. After the dance is over, the novices are taken to the houses of their parents by their instructors." [1]

Miss Kingsley informs us that "the great point of agreement between all these West African secret societies lies in the methods of initiation.   The boy, if he belongs to a tribe that goes in for tattooing, is tattooed, and is handed over to instructors in the societies' secrets and formulae.   He lives, with the other boys of his tribe undergoing initiation, usually under the rule of several instructors, and for the space of one year.   He lives always in the forest, and is naked and smeared with clay.   The boys are exercised so as to become inured to hardship ; in some districts, they make raids so as to perfect themselves in this useful accomplishment.   They always take a new name, and are supposed by the initiation process to become new beings in the magic wood, and on their return to their village at the end of their course, they pretend to have entirely forgotten their life before they entered the wood ; but this pretence is not kept up beyond the period of festivities given to welcome them home.   They all learn, to a certain extent, a new language, a secret language only understood by the initiated.   The same removal from home and instruction from initiated members is observed also with the girls. However, in their case, it is not always a forest-grove they are secluded in, sometimes it is done in huts.   Among the Grain Coast tribes, however, the girls go into a magic wood until they are married.   Should they have to leave the wood for any temporary reason, they must smear themselves with white clay.   A similar custom holds good in Okÿon, Calabar district, where, should a girl have to leave the fattening-house, she must be covered with white clay." [2]

Among the natives of the Sherbro, an island lying close

Miss Kingsley on the rites of initiation into secret societies in West Africa.

---

[1] O. Dapper, *Description de l'Afrique* (Amsterdam, 1686), pp. 268 *sq.* Dapper's account has been abridged in the text.

[2] Miss Mary H. Kingsley, *Travels in West Africa* (London, 1867), p. 531.   Perhaps the smearing with clay may be intended to indicate that the novices have undergone the new birth ; for the negro child, though born reddish-brown, soon turns slaty-grey (E. B. Tylor, *Anthropology*, London, 1881, p. 67), which would answer well enough to the hue of the clay-bedaubed novices.

The *purra*
or *poro*,
a secret
society
of Sierra
Leone.
to the coast of Sierra Leone, there is a secret society called the *purra* or *poro*, "which is partly of a religious, but chiefly of a political nature. It resembles free-masonry in excluding females, and in obliging every member by a solemn oath, which I believe is seldom violated, not to divulge the sacred mysteries, and to yield a prompt and implicit obedience to every order of their superiors. Boys of seven or eight years of age are admitted, or rather serve a novitiate until they arrive at a proper age ; for it is difficult to procure exact information, and even somewhat dangerous to make many inquiries. Every person on entering the society lays aside his former name and assumes a new one ; to call him by his old name would produce a dispute. They have a superior or head *purra* man, assisted by a grand council, whose commands are received with the most profound reverence and absolute submission, both by the subordinate councils and by individuals. Their meetings are held in the most retired spots, amid the gloom of night, and carried on with inquisitorial secrecy. When the *purra* comes into a town, which is always at night, it is accompanied with the most dreadful howlings, screams, and other horrid noises. The inhabitants, who are not members of the society, are obliged to secure themselves within doors ; should any one be discovered without, or attempting to peep at what is going forward, he would inevitably be put to death. To restrain the curiosity of the females, they are ordered to continue within doors, clapping their hands incessantly, so long as the *purra* remains. Like the secret tribunal, which formerly existed in Germany, it takes cognizance of offences, particularly of witchcraft and murder, but above all of contumacy and disobedience in any of its own members, and punishes the guilty with death in so secret and sudden a manner, that the perpetrators are never known : indeed, such is the dread created by this institution, that they are never even inquired after."[1]   When the members of the *purra* or

---

[1] Thomas Winterbottom, *An Account of the Native Africans in the Neighbourhood of Sierra Leone* (London, 1803), pp. 135 *sq.* Compare John Matthews, *A Voyage to the River Sierra-Leone* (London, 1791), pp. 82-85 ; J. B. L. Durand, *Voyage au Sénégal* (Paris, 1802), pp. 183 *sq.* (whose account is copied without acknowledgment from Matthews). The *purra* or *poro* society also exists among the Timmes of Sierra Leone;

poro society visit a town, the leader of the troop, whom an English writer calls " the Poro devil," draws discordant notes from a sort of reed flute, the holes of which are covered with spiders' webs. The only time when this devil and his rout make a prolonged stay in the town is on the evening before the day on which the newly initiated lads are to be brought back from the forest. Then the leader and his satellites parade the streets for hours, while all the uninitiated men, women, and children remain shut up in their houses, listening to the doleful strains of the flute, which signify that the devil is suffering the pangs of childbirth before he brings forth the initiated lads ; for he is supposed to have been pregnant with them the whole of the rainy season ever since they entered into the forest. When they come forth from the wood, they wear four or five coils of twisted ferns round their waists in token of their being initiated members of the order.[1] Among the Soosoos of Senegambia there is a similar secret society called *semo* : " the natives who speak English call it African masonry. As the whole ceremonies are kept very private, it is difficult to discover in what they consist : but it is said that the novices are met in the woods by the old men, who cut marks on several parts of their bodies, but most commonly on the belly ; they are also taught a language peculiar to the *semo*, and swear dreadful oaths never to divulge the secrets revealed to them. The young men are then made to live in the woods for twelve months, and are supposed to be at liberty to kill any one who approaches and does not understand the language of the *semo*. . . . It is said, when women are so unfortunate as to intrude upon the *semo*, they kill them, cut off their breasts, and hang them up by the side of the paths as a warning

The new birth.

The semo, *a secret society of Senegambia.*

in this tribe the novices are sometimes secluded from their families for ten years in the wood, they are tattooed on their backs and arms, and they learn a language which consists chiefly of names of plants and animals used in special senses. Women are not admitted to the society. See Zweifel et Moustier, " Voyage aux sources du Niger," *Bulletin de la Société de Géographie* (Paris), VI. Série, xv. (1878) pp. 108 *sq.*

[1] T. J. Alldridge, *The Sherbro and its Hinterland* (London, 1901), p. 130. This work contains a comparatively full account of the *purra* or *poro* society (pp. 124-131) and of the other secret societies of the country (pp. 131-149, 153-159). Compare L. Frobenius, *Die Masken und Geheimbünde Afrikas* (Halle, 1898), pp. 138-144 (*Nova Acta, Abh. der Kaiserl. Leop.-Carol. Deutschen Akademie der Naturforscher*, vol. lxxiv. No. 1).

to others. This circumstance is perhaps less deserving of credit, because the Soosoos are fond of telling wonderful and horrid stories respecting this institution. They say, for instance, that when first initiated their throats are cut, and they continue dead for some time ; at length they are reanimated and initiated into the mysteries of the institution, and are enabled to ramble about with much more vigour than they possessed before." [1]

Death and resurrection at initiation.

While the belief or the pretence of death and resurrection at initiation is common among the negroes of West Africa, few traces of it appear to be found among the tribes in the southern, central, and eastern parts of that continent ; and it is notable that in these regions secret societies, which flourish in the West, are also conspicuously absent. However, the Akikuyu of British East Africa " have a curious custom which requires that every boy just before circumcision must be born again. The mother stands up with the boy crouching at her feet ; she pretends to go through all the labour pains, and the boy on being reborn cries like a babe and is washed. He lives on milk for some days afterwards." [2] A fuller description of the ceremony was given by a member of the Kikuyu tribe as follows : " A day is appointed, any time of year, by father and mother. If the father is dead another elder is called in to act as proxy in his stead, or if the mother is not living another woman to act in her place. Any woman thus acting as representative is looked upon in future by the boy as his own mother. A goat or sheep is killed in the afternoon by any one, usually not by the father, and the stomach and intestines reserved. The ceremony begins in the evening. A piece of skin is cut in a circle, and passed over one shoulder of the candidate and under the other arm. The stomach of the goat is similarly treated and passed over the other shoulder and under the other arm. All the boy's ornaments are removed, but not his clothes. No men are allowed inside the hut, but women are present. The mother sits on a hide on the floor with the boy between

Ritual of the new birth among the Akikuyu of British East · Africa.

---

[1] Thomas Winterbottom, *An Account of the Native Africans in the Neighbourhood of Sierra Leone* (London, 1803), pp. 137-139. As to the *semo* or *simo* society see further L.

Frobenius, *op. cit.* pp. 130-138.

[2] Extract from a letter of Mr. A. C. Hollis to me. Mr. Hollis's authority is Dr. T. W. W. Crawford of the Kenia Medical Mission.

her knees. The sheep's gut is passed round the woman and brought in front of the boy. The woman groans as in labour, another woman cuts the gut, and the boy imitates the cry of a new-born infant. The women present all applaud, and afterwards the assistant and the mother wash the boy. That night the boy sleeps in the same hut as the mother." [1] Here the cutting of the sheep's gut, which unites the mother to the boy, is clearly an imitation of severing the navel string. Nor is it boys alone who are born again among the Akikuyu. " Girls go through the rite of second birth as well as boys. It is sometimes administered to infants. At one time the new birth was combined with circumcision, and so the ceremony admitted to the privileges and religious rites of the tribe. Afterwards trouble took place on account of mere boys wishing to take their place alongside of the young men and maintaining they were justified in doing so. The old men then settled the matter by separating the two. Unless the new birth has been administered the individual is not in a position to be admitted to circumcision, which is the outward sign of admittance to the nation. Any who have not gone through the rite cannot inherit property, nor take any part in the religious rites of the country." [2] For example, a man who has not been born again is disqualified for carrying his dying father out into the wilds and for disposing of his body after death. The new birth seems to take place usually about the tenth year, but the age varies with the ability of the father to provide a goat, whose guts are necessary to enable the boy or girl to be born again in due form. [3]

Among the Bondeis, a tribe on the coast of German East Africa, opposite to the island of Pemba, one of the rites of initiation into manhood consists in a pretence of

Rites of initiation among the Bondeis of East Africa.

[1] W. Scoresby Routledge and Katherine Routledge, *With a Prehistoric People, the Akikuyu of British East Africa* (London, 1910), p. 152. Compare C. W. Hobley, " Kikuyu Customs and Beliefs," *Journal of the Royal Anthropological Institute,* xl. (1910) p. 441.

[2] Mr. A. W. McGregor, of the Church Missionary Society, quoted by

W. S. Routledge and K. Routledge, *With a Prehistoric People,* p. 151, note.[1] Mr. McGregor " has resided amongst the Akikuyu since 1901. He has by his tact and kindness won the confidence of the natives, and is the greatest authority on their language " (*id.,* p. xxi).

[3] W. S. Routledge and K. Routledge, *op. cit.* p. 151.

slaying one of the lads with a sword; the entrails of a
fowl are placed on the boy's stomach to make the pretence
seem more real.[1]   Among the Bushongo, who inhabit a
district of the Belgian Congo bounded on the north and
east by the Sankuru River and on the west by the Kasai,
young boys had formerly to undergo certain rites of initiation, amongst which a simulation of killing them would seem
to have had a place, though in recent times the youths have
been allowed to escape the ordeal by the payment of a fine.
The supreme chief of the tribe, who in old days bore the
title of God on Earth (*Chembe Kunji*), used to assemble
all the lads who had just reached puberty and send them
away into the forest, where they remained for several
months under the care of one of his sons.   During their
seclusion they were deemed unclean and might see no one ;
if they chanced to meet a woman, she had to flee before
them.   By night the old men marched round the quarters
of the novices, raising hideous cries and whirling bull-roarers,
the noise of which the frightened lads took to be the
voices of ghosts.   They wore nothing but a comb, and
passed their leisure hours in learning to make mats and
baskets.   After about a month they had to submit to the first
ordeal.   A trench about ten feet deep was dug in the ground
and roofed over with sticks and earth so as to form a dark
tunnel.   In the sides of the tunnel were cut niches, and in
each niche a man took post, whose business it was to terrify
the novices.   For this purpose one of them was disguised in
the skin of a leopard, a second was dressed as a warrior with
a knife in his hand, a third was a smith with his furnace and
red-hot irons, and a fourth was masked to look like an ugly
ape, while he too gripped a knife in his hand.   The novices
generally recoiled in dismay from each of these apparitions,
and it was only by means of reiterated taunts and threats that
the elders forced them to traverse the whole length of the
tunnel.   After the lapse of another month the youths had to
face another ordeal of a similar character.   A low tunnel, about
three feet deep, was dug in the earth, and sticks were inserted

Rites
of initiation
among the
Bushongo
of the
Congo.

The first
ordeal.

The second
ordeal.

[1] Rev. G. Dale, "An Account of
the principal Customs and Habits of
the Natives inhabiting the Bondei
Country," *Journal of the Anthropological Institute*, xxv. (1896) p. 189.

in it so that their tops projected from the surface of the ground.
At the end of the tunnel a calabash was set full of goat's blood.
By way of encouraging the timid novices the master of the
ceremonies himself crawled through the tunnel, his progress
under ground being revealed to the novices above ground by
the vibrations of the sticks with which he collided in the
dark passage.   Then having bedabbled his nose, his mouth,
and all the rest of his body with the goat's blood, he emerged
from the tunnel on hands and knees, dripping with gore and
to all appearance in the last stage of exhaustion.   Then he
lay prostrate on his stomach in a state of collapse ; the elders
declared him to be dead and carried him off.   The chief
now ordered the lads to imitate the example set them by
the master of the ceremonies, but they begged and prayed
to be excused.   At first the chief was inexorable, but in time
he relented and agreed to accept a fine of so many cowries as
a ransom paid by the youths for exemption from the ordeal.
A month later the last of the ordeals took place.   A great   The last
trunk of a tree was buried with its lower end in the earth   ordeal: the
and surrounded for three-quarters of its circumference with   descent
arrows stuck in the ground so that the barbs were pointed   from the
towards the tree.   The chief and the leading men sat down   tree.
at the gap in the circle of arrows, so as to conceal the gap
from the eyes of the novices and other spectators, among whom
the women were allowed to be present.   To the eyes of the
uninitiated it now seemed that the tree was surrounded by a
bristling hedge of arrows, to fall upon which would be death.
All being ready the master of the ceremonies climbed the
tree amid breathless silence, and having reached the top,
which was decorated with a bunch of leaves, he looked about
him and asked the women, " Shall I come down ? "   " No !
no ! " they shrieked, " you will be killed by the arrows."
Then, turning disdainfully from these craven souls, the
gallant man addressed himself to the youths and repeated
his question, " Shall I come down ? "   A shout of " Yes ! "
gave the answer that might have been expected from these
heroic spirits.   In response the master of the ceremonies at
once slid down the tree and, dropping neatly to the ground
just at the gap in the hedge of arrows, presented himself
unscathed to the gaze of the excited assembly.   The chief

now ordered the young men to go up and do likewise. But the dauntless courage with which they had contemplated the descent of the master of the ceremonies entirely forsook them when it came to their turn to copy his shining example. Their mothers, too, raised a loud cry of protest, joining their prayers and entreaties to those of their hopeful sons. After some discussion the chief consented to accept a ransom, and the novices were dispensed from the ordeal. Then they bathed and were deemed to have rid themselves of their uncleanness, but they had still to work for the chief for three months before they ranked as full-grown men and might return to their villages.[1]

Rites of initiation among the Indians of Virginia: pretence of the novices that they have forgotten their former life.

Among the Indians of Virginia, an initiatory ceremony, called *Huskanaw*, took place every sixteen or twenty years, or oftener, as the young men happened to grow up. The youths were kept in solitary confinement in the woods for several months, receiving no food but an infusion of some intoxicating roots, so that they went raving mad, and continued in this state eighteen or twenty days. "Upon this occasion it is pretended that these poor creatures drink so much of the water of Lethe that they perfectly lose the remembrance of all former things, even of their parents, their treasure, and their language. When the doctors find that they have drunk sufficiently of the Wysoccan (so they call this mad potion), they gradually restore them to their senses again by lessening the intoxication of their diet ; but before they are perfectly well they bring them back into their towns, while they are still wild and crazy through the violence of the medicine. After this they are very fearful of discovering anything of their former remembrance ; for if such a thing should happen to any of them, they must immediately be *Huskanaw'd* again ; and the second time the usage is so severe that seldom any one escapes with life. Thus they must pretend to have forgot the very use of their tongues, so as not to be able to speak, nor understand anything that is spoken, till they learn it again. Now, whether this be real or counterfeit, I don't know ; but certain it is that they

[1] E. Torday et T. A. Joyce, *Les Bushongo* (Brussels, 1910), pp. 82-85. As for the title "God on Earth," applied to the principal chief or king, see *id.*, p. 53.

will not for some time take notice of anybody nor anything with which they were before acquainted, being still under the guard of their keepers, who constantly wait upon them everywhere till they have learnt all things perfectly over again.   Thus they unlive their former lives, and commence men by forgetting that they ever have been boys." [1]

Among some of the Indian tribes of North America there exist certain religious associations which are only open to candidates who have gone through a pretence of being killed and brought to life again.   In 1766 or 1767 Captain Jonathan Carver witnessed the admission of a candidate to an association called " the friendly society of the Spirit " (*Wakon-Kitchewah*) among the Naudowessies, a Siouan or Dacotan tribe in the region of the great lakes.   The candidate knelt before the chief, who told him that " he himself was now agitated by the same spirit which he should in a few moments communicate to him ; that it would. strike him dead, but that he would instantly be restored again to life ; to this he added, that the communication, however terrifying, was a necessary introduction to the advantages enjoyed by the community into which he was on the point of being admitted.   As he spoke this, he appeared to be greatly agitated ; till at last his emotions became so violent, that his countenance was distorted, and his whole frame convulsed.   At this juncture he threw something that appeared both in shape and colour like a small bean, at the young man, which seemed to enter his mouth, and he instantly fell as motionless as if he had been shot."   For a time the man lay like dead, but under a shower of blows he shewed signs of consciousness, and finally, discharging from his mouth the bean, or whatever it was that the chief had thrown at him, he came to life. [2]   In other tribes, for example, the

Ritual of death and resurrection at initiation into the secret societies of North America.

---

[1] (Beverley's) *History of Virginia* (London, 1722), pp. 177 *sq.*   Compare J. Bricknell, *The Natural History of North Carolina* (Dublin, 1737), pp. 405 *sq.*

[2] J. Carver, *Travels through the Interior Parts of North America*, Third Edition (London, 1781), pp. 271-275.   The thing thrown at the man and afterwards vomited by him was probably not a bean but a small white sea-shell (*Cypraea moneta*).   See H. R. Schoolcraft, *Indian Tribes of the United States* (Philadelphia, 1853–1856), iii. 287 ; J. G. Kohl, *Kitschi-Gami* (Bremen, 1859), i. 71 ; *Seventh Annual Report of the Bureau of Ethnology* (Washington, 1891), pp. 191, 215 ; *Fourteenth Annual Report of the Bureau of Ethnology* (Washington, 1896), p. 101.

The medi-
cine-bag
as an in-
strument
of death
and resur-
rection.

Ojebways, Winnebagoes, and Dacotas or Sioux, the instrument by which the candidate is apparently slain is the
medicine-bag.   The bag is made of the skin of an animal
(such as the otter, wild cat, serpent, bear, raccoon, wolf, owl,
weasel),. of which it roughly preserves the shape.   Each
member of the society has one of these bags, in which he
keeps the odds and ends that make up his " medicine " or
charms.   " They believe that from the miscellaneous contents
in the belly of the skin bag or animal there issues a spirit or
breath, which has the power, not only to knock down and
kill a man, but also to set him up and restore him to life."
The mode of killing a man with one of these medicine-bags
is to thrust it at him ; he falls like dead, but a second thrust
of the bag restores him to life.[1]   Among the Dacotas the
institution of the medicine-bag or mystery-sack was attributed
to Onktehi, the great spirit of the waters, who ordained that
the bag should consist of the skin of the otter, raccoon,
weasel, squirrel, or loon, or a species of fish and of serpents.
Further, he decreed that the bag should contain four sorts of
medicines of magical qualities, which should represent fowls,
quadrupeds, herbs, and trees.   Accordingly, swan's down,
buffalo hair, grass roots, and bark from the roots of trees are
kept by the Dacotas in their medicine-bags.   From this
combination there proceeds a magical influence (*tonwan*)
so powerful that no human being can of his own strength
withstand it.   When the god of the waters had prepared the
first medicine-bag, he tested its powers on four candidates
for initiation, who all perished under the shock.   So he
consulted with his wife, the goddess of the earth, and by

[1] J. Carver, *op. cit.* pp. 277 *sq.* ;
H. R. Schoolcraft, *Indian Tribes of
the United States*, iii. 287 (as to the
Winnebagoes), v. 430 *sqq.* (as to the
Chippeways and Sioux) ; J. G. Kohl,
Kitschi-Gami, i. 64-70 (as to the
Ojebways).   For a very detailed
account of the Ojebway ceremonies,
see W. J. Hoffman, " The Midewiwin
or Grand Medicine Society of the
Ojibwa," *Seventh Annual Report of
the Bureau of Ethnology* (Washington,
1891), especially pp. 215 *sq.*, 234 *sq.*,
248, 265.   For similar ceremonies
among the Menomini, see *id.*, "The

Menomini Indians,"*Fourteenth Annual
Report of the Bureau of Ethnology*
(Washington, 1896), pp. 99-102 ; and
among the Omahas, see J. Owen
Dorsey, "Omaha Sociology," *Third
Annual Report of the Bureau of Ethnology* (Washington, 1884), pp. 342-
346.   I have dealt more fully with
the ritual in *Totemism and Exogamy*,
iii. 462 *sqq.*   Compare also P. Radin,
" Ritual and Significance of the Win-
nebago Medicine Dance," *Journal of
American Folk-lore*, xxiv. (1911) pp.
149-208.

holding up his left hand and pattering on the back of it with the right, he produced myriads of little shells, whose virtue is to restore life to those who have been slain by the medicine-bag.   Having taken this precaution, the god chose four other candidates and repeated the experiment of initiation with success, for after killing them with the bag he immediately resuscitated them by throwing one of the shells into their vital parts, while he chanted certain words assuring them that it was only sport and bidding them rise to their feet.   That is why to this day every initiated Dacota has one of these shells in his body.   Such was the divine origin of the medicine-dance of the Dacotas.   The initiation takes place in a special tent.   The candidate, after being steamed in a vapour-bath for four successive days, plants himself on a pile of blankets, and behind him stands an aged member of the order.   " Now the master of the ceremonies, with the joints of his knees and hips considerably bent, advances with an unsteady, uncouth hitching, sack in hand, wearing an aspect of desperate energy, and uttering his ' Heen, heen, heen' with frightful emphasis, while all around are enthusiastic demonstrations of all kinds of wild passions. At this point the sack is raised near a painted spot on the breast of the candidate, at which the *tonwan* is discharged. At the instant the brother from behind gives him a push and he falls dead, and is covered with blankets.   Now the frenzied dancers gather around, and in the midst of bewildering and indescribable noises, chant the words uttered by the god at the institution of the ceremony, as already recorded. Then the master throws off the covering, and chewing a piece of the bone of the Onktehi, spirts it over him, and he begins to show signs of returning life.   Then as the master pats energetically upon the breast of the initiated person, he, convulsed, strangling, struggling, and agonizing, heaves up the shell which falls from his mouth on a sack placed in readiness to receive it.   Life is restored and entrance effected into the awful mysteries.   He belongs henceforth to the medicine-dance, and has a right to enjoy the medicine-feast." [1]

[margin note:] Ritual of death and resurrection at initiation among the Dacotas.

[1] G. H. Pond, " Dakota superstitions," *Collections of the Minnesota* *Historical Society for the year 1867* (Saint Paul, 1867), pp. 35, 37-40.   A

Ritual
of mimic
death
among the
Indians
of Nootka
Sound.

A ceremony witnessed by the castaway John R. Jewitt during his captivity among the Indians of Nootka Sound doubtless belongs to this class of customs. The Indian king or chief "discharged a pistol close to his son's ear, who immediately fell down as if killed, upon which all the women of the house set up a most lamentable cry, tearing handfuls of hair from their heads, and exclaiming that the prince was dead ; at the same time a great number of the inhabitants rushed into the house armed with their daggers, muskets, etc., enquiring the cause of their outcry. These were immediately followed by two others dressed in wolf skins, with masks over their faces representing the head of that animal. The latter came in on their hands and feet in the manner of a beast, and taking up the prince, carried him off upon their backs, retiring in the same manner they entered."[1] In another place Jewitt mentions that the young prince—a lad of about eleven years of age—wore a mask in imitation of a wolf's head.[2] Now, as the Indians of this part of America are divided into totem clans, of which the Wolf clan is one of the principal, and as the members of each clan are in the habit of wearing some portion of the totem animal about their person,[3] it is probable that the prince belonged to the Wolf clan, and that the ceremony described by Jewitt represented the killing of the lad in order that he might be born anew as a wolf, much in the same way that the Basque hunter supposed himself to have been killed and to have come to life again as a bear.

Rite of
death and
resurrec-
tion at

This conjectural explanation of the ceremony has, since it was first put forward, been confirmed by the researches of Dr. Franz Boas among these Indians ; though it would seem

---

similar but abridged account of the Dakota tradition and usage is given by S. R. Riggs in his *Dakota Grammar, Texts, and Ethnography* (Washington, 1893), pp. 227-229 (*Contributions to North American Ethnology*, vol. ix.).

[1] *Narrative of the Adventures and Sufferings of John R. Jewitt* (Middletown, 1820), p. 119.

[2] *Id.*, p. 44. For the age of the prince, see *id.*, p. 35.

[3] H. J. Holmberg, "Ueber die Völker des russischen Amerika," *Acta Societatis Scientiarum Fennicae*, iv. (Helsingfors, 1856) pp. 292 *sqq.*, 328 ; Ivan Petroff, *Report on the Population, Industries and Resources of Alaska*, pp. 165 *sq.* ; A. Krause, *Die Tlinkit-Indianer* (Jena, 1885), p. 112 ; R. C. Mayne, *Four Years in British Columbia and Vancouver Island* (London, 1862), pp. 257 *sq.*, 268 ; *Totemism and Exogamy*, iii. 264 *sqq.*

that the community to which the chief's son thus obtained admission was not so much a totem clan as a secret society called Tlokoala, whose members imitated wolves. The name Tlokoala is a foreign word among the Nootka Indians, having been borrowed by them from the Kwakiutl Indians, in whose language the word means the finding of a *manitoo* or personal totem. The Nootka tradition runs that this secret society was instituted by wolves who took away a chief's son and tried to kill him, but, failing to do so, became his friends, taught him the rites of the society, and ordered him to teach them to his friends on his return home. Then they carried the young man back to his village. They also begged that whenever he moved from one place to another he would kindly leave behind him some red cedar-bark to be used by them in their own ceremonies ; and to this custom the Nootka tribes still adhere. Every new member of the society must be initiated by the wolves. At night a pack of wolves, personated by Indians dressed in wolf-skins and wearing wolf-masks, make their appearance, seize the novice, and carry him into the woods. When the wolves are heard outside the village, coming to fetch away the novice, all the members of the society blacken their faces and sing, " Among all the tribes is great excitement, because I am Tlokoala." Next day the wolves bring back the novice dead, and the members of the society have to revive him. The wolves are supposed to have put a magic stone into his body, which must be removed before he can come to life. Till this is done the pretended corpse is left lying outside the house. Two wizards go and remove the stone, which appears to be quartz, and then the novice is resuscitated.[1] Among the Niska Indians of British Columbia, who are divided into four principal clans with the raven, the wolf, the eagle, and the bear for their respective totems, the novice at initiation is always brought back by an artificial totem animal. Thus when a

---

[1] Fr. Boas, in *Sixth Report on the North-Western Tribes of Canada*, pp. 47 *sq.* (separate reprint from the *Report of the British Association*, Leeds meeting, 1890) ; *id.*, " The Social Organization and the Secret Societies of the Kwakiutl Indians," *Report of the United States National Museum for* *1895* (Washington, 1897), pp. 632 *sq.* But while the initiation described in the text was into a wolf society, not into a wolf clan, it is to be observed that the wolf is one of the regular totems of the Nootka Indians. See Fr. Boas, in *Sixth Report on the North-Western Tribes of Canada*, p. 32.

man was about to be initiated into a secret society called Olala, his friends drew their knives and pretended to kill him.   In reality they let him slip away, while they cut off the head of a dummy which had been adroitly substituted for him. Then they laid the decapitated dummy down and covered it over, and the women began to mourn and wail.   His relations gave a funeral banquet and solemnly burnt the effigy. In short, they held a regular funeral.   For a whole year the novice remained absent and was seen by none but members of the secret society.   But at the end of that time he came back alive, carried by an artificial animal which represented his totem.[1]

In these initiatory rites the novice seems to be killed as a man and restored to life as an animal.

In these ceremonies the essence of the rite appears to be the killing of the novice in his character of a man and his restoration to life in the form of the animal which is thenceforward to be, if not his guardian spirit, at least linked to him in a peculiarly intimate relation.   It is to be remembered that the Indians of Guatemala, whose life was bound up with an animal, were supposed to have the power of appearing in the shape of the particular creature with which they were thus sympathetically united.[2]   Hence it seems not unreasonable to conjecture that in like manner the Indians of British Columbia may imagine that their life depends on the life of some one of that species of creature to which they assimilate themselves by their costume.   At least if that is not an article of belief with the Columbian Indians of the present day, it may very well have been so with their ancestors in the past, and thus may have helped to mould the rites and ceremonies both of the totem clans and of the

[1] Fr. Boas, in *Tenth Report on the North-Western Tribes of Canada*, pp. 49 *sq.*, 58 *sq.* (separate reprint from the *Report of the British Association*, Ipswich meeting, 1895).   It is remarkable, however, that in this tribe persons who are being initiated into the secret societies, of which there are six, are not always or even generally brought back by an artificial animal which represents their own totem.   Thus while men of the eagle totem are brought back by an eagle which rises from underground, men of the bear clan return on the back of an artificial killer-whale which is towed across the river by ropes. Again, members of the wolf clan are brought back by an artificial bear, and members of the raven clan by a frog. In former times the appearance of the artificial totem animal, or of the guardian spirit, was considered a matter of great importance, and any failure which disclosed the deception to the uninitiated was deemed a grave misfortune which could only be atoned for by the death of the persons concerned in the disclosure.

[2] See above, p. 213.

secret societies. For though these two sorts of communities differ in respect of the mode in which membership of them is obtained—a man being born into his totem clan but admitted into a secret society later in life—we can hardly doubt that they are near akin and have their root in the same mode of thought.[1] That thought, if I am right, is the possibility of establishing a sympathetic relation with an animal, a spirit, or other mighty being, with whom a man deposits for safe-keeping his soul or some part of it, and from whom he receives in return a gift of magical powers.

The Carrier Indians, who dwell further inland than the tribes we have just been considering, are divided into four clans with the grouse, the beaver, the toad, and the grizzly bear for their totems. But in addition to these clan totems the tribe recognized a considerable number of what Father Morice calls honorific totems, which could be acquired, through the performance of certain rites, by any person who wished to improve his social position. Each totem clan had a certain number of honorific totems or crests, and these might be assumed by any member of the clan who fulfilled the required conditions ; but they could not be acquired by members of another clan. Thus the Grouse clan had for its honorific totems or crests the owl, the moose, the weasel, the crane, the wolf, the full moon, the wind, and so on ; the Toad clan had the sturgeon, the porcupine, the wolverine, the red-headed woodpecker, the "darding knife," and so forth ; the Beaver clan had the mountain-goat for one of its

Honorific
totems
among the
Carrier
Indians.

---

[1] This is the opinion of Dr. F. Boas, who writes : " The close similarity between the clan legends and those of the acquisition of spirits presiding over secret societies, as well as the intimate relation between these and the social organizations of the tribes, allow us to apply the same argument to the consideration of the growth of the secret societies, and lead us to the conclusion that the same psychical factor that molded the clans into their present shape molded the secret societies " (" The Social Organization and the Secret Societies of the Kwakiutl Indians," *Report of the United States National* *Museum for 1895*, p. 662). Dr. Boas would see in the acquisition of a *manitoo* or personal totem the origin both of the secret societies and of the totem clans ; for according to him the totem of the clan is merely the *manitoo* or personal totem of the ancestor transmitted by inheritance to his descendants. As to personal totems or guardian spirits (*manitoos*) among the North American Indians, see *Totemism and Exogamy*, iii. 370 *sqq.* ; as to their secret societies, see *id.*, iii. 457 *sqq.* ; as to the theory that clan totems originated in personal or individual totems, see *id.*, iv. 48 *sqq.*

honorific totems; and the goose was a honorific totem of the Grizzly Bear clan.   But the common bear, as a honorific totem or crest, might be assumed by anybody, whatever his clan.   The common possession of a honorific totem appears to have constituted the same sort of bond among the Carrier Indians as the membership of a secret society does among the coast tribes of British Columbia; certainly the rites of initiation were similar.   This will be clear from Father Morice's account of the performances, which I will subjoin in his own words.   " The connection of the individual with his crest appeared more especially during ceremonial dances, when the former, attired, if possible, with the spoils of the latter, was wont to personate it in the gaze of an admiring

Initiatory rites at the adoption of a honorific totem.

assemblage.   On all such occasions, man and totem were also called by the same name.   The adoption of any such ' rite ' or crest was usually accompanied by initiatory ceremonies or observances corresponding to the nature of the crest, followed in all cases by a distribution of clothes to all

Simulated transformation of a novice into a bear.

present.   Thus whenever anybody resolved upon getting received as *Lulem* or Bear, he would, regardless of the season, divest himself of all his wearing apparel and don a bear-skin, whereupon he would dash into the woods there to remain for the space of three or four days and nights in deference to the wonts of his intended totem animal.   Every night a party of his fellow-villagers would sally out in search of the missing ' bear.'   To their loud calls : *Yi ! Kelulem* (Come on, Bear!) he would answer by angry growls in imitation of the bear.   The searching party making for the spot where he had been heard, would find by a second call followed by a similar answer that he had dexterously shifted to some opposite quarter in the forest.   As a rule, he could not be found, but had to come back of himself, when he was speedily apprehended and conducted to the ceremonial lodge, where he would commence his first bear-dance in conjunction with all the other totem people, each of whom would then personate his own particular totem.   Finally would take place the *potlatch* [distribution of property] of the newly initiated ' bear,' who would not forget to present his captor with at least a whole dressed skin.   The initiation to the ' Darding Knife ' was quite a theatrical performance.   A lance was prepared

which had a very sharp point so arranged that the slightest
pressure on its tip would cause the steel to gradually sink
into the shaft.   In the sight of the multitude crowding the
lodge, this lance was pressed on the bare chest of the
candidate and apparently sunk in his body to the shaft,
when he would tumble down simulating death.   At the
same time a quantity of blood—previously kept in the
mouth—would issue from the would-be corpse, making it
quite clear to the uninitiated gazers-on that the terrible
knife had had its effect, when lo! upon one of the actors
striking up one of the chants specially made for the circumstance and richly paid for, the candidate would gradually
rise up a new man, the particular *protégé* of the 'Darding
Knife.'" [1]

Pretence of
death and
resurrec-
tion at
initiation.

In the former of these two initiatory rites of the Carrier
Indians the prominent feature is the transformation of the
man into his totem animal; in the latter it is his death and
resurrection.   But in substance, probably, both are identical.
In both the novice dies as a man and revives as his totem,
whether that be a bear, a "darding" knife, or what not; in
other words, he has deposited his life or some portion of it in
his totem, with which accordingly for the future he is more
or less completely identified.   Hard as it may be for us to
conceive why a man should choose to identify himself with a
knife, whether "darding" or otherwise, we have to remember
that in Celebes it is to a chopping-knife or other iron tool
that the soul of a woman in labour is transferred for safety; [2]
and the difference between a chopping-knife and a "darding"
knife, considered as a receptacle for a human soul, is perhaps not very material.   Among the Thompson Indians of
British Columbia warriors who had a knife, an arrow, or
any other weapon for their personal totem or guardian
spirit, enjoyed this signal advantage over their fellows that
they were for all practical purposes invulnerable.   If an
arrow did hit them, which seldom happened, they vomited

Signifi-
cance of
these
initiatory
rites.

Supposed
invulner-
ability of
men who
have
weapons
for their
guardian
spirits.

[1] A. G. Morice, "Notes, archaeological, industrial, and sociological, on
the Western Dénés," *Transactions of
the Canadian Institute,* iv. (1892–93)
pp. 203-206.   The honorific totems
of the Carrier Indians may perhaps
correspond in some measure to the
sub-totems or multiplex totems of the
Australians.   As to these latter see
Totemism and Exogamy, i. 78 *sqq.,*
133 *sqq.*
[2] See above, pp. 153 *sq.*

the blood up, and the hurt soon healed. Hence these arrow-proof warriors rarely wore armour, which would indeed have been superfluous, and they generally took the most dangerous posts in battle. So convinced were the Thompson Indians of the power of their personal totem or guardian spirit to bring them back to life, that some of them killed themselves in the sure hope that the spirit would immediately raise them up from the dead. Others, more prudently, experimented on their friends, shooting them dead and then awaiting more or less cheerfully their joyful resurrection. We are not told that success crowned these experimental demonstrations of the immortality of the soul.[1]

Initiatory rite of the Toukaway Indians.

The Toukaway Indians of Texas, one of whose totems is the wolf, have a ceremony in which men, dressed in wolf-skins, run about on all fours, howling and mimicking wolves. At last they scratch up a living tribesman, who has been buried on purpose, and putting a bow and arrows in his hands, bid him do as the wolves do—rob, kill, and murder.[2] The ceremony probably forms part of an initiatory rite like the resurrection from the grave of the old man in the Australian rites.

Traces of the rite of death and resurrection among more advanced peoples.

The simulation of death and resurrection or of a new birth at initiation appears to have lingered on, or at least to have left traces of itself, among peoples who have advanced far beyond the stage of savagery. Thus, after his investiture with the sacred thread—the symbol of his order—a Brahman is called "twice born." Manu says, "According to the injunction of the revealed texts the first birth of an

---

[1] James Teit, *The Thompson Indians of British Columbia*, p. 357 (*The Jesup North Pacific Expedition, Memoir of the American Museum· of Natural History*, April, 1900). Among the Shuswap of British Columbia, when a young man has obtained his personal totem or guardian spirit, he is supposed to become proof against bullets and arrows (Fr. Boas, in *Sixth Report of the Committee on the North-Western Tribes of Canada*, p. 93, separate reprint from the *Report of the British Association*, Leeds meeting, 1890).

[2] H. R. Schoolcraft, *Indian Tribes of the United States* (Philadelphia, 1853–1856), v. 683. In a letter dated 16th Dec. 1887, Mr. A. S. Gatschet, formerly of the Bureau of Ethnology, Washington, wrote to me : "Among the Toukawe whom in 1884 I found at Fort Griffin [?], Texas, I noticed that they never kill the big or grey wolf, *hatchukunän*, which has a mythological signification, 'holding the earth' (*hatch*). He forms one of their totem clans, and they have had a dance in his honor, danced by the males only, who carried sticks."

Aryan is from his natural mother, the second happens on the tying of the girdle of Muṅga grass, and the third on the initiation to the performance to a *S*rauta sacrifice."[1]   A pretence of killing the candidate perhaps formed part of the initiation to the Mithraic mysteries.[2]

Thus, on the theory here suggested, wherever totemism is found, and wherever a pretence is made of killing and bringing to life again the novice at initiation, there may exist or have existed not only a belief in the possibility of permanently depositing the soul in some external object—animal, plant, or what not—but an actual intention of so doing.   If the question is put, why do men desire to deposit their life outside their bodies? the answer can only be that, like the giant in the fairy tale, they think it safer to do so than to carry it about with them, just as people deposit their money with a banker rather than carry it on their persons.   We have seen that at critical periods the life or soul is sometimes temporarily stowed away in a safe place till the danger is past.   But institutions like totemism are not resorted to merely on special occasions of danger ; they are systems into which every one, or at least every male, is obliged to be initiated at a certain period of life.   Now the period of life at which initiation takes place is regularly puberty ; and this fact suggests that the special danger which totemism and systems like it are intended to obviate is supposed not to arise till sexual maturity has been attained, in fact, that the danger apprehended is believed to attend the relation of the sexes to each other.   It would be easy to prove by a long array of facts that the sexual relation is associated in the primitive mind with many serious perils ; but the exact nature of the danger apprehended is still

The motive for attempting to deposit the soul in a safe place outside of the body at puberty may have been a fear of the dangers which, according to primitive notions, attend the union of the sexes.

---

[1] *The Laws of Manu*, ii.   169, translated by G. Bühler (Oxford, 1886), p. 61 (*The Sacred Books of the East*, vol. xxv.) ; J. A. Dubois, *Mœurs, Institutions et Cérémonies des Peuples de l'Inde* (Paris, 1825), i.   125 ; Monier Williams, *Religious Thought and Life in India* (London, 1883), pp. 360 *sq.*, 396 *sq.* ; H. Oldenberg, *Die Religion des Veda* (Berlin, 1894), pp. 466 *sqq.*

[2] Lampridius, *Commodus*, 9 ; C. W. King, *The Gnostics and their Remains*, Second Edition (London, 1887), pp. 127, 129.   Compare Fr. Cumont, *Textes et Monuments figurés relatifs aux mystères de Mithra*, i. (Brusseis, 1899) pp. 69 *sq.*, 321 *sq.* ; E. Rohde, *Psyche* [3] (Tübingen and Leipsic, 1903), ii. 400 *n.*[1] ; A. Dieterich, *Eine Mithrasliturgie* (Leipsic, 1903), pp. 91, 157 *sqq.*

obscure. We may hope that a more exact acquaintance with savage modes of thought will in time disclose this central mystery of primitive society, and will thereby furnish the clue, not only to totemism, but to the origin of the marriage system.

CHAPTER XII

THE GOLDEN BOUGH

THUS the view that Balder's life was in the mistletoe is Balder's entirely in harmony with primitive modes of thought. It life or death in the may indeed sound like a contradiction that, if his life was in mistletoe. the mistletoe, he should nevertheless have been killed by a blow from the plant. But when a person's life is conceived as embodied in a particular object, with the existence of which his own existence is inseparably bound up, and the destruction of which involves his own, the object in question may be regarded and spoken of indifferently as his life or his death, as happens in the fairy tales. Hence if a man's death is in an object, it is perfectly natural that he should be killed by a blow from it. In the fairy tales Koshchei the Deathless is killed by a blow from the egg or the stone in which his life or death is secreted;[1] the ogres burst when a certain grain of sand—doubtless containing their life or death—is carried over their heads;[2] the magician dies when the stone in which his life or death is contained is put under his pillow;[3] and the Tartar hero is warned that he may be killed by the golden arrow or golden sword in which his soul has been stowed away.[4]

[1] Above, p. 110; compare pp. 107, 120 sq., 132, 133.

[2] Above, p. 120.

[3] Above, p. 106.

[4] Above, p. 145. In the myth the throwing of the weapons and of the mistletoe at Balder and the blindness of Hother who slew him remind us of the custom of the Irish reapers who kill the corn-spirit in the last sheaf by throwing their sickles blindfold at it.

See *Spirits of the Corn and of the Wild*, i. 144. In Mecklenburg a cock is sometimes buried in the ground and a man who is blindfolded strikes at it with a flail. If he misses it, another tries, and so on till the cock is killed. See K. Bartsch, *Sagen, Märchen und Gebräuche aus Mecklenburg* (Vienna, 1879–1880), ii. 280. In England on Shrove Tuesday a hen used to be tied upon a man's back, and other men blind-

   The idea that the life of the oak was in the mistletoe
was probably suggested, as I have said, by the observation
that in winter the mistletoe growing on the oak remains
green while the oak itself is leafless.   But the position of
the plant—growing not from the ground but from the trunk
or branches of the tree—might confirm this idea.   Primitive
man might think that, like himself, the oak-spirit had sought
to deposit his life in some safe place, and for this purpose
had pitched on the mistletoe, which, being in a sense neither
on earth nor in heaven, might be supposed to be fairly out
of harm's way.   In the first chapter we saw that primitive
man seeks to preserve the life of his human divinities by
keeping them poised between earth and heaven, as the
place where they are least likely to be assailed by the
dangers that encompass the life of man on earth.   We
can therefore understand why it has been a rule both of
ancient and of modern folk-medicine that the mistletoe
should not be allowed to touch the ground ; were it to
touch the ground, its healing virtue would be gone.[1]   This
may be a survival of the old superstition that the plant in
which the life of the sacred tree was concentrated should
not be exposed to the risk incurred by contact with the

earth.   In an Indian legend, which offers a parallel to the
Balder myth, Indra swore to the demon Namuci that he
would slay him neither by day nor by night, neither with
staff nor with bow, neither with the palm of the hand nor
with the fist, neither with the wet nor with the dry.   But
he killed him in the morning twilight by sprinkling over
him the foam of the sea.[2]   The foam of the sea is just such

---

folded struck at it with branches till they
killed it. See T. F. Thiselton Dyer,
British Popular Customs (London,
1876), p. 68.   W. Mannhardt (*Die
Korndämonen*, Berlin, 1868, pp. 16 *sq.*)
has made it probable that such sports are
directly derived from the custom of killing a cock upon the harvest-field as a
representative of the corn-spirit. See
Spirits of the Corn and of the Wild, i.
277 *sq.* These customs, therefore, combined with the blindness of Hother in the
myth, suggest that the man who killed
the human representative of the oak-

spirit was blindfolded, and threw his
weapon or the mistletoe from a little
distance.   After the Lapps had killed
a bear—which was the occasion of
many superstitious ceremonies — the
bear's skin was hung on a post, and
the women, blindfolded, shot arrows at
it.   See J. Scheffer, *Lapponia* (Frankfort, 1673), p. 240.

[1] Pliny, *Nat. Hist.* xxiv. 12 ; J.
Grimm, *Deutsche Mythologie*,[4] ii. 1010.
Compare below, p. 282.

[2] *The Satapatha Brahmana*, xii. 7.
3. 1·3, translated by J. Eggeling,

an object as a savage might choose to put his life in, because it occupies that sort of intermediate or nondescript position between earth and sky or sea and sky in which primitive man sees safety. It is therefore not surprising that the foam of the river should be the totem of a clan in India.[1]

Again, the view that the mistletoe owes its mystic char- *Analogous* acter partly to its not growing on the ground is confirmed by *superstitions* a parallel superstition about the mountain-ash or rowan-tree. *attaching* In Jutland a rowan that is found growing out of the top *to a para-sitic rowan.* of another tree is esteemed " exceedingly effective against witchcraft : since it does not grow on the ground witches have no power over it ; if it is to have its full effect it must be cut on Ascension Day."[2]   Hence it is placed over doors to prevent the ingress of witches.[3]   In Sweden and Norway, also, magical properties are ascribed to a " flying-rowan " (*flögrönn*), that is to a rowan which is found growing not in the ordinary fashion on the ground but on another tree, or on a roof, or in a cleft of the rock, where it has sprouted from seed scattered by birds.   They say that a man who is out in the dark should have a bit of " flying-rowan " with him to chew ; else he runs a risk of being bewitched and of being unable to stir from the spot.[4]   A Norwegian story relates how once on a time a Troll so bewitched some men who were ploughing in a field that they could not drive a straight furrow ; only one of the ploughmen was able to resist the enchantment because by good luck his plough was made out of a " flying-rowan."[5]   In Sweden, too, the " flying-rowan " is used to make the divining rod, which discovers hidden treasures.   This useful art has nowadays unfor-

Part v. (Oxford, 1900) pp. 222 *sq.* (*The Sacred Books of the East*, vol. xliv.) ; Denham Rouse, in *Folk - lore Journal*, vii. (1889) p. 61, quoting *Taittirya Brāhmana*, I. vii. 1.

[1] Col. E. T. Dalton, "The Kols of Chota - Nagpore," *Transactions of the Ethnological Society*, N.S. vi. (1868) p. 36.

[2] Jens Kamp, *Danske Folkeminder* (Odense, 1877), pp. 172, 65 *sq.*, referred to in Feilberg's *Bidrag til en Ordbog over Jyske Almuesmål*, Fjerde hefte (Copenhagen, 1888), p. 320. For a sight of Feilberg's work I am indebted to the kindness of the late Rev. Walter Gregor, M.A., of Pitsligo, who pointed out the passage to me.

[3] E. T. Kristensen, *Jydske Folkeminder*, vi. 380₂₆₂, referred to by Feilberg, *l.c.*   According to Marcellus (*De Medicamentis*, xxvi. 115), ivy which springs from an oak is a remedy for stone, provided it be cut with a copper instrument.

[4] A. Kuhn, *Die Herabkunft des Feuers und des Göttertranks*[2] (Gütersloh, 1886), pp. 175 *sq.*, quoting Dybeck's *Runa*, 1845, pp. 62 *sq.*

[5] A. Kuhn, *op. cit.* p. 176.

tunately been almost forgotten, but three hundred years ago
it was in full bloom, as we gather from the following contemporary account. "If in the woods or elsewhere, on old
walls or on high mountains or rocks you perceive a rowan-
tree (*runn*) which has sprung from a seed that a bird has
dropped from its bill, you must either knock or break off
that rod or tree in the twilight between the third day and
the night after Ladyday. But you must take care that
neither iron nor steel touches it and that in carrying it
home you do not let it fall on the ground. Then place it
under the roof on a spot under which you have laid various
metals, and you will soon be surprised to see how that rod
under the roof gradually bends in the direction of the metals.
When your rod has sat there in the same spot for fourteen
days or more, you take a knife or an awl, which has been
stroked with a magnet, and with it you slit the bark on all
sides, and pour or drop the blood of a cock (best of all the
blood from the comb of a cock which is all of one colour) on
the said slits in the bark ; and when the blood has dried,
the rod is ready and will give public proof of the efficacy of
its marvellous properties."[1] Just as in Scandinavia the
parasitic rowan is deemed a countercharm to sorcery, so in
Germany the parasitic mistletoe is still commonly considered a protection against witchcraft, and in Sweden, as
we saw, the mistletoe which is gathered on Midsummer Eve
is attached to the ceiling of the house, the horse's stall or
the cow's crib, in the belief that this renders the Troll powerless to injure man or beast.[2]

[1] Quoted by A. Kuhn, *op. cit.* pp.
180 *sq.* In Zimbales, a province of the
Philippine Islands, "a certain parasitic
plant that much resembles yellow moss
and grows high up on trees is regarded
as a very powerful charm. It is called
gay-u-ma, and a man who possesses
it is called *nanara gayuma*. If his
eyes rest on a person during the new
moon he will become sick at the
stomach, but he can cure the sickness
by laying hands on the afflicted part."
See W. A. Reed, *Negritos of Zambales*
(Manilla, 1904), p. 67 (*Department of
the Interior, Ethnological Survey Pub-
lications*, vol. ii. part i.). Mr. Reed

seems to mean that if a man who possesses
this parasitic plant sees a person at the
new moon, the person on whom his
eye falls will be sick in his stomach,
but that the owner of the parasite
can cure the sufferer by laying his (the
owner's) hands on his (the patient's)
stomach. It is interesting to observe
that the magical virtue of the parasitic
plant appears to be especially effective
at the new moon.

[2] A. Wuttke, *Der deutsche Volksaberglaube*[2] (Berlin, 1869), p. 97 §
128; L. Lloyd, *Peasant Life in
Sweden* (London, 1870), p. 269. See
above, p. 86.

The view that the mistletoe was not merely the instrument of Balder's death, but that it contained his life, is countenanced by the analogy of a Scottish superstition. Tradition ran that the fate of the Hays of Errol, an estate in Perthshire, near the Firth of Tay, was bound up with the mistletoe that grew on a certain great oak. A member of the Hay family has recorded the old belief as follows : "Among the low country families the badges are now almost generally forgotten ; but it appears by an ancient MS. and the tradition of a few old people in Perthshire, that the badge of the Hays was the mistletoe. There was formerly in the neighbourhood of Errol, and not far from the Falcon stone, a vast oak of an unknown age, and upon which grew a profusion of the plant : many charms and legends were considered to be connected with the tree, and the duration of the family of Hay was said to be united with its existence. It was believed that a sprig of the mistletoe cut by a Hay on Allhallowmas eve, with a new dirk, and after surrounding the tree three times sunwise, and pronouncing a certain spell, was a sure charm against all glamour or witchery, and an infallible guard in the day of battle. A spray gathered in the same manner was placed in the cradle of infants, and thought to defend them from being changed for elf-bairns by the fairies. Finally, it was affirmed, that when the root of the oak had perished, 'the grass should grow in the hearth of Errol, and a raven should sit in the falcon's nest.' The two most unlucky deeds which could be done by one of the name of Hay was, to kill a white falcon, and to cut down a limb from the oak of Errol. When the old tree was destroyed I could never learn. The estate has been some time sold out of the family of Hay, and of course it is said that the fatal oak was cut down a short time before."[1] The old superstition is recorded in verses which are traditionally ascribed to Thomas the Rhymer :—

> " *While the mistletoe bats on Errol's aik,*
> *And that aik stands fast,*
> *The Hays shall flourish, and their good grey hawk*
> *Shall nocht flinch before the blast.*

The fate of the Hays believed to be bound up with the mistletoe on Errol's oak.

---

[1] John Hay Allan, *The Bridal of Caölchairn* (London, 1822), pp. 337 *sq.*

> *" But when the root of the aik decays,*
> *And the mistletoe dwines on its withered breast,*
> *The grass shall grow on Errol's hearthstane,*
> *And the corbie roup in the falcon's nest."* [1]

The idea that the fate of a family, as distinct from the lives of its members, is bound up with a particular plant or tree, is no doubt comparatively modern. The older view may have been that the lives of all the Hays were in this particular mistletoe, just as in the Indian story the lives of all the ogres are in a lemon ; to break a twig of the mistletoe would then have been to kill one of the Hays. Similarly in the island of Rum, whose bold mountains the voyager from Oban to Skye observes to seaward, it was thought that if one of the family of Lachlin shot a deer on the mountain of Finchra, he would die suddenly or contract a distemper which would soon prove fatal.[2] Probably the life of the Lachlins was bound up with the deer on Finchra, as the life of the Hays was bound up with the mistletoe on Errol's oak, and the life of the Dalhousie family with the Edgewell Tree.

It is not a new opinion that the Golden Bough was the mistletoe.[3] True, Virgil does not identify but only compares

The life of the Lachlins and the deer of Finchra.

[1] Rev. John B. Pratt, *Buchan,* Second Edition (Aberdeen, Edinburgh, and London, 1859), p. 342. "*The corbie roup*" means "the raven croak." In former editions of this work my only source of information as to the mistletoe and oak of the Hays was an extract from a newspaper which was kindly copied and sent to me, without the name of the newspaper, by the late Rev. Walter Gregor, M.A., of Pitsligo. For my acquaintance with the works of J. H. Allan and J. B. Pratt I am indebted to the researches of my learned friend Mr. A. B. Cook, who has already quoted them in his article "The European Sky-God," *Folk-lore,* xvii. (1906) pp. 318 *sq.*

[2] M. Martin, "Description of the Western Islands of Scotland," in J. Pinkerton's *Voyages and Travels* (London, 1808–1814), iii. 661.

[3] See James Sowerby, *English Botany,* xxi. (London, 1805), p. 1470: "The Misseltoe is celebrated in story

as the sacred plant of the Druids, and the Golden Bough of Virgil, which was Aeneas's passport to the infernal regions." Again, the author of the *Lexicon Mythologicum* concludes, "*cum Jonghio nostro,*" that the Golden Bough "was nothing but the mistletoe glorified by poetical license." See *Edda Rhythmica seu Antiquior, vulgo Saemundina dicta,* iii. (Copenhagen, 1828) p. 513 note. C. L. Rochholz expresses the same opinion (*Deutscher Glaube und Brauch,* Berlin, 1867, i. 9). The subject is discussed at length by E. Norden, *P. Vergilius Maro, Aeneis Buch VI.* (Leipsic, 1903) pp. 161-171, who, however, does not even mention the general or popular view (*publica opinio*) current in the time of Servius, that the Golden Bough was the branch which a candidate for the priesthood of Diana had to pluck in the sacred grove of Nemi. I confess I have more respect for the general opinion of antiquity than to dismiss it thus cavalierly without a hearing.

it with mistletoe.   But this may be only a poetical device to The Golden Bough seems to have been a glorified mistletoe. cast a mystic glamour over the humble plant.   Or, more probably, his description was based on a popular superstition that at certain times the mistletoe blazed out into a supernatural golden glory.   The poet tells how two doves, guiding Aeneas to the gloomy vale in whose depth grew the Golden Bough, alighted upon a tree, " whence shone a flickering gleam of gold.   As in the woods in winter cold the mistletoe —a plant not native to its tree—is green with fresh leaves and twines its yellow berries about the boles ; such seemed upon the shady holm-oak the leafy gold, so rustled in the gentle breeze the golden leaf." [1]   Here Virgil definitely describes the Golden Bough as growing on a holm-oak, and compares it with the mistletoe.   The inference is almost inevitable that the Golden Bough was nothing but the mistletoe seen through the haze of poetry or of popular superstition.

Now grounds have been shewn for believing that the If the Golden Bough was the mistletoe, the King of the Wood at Nemi may have personated an oak spirit and perished in an oak fire. priest of the Arician grove—the King of the Wood—personified the tree on which grew the Golden Bough.[2]   Hence if that tree was the oak, the King of the Wood must have been a personification of the oak-spirit.   It is, therefore, easy to understand why, before he could be slain, it was necessary to break the Golden Bough.   As an oak-spirit, his life or death was in the mistletoe on the oak, and so long as the mistletoe remained intact, he, like Balder, could not die.   To slay him, therefore, it was necessary to break the mistletoe, and probably, as in the case of Balder, to throw it at him.   And to complete the parallel, it is only necessary to suppose that the King of the Wood was formerly burned, dead or alive, at the midsummer fire festival which, as we have seen, was annually celebrated in the Arician grove.[3] The perpetual fire which burned in the grove, like the per-

---

[1] Virgil, *Aen.* vi. 203 *sqq.*, compare 136 *sqq.* See Note IV. "The Mistletoe and the Golden Bough" at the end of this volume.

[2] *The Magic Art and the Evolution of Kings*, i. 40 *sqq.*, ii. 378 *sqq.* Virgil (*Aen.* vi. 201 *sqq.*) places the Golden Bough in the neighbourhood of Lake Avernus.   But this was probably a poetical liberty, adopted for the convenience of Aeneas's descent to the infernal world.   Italian tradition, as we learn from Servius (on Virgil, *Aen.* vi. 136), placed the Golden Bough in the grove at Nemi.

[3] *The Magic Art and the Evolution of Kings*, i. 12.

petual fire which burned in the temple of Vesta at Rome
and under the oak at Romove,[1] was probably fed with the
sacred oak-wood ; and thus it would be in a great fire of oak
that the King of the Wood formerly met his end.   At a
later time, as I have suggested, his annual tenure of office
was lengthened or shortened, as the case might be, by the
rule which allowed him to live so long as he could prove his
divine right by the strong hand.   But he only escaped the
fire to fall by the sword.

A similar   Thus it seems that at a remote age in the heart of Italy,
tragedy
may have   beside the sweet Lake of Nemi, the same fiery tragedy was
been   annually enacted which Italian merchants and soldiers were
enacted
over the   afterwards to witness among their rude kindred, the Celts of
human   Gaul, and which, if the Roman eagles had ever swooped on
representa-
tive of   Norway, might have been found repeated with little differ-
Balder in   ence among the barbarous Aryans of the North.   The rite
Norway.
was   probably an essential feature in the ancient Aryan
worship of the oak.[2]

The   It only remains to ask, Why was the mistletoe called
name of the
Golden   the Golden Bough ?[3]   The whitish-yellow of the mistletoe
Bough may   berries is hardly enough to account for the name, for
have been
applied   Virgil says that the bough was altogether golden, stem
to the   as well as leaves.[4]   Perhaps the name may be derived
mistletoe
on account   from the rich golden yellow which a bough of mistletoe
of the   assumes when it has been cut and kept for some months ;
golden
tinge which   the bright tint is not confined to the leaves, but spreads
the plant   to the stalks as well, so that the whole branch appears
assumes in
withering.   to be indeed a Golden Bough.   Breton peasants hang up

---

[1] *The Magic Art and the Evolution
of Kings*, ii. 186, 366 note [2].

[2] A custom of annually burning or
otherwise sacrificing a human representative of the corn-spirit has been
noted among the Egyptians, Pawnees,
and Khonds.   See *Spirits of the Corn
and of the Wild*, i. 238 *sq.*, 245 *sqq.*,
259 *sq.*   We have seen that in Western
Asia there are strong traces of a practice
of annually burning a human god.   See
Adonis, Attis, Osiris, Second Edition,
pp. 84 *sqq.*, 98 *sq.*, 137 *sq.*, 139 *sqq.*,
155 *sq.*   The Druids appear to have
eaten portions of the human victim
(Pliny, *Nat. Hist.* xxx. 13).   Perhaps

portions of the flesh of the King of the
Wood were eaten by his worshippers
as a sacrament.   We have found traces
of the use of sacramental bread at
Nemi.   See *Spirits of the Corn and of
the Wild*, ii. 94 *sqq.*

[3] It has been said that in Welsh a
name for mistletoe is "the tree of pure
gold" (*pren puraur*).   See J. Grimm,
Deutsche Mythologie,[4] ii. 1009, referring to Davies.   But my friend Sir
John Rhys tells me that the statement
is devoid of foundation.

[4] Virgil, *Aen.* vi. 137 *sq.*:—

   " *Latet arbore opaca
Aureus et foliis et lento vimine ramus.*"

great bunches of mistletoe in front of their cottages, and in the month of June these bunches are conspicuous for the bright golden tinge of their foliage.[1] In some parts of Brittany, especially about Morbihan, branches of mistletoe are hung over the doors of stables and byres to protect the horses and cattle,[2] probably against witchcraft.

The yellow colour of the withered bough may partly explain why the mistletoe has been sometimes supposed to possess the property of disclosing treasures in the earth;[3] for on the principles of homoeopathic magic there is a natural affinity between a yellow bough and yellow gold. This suggestion is confirmed by the analogy of the marvellous properties popularly ascribed to the mythical fern-seed or fern-bloom. We saw that fern-seed is popularly supposed to bloom like gold or fire on Midsummer Eve.[4] Thus in Bohemia it is said that "on St. John's Day fern-seed blooms with golden blossoms that gleam like fire."[5] Now it is a property of this mythical fern-seed that whoever has it, or will ascend a mountain holding it in his hand on Midsummer Eve, will discover a vein of gold or will see the treasures of the earth shining with a bluish flame.[6] In Russia they say that if you

The yellow hue of withered mistletoe may partly explain why the plant is thought to disclose yellow gold in the earth. Similarly fern-seed is thought to bloom like gold or fire and to reveal buried treasures on Midsummer Eve.

[1] This suggestion as to the origin of the name has been made to me by two correspondents independently. Miss Florence Grove, writing to me from 10 Milton Chambers, Cheyne Walk, London, on May 13th, 1901, tells me that she regularly hangs up a bough of mistletoe every year and allows it to remain till it is replaced by the new branch next year, and from her observation "the mistletoe is actually a golden bough when kept a sufficiently long time." She was kind enough to send me some twigs of her old bough, which fully bore out her description. Again, Mrs. A. Stuart writes to me from Crear Cottage, Morningside Drive, Edinburgh, on June 26th, 1901: "As to why the mistletoe might be called the Golden Bough, my sister Miss Haig wishes me to tell you that last June, when she was in Brittany, she saw great bunches of mistletoe hung up in front of the houses in the villages. The leaves were *bright golden*. You should hang up a branch next Christmas and keep it till June!" The

great hollow oak of Saint-Denis-des-Puits, in the French province of Perche, is called "the gilded or golden oak" (*Chêne-Doré*) "in memory of the Druidical tradition of the mistletoe cut with a golden sickle." See Félix Chapiseau, *Le Folk-lore de la Beauce et du Perche* (Paris, 1902), i. 97. Perhaps the name may be derived from bunches of withered mistletoe shining like gold in the sunshine among the branches.

[2] H. Gaidoz, "Bulletin critique de la Mythologie Gauloise," *Revue de l'Histoire des Religions*, ii. (Paris, 1880) p. 76.

[3] See below, pp. 291 *sq.*

[4] See above, pp. 65 *sq.*

[5] J. V. Grohmann, *Aberglauben und Gebräuche aus Böhmen und Mähren* (Prague and Leipsic, 1864), p. 97, § 673.

[6] J. V. Grohmann, *op. cit.* p. 97, § 676; A. Wuttke, *Der deutsche Volksaberglaube*[2] (Berlin, 1869), p. 94, § 123; I. V. Zingerle, *Sitten, Bräuche und Meinungen des Tiroler Volkes*[2] (Innsbruck, 1871), p. 158, § 1350.

succeed in catching the wondrous bloom of the fern at midnight on Midsummer Eve, you have only to throw it up into the
air, and it will fall like a star on the very spot where a treasure
lies hidden.[1]   In Brittany treasure-seekers gather fern-seed
at midnight on Midsummer Eve, and keep it till Palm
Sunday of the following year ; then they strew the seed on
ground where they think a treasure is concealed.[2]   Tyrolese
peasants imagine that hidden treasures can be seen glowing
like flame on Midsummer Eve, and that fern-seed, gathered
at this mystic season, with the usual precautions, will help to
bring the buried gold to the surface.[3]   In the Swiss canton
of Freiburg people used to watch beside a fern on St. John's
night in the hope of winning a treasure, which the devil
himself sometimes brought to them.[4]   In Bohemia they say
that he who procures the golden bloom of the fern at this
season has thereby the key to all hidden treasures ; and that
if maidens will spread a cloth under the fast-fading bloom,
red gold will drop into it.[5]   And in the Tyrol and Bohemia
if you place fern-seed among money, the money will never
decrease, however much of it you spend.[6]   Sometimes the

[1] C. Russwurm, "Aberglaube in
Russland," *Zeitschrift für deutsche
Mythologie und Sittenkunde*, iv. (1859),
pp. 152 *sq.*; Angelo de Gubernatis,
Mythologie des Plantes (Paris, 1878–
1882), ii. 146.

[2] P. Sébillot, *Traditions et Superstitions de la Haute-Bretagne* (Paris,
1882), ii. 336; *id.*, *Coutumes populaires
de la Haute-Bretagne* (Paris, 1886), p.
217.

[3] J. E. Waldfreund, "Volksge-
bräuche und Aberglauben in Tirol und
dem Salzburger Gebirg," *Zeitschrift für
deutsche Mythologie und Sittenkunde*,
iii. (1855), p. 339.

[4] H. Runge, "Volksglaube in der
Schweiz," *Zeitschrift für deutsche
Mythologie und Sittenkunde*, iv. (1859),
p. 175.

[5] O. Frh. von Reinsberg-Düringsfeld, *Fest-Kalendar aus Böhmen* (Prague,
N.D.), pp. 311 *sq.*   Compare Theodor
Vernaleken, *Mythen und Bräuche des
Volkes in Oesterreich* (Vienna, 1859),
pp. 309 *sq.* ; M. Töppen, *Aberglauben
aus Masuren*[2] (Danzig, 1867), pp. 72
sq.   Even without the use of fern-seed

treasures are sometimes said to bloom
or burn in the earth, or to reveal their
presence by a bluish flame, on Midsummer Eve ; in Transylvania only
children born on a Sunday can see
them and fetch them up.   See J. Haltrich, *Zur Volkskunde der Siebenbürger
Sachsen* (Vienna, 1885), p. 287 ; I. V.
Zingerle, *Sitten, Bräuche und Meinungen des Tiroler Volkes*[2] (Innsbruck,
1871), p. 159, §§ 1351, 1352 ; K.
Bartsch, *Sagen, Märchen und Gebräuche
aus Mecklenburg* (Vienna, 1879–1880),
ii. 285, § 1431 ; E. Monseur, *Folklore
Wallon* (Brussels, N.D.), p. 6, § 1789 ;
K. Haupt, *Sagenbuch der Lausitz*
(Leipsic, 1862–1863), i. 231 *sq.*, No.
275 ; A. Wuttke, *Der deutsche Volksaberglaube*[2] (Berlin, 1869), p. 76, § 92 ;
F. J. Wiedemann, *Aus dem inneren
und äusseren Leben der Ehsten* (St.
Petersburg, 1876), p. 363.

[6] I. V. Zingerle, *op. cit.* p. 103, §
882 ; *id.*, in *Zeitschrift für deutsche
Mythologie und Sittenkunde*, i. (1853),
p. 330 ; W. Müller, *Beiträge zur Volkskunde der Deutschen in Mähren* (Vienna
and Olmütz, 1893), p. 265.   At Per-

fern-seed is supposed to bloom on Christmas night, and
whoever catches it will become very rich.[1]   In Styria they
say that by gathering fern-seed on Christmas night you can
force the devil to bring you a bag of money.[2]   In Swabia
likewise you can, by taking the proper precautions, compel
Satan himself to fetch you a packet of fern-seed on Christmas
night.   But for four weeks previously, and during the whole
of the Advent season, you must be very careful never to
pray, never to go to church, and never to use holy water ;
you must busy yourself all day long with devilish thoughts,
and cherish an ardent wish that the devil would help you to
get money.   Thus prepared you take your stand, between
eleven and twelve on Christmas night, at the meeting of two
roads, over both of which corpses have been carried to the
churchyard.   Here many people meet you, some of them
dead and buried long ago, it may be your parents or grand-
parents, or old friends and acquaintances, and they stop and
greet you, and ask, " What are you doing here ? "   And tiny
little goblins hop and dance about and try to make you laugh.
But if you smile or utter a single word, the devil will tear you
to shreds and tatters on the spot.   If, however, you stand
glum and silent and solemn, there will come, after all the
ghostly train has passed by, a man dressed as a hunter, and
that is the devil.   He will hand you a paper cornet full of
fern-seed, which you must keep and carry about with you as
long as you live.   It will give you the power of doing as
much work at your trade in a day as twenty or thirty ordinary
men could do in the same time.   So you will grow very
rich.   But few people have the courage to go through with
the ordeal.   The people of Rotenburg tell of a weaver of
their town, who lived some two hundred and fifty years
ago and performed prodigies of weaving by a simple application of fern-seed which he had been so fortunate as to obtain,
no doubt from the devil, though that is not expressly alleged

Sometimes fern-seed is thought to bloom on Christmas night.

The wicked weaver of Rotenburg.

---

gine, in the Tyrol, it was thought that
fern-seed gathered with the dew on St.
John's night had the power of transforming metals (into gold ?). See Ch.
Schneller, *Märchen und Sagen aus
Wälschtirol* (Innsbruck, 1867), p. 237,
§ 23.

[1] I. V. Zingerle, *Sitten, Bräuche
und Meinungen des Tiroler Volkes,*[2] pp.
190 *sq.,* § 1573.
[2] A. Schlossar, " Volksmeinung und
Volksaberglaube aus der deutschen
Steiermark," *Germania,* N.R., xxiv.
(1891) p. 387.

by tradition. Rich in the possession of this treasure, the lazy rascal worked only on Saturdays and spent all the rest of the week playing and drinking; yet in one day he wove far more cloth than any other skilled weaver who sat at his loom from morning to night every day of the week. Naturally he kept his own counsel, and nobody might ever have known how he did it, if it had not been for what, humanly speaking, you might call an accident, though for my part I cannot but regard it as the manifest finger of Providence. One day—it was the octave of a festival—the fellow had woven a web no less than a hundred ells long, and his mistress resolved to deliver it to her customer the same evening. So she put the cloth in a basket and away she trudged with it. Her way led her past a church, and as she passed the sacred edifice, she heard the tinkle of the holy bell which announced the elevation of the Host. Being a good woman she put her basket down, knelt beside it, and there, with the shadows gathering round her, committed herself to the care of God and his good angels and received, along with the kneeling congregation in the lighted church, the evening benediction, which kept her and them from all the perils and dangers of the night. Then rising refreshed she took up her basket. But what was her astonishment on looking into it to find the whole web reduced to a heap of yarn! The blessed words of the priest at the altar had undone the cursed spell of the Enemy of Mankind.[1]

The golden or fiery fern-seed appears to be an emanation of the sun's fire.   Thus, on the principle of like by like, fern-seed is supposed to discover gold because it is itself golden; and for a similar reason it enriches its possessor with an unfailing supply of gold. But while the fern-seed is described as golden, it is equally described as glowing and fiery.[2] Hence, when we consider that two great days for gathering the fabulous seed are Midsummer Eve and Christmas—that is, the two solstices (for Christmas is nothing but an old heathen celebration of the winter solstice)—we are led to

---

[1] Ernst Meier, *Deutsche Sagen, Sitten und Gebräuche aus Schwaben* (Stuttgart, 1852), pp. 242-244.

[2] J. V. Grohmann, *Aberglauben und Gebräuche aus Böhmen und Mähren*, p. 97, § 675; W. R. S. Ralston, *Songs of the Russian People*, Second Edition (London, 1872), p. 98; C. Russwurm, "Aberglaube in Russland," *Zeitschrift für deutsche Mythologie und Sittenkunde*, iv. (1859) p. 152.

regard the fiery aspect of the fern-seed as primary, and its golden aspect as secondary and derivative. Fern-seed, in fact, would seem to be an emanation of the sun's fire at the two turning-points of its course, the summer and winter solstices. This view is confirmed by a German story in which a hunter is said to have procured fern-seed by shooting at the sun on Midsummer Day at noon ; three drops of blood fell down, which he caught in a white cloth, and these blood-drops were the fern-seed.[1] Here the blood is clearly the blood of the sun, from which the fern-seed is thus directly derived. Thus it may be taken as probable that fern-seed is golden, because it is believed to be an emanation of the sun's golden fire.

Now, like fern-seed, the mistletoe is gathered either at Midsummer or Christmas[2]—that is, at the summer and winter solstices — and, like fern-seed, it is supposed to possess the power of revealing treasures in the earth. On Midsummer Eve people in Sweden make divining-rods of mistletoe, or of four different kinds of wood one of which must be mistletoe. The treasure-seeker places the rod on the ground after sun-down, and when it rests directly over treasure, the rod begins to move as if it were alive.[3] Now,

Like fern-seed the mistletoe is gathered at the solstices (Midsummer and Christmas) and is supposed to reveal treasures in the earth ;

---

[1] L. Bechstein, *Deutsches Sagenbuch* (Leipsic, 1853), p. 430, No. 500 ; *id.*, *Thüringer Sagenbuch* (Leipsic, 1885), ii. pp. 17 *sq.*, No. 161.

[2] For gathering it at midsummer, see above, pp. 86 *sq.* The custom of gathering it at Christmas still commonly survives in England. At York " on the eve of Christmas-day they carry mistletoe to the high altar of the cathedral, and proclaim a public and universal liberty, pardon and freedom to all sorts of inferior and even wicked people at the gates of the city, toward the four quarters of heaven." See W. Stukeley, *The Medallic History of Marcus Aurelius Valerius Carausius, Emperor in Britain* (London, 1757–1759), ii. 164 ; J. Brand, *Popular Antiquities of Great Britain* (London, 1882–1883), i. 525. This last custom, which is now doubtless obsolete, may have been a relic of an annual period of license like the Saturnalia. The traditional privilege accorded to men of kissing any woman found under

mistletoe is probably another relic of the same sort. See Washington Irving, *Sketch-Book*, " Christmas Eve," p. 147 (Bohn's edition) ; Marie Trevelyan, *Folk-lore and Folk-stories of Wales* (London, 1909), p. 88.

[3] A. A. Afzelius, *Volkssagen und Volkslieder aus Schwedens älterer und neuerer Zeit* (Leipsic, 1842), i. 41 *sq.*; J. Grimm, *Deutsche Mythologie*,[4] iii. 289 ; L. Lloyd, *Peasant Life in Sweden* (London, 1870), pp. 266 *sq.* See above, p. 69. In the Tyrol they say that if mistletoe grows on a hazel-tree, there must be a treasure under the tree. See J. N. Ritter von Alpenburg, *Mythen und Sagen Tirols* (Zurich, 1857), p. 398. In East Prussia a similar belief is held in regard to mistletoe that grows on a thorn. See C. Lemke, *Volksthümliches in Ostpreussen* (Mohrungen, 1884–1887), ii. 283. We have seen that the divining-rod which reveals treasures is commonly cut from a hazel (above, pp. 67 *sq.*).

perhaps,
therefore,
it too is
deemed an
emanation
of the sun's
golden fire.
if the mistletoe discovers gold, it must be in its character of the Golden Bough; and if it is gathered at the solstices, must not the Golden Bough, like the golden fern-seed, be an emanation of the sun's fire? The question cannot be answered with a simple affirmative. We have seen that the old Aryans perhaps kindled the solstitial and other ceremonial fires in part as sun-charms, that is, with the intention of supplying the sun with fresh fire; and as these fires were usually made by the friction or combustion of oak-wood,[1] it may have appeared to the ancient Aryan that the sun was periodically recruited from the fire which resided in the sacred oak. In other words, the oak may have seemed to him the original storehouse or reservoir of the fire which was from time to time drawn out to feed the sun. But if the life of the oak was conceived to be in the mistletoe, the mistletoe must on that view have contained the seed or germ of the fire which was elicited by friction from the wood of the oak. Thus, instead of saying that the mistletoe was an emanation of the sun's fire, it might be more correct to say that the sun's fire was regarded as an emanation of the mistletoe. No wonder, then, that the mistletoe shone with a golden splendour, and was called the Golden Bough. Probably, however, like fern-seed, it was thought to assume its golden aspect only at those stated times, especially midsummer, when fire was drawn from the oak to light up the sun.[2] At Pulverbatch, in Shropshire, it was believed within living memory that the oak-tree blooms on Midsummer Eve and the blossom withers before daylight. A maiden who wishes to know her lot in marriage should spread a white cloth under the tree at night, and in the morning she will find a little dust, which is all that remains of the flower. She should place the pinch of dust under her pillow, and then her future husband will appear to her in her dreams.[3] This fleeting bloom of the oak, if I am right, was probably the mistletoe in its character of the Golden Bough. The conjecture is confirmed by the obser-

---

[1] Above, pp. 90-92.

[2] Fern-seed is supposed to bloom at Easter as well as at Midsummer and Christmas (W. R. S. Ralston, *Songs of the Russian People*, pp. 98 *sq.*); and Easter, as we have seen, is one of the times when fires are ceremonially kindled, perhaps to recruit the fire of the sun.

[3] Miss C. S. Burne and Miss G. F. Jackson, *Shropshire Folk-lore* (London, 1883), p. 242.

vation that in Wales a real sprig of mistletoe gathered on Midsummer Eve is similarly placed under the pillow to induce prophetic dreams ;[1] and further the mode of catching the imaginary bloom of the oak in a white cloth is exactly that which was employed by the Druids to catch the real mistletoe when it dropped from the bough of the oak, severed by the golden sickle.[2] As Shropshire borders on Wales, the belief that the oak blooms on Midsummer Eve may be Welsh in its immediate origin, though probably the belief is a fragment of the primitive Aryan creed.   In some parts of Italy, as we saw,[3] peasants still go out on Midsummer morning to search the oak-trees for the "oil of St. John," which, like the mistletoe, heals all wounds, and is, perhaps, the mistletoe itself in its glorified aspect. Thus it is easy to understand how a title like the Golden Bough, so little descriptive of its usual appearance on the tree, should have been applied to the seemingly insignificant parasite. Further, we can perhaps see why in antiquity mistletoe was believed to possess the remarkable property of extinguishing fire,[4] and why in Sweden it is still kept in houses as a safeguard against conflagration.[5]   Its fiery nature marks it out, on homoeopathic principles, as the best possible cure or preventive of injury by fire.

These considerations may partially explain why Virgil makes Aeneas carry a glorified bough of mistletoe with him on his descent into the gloomy subterranean world. The poet describes how at the very gates of hell there stretched a vast and gloomy wood, and how the hero, following the flight of two doves that lured him on, wandered into the depths of the immemorial forest till he saw afar off through the shadows of the trees the flickering light of the Golden Bough illuminating the matted boughs overhead.[6] If the mistletoe, as a yellow withered bough in the sad autumn woods, was conceived to contain the seed of fire, what better companion could a forlorn wanderer in the nether shades

Aeneas and the Golden Bough.

---

[1] Marie Trevelyan, *Folk-lore and Folk-stories of Wales* (London, 1909), p. 88.

[2] Pliny, *Nat. Hist.* xvi. 251.

[3] Above, pp. 82 *sq.*

[4] Pliny, *Nat. Hist.* xxxiii. 94 :

"*Calx aqua accenditur et Thracius lapis, idem oleo restinguitur, ignis autem aceto maxime et visco et ovo.*"

[5] See above, p. 85.

[6] Virgil, *Aen.* vi. 179-209.

take with him than a bough that would be a lamp to his feet as well as a rod and staff to his hands? Armed with it he might boldly confront the dreadful spectres that would cross his path on his adventurous journey. Hence when Aeneas, emerging from the forest, comes to the banks of Styx, winding slow with sluggish stream through the infernal marsh, and the surly ferryman refuses him passage in his boat, he has but to draw the Golden Bough from his bosom and hold it up, and straightway the blusterer quails at the sight and meekly receives the hero into his crazy bark, which sinks deep in the water under the unusual weight of the living man.[1] Even in recent times, as we have seen, mistletoe has been deemed a protection against witches and trolls,[2] and the ancients may well have credited it with the same magical virtue. And if the parasite can, as some of our peasants believe, open all locks,[3] why should it not have served as an "open Sesame" in the hands of

Orpheus and the willow.
Aeneas to unlock the gates of death? There is some reason to suppose that when Orpheus in like manner descended alive to hell to rescue the soul of his dead wife Eurydice from the shades, he carried with him a willow bough to serve as a passport on his journey to and from the land of the dead ; for in the great frescoes representing the nether world, with which the master hand of Polygnotus adorned the walls of a loggia at Delphi, Orpheus was depicted sitting pensively under a willow, holding his lyre, now silent and useless, in his left hand, while with his right he grasped the drooping boughs of the tree.[4] If the willow in the picture had indeed the significance which an ingenious scholar has attributed to it,[5] the painter meant to represent the dead musician dreaming wistfully of the time when the willow had carried him safe back across the Stygian ferry to that bright world of love and music which he was now to see no more. Again, on an ancient sarcophagus, which exhibits in sculptured relief the parting of Adonis from Aphrodite, the hapless youth, reclining in the lap of his leman, holds a

[1] Virgil, *Aen.* vi. 384-416.
[2] Above, pp. 86, 282.
[3] Above, p. 85.
[4] Pausanias, x. 30. 6.
[5] J. Six, "Die Eriphyle des Polyg-

not," *Mittheilungen des kaiserlich deutschen Archaeologischen Instituts, Athenische Abtheilung,* xix. (1894) pp. 338 *sq.* Compare my commentary on Pausanias, vol. v. p. 385.

branch, which has been taken to signify that he, too, by the
help of the mystic bough, might yet be brought back from
the gates of death to life and love.[1]

Now, too, we can conjecture why Virbius at Nemi came
to be confounded with the sun.[2] If Virbius was, as I have
tried to shew, a tree-spirit, he must have been the spirit of
the oak on which grew the Golden Bough ; for tradition
represented him as the first of the Kings of the Wood. As
an oak-spirit he must have been supposed periodically to
rekindle the sun's fire, and might therefore easily be confounded with the sun itself. Similarly we can explain why
Balder, an oak-spirit, was described as " so fair of face and
so shining that a light went forth from him,"[3] and why he
should have been so often taken to be the sun. And in
general we may say that in primitive society, when the only
known way of making fire is by the friction of wood, the
savage must necessarily conceive of fire as a property stored
away, like sap or juice, in trees, from which he has labori-
ously to extract it. The Senal Indians of California " profess
to believe that the whole world was once a globe of fire,
whence that element passed up into the trees, and now
comes out whenever two pieces of wood are rubbed
together."[4] Similarly the Maidu Indians of California hold
that " the earth was primarily a globe of molten matter, and
from that the principle of fire ascended through the roots
into the trunk and branches of trees, whence the Indians can
extract it by means of their drill."[5] In Namoluk, one of
the Caroline Islands, they say that the art of making fire
was taught men by the gods. Olofaet, the cunning master
of flames, gave fire to the bird *mwi* and bade him carry it to
earth in his bill. So the bird flew from tree to tree and
stored away the slumbering force of the fire in the wood,
from which men can elicit it by friction.[6] In the ancient

Trees thought by the savage to be the seat of fire because he elicits it by friction from their wood.

---

[1] The sarcophagus is in the Lateran
Museum at Rome. See W. Helbig,
*Führer durch die öffentlichen Samm-
lungen Klassischer Altertümer in Rom* [2]
(Leipsic, 1899), ii. 468.

[2] See *The Magic Art and the Evolution of Kings*, i. 19 *sqq.*

[3] *Die Edda*, übersetzt von K.

Simrock [8] (Stuttgart, 1882), p. 264.

[4] S. Powers, *Tribes of California*
(Washington, 1877), p. 171.

[5] S. Powers, *Tribes of California*,
p. 287.

[6] Max Girschner, "Die Karolinen-
insel Namõluk und ihre Bewohner,"
Baessler-Archiv, ii. (1912) p. 141.

Vedic hymns of India the fire-god Agni "is spoken of as born in wood, as the embryo of plants, or as distributed in plants. He is also said to have entered into all plants or to strive after them. When he is called the embryo of trees or of trees as well as plants, there may be a side-glance at the fire produced in forests by the friction of the boughs of trees." [1]   In some Australian languages the words for wood and fire are said to be the same. [2]

Trees that have been struck by lightning are deemed by the savage to be charged with a double portion of fire.

A tree which has been struck by lightning is naturally regarded by the savage as charged with a double or triple portion of fire; for has he not seen the mighty flash enter into the trunk with his own eyes?   Hence perhaps we may explain some of the many superstitious beliefs concerning trees that have been struck by lightning. Thus in the opinion of the Cherokee Indians " mysterious properties attach to the wood of a tree which has been struck by lightning, especially when the tree itself still lives, and such wood enters largely into the secret compounds of the conjurers. An ordinary person of the laity will not touch it, for fear of having cracks come upon his hands and feet, nor is it burned for fuel, for fear that lye made from the ashes will cause consumption. In preparing ballplayers for the contest, the medicine-man sometimes burns splinters of it to coal, which he gives to the players to paint themselves with, in order that they may be able to strike their opponents with all the force of a thunderbolt. Bark or wood from a tree struck by lightning, but still green, is beaten up and put into the water in which seeds are soaked before planting, to insure a good crop, but, on the other hand, any lightning-struck wood thrown into the field will cause the crop to wither, and it is believed to have a bad effect even to go into the field immediately after having been near such a tree." [3]   Apparently the Cherokees imagine that when wood struck by lightning is soaked in

[1] A. A. Macdonell, *Vedic Mythology* (Strasburg, 1897), pp. 91 *sq.*, referring to *Rigveda*, vi. 3. 3, x. 79. 7, ii. 1. 14, iii. 1. 13, x. 1. 2, viii. 43. 9, i. 70. 4, ii. 1. 1.   Compare H. Oldenberg, *Die Religion des Veda* (Berlin, 1894), pp. 120 *sq.*

[2] Edward M. Curr, *The Australian Race* (Melbourne and London, 1886–1887), i. 9, 18.

[3] James Mooney, "Myths of the Cherokee," *Nineteenth Annual Report of the Bureau of American Ethnology*, Part i. (Washington, 1900) p. 422, compare p. 435.

water the fierce heat of the slumbering fire in its veins is tempered to a genial warmth, which promotes the growth of the crops ; but that when the force of the fire has not been thus diluted it blasts the growing corn.   When the Thompson Indians of British Columbia wished to set fire to the houses of their enemies, they shot at them arrows which were either made from a tree that had been struck by lightning or had splinters of such wood attached to them.[1] They seem to have thought that wood struck by lightning was so charged with fire that it would ignite whatever it struck, the mere concussion sufficing to explode it like gunpowder. Yet curiously enough these Indians supposed that if they burned the wood of trees that had been struck by lightning, the weather would immediately turn cold.[2]   Perhaps they conceived such trees as reservoirs of heat, and imagined that by using them up they would exhaust the supply and thus lower the temperature of the atmosphere.[3] Wendish peasants of Saxony similarly refuse to burn in their stoves the wood of trees that have been struck by lightning ; but the reason they give for their refusal is different.   They say that with such fuel the house would be burnt down.[4]   No doubt they think that the electric flash, inherent in the wood, would send such a roaring flame up the chimney that nothing could stand before it.   In like manner the Thonga of South Africa will not use such wood as fuel nor warm themselves at a fire which has been kindled with it ; but what danger they apprehend from the wood we are not told.[5] On the contrary, when lightning sets fire to a tree, the Winamwanga of Northern Rhodesia put out all the fires in the village and plaster the fireplaces afresh, while the head men convey the lightning-kindled fire to the chief, who prays over it.   The chief then sends out

[1] James Teit, *The Thompson Indians of British Columbia*, p. 346 (*The Jesup North Pacific Expedition, Memoir of the American Museum of Natural History*, April, 1900).

[2] J. Teit, *op. cit.* p. 374.

[3] The Shuswap Indians of British Columbia entertain a similar belief. It has been suggested that the fancy may be based on the observation that cold follows a thunder-storm. See G. M. Dawson, "Notes on the Shuswap

people of British Columbia," *Transactions of the Royal Society of Canada*, ix. (1891) Section ii. p. 38.

[4] R. Wuttke, *Sächsische Volkskunde* [2] (Dresden, 1901), p. 369.

[5] Henri A. Junod, *The Life of a South African Tribe* (Neuchatel, 1912–1913), ii. 291.   The Thonga imagine that lightning is caused by a great bird, which sometimes buries itself in the ground to a depth of several feet. See H. A. Junod, *op. cit.* ii. 290 *sq.*

the new fire to all his villages, and the villagers reward his messengers for the boon.   This shews that they look upon fire kindled by lightning with reverence, and the reverence is intelligible, for they speak of thunder and lightning as God himself coming down to earth.[1]   Similarly the Maidu Indians of California believe that a Great Man created the world and all its inhabitants, and that lightning is nothing but the Great Man himself descending swiftly out of heaven and rending the trees with his flaming arm.[2]

Theory that the sanctity of the oak and the relation of the tree to the sky-god were suggested by the frequency with which oaks are struck by lightning.

It is a plausible theory that the reverence which the ancient peoples of Europe paid to the oak, and the connexion which they traced between the tree and their sky-god,[3] were derived from the much greater frequency with which the oak appears to be struck by lightning than any other tree of our European forests.   Some remarkable statistics have been adduced in support of this view by Mr. W. Warde Fowler.[4]   Observations, annually made in the forests of Lippe-Detmold for seventeen years, yielded the result that while the woods were mainly stocked with beech and only to a small extent with oak and Scotch pine, yet far more oaks and Scotch pines were struck by lightning than beeches, the number of stricken Scotch pines exceeding the number of stricken beeches in the proportion of thirty-seven to one, and the number of stricken oaks exceeding the number of stricken beeches in the proportion

[1] Dr. James A. Chisholm (of the Livingstonia Mission, Mwenzo, N.E. Rhodesia), "Notes on the Manners and Customs of the Winamwanga and Wiwa," *Journal of the African Society*, No. 36 (July, 1910), p. 363.

[2] S. Powers, *Tribes of California* (Washington, 1877), p. 287.   The dread of lightning is prominent in some of the customs observed in Patiko, a district of the Uganda Protectorate. If a village has suffered from lightning, ropes made of twisted grass are strung from peak to peak of the houses to ward off further strokes.   And if a person has been struck or badly shaken, "an elaborate cure is performed upon him. A red cock is taken, his tongue torn out, and his body dashed upon the house where the stroke fell.   Then the scene changes to the bank of a small running stream, where the patient is made to kneel while the bird is sacrificed over the water.   A raw egg is next given to the patient to swallow, and he is laid on his stomach and encouraged to vomit.   The lightning is supposed to be vomited along with the egg, and all ill effects prevented." See Rev. A. L. Kitching, *On the Backwaters of the Nile* (London, 1912), p. 263.

[3] See *The Magic Art and the Evolution of Kings*, ii. 349 *sqq.*

[4] W. Warde Fowler, "The Oak and the Thunder-god," *Archiv für Religionswissenschaft*, xvi. (1913) pp. 318 *sq.*   My friend Mr. Warde Fowler had previously called my attention to the facts in a letter dated September 17th, 1912.

of no less than sixty to one.   Similar results have been obtained from observations made in French and Bavarian forests.[1]   In short, it would seem from statistics compiled by scientific observers, who have no mythological theories to maintain, that the oak suffers from the stroke of lightning far oftener than any other forest tree in Europe.   However we may explain it, whether by the easier passage of electricity through oakwood than through any other timber,[2] or in some other way, the fact itself may well have attracted the notice of our rude forefathers, who dwelt in the vast forests which then covered a large part of Europe ; and they might naturally account for it in their simple religious way by supposing that the great sky-god, whom they worshipped and whose awful voice they heard in the roll of thunder, loved the oak above all the trees of the wood and often descended into it from the murky cloud in a flash of lightning, leaving a token of his presence or of his passage in the riven and blackened trunk and the blasted foliage.   Such trees would thenceforth be encircled by a nimbus of glory as the visible seats of the thundering sky-god.   Certain it is that, like some savages, both Greeks and Romans identified their great god of the sky and of the oak with the lightning flash which struck the ground ; and they regularly enclosed such a stricken spot and treated it thereafter as sacred.[3]   It

[1] Dr. W. Schlich's *Manual of Forestry*, vol. iv. *Forest Protection*, by W. R. Fisher, Second Edition (London, 1907), pp. 662 *sq.*   Mr. W. Warde Fowler was the first to call the attention of mythologists to this work.

[2] Experiments on the conductivity of electricity in wood go to shew that starchy trees (oak, poplar, maples, ash, elm, *sorbus*) are good conductors, that oily trees (beech, walnut, birch, lime) are bad conductors, and that the conifers are intermediate, the Scotch pine in summer being as deficient in oil as the starchy trees, but rich in oil during winter.   It was found that a single turn of Holz's electric machine sufficed to send the spark through oakwood, but that from twelve to twenty turns were required to send it through beech-wood.   Five turns of the machine were needed to send the spark through

poplar and willow wood.   See Dr. W. Schlich, *Manual of Forestry*, vol. iv. *Forest Protection*, Second Edition (London, 1907), p. 664.   In the tropics lightning is said to be especially attracted to coco-nut palms.   See P. Amaury Talbot, *In the Shadow of the Bush* (London, 1913), p. 73.

[3] As to the Greek belief and custom, see H. Usener, *Kleine Schriften*, iv. (Leipsic and Berlin, 1913), " Keraunos," pp. 471 *sqq.* ; *The Magic Art and the Evolution of Kings*, ii. 361.   As to the Roman belief and custom, see Festus, *svv. Fulguritum* and *Provorsum fulgur*, pp. 92, 229, ed. C. O. Müller (Leipsic, 1839) ; H. Dessau, *Inscriptiones Latinae Selectae*, vol. ii. pars i. (Berlin, 1902) pp. 10 *sq.*, Nos. 3048-3056 ; L. Preller, *Römische Mythologie*[3] (Berlin, 1881–1883), i. 190-193 ; G. Wissowa, *Religion und*

is not rash to suppose that the ancestors of the Celts and Germans in the forests of Central Europe paid a like respect for like reasons to a blasted oak.

The margin note: "This explanation of the Aryan worship of the oak is preferable to the one formerly adopted by the author."

This explanation of the Aryan reverence for the oak and of the association of the tree with the great god of the thunder and the sky, was suggested or implied long ago by Jacob Grimm,[1] and has been of late powerfully reinforced by Mr. W. Warde Fowler.[2] It appears to be simpler and more probable than the explanation which I formerly adopted, namely, that the oak was worshipped primarily for the many benefits which our rude forefathers derived from the tree, particularly for the fire which they drew by friction from its wood; and that the connexion of the oak with the sky was an after-thought based on the belief that the flash of lightning was nothing but the spark which the sky-god up aloft elicited by rubbing two pieces of oak wood against each other, just as his savage worshipper kindled fire in the forest on earth.[3] On that theory the god of the thunder and the sky was derived from the original god of the oak; on the present theory, which I now prefer, the god of the sky and the thunder was the great original deity of our Aryan ancestors, and his association with the oak was merely an inference based on the frequency with which the oak was seen to be struck by lightning. If the Aryans, as some think, roamed the wide steppes of Russia or Central Asia with their flocks and herds before they plunged into the gloom of the European forests, they may have worshipped the god of the blue or cloudy firmament and the flashing thunderbolt long before they thought of associating him with the blasted oaks in their new home.[4]

Kultus der Römer[2] (Munich, 1912), pp. 121 *sq.* By a curious refinement the Romans referred lightning which fell by day to Jupiter, but lightning which fell by night to a god called Summanus (Festus, p. 229).

[1] J. Grimm, *Deutsche Mythologie*,[4] iii. 64, citing a statement that lightning strikes twenty oaks for one beech. The statistics adduced by Mr. W. Warde Fowler seem to shew that this

statement is no exaggeration but rather the contrary.

[2] W. Warde Fowler, "The Oak and the Thunder-god," *Archiv für Religionswissenschaft*, xvi. (1913) pp. 317-320.

[3] *The Magic Art and the Evolution of Kings*, ii. 356 *sqq.*

[4] The suggestion is Mr. W. Warde Fowler's (*op cit.* pp. 319 *sq.*).

Perhaps the new theory has the further advantage of throwing light on the special sanctity ascribed to mistletoe which grows on an oak.   The mere rarity of such a growth on an oak hardly suffices to explain the extent and the persistence of the superstition.   A hint of its real origin is possibly furnished by the statement of Pliny that the Druids worshipped the plant because they believed it to have fallen from heaven and to be a token that the tree on which it grew was chosen by the god himself.[1]   Can they have thought that the mistletoe dropped on the oak in a flash of lightning? The conjecture is confirmed by the name thunder-besom which is applied to mistletoe in the Swiss canton of Aargau,[2] for the epithet clearly implies a close connexion between the parasite and the thunder; indeed "thunder-besom" is a popular name in Germany for any bushy nest-like excrescence growing on a branch, because such a parasitic growth is actually believed by the ignorant to be a product of lightning.[3] If there is any truth in this conjecture, the real reason why the Druids worshipped a mistletoe-bearing oak above all other trees of the forest was a belief that every such oak had not only been struck by lightning but bore among its branches a visible emanation of the celestial fire ; so that in cutting the mistletoe with mystic rites they were securing for themselves all the magical properties of a thunderbolt.   If that was so, we must apparently conclude that the mistletoe was deemed an emanation of the lightning rather than, as I have thus far argued, of the midsummer sun.   Perhaps, indeed, we might combine the two seemingly divergent views by supposing that in the old Aryan creed the mistletoe descended from the sun on Midsummer Day in a flash of lightning.   But such a combination is artificial and unsupported, so far as I know, by any positive evidence.   Whether on mythical principles the two interpretations can really be reconciled with each other or not, I will not presume to say ; but even should they prove to be discrepant, the inconsistency need not have prevented our rude forefathers from embracing both of them at the same time with an equal fervour of conviction ; for like the great majority of mankind the savage is above being

---

[1] Pliny, *Natur. Hist.* xvi. 249
[2] See above, p. 85.

[3] J. Grimm, *Deutsche Mythologie,*[4] i. 153.   See above, p. 85.

hidebound by the trammels of a pedantic logic. In attempting to track his devious thought through the jungle of crass ignorance and blind fear, we must always remember that we are treading enchanted ground, and must beware of taking for solid realities the cloudy shapes that cross our path or hover and gibber at us through the gloom. We can never completely replace ourselves at the standpoint of primitive man, see things with his eyes, and feel our hearts beat with the emotions that stirred his. All our theories concerning him and his ways must therefore fall far short of certainty ; the utmost we can aspire to in such matters is a reasonable degree of probability.

Hence the stroke of mistletoe that killed Balder may have been a stroke of lightning.

To conclude these enquiries we may say that if Balder was indeed, as I have conjectured, a personification of a mistletoe-bearing oak, his death by a blow of the mistletoe might on the new theory be explained as a death by a stroke of lightning. So long as the mistletoe, in which the flame of the lightning smouldered, was suffered to remain among the boughs, so long no harm could befall the good and kindly god of the oak, who kept his life stowed away for safety between earth and heaven in the mysterious parasite ; but when once that seat of his life, or of his death, was torn from the branch and hurled at the trunk, the tree fell—the god died—smitten by a thunderbolt.[1]

The King of the Wood and the Golden Bough.

And what we have said of Balder in the oak forests of Scandinavia may perhaps, with all due diffidence in a question so obscure and uncertain, be applied to the priest of Diana, the King of the Wood, at Aricia in the oak forests of Italy. He may have personated in flesh and blood the great Italian god of the sky, Jupiter,[2] who had kindly come down from heaven in the lightning flash to dwell among men in the mistletoe—the thunder-besom—the Golden Bough—growing

---

[1] This interpretation of Balder's death was anticipated by W. Schwartz (*Der Ursprung der Mythologie*, Berlin, 1860, p. 176), who cut the whole knot by dubbing Balder "the German thunder-and-lightning god" and mistletoe "the wonderful thunder-and-lightning flower." But as this learned writer nursed a fatal passion for thunder and lightning, which he detected lurking in the most unlikely places, we need not wonder that he occasionally found it in places where there were some slight grounds for thinking that it really existed.

[2] On the relation of the priest to Jupiter, and the equivalence of Jupiter and Juno to Janus (Dianus) and Diana, see *The Magic Art and the Evolution of Kings*, ii. 376 *sqq.*

on the sacred oak beside the still waters of the lake of Nemi. If that was so, we need not wonder that the priest guarded with drawn sword the mystic bough which contained the god's life and his own. The goddess whom he served and married was herself, if I am right, no other than the Queen of Heaven, the true wife of the sky-god. For she, too, loved the solitude of the woods and the lonely hills, and sailing overhead on clear nights in the likeness of the silver moon she looked down with pleasure on her own fair image reflected on the calm, the burnished surface of the lake, Diana's Mirror.

CHAPTER XIII

FAREWELL TO NEMI

Looking back at the end of the journey. WE are at the end of our enquiry, but as often happens in the search after truth, if we have answered one question, we have raised many more; if we have followed one track home, we have had to pass by others that opened off it and led, or seemed to lead, to far other goals than the sacred grove at Nemi. Some of these paths we have followed a little way; others, if fortune should be kind, the writer and the reader may one day pursue together. For the present we have journeyed far enough together, and it is time to part. Yet before we do so, we may well ask ourselves whether there is not some more general conclusion, some lesson, if possible, of hope and encouragement, to be drawn from the melancholy record of human error and folly which has engaged our attention in these volumes.

The movement of human thought in the past from magic to religion. If then we consider, on the one hand, the essential similarity of man's chief wants everywhere and at all times, and on the other hand, the wide difference between the means he has adopted to satisfy them in different ages, we shall perhaps be disposed to conclude that the movement of the higher thought, so far as we can trace it, has on the whole been from magic through religion to science. In magic man depends on his own strength to meet the difficulties and dangers that beset him on every side. He believes in a certain established order of nature on which he can surely count, and which he can manipulate for his own ends. When he discovers his mistake, when he recognizes sadly that both the order of nature which he had assumed and the control which he had believed himself to exercise over it were purely imaginary, he ceases to rely on his own intelligence and his own unaided efforts, and throws himself humbly on the mercy of certain great invisible beings behind the veil of nature, to whom he now ascribes all those far-reaching powers which he once arrogated to himself. Thus in the acuter minds magic is gradually superseded by religion, which explains the succession of natural phenomena as regulated by the will, the passion, or the caprice of spiritual beings like man in kind, though vastly superior to him in power.

But as time goes on this explanation in its turn proves to be unsatisfactory. For it assumes that the succession of natural events is not determined by immutable laws, but is to some extent variable and irregular, and this assumption is not borne out by closer observation. On the contrary, the more we scrutinize that succession the more we are struck by the rigid uniformity, the punctual precision with which, wherever we can follow them, the operations of nature are carried on. Every great advance in knowledge has extended the sphere of order and correspondingly restricted the sphere of apparent disorder in the world, till now we are ready to anticipate that even in regions where chance and confusion appear still to reign, a fuller knowledge would everywhere reduce the seeming chaos to cosmos. Thus the keener minds, still pressing forward to a deeper solution of the mysteries of the universe, come to reject the religious theory of nature as inadequate, and to revert in a measure to the older standpoint of magic by postulating explicitly, what in magic had only been implicitly assumed, to wit, an inflexible regularity in the order of natural events, which, if carefully observed, enables us to foresee their course with certainty and to act accordingly. In short, religion, regarded as an explanation of nature, is displaced by science.

The movement of thought from religion to science.

But while science has this much in common with magic that both rest on a faith in order as the underlying principle of all things, readers of this work will hardly need to be reminded that the order presupposed by magic differs widely from that which forms the basis of science. The difference flows naturally from the different modes in which the two orders have been reached. For

Contrast between the views of natural order postulated by magic and by science respectively.

whereas the order on which magic reckons is merely an extension, by false analogy, of the order in which ideas present themselves to our minds, the order laid down by science is derived from patient and exact observation of the phenomena themselves. The abundance, the solidity, and the splendour of the results already achieved by science are well fitted to inspire us with a cheerful confidence in the soundness of its method. Here at last, after groping about in the dark for countless ages, man has hit upon a clue to the labyrinth, a golden key that opens many locks in the treasury of nature. It is probably not too much to say that the hope of progress—moral and intellectual as well as material—in the future is bound up with the fortunes of science, and that every obstacle placed in the way of scientific discovery is a wrong to humanity.

The scientific theory of the world not necessarily final.

Yet the history of thought should warn us against concluding that because the scientific theory of the world is the best that has yet been formulated, it is necessarily complete and final. We must remember that at bottom the generalizations of science or, in common parlance, the laws of nature are merely hypotheses devised to explain that ever-shifting phantasmagoria of thought which we dignify with the high-sounding names of the world and the universe. In the last analysis magic, religion, and science are nothing but theories of thought; and as science has supplanted its predecessors, so it may hereafter be itself superseded by some more perfect hypothesis, perhaps by some totally different way of looking at the phenomena—of registering the shadows on the screen—of which we in this generation can form no idea. The advance of knowledge is an infinite progression towards a goal that for ever recedes. We need not murmur at the endless pursuit :—

> " *Fatti non foste a viver come bruti*
> *Ma per seguir virtute e conoscenza.*"

Great things will come of that pursuit, though we may not enjoy them. Brighter stars will rise on some voyager of the future—some great Ulysses of the realms of thought—than shine on us. The dreams of magic may one day be

the waking realities of science. But a dark shadow lies The
athwart the far end of this fair prospect. For however vast shadow
the increase of knowledge and of power which˙the future across the
may have in store for man, he can· scarcely hope to stay path.
the sweep of those great forces which seem to be making
silently but relentlessly for the destruction of all this starry
universe in which our earth swims as a speck or mote.   In
the ages to come man may be able to predict, perhaps even
to control, the wayward courses of the winds and clouds,
but hardly will his puny hands have strength to speed
afresh our slackening planet in its orbit or rekindle the
dying fire of the sun.[1] Yet the philosopher who trembles
at the idea of such distant catastrophes may console himself
by reflecting that these gloomy apprehensions, like the
earth and the sun themselves, are only parts of that un-
substantial world which thought has conjured up out of the
void, and that the phantoms which the subtle enchantress
has evoked to-day she may ban to-morrow.   They too, like
so much that to common eyes seems solid, may melt into
air, into thin air.[2]

Without dipping so far into the future, we may illustrate The web
the course which thought has hitherto run by likening it to of thought.

[1] " I quite agree how humiliating
the slow progress of man is, but every
one has his own pet horror, and this
slow progress or even personal anni-
hilation sinks in my mind into insig-
nificance compared with the idea or
rather I presume certainty of the sun
some day cooling and we all freezing.
To think of the progress of millions of
years, with every continent swarming
with good and enlightened men, all
ending in this, and with probably no
fresh start until this our planetary
system has been again converted into
red-hot gas. *Sic transit gloria mundi,*
with a vengeance " (*More Letters of
Charles Darwin,* edited by Francis
Darwin, London, 1903, i. 260 *sq.*).

[2] Since this passage was written the
hope which it expresses has been to
some extent strengthened by the discovery of radium, which appears to
prolong indefinitely the prospect of the
duration of the sun's heat, and with it
the duration of life on its attendant
planets. See (Sir) George Howard
Darwin's Presidential Address to the
British Association, *Report of the 75th
Meeting of the British Association for
the Advancement of Science* (South
Africa, 1905), pp. 28 *sq.* ; F. Soddy,
The Interpretation of Radium, Third
Edition (London, 1912), pp. 240 *sqq.* ;
E. Rutherford, *Radio-active Substances
and their Radiations* (Cambridge,
1913), pp. 653-656.   At the same
time it should be borne in mind that
even if the atomic disintegration and
accompanying liberation of energy,
which characterize radium and kindred
elements, should prove to be common
in different degrees to all the other
elements and to form a vast and till
lately unsuspected store of heat to the
sun, this enormous reserve of fuel
would only defer but could not avert
that final catastrophe with which the
solar system and indeed the whole
universe is remorselessly threatened by
the law of the dissipation of energy.

a web woven of three different threads—the black thread of magic, the red thread of religion, and the white thread of science, if under science we may include those simple truths, drawn from observation of nature, of which men in all ages have possessed a store.   Could we then survey the web of thought from the beginning, we should probably perceive it to be at first a chequer of black and white, a patchwork of true and false notions, hardly tinged as yet by the red thread of religion.   But carry your eye further along the fabric and you will remark that, while the black and white chequer still runs through it, there rests on the middle portion of the web, where religion has entered most deeply into its texture, a dark crimson stain, which shades off insensibly into a lighter tint as the white thread of science is woven more and more into the tissue.   To a web thus chequered and stained, thus shot with threads of diverse hues, but gradually changing colour the farther it is unrolled, the state of modern thought, with all its divergent aims and conflicting tendencies, may be compared.   Will the great movement which for centuries has been slowly altering the complexion of thought be continued in the near future ? or will a reaction set in which may arrest progress and even undo much that has been done ?   To keep up our parable, what will be the colour of the web which the Fates are now weaving on the humming loom of time ? will it be white or red ?   We cannot tell.   A faint glimmering light illumines the backward portion of the web.   Clouds and thick darkness hide the other end.

Nemi at evening: the *Ave Maria* bell.   Our long voyage of discovery is over and our bark has drooped her weary sails in port at last.   Once more we take the road to Nemi.   It is evening, and as we climb the long slope of the Appian Way up to the Alban Hills, we look back and see the sky aflame with sunset, its golden glory resting like the aureole of a dying saint over Rome and touching with a crest of fire the dome of St. Peter's.   The sight once seen can never be forgotten, but we turn from it and pursue our way darkling along the mountain side, till we come to Nemi and look down on the lake in its deep hollow, now fast disappearing in the evening shadows.   The place has changed but little since Diana received the homage of her worshippers in the sacred grove. The temple of the sylvan goddess, indeed, has vanished and the King of the Wood no longer stands sentinel over the Golden Bough. But Nemi's woods are still green, and as the sunset fades above them in the west, there comes to us, borne on the swell of the wind, the sound of the church bells of Ariccia ringing the Angelus. *Ave Maria!* Sweet and solemn they chime out from the distant town and die lingeringly away across the wide Campagnan marshes. *Le roi est mort, vive le roi! Ave Maria!*

NOTES

I

SNAKE STONES [1]

THE belief of the Scottish Highlanders as to the so-called Snake Snake Stones has been recorded as follows by a good authority at the end Stones in the of the nineteenth century :— Highlands.

"A product called *clach-nathrach*, serpent stone, is found on the root of the long ling. It is of steel-grey colour, has the consistency of soft putty when new and of hard putty when old, and is as light as pumice-stone, which it resembles. It is of a globular form, and from one to three inches in diameter. There is a circular hole, about a quarter of an inch in width, through the centre. This substance is said to be produced by the serpent emitting spume round the root of a twig of heather. The *clach-nathrach* is greatly prized by the people, who transmit it as a talisman to their descendants." [2]

II

THE TRANSFORMATION OF WITCHES INTO CATS

THE European belief that witches can turn themselves into cats, Witches and that any wounds inflicted on the witch-cat will afterwards be as cats found on the body of the witch herself,[3] has its exact parallel among the Oraons. among the Oraons or Uraons, a primitive hill tribe of Bengal. The following is the account given of the Óraon belief by a Jesuit missionary, who laboured for years among these savages and was intimately acquainted with their superstitions :—

[1] See above, vol. i. pp. 15 *sq.*
[2] Alexander Carmichael, *Carmina Gadelica, Hymns and Incantations with Illustrative Notes on Words, Rites, and Customs, dying and obso-* *lete : orally collected in the Highlands and Islands of Scotland and translated into English* (Edinburgh, 1900), ii. 312.
[3] Above, vol. i. pp. 315 *sqq.*

" *Chordewa* is a witch rather than a *bhut* [demon]. It is believed that some women have the power to change their soul into a black cat, who then goes about in the houses where there are sick people. Such a cat has a peculiar way of mewing quite different from its brethren, and is easily recognised. It steals quietly into the house, licks the lips of the sick man and eats of the food that has been prepared for him. The sick man soon gets worse and dies. They say it is very difficult to catch the cat, as it has all the nimbleness of its nature and the cleverness of a *bhut*. However, they sometimes succeed, and then something wonderful happens. The woman out of whom the cat has come remains insensible, as it were in a state of temporary death, until the cat re-enters her body. Any wound inflicted on the cat will be inflicted on her ; if they cut its ears or break its legs or put out its eyes the woman will suffer the same mutilation. The Uraons say that formerly they used to burn any woman that was suspected to be a *Chordewa*." [1]

III

AFRICAN BALDERS

African parallels to Balder.

IN various parts of Africa stories are told of men who could only be killed, like Balder, by the stroke of an apparently insignificant weapon ; and some at least of these men were not mythical beings but real men of flesh and blood who lived not long ago and whose memory is still comparatively fresh among their people. The Wadoe of German East Africa tell such a story of a great sorcerer, whom they now worship as a dispenser of sunshine and rain. The legend and the worship are reported as follows by a native African traveller :—

The worshipful ghost in the cave.

"If drought sets in, all the chiefs meet in council and resolve : 'This year we have had nothing but sunshine ; when we plant, the fruits will not ripen ; therefore we must betake ourselves to our spirits of the dead (*mizimu*).' Then they take some woollen stuff dyed blue and a red cloth, and set out together on the way and go to the district Nguu, where their principal ghost (*mzimu*) resides, in order to lay the matter before him. The ghost dwells in a very spacious cave. On their coming the chiefs greet him. His answer consists in a humming noise, which sounds like the patter of rain. If one among them is a bad man, the ghost says to them, 'There is come with you in the caravan a rascal who wears such and such clothes.' If such a man there is, he is driven away. Now they

[1] The late Rev. P. Dehon, S.J., "Religion and Customs of the Uraons," *Memoirs of the Asiatic* *Society of Bengal*, vol. i. No. 9 (Calcutta, 1906), p. 141.

tell the ghost all that they wish to say, to wit: 'This year thou hast given us much sunshine; the fruits in the fields do not grow tall, everywhere there is sickness, therefore we beg thee, give us rain.' Thereupon the ghost hums a second time, and all are glad, because he has answered them. But if the ghost is angry, he does not answer but holds his peace. If he has made them glad and given an answer, much rain will fall; otherwise they return as they went in sunshine.

"Originally this ghost was a man, a village elder (*jumbe*) of Ukami. He was a great sorcerer. One day people wished to conquer him, but they could do him no harm, for neither lead nor sword nor arrow could pierce his body. But he lived at strife with his wife. She said to his enemies, 'If you would kill my husband, I will tell you how it can be done.' They asked her, 'How can it be done?' She answered, 'My husband is a great sorcerer; you all know that.' They answered, 'That is true.' Then she said further, 'If you would kill him so that he dies on the spot, seek a stalk of a gourd and smite him with it; then he will die at once, for that has always been to him a forbidden thing.'[1] They sought the stalk of a gourd, and when they smote him with it, he died at once without so much as setting one foot from the spot. But of him and his departure there was nothing more to be seen, for suddenly a great storm blew, and no man knew whither he had gone. The storm is said to have carried him to that cave which is still there to this day. After some days people saw in the cave his weapons, clothes, and turban lying, and they brought word to the folk in the town, 'We have seen the clothes of the elder in the cave, but of himself we have perceived nothing.' The folk went thither to look about, and they found that it was so. So the news of this ghost spread, all the more because people had seen the marvel that a man died and nobody knew where he had gone. The wonderful thing in this wood is that the spirits dwell in the midst of the wood and that everywhere a bright white sand lies on the ground, as if people had gone thither for the purpose of keeping everything clean. On many days they hear a drumming and shouts of joy in this wood, as if a marriage feast were being held there. That is the report about the ghost of Kolelo.[2] All village elders, who dwell in the interior, see in this ghost the greatest ghost of all. All the chiefs (*mwene*) and headmen (*pazi*) and the village elders (*jumben*) of the clan Kingaru[3] respect that ghost."[4]

The man who could only be killed by the stalk of a gourd.

[1] "Every clan (*Familienstamm*) has a definite thing which is forbidden to all the members of the clan, whether it be a particular kind of meat, or a certain fish, or as here the stalk of a gourd."

[2] "The place in Nguu, where the ghost is said to dwell."

[3] "In Ukami."

[4] C. Velten, *Schilderungen der Suaheli* (Göttingen, 1901), pp. 195-197.

Miss Alice Werner, who kindly called my attention to this and the following cases of African Balders, tells me that this worshipful ghost in the cave appears to have been in his time a real man. Again, she was assured by some natives that "Chikumbu, a Yao chief, who at one time gave the Administration some trouble, was invulnerable by shot or steel; the only thing that could kill him—since he had not been fortified against it by the proper medicine—was a sharp splinter of bamboo. This reminds one of Balder and the mistletoe."[1] Again, a Nyanja chief named Chibisa, who was a great man in this part of Africa when Livingstone travelled in it,[2] "stood firm upon his ant-heap, while his men fell round him, shouting his war-song, until one who knew the secret of a sand-bullet brought him down."[3]

Once more the Swahili tell a story of an African Samson named Liongo who lived in Shanga, while it was a flourishing city. By reason of his great strength he oppressed the people exceedingly, and they sought to kill him, but all in vain. At last they bribed his nephew, saying, "Go and ask your father what it is that will kill him. When you know, come and tell us, and when he is dead we will give you the kingdom." So the treacherous nephew went to his uncle and asked him, "Father, what is it that can kill you?" And his uncle said, "A copper needle. If any one stabs me in the navel, I die." So the nephew went to the town and said to the people, "It is a copper needle that will kill him." And they gave him a needle, and he went back to his uncle; and while his uncle slept the wicked nephew stabbed him with the needle in the navel. So he died, and they buried him, and his grave is to be seen at Ozi to this day. But they seized the nephew and killed him; they did not give the kingdom to that bad young man.[4]

When we compare the story of Balder with these African stories, the heroes of which were probably all real men, and when further we remember the similar tale told of the Persian hero Isfendiyar, who may well have been an historical personage,[5] we are confirmed

Sidenotes: The man who could only be killed by a splinter of bamboo. The man who could only be killed by a copper needle. These stories confirm the view that Balder may

---

[1] Miss Alice Werner, *The Natives of British Central Africa* (London, 1906), p. 82. In a letter Miss Werner tells me that she learned these particulars at Blantyre in 1893, and that the chief lived in the neighbourhood of Mlanje.

[2] Rev. Henry Rowley, *Twenty Years in Central Africa* (London, N.D.), pp. 36 *sqq.* For a reference to this and all the other works cited in this Note I am indebted to the kindness of Miss Alice Werner.

[3] Rev. David Clement Scott, *A Cyclopaedic Dictionary of the Mang'anja Language spoken in British Central Africa* (Edinburgh, 1892), p. 315.

[4] Edward Steere, *Swahili Tales* (London, 1870), pp. 441-453. The young man in the story is spoken of now as the nephew and now as the son of the man he murdered. Probably he was what we should call a nephew or brother's son of his victim; for under the classificatory system of relationship, which seems to prevail among the Bantu stock, to whom the Swahili belong, a man regularly calls his paternal uncle his father.

[5] Above, vol. i. pp. 104 *sq.*

in the suspicion that Balder himself may have been a real man, have been
admired and beloved in his lifetime and deified after his death, a real man
like the African sorcerer, who is now worshipped in a cave and deified
bestows rain or sunshine on his votaries. On the whole I incline after death.
to regard this solution of the Balder problem as more probable than
the one I have advocated in the text, namely that Balder was a
mythical personification of a mistletoe-bearing oak. The facts
which seem to incline the balance to the side of Euhemerism
reached me as my book was going to press and too late to be
embodied in their proper place in the volumes. The acceptance
of this hypothesis would not necessarily break the analogy which I
have traced between Balder in his sacred grove on the Sogne fiord
of Norway and the priest of Diana in the sacred grove of Nemi;
indeed, it might even be thought rather to strengthen the
resemblance between the two, since there is no doubt at all that
the priests of Diana at Nemi were men who lived real lives and
died real deaths.

IV

THE MISTLETOE AND THE GOLDEN BOUGH

THAT Virgil compares the Golden Bough to the mistletoe[1] is Two
certain and admitted on all hands. The only doubt that can arise species
is whether the plant to which he compares the mystic bough is the of mistle-
ordinary species of mistletoe (*Viscum album*) or the species known *Viscum*
to botanists as *Loranthus europaeus*. The common mistletoe (*Viscum* *album*
album, L.) "lives as a semi-parasite (obtaining carbon from the air, *Loranthus*
but water, nitrogen, and mineral matter from the sap of its host) on *europaeus.*
many conifers and broadleaved trees, and chiefly on their branches. Common
The hosts, or trees on which it lives, are, *most frequently*, the apple (*Viscum*
tree, both wild and cultivated varieties; *next*, the silver-fir; *fre-* *album*)
quently, birches, poplars (except aspen), limes, willows, Scots pine,
mountain-ash, and hawthorn; *occasionally*, robinia, maples, horse-
chestnut, hornbeam, and aspen. It is very rarely found on oaks,
but has been observed on pedunculate oak at Thornbury, Gloucestershire, and elsewhere in Europe, also on *Quercus coccinea*, Moench.,
and *Q. palustris*, Moench. The alders, beech and spruce appear
to be always free from mistletoe, and it very rarely attacks pear-
trees. It is commoner in Southern Europe than in the North,

---

[1] Virgil, *Aen.* vi. 205 *sqq.* :—
" *Quale solet silvis brumali frigore*
    viscum
Fronde virere nova, quod non sua
    seminat arbos,

Et croceo fetu teretis circumdare
    truncos :
Talis erat species auri frondentis
    opaca
Ilice, sic leni crepitabat bractea vento."

and is extremely abundant where cider is made. In the N.-W. Himalayan districts, it is frequently found on apricot-trees, which are the commonest fruit-trees there. Its white berries are eaten by birds, chiefly by the missel-thrush (*Turdus viscivorus*, L.), and the seeds are either rubbed by the beak against branches of trees, or voided on to them; the seeds, owing to the viscous nature of the pulp surrounding them, then become attached to the branches." [1] The large smooth pale-green tufts of the parasite, clinging to the boughs of trees, are most conspicuous in winter, when they assume a yellowish hue. [2] In Greece at the present time mistletoe grows most commonly on firs, especially at a considerable elevation (three thousand feet or more) above the level of the sea. [3] Throughout Italy mistletoe now grows on fruit-trees, almond-trees, hawthorn, limes, willows, black poplars, and firs, but never, it is said, on oaks. [4] In England seven authentic cases of mistletoe growing on oaks are said to be reported. [5] In Gloucestershire mistletoe grows on the Badham Court oak, Sedbury Park, Chepstow, and on the Frampton-on-Severn oak. [6] Branches of oak with mistletoe growing on them were exhibited to more than one learned society in France during the nineteenth century; one of the branches was cut in the forest of Jeugny. [7] It is a popular French superstition that mandragora or "the hand of glory," as it is called by the people, may be found by digging at the root of a mistletoe-bearing oak. [8]

[1] W. Schlich, *Manual of Forestry*, vol. iv. *Forest Protection*, by W. R. Fisher, M.A., Second Edition (London, 1907), p. 412. French peasants about Coulommiers think that mistletoe springs from birds' dung. See H. Gaidoz, "Bulletin critique de la Mythologie Gauloise," *Revue de l'Histoire des Religions*, ii. (1880) p. 76. The ancients were well aware that mistletoe is propagated from tree to tree by seeds which have been voided by birds. See Theophrastus, *De Causis Plantarum*, ii. 17. 5; Pliny, *Naturalis Historia*, xvi. 247. Pliny tells us that the birds which most commonly deposited the seeds were pigeons and thrushes. Can this have been the reason why Virgil (*Aen.* vi. 190 *sqq.*) represents Aeneas led to the Golden Bough by a pair of doves?

[2] James Sowerby, *English Botany*, xxi. (London, 1805) p. 1470.

[3] C. Fraas, *Synopsis Plantarum Florae Classicae* (Munich, 1845), p. 152.

[4] H. O. Lenz, *Botanik der alten Griechen und Römer* (Gotha, 1859), p. 597, quoting Pollini.

[5] J. Lindley and T. Moore, *The Treasury of Botany*, New Edition (London, 1874), ii. 1220. A good authority, however, observes that mistletoe is "frequently to be observed on the branches of old apple-trees, hawthorns, lime-trees, oaks, etc., where it grows parasitically." See J. Sowerby, *English Botany*, xxi. (London, 1805) p. 1470.

[6] *Encyclopaedia Britannica*, Ninth Edition, x. 689, *s.v.* "Gloucester."

[7] H. Gaidoz, "Bulletin critique de la Mythologie Gauloise," *Revue de l'Histoire des Religions*, ii. (1880) pp. 75 *sq.*

[8] Angelo de Gubernatis, *La Mythologie des Plantes* (Paris, 1878–1882), ii. 216 *sq.* As to the many curious superstitions that have clustered round mandragora, see P. J. Veth, "De Mandragora," *Internationales Archiv für Ethnographie*, vii. (1894) pp. 199-205; C. B. Randolph, "The Mandragora of the Ancients in Folk-lore and Medicine," *Proceedings of the American Academy of Arts and Sciences*, vol. xl. No. 12 (January, 1905), pp. 487-537.

The species of mistletoe known as *Loranthus europaeus* resembles *Loranthus*
the ordinary mistletoe in general appearance, but its berries are bright *europaeus.*
yellow instead of white. "This species attacks chiefly oaks, *Quercus
cerris*, L., *Q. sessiliflora*, Salisb., less frequently, *Q. pedunculata*, Ehrh.,
and *Castanea vulgaris*, Lam. ; also lime. It is found throughout
Southern Europe and as far north as Saxony, not in Britain. It
grows chiefly on the branches of standards over coppice." The
injury which it inflicts on its hosts is even greater than that inflicted
by the ordinary mistletoe ; it often kills the branch on which it
settles. The seeds are carried to the trees by birds, chiefly by
the missel-thrush. In India many kinds of *Loranthus* grow on
various species of forest trees, for example, on teak ;[1] one variety
(*Loranthus vestitus*) grows on two species of oak, the *Quercus
dilatata*, Lindl., and the *Quercus incana*, Roxb.[2] A marked distinction between the two sorts of mistletoe is that whereas ordinary
mistletoe (*Viscum album*) is evergreen, the *Loranthus* is deciduous.[3]
In Greece the *Loranthus* has been observed on many old chestnut-
trees at Stheni, near Delphi.[4] In Italy it grows chiefly on the various
species of oaks and also on chestnut-trees. So familiar is it on oaks
that it is known as "oak mistletoe" both in popular parlance (*visco
quercino*) and in druggists' shops (*viscum quernum*). Bird-lime is
made from it in Italy.[5]

Both sorts of mistletoe were known to the ancient Greeks and Both sorts
Romans, though the distinctive terms which they applied to each of mistle-
appear not to be quite certain. Theophrastus, and Pliny after him, toe known
seem to distinguish three sorts of mistletoe, to which Theophrastus ancients
gives the names of *ixia*, *hyphear*, and *stelis* respectively. He says and desig-
that the *hyphear* and the *stelis* grow on firs and pines, and that the nated by
ixia grows on the oak (δρῦς), the terebinth, and many other kinds different
of trees. He also observes that both the *ixia* and the *hyphear* grow words.
on the ilex or holm-oak (πρῖνος), the same tree sometimes bearing
both species at the same time, the *ixia* on the north and the *hyphear*
on the south. He expressly distinguishes the evergreen species of
ixia from the deciduous, which seems to prove that he included

---

[1] W. Schlich, *Manual of Forestry*, vol. iv. *Forest Protection*, Second Edition (London, 1907), pp. 415-417.

[2] E. B. Stebbing, "The Loranthus Parasite of the Moru and Ban Oaks," *Journal and Proceedings of the Asiatic Society of Bengal*, New Series, v. (Calcutta, 1910) pp. 189-195. The *Loranthus vestitus* "is a small branching woody plant with dirty yellowish green leaves which are dark shining green above. It grows in great clumps and masses on the trees, re-

sembling a giant mistletoe. The fruit is yellowish and fleshy, and is almost sessile on the stem, which it thickly studs" (*ib.*, p. 192). The writer shews that the parasite is very destructive to oaks in India.

[3] H. O. Lenz, *Botanik der alten Griechen und Römer* (Gotha, 1859), p. 598, notes [151 and 152].

[4] C. Fraas, *Synopsis Plantarum Florae Classicae* (Munich, 1845), p. 152.

[5] H. O. Lenz, *Botanik der alten Griechen und Römer* (Gotha, 1859), pp. 599 *sq.*

both the ordinary mistletoe (*Viscum album*) and the *Loranthus* under the general name of *ixia*.[1]

Doubts as to the identification of the ancient names for mistletoe.

Modern writers are not agreed as to the identification of the various species of mistletoe designated by the names *ixia*, *hyphear*, and *stelis*. F. Wimmer, the editor of Theophrastus in the Didot edition, takes *hyphear* to be common mistletoe (*Viscum album*), *stelis* to be *Loranthus europaeus*, and *ixia* to be a general name which includes the two species.[2] On the other hand F. Fraas, while he agrees as to the identification of *hyphear* and *stelis* with common mistletoe and *Loranthus* respectively, inclines somewhat hesitatingly to regard *ixia* or *ixos* (as Dioscorides has it) as a synonym for *stelis* (the *Loranthus*).[3] H. O. Lenz, again, regards both *hyphear* and *stelis* as synonyms for common mistletoe (*Viscum album*), while he would restrict *ixia* to the *Loranthus*.[4] But both these attempts to confine *ixia* to the single deciduous species *Loranthus* seem incompatible with the statement of Theophrastus, that *ixia* includes an evergreen as well as a deciduous species.[5]

Did Virgil compare the Golden Bough to common mistletoe or to *Loranthus*? Some enquirers decide in favour of *Loranthus*.

We have now to ask, Did Virgil compare the Golden Bough to the common mistletoe (*Viscum album*) or to the *Loranthus europaeus*? Some modern enquirers decide in favour of the *Loranthus*. Many years ago Sir Francis Darwin wrote to me:[6] "I wonder whether *Loranthus europaeus* would do for your Golden Bough. It is a sort of mistletoe growing on oaks and chestnuts in S. Europe. In the autumn it produces what are described as bunches of pretty yellow berries. It is not evergreen like the mistletoe, but deciduous, and as its leaves appear at the same time as the oak

[1] Theophrastus, *Historia Plantarum*, iii. 7. 5, iii. 16. 1, *De Causis Plantarum*, ii. 17 ; Pliny, *Nat. Hist.* xvi. 245-247. Compare Dioscorides, *De materia medica*, ii. 93 (103), vol. i. pp. 442 *sq.*, ed. C. Sprengel (Leipsic, 1829-1830), who uses the form *ixos* instead of *ixia*. Both Dioscorides (*l.c.*) and Plutarch (*Coriolanus*, 3) affirm that mistletoe (*ixos*) grows on the oak (δρῦς); and Hesychius quotes from Sophocles's play *Meleager* the expression "mistletoe-bearing oaks" (ἰξοφόρους δρύας, Hesychius, *s.v.*).

[2] Theophrastus, *Opera quae supersunt omnia*, ed. Fr. Wimmer (Paris, 1866), pp. 537, 545, 546, *s.vv.* ἰξία, στελίς, ὑφέαρ.

[3] F. Fraas, *Synopsis Plantarum Florae Classicae* (Munich, 1845), p. 152.

[4] H. O. Lenz, *Botanik der alten Griechen und Römer* (Gotha, 1859), p. 597, notes [147 and 148].

[5] Theophrastus, *De Causis Plantarum*, ii. 17. 2, ἐπεὶ τό γε τὴν μὲν ἀείφυλλον εἶναι τῶν ἰξιῶν (τὴν δὲ φυλλοβόλον) οὐθὲν ἄτοπον, κἂν ἡ μὲν (ἐν) ἀειφύλλοις ἡ δὲ ἐν φυλλοβόλοις ἐμβιώῃ.

[6] His letter is undated, but the postmark is April 28th, 1889. Sir Francis Darwin has since told me that his authority is Kerner von Marilaun, *Pflanzenleben* (1888), vol. i. pp. 195, 196. See Anton Kerner von Marilaun, *The Natural History of Plants*, translated and edited by F. W. Oliver (London, 1894–1895), i. 204 *sqq.* According to this writer "the mistletoe's favourite tree is certainly the Black Poplar (*Populus nigra*). It flourishes with astonishing luxuriance on the branches of that tree. . . . Mistletoe has also been found by way of exception upon the oak and the maple, and upon old vines" (*op. cit.* i. 205).

leaves and drop at the same time in autumn, it must look like a branch of the oak, more especially as it has rough bark with lichens often growing on it. *Loranthus* is said to be a hundred years old sometimes." Professor P. J. Veth, after quoting the passage from Virgil, writes that "almost all translators (including Vondel) and commentators of the Mantuan bard think that the mistletoe is here meant, probably for the simple reason that it was better known to them than *Loranthus europaeus*. I am convinced that Virgil can only have thought of the latter. On the other side of the Alps the *Loranthus* is much commoner than the mistletoe; on account of its splendid red blossoms, sometimes twenty centimetres long, it is a far larger and more conspicuous ornament of the trees; it, bears really golden yellow fruit (*Croceus fetus*), whereas the berries of the mistletoe are almost white; and it attaches itself by preference to the oak, whereas the mistletoe is very seldom found on the oak."[1] Again, Mr. W. R. Paton writes to me from Mount Athos:[2] "The oak is here called *dendron, the* tree. As for the mistletoe there are two varieties, both called *axo* (ancient ἰξός). Both are used to make bird-lime. The real *Golden Bough* is the variety with yellow berries and no leaves. It is the parasite of the oak and rarely grows on other trees. It is very abundant, and now in winter the oak-trees which have adopted it seem from a distance to be draped in a golden tissue. The other variety is our own mistletoe and is strictly a parasite of the fir (a spruce fir, I don't know its scientific name). It is also very abundant."

Thus in favour of identifying Virgil's mistletoe (*viscum*) with *Loranthus* rather than with common mistletoe it has been urged, first, that the berries of *Loranthus* are bright yellow, whereas those of the mistletoe are of a greenish white; and, second, that the *Loranthus* commonly grows on oaks, whereas mistletoe seldom does so, indeed in Italy mistletoe is said never to be found on an oak. Both these circumstances certainly speak strongly in favour of *Loranthus*; since Virgil definitely describes the berries as of a saffron-yellow (*croceus*) and says that the plant grew on a holm-oak. Yet on the other hand Virgil tells us that the plant put forth fresh leaves in the depths of winter (*brumali frigore*, strictly speaking, "the cold of the winter solstice"); and this would best apply to the common mistletoe, which is evergreen, whereas *Loranthus* is deciduous.[3] Accordingly, if we must decide between the two species, this single circumstance appears to incline the balance in favour of

Reason for preferring common mistletoe.

---

[1] Prof. P. J. Veth, "De leer der signatuur, III. De mistel en de riembloem," *Internationales Archiv für Ethnographie*, vii. (1894) p. 105. The Dutch language has separate names for the two species: mistletoe is *mistel*, and *Loranthus* is *riembloem*.

[2] His letter is dated 18th February, 1908.

[3] But Sir Francis Darwin writes to me:—"I do not quite see why *Loranthus* should not put out leaves in winter as easily as *Viscum*, in both cases it would be due to unfolding

Perhaps
Virgil
confused
the two
species.

common mistletoe.   But is it not possible that Virgil, whether consciously or unconsciously, confused the two plants and combined traits from both in his description?   Both parasites are common in Italy and in appearance they are much alike except for the colour of the berries.   As a loving observer of nature, Virgil was probably familiar by sight with both, but he may not have examined them closely; and he might be excused if he thought that the parasite which he saw growing, with its clusters of bright yellow berries, on oaks in winter, was identical with the similar parasite which he saw growing, with its bunches of greenish white berries and its pale green leaves, on many other trees of the forest.   The confusion would be all the more natural if the Celts of northern Italy, in whose country the poet was born, resembled the modern Celts of Brittany in attaching bunches of the common mistletoe to their cottages and leaving them there till the revolving months had tinged the pale berries, leaves, and twigs with a golden yellow, thereby converting the branch of mistletoe into a true Golden Bough.

---

leaf buds; the fact that *Viscum* has adult leaves at the time, while *Loranthus* has not, does not really affect the matter."   However, Mr. Paton tells us, as we have just seen, that in winter the *Loranthus* growing on the oaks of Mount Athos has no leaves, though its yellow berries are very conspicuous.

INDEX

Dances of fasting men and women at festival, i. 8 *sq.* ; of Duk-duk society, 11 ; of girls at puberty, 28, 29, 30, 37, 42, 50, 58, 59 ; round bonfires, 108, 109, 110, 111, 114, 116, 120, 131, 142, 145, 148, 153 *sq.*, 159, 166, 172, 173, 175, 178, 182, 183, 185, 187, 188, 189, 191, 193, 194, 195, 198, 246, ii. 2, 39; masked, bull-roarers used at, 230 *n.* ; of novices at initiation, 258, 259

Dancing with the fairies at Hallowe'en, i. 227

Dandelions gathered at Midsummer, ii. 49

Danger apprehended from the sexual relation, ii. 277 *sq.*

Dangers thought to attend women at menstruation, i. 94

Danish stories of the external soul, ii. 120 *sqq.*

—— story of a girl who was forbidden to see the sun, i. 70 *sqq.*

Danserosse or *danseresse*, a stone, i. 110

Danube, worship of Grannus on the, i. 112

Danzig, the immortal lady of, i. 100

Daphne gnidium gathered at Midsummer, ii. 51

Dapper, O., on ritual of death and resurrection at initiation in the Belli-Paaro society, ii. 257 *sqq.*

Daramulun, a mythical being who instituted and superintends the initiation of lads in Australia, ii. 228, 233, 237 ; his voice heard in the sound of the bull-roarer, 228. *See also* Thrumalun and Thuremlin

"Darding Knife," pretence of death and resurrection at initiation to the, ii. 274 *sq.*

Darling River, the Ualaroi of the, ii. 233

Darma Rajah, Hindoo god, ii. 6

Darowen, in Wales, Midsummer fires at, i. 201

Darwin, Charles, on the cooling of the sun, ii. 307

Darwin, 'Sir Francis, on the Golden Bough, ii. 318, 319 *n.*[3]

Dashers of churns, witches ride on, ii. 73 *sq.*

Date of Chinese festival changed, i. 137

Dathi, king of Ireland, and his Druid, i. 228 *sq.*

Davies, J. Ceredig, as to witches in Wales, i. 321 *n.*[2]

Dawn of the Day, prayers to the, i. 50 *sq.*, 53 ; prayer of adolescent girl to the, 98 *n.*[1]

Dawson, James, on sex totems in Victoria, ii. 216

Dead, festival of the, i. 223 *sq.*, 225 *sq.* ; souls of the, sit round the Midsummer fire, 183, 184 ; sacrifice of reindeer to the, ii. 178; incarnate in serpents, 211 *sq.* ; bull-roarers sounded at festivals of the, 230. *n.* ; first-fruits offered to the souls of the, 243

"Death, carrying out," i. 119; "the burying of," 119; effigies of, burnt in spring fires, ii. 21 *sq.* ; omens of, 54, 64; customs observed by mourners after a death in order to escape from the ghost, 174 *sqq.* ; identified with the sun, 174 *n.*[1]

Death and resurrection, ritual of, ii. 225 *sqq.* ; in Australia, 227 *sqq.* ; in New Guinea, 239 *sqq.* ; in Fiji, 243 *sqq.* ; in Rook, 246 ; in New Britain, 246 *sq.* ; in Ceram, 249 *sqq.* ; in Africa, 251 *sqq.* ; in North America, 266 *sqq.* ; traces of it elsewhere, 276 *sq.*

Debregeasia velutina, used to kindle fire by friction, ii. 8

December, the last day of, Hogmanay, i. 266 ; the twenty-first, St. Thomas's Day, 266

Decle, L., quoted, i. 4 *n.*[1]

Dee, holed stone used by childless women in the Aberdeenshire, ii. 187

Deer and the family of Lachlin, superstition concerning, ii. 284

Deffingin, in Swabia, Midsummer bon-fires at, i. 166 *sq.*

Dehon, P., on witches as cats among the Oraons, ii. 312

Deiseal, deisheal, dessil, the right-hand turn, in the Highlands of Scotland, i. 150 *n.*[1], 154

Delagoa Bay, the Thonga of, i. 29

Delaware Indians, seclusion of girls at puberty among the, i. 54

Delivery, charms to ensure women an easy, i. 49, 50 *sq.*, 52 ; women creep through a rifted rock to obtain an easy, ii. 189

Delmenhorst, in Oldenburg, Easter fires at, i. 142

Delos, new fire brought from, i. 136

Delphi, perpetual fire at, ii. 91 *n.*[7]; the picture of Orpheus at, 294 ; Stheni, near, 317

Demeter, the torches of, i. 340 *n.*[1]; serpents in the worship of, ii. 44 *n.*

Demnat, in the Atlas, New Year rites at, i. 217, 218

Demon supposed to attack girls at puberty, i. 67 *sq.* ; festival of fire instituted to ban a, ii. 3

Demons attack women at puberty and childbirth, i. 24 *n.*[2]; expelled at the New Year, 134 *sq.* ; abroad on Midsummer Eve, 172 ; ashes of holy

Franken, Middle, fire custom at Easter in, i. 143

Frankenstein, precautions against witches in, ii. 20 *n.*

Fraser Lake in British Columbia, i. 47

Freiburg, in Switzerland, Lenten fires in, i. 119 ; fern and treasure on St. John's Night in, ii. 288

Freising, in Bavaria, creeping through a narrow opening in the cathedral of, ii. 189

French cure for whooping - cough, ii. 192 *n.*[1]

—— Islands, use of bull-roarers in, ii. 229 *n.*

—— peasants, their superstition as to a virgin and a flame, i. 137 *n.*

Friction of wood, fire made by the, i. 132, 133, 135, 136, 137, 138, 144 *sq.*, 148, 155, 169 *sq.*, 175, 177, 179, 220, 264, 270 *sqq.*, 335 *sq.*, ii. 8 ; the most primitive mode of making fire, 90, 295

"Friendly Society of the Spirit" among the Naudowessies, ii. 267

Frigg or Frigga, the goddess, and Balder, i. 101, 102

Fringes worn over the eyes by girls at puberty, i. 47, 48

Fruit-trees threatened, i. 114 ; Midsummer fires lit under, 215 ; shaken at Christmas to make them bear fruit, 248 ; fumigated with smoke of need-fire, 280 ; fertilized by burning torches, 340

Fuga daemonum, St. John's wort, ii. 55

Fulda, the Lord of the Wells at, ii. 28

Fumigating crops with smoke of bonfires, i. 201, 337

—— sheep and cattle, ii. 12, 13

Fumigation of pastures at Midsummer to drive away witches and demons, i. 179 ; of fruit-trees, nets, and cattle with smoke of need-fire, 280 ; of byres with juniper, 296 ; of trees with wild thyme on Christmas Eve, ii. 64

Fünen, in Denmark, cure for childish ailments at, ii. 191

Funeral, customs observed by mourners after a funeral in order to escape from the ghost, ii. 174 *sqq.*

—— ceremony among the Michemis, i. 5

Furnace, walking through a fiery, ii. 3 *sqq.*

Furness, W. H., on passing under an archway, ii. 179 *sq.*, 180 *n.*[1]

Gabb, W. M., on ceremonial uncleanness, i. 65 *n.*[1]

Gablonz, in Bohemia, Midsummer bed of flowers at, ii. 57

Gaboon, birth-trees in the, ii. 160 ; theory of the external soul in, 200 *sq.*

Gacko, need-fire at, i. 286

Gaidoz, H., on the custom of passing sick people through cleft trees, ii. 171

Gage, Thomas, on *naguals* among the Indians of Guatemala, ii. 213

Gaj, in Slavonia, need-fire at, i. 282

Galatian senate met in Drynemetum, "the temple of the oak," ii. 89

Galatians kept their old Celtic speech, ii. 89 *n.*[2]

Galela, dread of women at menstruation in, i. 79

Galelareese of Halmahera, their rites of initiation, ii. 248

Gallic Councils, their prohibition of carrying torches, i. 199

Gallows Hill, magical plants gathered on the, ii. 57

—— -rope used to kindle need-fire, i. 277

Gandersheim, in Brunswick, need-fire at, i. 277

Gap, in the High Alps, cats roasted alive in the Midsummer fire at, ii. 39 *sq*

Gardner, Mrs. E. A., i. 131 *n.*[1]

Garlands of flowers placed on wells at Midsummer, ii. 28 ; thrown on trees, a form of divination, 53

Garlic roasted at Midsummer fires, i. 193

Garonne, Midsummer fires in the valley of the, i. 193

Gatschet, A. S., on the Toukawe Indians, ii. 276 *n.*[2]

Gaul, "serpents' eggs" in ancient, i. 15 ; human sacrifices in ancient, ii. 32 *sq.*

Gauls, their fortification walls, i. 267 *sq.*

Gazelle Peninsula, New Britain, the Ingniet society in the, ii. 156

Gem, external soul of magician in a, ii. 105 *sq.* ; external soul of giant in a, 130

Geneva, Midsummer fires in the canton of, i. 172

Genius, the Roman, ii. 212 *n.*

Geranium burnt in Midsummer fire, i. 213

Gerhausen, i. 166

German stories of the external soul, ii. 116 *sqq.*

Germans, human sacrifices offered by the ancient, ii. 28 *n.*[1] ; the oak sacred among the, 89

Germany, Lenten fires in, i. 115 *sq.* ; Easter bonfires in, 140 *sqq.* ; custom at eclipses in, 162 *n.* ; the Midsummer fires in, 163 *sqq.* ; the Yule log in, 247 *sqq.* ; belief in the transformation of witches into animals in, 321 *n.*[2] ; colic, sore eyes, and stiffness of the

Kabenau river, in German New Guinea, ii. 193

Kabyle tale, milk-tie in a, ii. 138 $n.$[1]; the external soul in a, i. 139

Kahma, in Burma, annual extinction of fires in, i. 136

Kai of New Guinea, their seclusion of women at menstruation, i. 79 ; their use of a cleft stick as a cure, ii. 182 ; their rites of initiation, 239 *sqq.*

Kail, divination by stolen, i. 234 *sq.*

Kakian association in Ceram, rites of initiation in the, ii. 249 *sqq.*

Kalmuck story of the external soul, ii. 142

Kamenagora in Croatia, Midsummer fires at, i. 178

Kamtchatkans, their purification after a death, ii. 178

Kanna district, Northern Nigeria, ii. 210

Kappiliyans of Madura, their seclusion of girls at puberty, i. 69

Karens of Burma, their custom at childbirth, ii. 157

Kasai River, ii. 264

Katajalina, a spirit who eats up boys at initiation and restores them to life, ii. 234 *sq.*

Katrine, Loch, i. 231

Kauffmann, Professor F., 1. 102 $n.$[1], 103 $n.$; on the external soul, ii. 97 $n.$

Kaupole, a Midsummer pole in Eastern Prussia, ii. 49

Kawars, of India, their cure for fever, ii. 190

Kaya-Kaya or Tugeri of Dutch New Guinea, their use of bull-roarers, ii. 242 *sq.*

Kayans or Bahaus of Central Borneo, i. 4 *sq.* ; custom observed by them after a funeral, ii. 175 *sq.* ; their way of giving the slip to a demon, 179 *sq.*

Keating, Geoffrey, Irish historian, quoted, i. 139 ; on the Beltane fires, 158 *sq.*

Keating, W. H., quoted, i. 89

Kei Islands, birth-custom in the, ii. 155

Keitele, Lake, in Finland, ii. 165

Kemble, J. M., on need-fire, i. 288

Kerry, Midsummer fires in, i. 203

Kersavondblok, the Yule log, i. 249

Kersmismot, the Yule log, i. 249

Khambu caste in Sikkhim, their custom after a funeral, ii. 18

Kharwars of Mirzapur, their dread of menstruous women, i. 84

Khasis of Assam, story of the external soul told by the, i. 146 *sq.*

Khnumu, Egyptian god, fashions a wife for Bata, ii. 135

Khonds, human sacrifices among the, ii. 286 $n.$[2]

Kia blacks of Queensland, their treatment of girls at puberty, i. 39

Kidd, Dudley, on external souls of chiefs, ii. 156 $n.$[2]

Kildare, Midsummer fires in, i. 203

Kilkenny, Midsummer fires in, i. 203

Killin, the hill of the fires at, i. 149

Killing a totem animal, ii. 220

—— the novice and bringing him to life again at initiation, pretence of, ii. 225 *sqq.*

King, nominal, chosen at Midsummer, i. 194, ii. 25 ; presides at summer bonfire, 38

—— and Queen of Roses, i. 195

—— of the Bean, i. 153 $n.$[3]

—— of Summer chosen on St. Peter's Day, i. 195

—— of the Wood at Nemi put to death, i. 2 ; in the Arician grove a personification of an oak-spirit, ii. 285 ; the priest of Diana at Aricia, perhaps personified Jupiter, 302 *sq. See also* Kings

Kingaru, clan of the Wadoe, ii. 313

Kings, sacred or divine, put to death, i. 1 *sq.* ; subject to taboos, 2

—— and priests, their sanctity analogous to the uncleanness of women at menstruation, i. 97 *sq.*

—— of Uganda, their life bound up with barkcloth trees, ii. 160

Kings, The Epic of, i. 104

Kingsley, Miss Mary H., on external or bush souls, ii. 204 *sq.* ; on rites of initiation in West Africa, 259

Kingussie, in Inverness-shire, Beltane cakes at, i. 153

Kinship created by the milk-tie, ii. 138 $n.$[1]

Kirchmeyer, Thomas, author of *Regnum Papisticum*, i. 124, 125 $n.$[1]; his account of Midsummer customs, 162 *sq.*

Kirghiz story of girl who might not see the sun, i. 74

Kirk Andreas, in the Isle of Man, i. 306

Kirkmichael, in Perthshire, Beltane fires and cakes at, i. 153

Kirton Lindsey, in Lincolnshire, i. 318 ; medical use of mistletoe at, ii. 84

Kitching, Rev. A. L., on cure for lightning stroke, ii. 298 $n.$[2]

Kiwai, island off New Guinea, use of bull-roarers in, ii. 232

Kiziba, to the west of Victoria Nyanza, theory of the afterbirth in, ii. 162 $n.$[2]

Kloo, in the Queen Charlotte Islands, i. 45

Knawel, St. John's blood on root of, ii. 56

Lungs or liver of bewitched animal burnt or boiled to compel the witch to appear, i. 321 *sq.*

Lushais of Assam, sick children passed through a coil among the, ii. 185 *sq.*

Lussac, in Poitou, Midsummer fires at, i. 191

Luther, Martin, burnt in effigy at Midsummer, i. 167, 172 *sq.*, ii. 23

Luxemburg, "Burning the Witch". in, ii. 116

Lythrum salicaria, purple loosestrife, gathered at Midsummer, ii. 65

Mabuiag, seclusion of girls at puberty in, i. 36 *sq.* ; dread and seclusion of women at menstruation in, 78 *sq.* ; girls at puberty in, 92 *n.*[1]; belief as to a species of mistletoe in, ii. 79

Mac Crauford, the great arch witch, i. 293

Macassar in Celebes, magical unguent in, i. 14

Macdonald, Rev. James, on the story of Headless Hugh, ii. 131 *n.*[1]; on external soul in South Africa, 156

Macdonell, A. A., on Agni, ii. 296

McDougall, W., and C. Hose, on creeping through a cleft stick after a funeral, ii. 176 *n.*[1]

Macedonia, Midsummer fires among the Greeks of, i. 212 ; bonfires on August 1st in, 220 ; need - fire among the Serbs of Western, 281 ; St. John's flower at Midsummer in, ii. 50

Macedonian peasantry burn effigies of Judas at Easter, i. 131

McGregor, A. W., on the rite of new birth among the Akikuyu, ii. 263

Mackay, Alexander, on need - fire, i. 294 *sq.*

Mackays, sept of the "descendants of the seal," ii. 131 *sq.*

Mackenzie, E., on need-fire, i. 288

Mackenzie, Sheriff David J., i. 268 *n.*[1]

Macphail, John, on need-fire, i. 293 *sq.*

Macusis of British Guiana, seclusion of girls at puberty among the, i. 60

Madangs of Borneo, custom observed by them after a funeral, ii. 175 *sq.*

Madern, parish of, Cornwall, holed stone in, ii. 187

Madonie Mountains, in Sicily, Midsummer fires on the, i. 210

Madras Presidency, the fire-walk in the, ii. 6

Madura, the Káppiliyans of, i. 69 ; the Parivarams of, 69

Maeseyck, processions with torches at, i. 107 *sq.*

Magic, homoeopathic or imitative, i. 49, 133, 329, ii. 231, 287 ; dwindles into divination, i. 336 ; movement of thought from magic through religion to science, ii. 304 *sq.*

Magic and ghosts, mugwort a protection against, ii. 59

—— and science, different views of natural order postulated by the two, ii. 305 *sq.*

—— flowers of Midsummer Eve, ii. 45 *sqq.*

Magical bone in sorcery, i. 14

—— implements not allowed to touch the ground, i. 14 *sq.*

—— influence of medicine-bag, ii. 268

—— virtues of plants at Midsummer apparently derived from the sun, ii. 71 *sq.*

Magician's apprentice, Danish story of the, ii. 121 *sqq.*

—— Glass, the, i. 16

Magyars, Midsummer fires among the, i. 178 *sq.* ; stories of the external soul among the, ii. 139 *sq.*

Mahabharata, Draupadi and her five husbands in the, ii. 7

"Maiden-flax" at Midsummer, ii. 48

Maidu Indians of California, seclusion of girls at puberty among the, ii. 42 ; their notion as to fire in trees, ii. 295 ; their idea of lightning, 298

Maimonides, on the seclusion of menstruous women, i. 83

Makalanga, a Bantu tribe, i. 135 *n.*[2]

Makral, "the witch," i. 107

Malabar, the Iluvans of, i. 5 ; the Tiyans of, 68

Malassi, a fetish in West Africa, ii. 256

Malay belief as to sympathetic relation between man and animal, ii. 197

—— story of the external soul, ii. 147 *sq.*

Malayo-Siamese families of the Patani States, their custom as to the after-birth, ii. 163 *sq.*

Malays of the Peninsula, their doctrine of the plurality of souls, ii. 222

Male and female souls in Chinese philosophy, ii. 221

Malkin Tower, witches at the, i. 245

Malta, fires on St. John's Eve in, i. 210 *sq.*

Malurus cyaneus, superb warbler, women's "sister," among the Kurnai, ii. 216

Man and animal, sympathetic relation between, ii. 272 *sq.*

Man, the Isle of, Midsummer fires in, i. 201, 337 ; old New Year's Day in, 224 *sq.* ; Hallowe'en customs in, 243 *sq.* ; bonfires on St. Thomas's Day in, 266 ; cattle burnt alive to stop a murrain in, 325 *sqq.*; mugwort gathered on Midsummer Eve in, ii. 59. *See also* Isle of Man

ashes of Midsummer fires, 192 ; burnt to stop disease in the flock, 301 ; burnt alive as a sacrifice in the Isle of Man, 306 ; witch in shape of a black, 316 ; driven through fire, ii. 11 *sqq.* ; omens drawn from the intestines of, 13 ; passed through a hole in a rock to rid them of disease, 189 *sq.*

Shells used in ritual of death and resurrection, ii. 267 *n.*[2], 269

Sherbro, Sierra Leone, secret society in the, ii. 259 *sqq.*

Shirley Heath, cleft ash-tree at, ii. 168

Shirt, wet, divination by, i. 236, 241

Shoe, divination by thrown, i. 236

Shoes of boar's skin worn by king at inauguration, i. 4 ; magical plants at Midsummer put in, ii. 54, 60, 65

Shooting at the sun on Midsummer Day, ii. 291

—— at witches in the clouds, i. 345

"Shot-a-dead" by fairies, i. 303

Shropshire, the Yule log in, i. 257 ; fear of witchcraft in, 342 *n.*[4] ; the oak thought to bloom on Midsummer Eve in, ii. 292, 293

Shrove Tuesday, effigies burnt on, i. 120 ; straw-man burnt on, ii. 22 ; wicker giants on, 35 ; cats burnt alive on, 40 ; the divining-rod cut on, 68 ; custom of striking a hen dead on, 279 *n.*

Shuswap Indians of British Columbia, seclusion of girls at puberty among the, i. 53 *sq.* ; girls at puberty forbidden to eat anything that bleeds, 94 ; fence themselves with thorn bushes against ghosts, ii. 174 *n.*[2] ; personal totems among the, 276 *n.*[1] ; their belief as to trees struck by lightning, 297 *n.*[8]

Siam, king of, not allowed to set foot on ground, i. 3 ; tree-spirit in serpent form in, ii. 44 *n.*[1]

Siamese, their explanation of a first menstruation, i. 24 ; their story of the external soul, ii. 102

Siberia, marriage custom in, i. 75 ; external souls of shamans in, ii. 196 *sq.*

Sibyl, the Norse, her prophecy, i. 102 *sq.*

Sibyl's wish, the, i. 99

Sicily, Midsummer fires in, i. 210 ; St. John's Day (Midsummer Day) regarded as dangerous and unlucky in, ii. 29 ; bathing at Midsummer in, 29 ; St. John's wort in, 55

Sickness, bonfires a protection against, i. 108, 109 ; transferred to animal, ii. 181

Sieg, the Yule log in the valley of the, i. 248

Siena, the, of the Ivory Coast, their totemism, ii. 220 *n.*[2]

Sierck, town on the Moselle, i. 164

Sierra Leone, birth-trees in, ii. 160 ; secret society in, 260 *sq.*

Sieve, divination by, i. 236

Sikkhim, custom after a funeral in, ii. 18

Silence compulsory on girls at puberty, i. 29, 57 ; in ritual, 123, 124, ii. 63, 67, 171, 184

Silesia, Spachendorf in, i. 119 ; fires to burn the witches in, 160 ; Midsummer fires in, 170 *sq.*, 175 ; need-fire in, 278 ; witches as cats in, 319 *sq.* ; divination by flowers on Midsummer Eve in, ii. 53

Silius Italicus, on the fire-walk of the Hirpi Sorani, ii. 14 *n.*[8]

Sill of door, unlucky children passed under the, ii. 190

Silver sixpence or button used to shoot witches with, i. 316

Silvia and Mars, story of, ii. 102

Simeon, prince of Bulgaria, his life bound up with the capital of a column, ii. 156 *sq.*

Simla, i. 12

Simurgh and Rustem, i. 104

Sin-offering, i. 82

Singhalese, seclusion of girls at puberty among the, i. 69

Singleton, Miss A. H., ii. 192 *n.*[1]

Siouan tribes of North America, names of clans not used in ordinary conversation among the, ii. 224 *n.*[2]

Sioux or Dacotas, ritual of death and resurrection among the, ii. 268 *sq.*

Sipi in Northern India, i. 12

Sirius, how the Bushmen warm up the star, i. 332 *sq.*

Sister's Beam (*Sororium tigillum*) at Rome, ii. 194, 195 *n.*[4]

Sisyphus, the stone of, i. 298

Sixpence, silver, witches shot with a, i. 316

Sixth day of the moon, mistletoe cut on the, ii. 77

Sixty years, cycles of, ii. 77 *n.*[1]

Skin disease, traditional cure of, in India, ii. 192 ; leaping over ashes of fire as remedy for, 2

Sky, girls at puberty not allowed to look at the, i. 43, 45, 46, 69

Skye, island of, i. 289 ; the need-fire in, 148

Slane, the hill of, i. 158

Slave Coast, custom of widows on the, ii. 18 *sq.* ; use of bull-roarers on the, 229 *n.*

Slavonia, the Yule log in, i. 262 *sq.* ; need-fire in, 282

Suffering, intensity of, a means to break the spell of witchcraft, i. 304
Suffolk, belief as to menstruous women in, i. 96 *n.*[2]; duck baked alive as a sacrifice in, 303 *sq.*
Suk of British East Africa, their dread of menstruous women, i. 81
"Sultan of the Oleander," i. 18
Sumatra, the Minangkabauers of, i. 79; the Kooboos of, ii. 162 *n.*[2]; the Looboos of, 182 *sq.*; totemism among the Battas of, 222 *sqq.*; use of bull-roarers in, 229 *n.*
Summer, King of, chosen on St. Peter's Day, i. 195
Sun, rule not to see the, i. 18 *sqq.*; priest of the, uses a white umbrella, 20 *n.*[1]; not to shine on girls at puberty, 22, 35, 36, 37, 41, 44, 46, 47, 68; not to be seen by Brahman boys for three days, 68 *n.*[2]; impregnation of women by the, 74 *sq.*; made to shine on women at marriage, 75; sheep and lambs sacrificed to the, 132; temple of the, at Cuzco, 132; the Birthday of the, at the winter solstice, 246; Christmas an old heathen festival of the birth of the, 331 *sq.*; symbolized by a wheel, 334 *n.*[1], 335; in the sign of the lion, ii. 66 *sq.*; magical virtues of plants at Midsummer derived from the, 71 *sq.*; in the sign of Sagittarius, 82; calls men to himself through death, 173, 174 *n.*[1]; fern-seed procured by shooting at the sun on Midsummer Day, 291; the ultimate cooling of the, 307
Sun-charms, i. 331; the solstitial and other ceremonial fires perhaps sun-charms, ii. 292
—— -god, ii. 1, 16
Sundal, in Norway, need-fire in, i. 280
Sunday, children born on a Sunday can see treasures in the earth, ii. 288 *n.*[5]
—— of the Firebrands, i. 110
—— in Lent, the first, fire-festival on the, i. 107 *sqq.*
Sung-yang, were-tiger in, i. 310
Sunless, Prince, i. 21
Sunshine, use of fire as a charm to produce, i. 341 *sq.*
Superb warbler, called women's "sister" among the Kurnai, ii. 215 *n.*[1], 216, 218
Superstitions, Index of, i. 270; about trees struck by lightning, ii. 296 *sqq.*
Surenthal in Switzerland, new fire made by friction at Midsummer in the, i. 169 *sq.*
Sûrya, the sun-god, ii. 1
Sussex, cleft ash-trees used for the cure of rupture in, ii. 169 *sq.*
Sutherland, the need-fire in, i. 294 *sq.*

Sutherlandshire, sept of the Mackays, "the descendants of the seal," in, ii. 131 *sq.*
Swabia, "burning the witch" in, i. 116; custom of throwing lighted discs in, 116 *sq.*; Easter fires in, 144 *sq.*; custom at eclipses in, 162 *n.*; the Midsummer fires in, 166 *sq.*; witches as hares and horses in, 318 *sq.*; the divining-rod in, ii. 68 *n.*[4]; fern-seed brought by Satan on Christmas night in, 289
Swahili of East Africa, their ceremony of the new fire, i. 133, 140; birth-trees among the, ii. 160 *sq.*; their story of an African Samson, ii. 314
Swallows, stones found in stomachs of, i. 17
Swan-woman, Tartar story of the, ii. 144
Swan's bone, used by menstruous women to drink out of, i. 48, 49, 50, 90, 92
Swans' song in a fairy tale, ii. 124
Swanton, J. R., quoted, i. 45 *n.*[1]
Sweden, customs observed on Yule Night in, i. 20 *sq.*; Easter bonfires in, 146; bonfires on the Eve of May Day in, 159, 336; Midsummer fires in, 172; the need-fire in, 280; bathing at Midsummer in, ii. 29; "Midsummer Brooms" in, 54; the divining-rod in, 69, 291; mistletoe to be shot or knocked down with stones in, 82; mistletoe a remedy for epilepsy in, 83; medical use of mistletoe in, 84; mistletoe used as a protection against conflagration in, 85, 293; mistletoe cut at Midsummer in, 86; mystic properties ascribed to mistletoe on St. John's Eve in, 86; Balder's balefires in, 87; children passed through a cleft oak as a cure for rupture or rickets in, 170; crawling through a hoop as a cure in, 184; superstitions about a parasitic rowan in, 281
Switzerland, Lenten fires in, i. 118 *sq.*; new fire kindled by friction of wood in, 169 *sq.*; Midsummer fires in, 172; the Yule log in, 249; need-fire in, 279 *sq.*, 336; people warned against bathing at Midsummer in, ii. 27; the belief in witchcraft in, 42 *n.*[2]; divination by orpine at Midsummer in, 61
Sympathetic relation between cleft tree and person who has been passed through it, ii. 170, 171 *n.*[1], 172; between man and animal, 272 *sq.*
Syria, restrictions on menstruous women in, i. 84
Syrmia, the Yule log in, i. 262 *sq.*

Tabari, Arab chronicler, i. 82

Thor, a Norse god, i. 103

Thorn, external soul in a, ii. 129; mistletoe on a, 291 *n.*[3]

—— bushes used to keep off ghosts, ii. 174 *sq.*

Thought, the web of, ii. 307 *sq.*

Threatening fruit-trees, i. 114

Three Holy Kings, the divining-rod baptized in the name of the, ii. 68

—— leaps over bonfire, i. 214, 215

Threshold, shavings from the, burnt, ii. 53

Thrice to crawl under a bramble as a cure, ii. 180; to pass through a wreath of woodbine, 184

Throwing or striking blindfold, ii. 279 *n.*[4]

Thrumalun, a mythical being who kills and resuscitates novices at initiation, ii. 233. *See also* Daramulun *and* Thuremlin

Thrushes deposit seeds of mistletoe, ii. 316 *n.*[1]

Thunder associated with the oak, i. 145; Midsummer fires a protection against, 176; charred sticks of Midsummer bonfire a protection against, 184, 192; ashes of Midsummer fires a protection against, 190; brands from the Midsummer fires a protection against, 191; certain flowers at Midsummer a protection against, ii. 54, 58, 59; the sound of bull-roarers thought to imitate, 228 *sqq. See also* Lightning

Thunder and lightning, the Yule log a protection against, i. 248, 249, 250, 252, 253, 254, 258, 264; bonfires a protection against, 344; smoke of Midsummer herbs a protection against, ii. 48; vervain a protection against, 62; name given to bull-roarers, 231 *sq.*

—— and the oak, the Aryan god of the, i. 265

" —— -besom," name applied to mistletoe and other bushy excrescences on trees, ii. 85, 301; a protection against thunderbolts, 85

—— -bird, the mythical, i. 44

" —— -bolts," name given to celts, i. 14 *sq.*

" —— -poles," oak sticks charred in Easter bonfires, i. 145

Thunderstorms and hail caused by witches, i. 344; Midsummer flowers a protection against, ii. 48

Thuremlin, a mythical being who kills lads at initiation and restores them to life, ii. 227. *See also* Daramulun

Thuringia, custom at eclipses in, i. 162 *n.*; Midsummer fires in, 169, ii. 40; Schweina in, i. 265; belief as to magical properties of the fern in, ii. 66 *sq.*

Thursday, Maundy, i. 125 *n.*[1]

Thurso, witches as cats at, i. 317

Thurston, E., on the fire-walk, ii. 9

Thyme burnt in Midsummer fire, i. 213; wild, gathered on Midsummer Day, ii. 64

Tibet, sixty years' cycle in, ii. 78 *n.*

Ticunas of the Amazon, ordeal of young men among the, i. 62 *sq.*

Tiger, a Batta totem, ii. 223

Tiger's skin at inauguration of a king, i. 4

Timmes of Sierra Leone, their secret society, ii. 260 *n.*[1]

Tinneh Indians, seclusion of girls at puberty among the, i. 47 *sqq.*; their dread and seclusion of menstruous women, 91 *sqq.*

Tinnevelly, the Kappiliyans of, i. 69

Tipperary, county of, were-wolves in, i. 310 *n.*[1]; woman burnt as a witch in, 323 *sq.*

Tiree, the need-fire in, i. 148; the Beltane cake in, 149; witch as sheep in, 316

Tivor, god or victim, i. 103 *n.*

Tiyans of Malabar, their seclusion of girls at puberty, i. 68 *sq.*

Tlactga or Tlachtga in Ireland, i. 139

Tlingit (Thlinkeet) Indians of Alaska, seclusion of girls at puberty among the, i. 45 *sq.*

Tlokoala, a secret society of the Nootka Indians, ii. 271

Toad, witch in form of a, i. 323

—— clan, ii. 273

—— -stools thrown into Midsummer bonfires as a charm, i. 172

Toad's heart worn by a thief to prevent detection, i. 302 *n.*[2]

Toads burnt alive in Devonshire, i. 302

Toaripi of New Guinea, their rule as to menstruous women, i. 84

Tobas, Indian tribe of the Gran Chaco, their custom of secluding girls at puberty, i. 59

Tobelorese of Halmahera, their rites of initiation, ii. 248

Toboengkoe, the, of Central Celebes, custom observed by widower among the, ii. 178 *sq.*

Tocandeira, native name for the *Cryptocerus atratus*, F., ant, i. 62

Todas of the Neilgherry Hills, their ceremony of the new fire, i. 136

Tokio, the fire-walk at, ii. 9 *sq.*

Tokoelawi of Central Celebes, custom observed by mourners among the, ii. 178

Tomori, the Gulf of, in Celebes, i. 312

Tongue of medicine-man, hole in, ii. 238, 239

THE END

Printed by R. & R. CLARK, LIMITED, *Edinburgh.*